BECOMING AUSTRIANS

BECOMING AUSTRIANS

Jews and Culture between the World Wars

Lisa Silverman

OXFORD
UNIVERSITY PRESS

Oxford University Press is a department of the University of Oxford.
It furthers the University's objective of excellence in research, scholarship,
and education by publishing worldwide.

Oxford New York
Auckland Cape Town Dar es Salaam Hong Kong Karachi
Kuala Lumpur Madrid Melbourne Mexico City Nairobi
New Delhi Shanghai Taipei Toronto

With offices in
Argentina Austria Brazil Chile Czech Republic France Greece
Guatemala Hungary Italy Japan Poland Portugal Singapore
South Korea Switzerland Thailand Turkey Ukraine Vietnam

Published in the United States of America by
Oxford University Press
198 Madison Avenue, New York, NY 10016

First issued as an Oxford University Press paperback, 2015.

Library of Congress Cataloging-in-Publication Data
Silverman, Lisa
Becoming Austrians : Jews and culture between the World Wars / Lisa Silverman.
p. cm.
Includes bibliographical references and index.
ISBN 978-0-19-979484-3 (hardcover); 978-0-19-025781-1 (paperback)
1. Jews—Austria—History—20th century. 2. Jews—Austria—Social
conditions—20th century. 3. Jews—Austria—Vienna—History—20th
century. 4. Antisemitism—Austria. 5. Vienna (Austria)—Intellectual
life—20th century. 6. Vienna (Austria)—Ethnic relations. I. Title.
DS135.A9S55 2012
305.892′4043609041—dc23 2011045723

9 8 7 6 5 4 3 2 1

Printed in the United States of America
on acid-free paper

For my parents,
Paula and Harry Silverman, with love

CONTENTS

ACKNOWLEDGMENTS

I'm delighted to thank those who have given so generously of their time, support, and advice over the lengthy process of writing this book. At Yale, Paula Hyman (z"l) and Jeffrey Sammons provided invaluable expertise and insight at its earliest stages. In Vienna, a generous fellowship from the Internationales Forschungszentrum Kulturwissenschaften (IFK) allowed me to conduct fundamental research. I am grateful to Lutz Musner, the fellows and other members of the staff for making me feel so welcome. A grant from the Kohn Foundation allowed me to experience the stimulating environment of the Centre for German-Jewish Studies at the University of Sussex, where I found excellent mentors and consistent sources of encouragement and wisdom in Sander Gilman, Raphael Gross, and Edward Timms. Many other scholars in Europe and the United States took the time to offer constructive advice and point me to vital sources, including Leora Auslander, Judith Beniston, Brigitte Dalinger, Werner Hanak, Wolfgang Maderthaner, Pia Schölnberger, Monica Strauss, and Wolfgang Wieshaider. I'm especially grateful to Marsha Rozenblit and Murray Hall, who read and commented on the entire manuscript. Rebecca Steinitz's careful eye and skillful editing helped me say what I wanted to say. Emily Verch and Marcus Jobst's expertise in visualizing information let me show what I wanted to show. Many thanks are due to Jason Heilman for his savvy translation advice and careful editing, and to Michaela Sivich for her efficient research assistance. At Oxford University Press, I thank Nancy Toff for her helpful guidance in transforming my manuscript into a book, and Sonia Tycko for keeping me on track with efficiency and patience throughout the publication process. Thanks are due as well to two anonymous readers, whose suggestions and critiques greatly improved the manuscript.

I cannot say enough good things about my colleagues at the University of Wisconsin-Milwaukee, who have provided me with an ideal working environment for the past six years. I am deeply grateful for their enthusiasm, encouragement, and friendship. A fellowship from the Center for 21st Century Studies brought me much-needed time and space to complete the project, as well as a supportive group of fellows with whom to share ideas. Travel grants from the history department, graduate school, and Center for Jewish Studies made it possible to carry out necessary research abroad, as did a summer fellowship from the City of Salzburg. The helpfulness of the staff of all of the archives I visited in Austria and the United States was essential to the completion of this project. I owe a special debt of gratitude to Nicole Emanuel, Irene Halsman, and August Zirner, who were so generous with their precious family photographs and documents and who inspired me with their commitment to learning more about their families' pasts.

A group of incredible friends has greatly enriched the process of writing and kept it from being a lonely one. Chaya Halberstam and Ravit Reichman have never ceased reading, listening, challenging, encouraging, and providing comfort without my having to ask. They have read countless drafts of these chapters and have seen me through the emotional ups and downs that came with writing them—their generosity, intellect, humor, and friendship mean the world to me. I could not have completed this book without the boundless support of Dan Magilow. His erudition, keen editorial skills, and sharp sense of humor helped me clear innumerous hurdles and keep my sanity. Darcy Buerkle provided crucial insight and warm friendship when I needed it most. Paul Lerner's helpful comments arrived at just the right moment. Abigail Gillman offered invaluable advice. Christoph Meinrenken improved my translations and provided unending friendship and moral support, not to mention fantastic accommodations in the West Village, whenever I asked.

In Vienna, Elana Shapira has been part of this project from beginning to end, and the effects of her shrewd insight can be found in every chapter of this book. She and Anton Legerer forfeited innumerable hours of sleep, whether to indulge me in vigorous debate or just to keep me company. Dieter and Louise Hecht never hesitated to help me hone crucial details and to offer their sound judgment, and Sandra Brandeis-Crawford always managed to find time for an evening out. All five of them cheerfully allowed me to interrupt their hectic lives more times than I can count, and I owe them my deepest gratitude for their hospitality and friendship.

Whether discussing ideas on their balcony in Switzerland or accompanying me on adventures in the French countryside, Franka Marquardt and Patrick Buehler Marquardt have been an untiring source of friendship and inspiration. I couldn't have found better friends and colleagues than Deborah Holmes and Georg Spitaler, whose knowledge of Vienna and its past always kept me from going too far off track. More than a few conferences would have been truly unbearable without Marcus Pyka's sharp insight and wit. In Milwaukee, Winson Chu helped me keep my historical arguments in line, while Arijit Sen was willing to leap with me across the widest of disciplinary boundaries. Along with Aneesh

Aneesh, Erica Bornstein, Aparna Datei, Karolina May, Manu Sobti, and Vaishali Wagh, they heard much more about Austria and the Jews than they bargained for. They helped me make this work the best it could be with their warm companionship, constant encouragement, and delicious home cooking.

The love and support of my family has been indispensable. My dear sister Jill Silverman fielded calls from me at all hours of the day, provided a warm, sunny escape whenever I needed it, and offered top-notch pet care with no questions asked. I owe my deepest gratitude to my parents, Paula and Harry Silverman, without whom I could never have accomplished this project. From the start, they've encouraged me along whatever path I chose to take, no matter how far away it took me. It is to them that I dedicate this book, with love.

Portions of chapter 4 appeared as "Max Reinhardt between Yiddish Theatre and the Salzburg Festival" in *Jews and the Making of Modern German Theatre*, ed. Jeanette R. Malkin and Freddie Rokem (Iowa City: University of Iowa Press, 2010).

BECOMING AUSTRIANS

INTRODUCTION: THE PRICE OF INCLUSION

AUSTRIA'S FIRST REPUBLIC AND THE JEWS

Perhaps flattery *can* get you anywhere. In 1923, British writer J. L. Benvenisti scored a major coup for *The American Hebrew*: an interview with the renowned writer Arthur Schnitzler at his home in Vienna. When Schnitzler answered the door, however, he was not happy to see a reporter from the Jewish magazine: "'I never give interviews,' he said. 'All I have to say on the Jewish question is in my book, *Der Weg ins Freie*.'" *The Road to the Open* was Schnitzler's first novel, and in it he explicitly addressed issues of Jews and antisemitism. But Benvenisti had a ready reply: "'Herr Doctor,' I said, 'I have not read *Der Weg ins Freie* once but three times, and it is to discuss that book I have come to you.' Whereupon an extraordinarily sweet smile illuminated Schnitzler's face. 'You are very flattering,' he said, and motioned me to a seat."[1]

Despite his protests, Schnitzler had plenty to say that day about Jews, from their responses to antisemitism, to their creativity, to his own Jewish self-identification. He first disavowed Zionism, then proclaimed admiration for it; he staunchly defended his own rootedness in Vienna despite threatening attacks by violent antisemites; and he suggested that differences between Jews and Gentiles were mere social distinctions imposed by the outside world. Then, in a revealing change of opinion, he added that Jews were in part to blame for making themselves the target of "deep-rooted" hatred and weakening their own defenses due to their "excessive objectivity" and "a certain inclination to self-analysis." Despite his resigned response to the issue of antisemitism, however, he ended the interview on a high note. When Benvenisti asked whether he believed that Jews are a creative people, he answered, "I believe we are on the verge of a great Jewish renaissance. What is the nature of the artistic message Judaism has to convey to the world, I am unable to say. But there is a promise of springtime in the air. Time alone will show the nature of the blossom."[2]

The historical irony of Schnitzler's words, in the wake of the horrors that befell Austria's Jews scarcely a generation later, obscures the fact that, in the years between the World Wars, Jews flourished as creators of culture in Austria.[3] When Schnitzler gave his interview, Jews were running publishing houses and writing bestselling novels, Viennese cinemas screened films dealing with the topic of Jewish assimilation, and Max Reinhardt and Hugo von Hofmannsthal's national cultural festival in Salzburg was already in its third successful year.[4] Yiddish publishing in Vienna peaked around 1922, and Yiddish theater had experienced a revival among non-Yiddish-speaking Viennese audiences.[5] In fact, Schnitzler himself, along with a number of other Viennese cultural luminaries, enjoyed attending performances of *Der Dybbuk* by the Vilna Troupe, for example.[6] It would seem from the cultural evidence that Schnitzler was right on target.

But Schnitzler had another valuable rationale behind his prediction. By the end of 1923, as the economy recovered, the wave of postwar antisemitic action by those who held Jews responsible for the loss of the war had begun to ebb. Between 1926 and 1929, the only major act of public violence in Vienna was the burning of the Justizpalast (Palace of Justice) in 1927, which had nothing to do with Jews.[7] Sporadic eruptions notwithstanding, after 1923 there was little evidence to suggest that antisemitism, either casual or violent, would prevent Jews who sought to immerse themselves in Austrian culture from doing so. And indeed, it did not. However, the parameters of Jewish participation in Austrian culture were carefully circumscribed. Schnitzler's so-called Jewish renaissance in interwar Austria came with a price. Unspoken rules of behavior built upon notions of Jewish difference constantly and irrevocably shaped the experiences of Jews in Austrian culture.[8]

This book digs deep into the years between the World Wars to examine the role Jewish difference played in the lives, works, and deeds of a broad range of Austrians, from self-professed Jews to converts, from native Yiddish speakers to secular Viennese Jews, regardless of their degree of Jewish self-identification. Through careful readings of interwar novels, films, plays, and events like festivals and murder trials, it reveals how the social codings of politics, class, gender, nation, and geography received a powerful boost when articulated using the terms of Jewish difference. Paradoxically, the book ultimately shows that intensified engagements with the terms of Jewish difference—which inevitably located the "Jewish" as subordinate to the "not-Jewish"—characterized not only antisemitic acts but also the creation of culture by Jews and non-Jews alike in interwar Austria.

In doing so, this book powerfully calls into question long-standing descriptions of fin-de-siècle Vienna as the example *par excellence* of Jewish participation in modern urban culture on two counts. First, it challenges the myth of an unbroken line from the turn of the century to the *Anschluss*, along which a continuous era of cultural creativity, and Jews' participation in it, ran a steadily declining course. Austria between the World Wars is typically overshadowed by two monumental epochs: the celebrated years around 1900 on one end, and the bleak era that followed the *Anschluss* in 1938 on the other.[9] And it is true that after the collapse of the monarchy in 1918, Austria was rocked by financial and political crises that often overshadowed the concerns of art, literature, and culture that had occupied such a dominant public place in the period immediately preceding the First World War.

However, the collapse of the monarchy and the ensuing turmoil in no way resulted in an abandonment of art and culture, as has sometimes been assumed, but rather led to new and intensified forms of expression and reflection in literature, theater, music, dance, science, scholarship, and many other areas in which Jews played a significant role.[10] The newly politicized cultural climate of the interwar period affected both creative pursuits as well as the newfound drive with which Jews—and others—undertook them.[11] After the collapse of the Habsburg monarchy, all Austrians were forced to shape new self-understandings out of a world in political, social, and economic disarray, but Jews in particular found the lives they had enjoyed shaken to the core.[12] As a result, their investment in culture as a means of shaping the contours of their new self-understandings as Austrians was thus particularly strong—and particularly vexed.[13] Bracketing the years between the World Wars thus yields some of the strongest examples of the role of Jewish difference in articulating the terms of culture in Austria.

Second, this book counters the notion that the successful participation of Jews in Austrian culture represented an erasure of the social boundaries responsible for maintaining their status as "outsiders."[14] As Austrians uneasily reconceptualized themselves along new national and urban lines, their self-conceptions increasingly relied upon longstanding prejudices and stereotypes of the "Jew" as the ultimate Other. Both Jews and non-Jews used this age-old paradigm to interpret, clarify, and critique the terms of the country's altered political, social, and economic circumstances, even as Jews became leaders of political movements and rose to the forefront of social and cultural programs. Ultimately, this book shows that while Austria's First Republic may have provided a platform for Jews to shape mainstream culture, it had little room for the "Jewish" when it came to forming new conceptions of the "Austrian."[15]

In Austria-Hungary, by contrast, many of the most civic-minded Jews had considered themselves incomparably Austrian. According to Marsha L. Rozenblit, Austria's political structure before World War I allowed Jews to self-identify comfortably on a number of levels.[16] She notes that Jews could easily fashion themselves as proud members of a German *Kulturnation*, while maintaining their status as loyal citizens of Austria-Hungary. Choosing as well to identify as Jews along religious lines caused little conflict with either of these allegiances, and hardly posed a problem in a dual monarchy whose members stemmed from a myriad of national, ethnic, and religious groups.[17] The commitment to a multinational character and flexibility, upon which Jews in Austria-Hungary believed their state functioned, allowed them to live without fear of state-supported or state-tolerated acts of radical antisemitism.[18] Thus, while the monarchy's collapse and the ensuing political and social changes profoundly affected all its subjects, Jews had much more to lose with its demise.[19]

Joseph Samuel Bloch, a rabbi, member of the *Reichsrat* and publisher of the Jewish newspaper *Österreichische Wochenschrift*, suggested that because Jews remained loyal supporters of the monarchy and Kaiser Franz Joseph in the face of the rise of ethnic nationalisms, it followed that they should represent the ideal Austrians in the newly configured country. "If one could construct a specifically Austrian nationality, then the Jews would constitute its foundation."[20] For Bloch, Jews were the only "unconditional Austrians" and thus should logically form the core of a new, multinational state.[21] But his notion that the political loyalty of the Jews would translate directly and easily into a new Austrian national sensibility proved false. Thus, the most loyal citizens of the monarchy went from considering themselves the most Austrian to realizing that in the First Republic, they were in danger of becoming the *least* Austrian.

Because this book focuses on the role of Jews and the "Jewish" in shaping Austrian culture, it does not emphasize works created for the purpose of fostering a collective sense of Jewish self-identification.[22] Rather, it examines texts and events that deeply engage the socially constructed categories of Jewish difference. During this time, developing notions about how to define the new "Austrian" meshed with age-old stereotypes about the "Jew" in discursive and performative processes that *all* Austrians, Jews and non-Jews, used and understood to make sense of their world. Studies of Jewish history that restrict their inquiry to explicit manifestations of Jewish culture, or to works that Jews themselves called "Jewish," severely limit the depths to which we can probe these processes as they occurred on stages and in courtrooms, were narrated in fiction and in essays, and were revealed in the choices people made in their everyday lives about where to live, work, and entertain themselves.[23]

Contradictory as it may seem, this book thus seeks to examine the experiences of Austrian Jews *without* making Jewish self-identification the ontological foundation of Jewish experience and Jewish history. Instead, it foregrounds Jewish difference as one of a number of analytic categories or frameworks, like gender and class, that not only intersected and overlapped, but also used each others' terms in order to articulate their power. Unfortunately, in this case we lack a single term that refers to the relationship between the constructed categories of the frame, as "gender" does for "Man" and "Woman." For this reason,

I use the term "Jewish difference" to refer to the dialectical, hierarchical framework that encompasses the relationship between the socially constructed categories of "Jew" and "non-Jew." This term, which, like gender, refers to the relationship between two cultural ideals, allows us to avoid essentializing our understandings of what is "Jewish" and automatically implies that its definition is necessarily subject to change.[24] Thus, I neither deny nor ignore the "Jewish content" of a work and the degree of Jewish self-identification of its author, but I use neither as an a priori rule for identifying people, topics, and texts worthy of inclusion in a study about Austrian Jewish cultural history.[25] Instead, I show how the experiences of a variety of Austrians of varying levels of Jewish self-identification, as well as the culture they produced, can become powerful historical evidence for how Jewish difference functioned to constitute Austrian self-understandings.[26]

To identify this engagement with the terms of Jewish difference, this book considers Jews (as people) and the "Jewish" (as a socially constructed ideal that stems from, but is not equal to, Jews) as separate entities.[27] It does so primarily because their lives and works suggest that most Austrians did, too.[28] Here too, a comparison with gender as an analytical category is helpful. As Judith Butler points out, once gender boundaries are defined, they necessarily become invisible so that they can be invoked as the framework of the ideal definitions of the categories they attempt to represent. It is only in performing gender, in other words, that people actually evoke these boundaries—and they do so to engage in the process of self-identification.[29] I believe that we can identify a similar framework in operation for the performances of Jewish difference. When we do, we find that it played a critical role in interwar Austrian culture in particular, especially when it was least explicitly apparent.

Recent scholarship suggests other useful means for addressing the complexities of Austrian Jewish history.[30] Marsha L. Rozenblit, for example, deploys social anthropologist Fredrik Barth's definition of ethnic identity, which emphasizes the boundaries that distinguish members of a group from nonmembers, rather than the actual content of that which is bounded, to demonstrate how Jewish ethnic self-understandings were constructed in Austria before and during World War I.[31] This book foregrounds the imagined social boundary separating Jews from non-Jews, maintaining that in the increasingly politicized culture between the wars, it played a major role in determining how culture was both created and received. Klaus Hödl's approach to Jewish experiences around the fin-de-siècle incorporates the idea of performance as a methodological framework. Hödl convincingly shows that Jews constantly redetermined and redefined their self-understandings as Jews through the very act of engagement with non-Jewish individuals and practices. However, Hödl also admits that at the end of these cultural exchanges, the categories of the "Jewish" and the "non-Jewish" remained—even if in a different form. Thus, my study claims that even if no real, fixed essences of the "Jew" and "non-Jew" actually existed, we cannot overlook the fact that Austrians often clung to, and acted upon, their implicit belief that these binary essences did exist.[32]

To be sure, continuity as well as change characterized how Austrians used Jewish difference to articulate other social structures in the interwar period. I bracket the years 1918–1938 with the awareness of the important continuities in European culture, and I maintain that the terms of this analysis could also be applied to the study of Jews and Austrian culture before World War I, or to Jews and culture in other countries. But while Austrians' conceptions of the "Jewish" did not change overnight with the collapse of the monarchy, I claim that the political, social, and economic instability of the interwar years, combined with the urgency of forming new national and urban self-understandings, provided extremely fertile ground for Austrians to use Jewish difference to make legible other power relationships expressed in gender, and class, and politics. In other words, the use of Jewish difference as a method of articulating other power relationships intensified along with the highly charged and politicized culture of the period.[33]

The intensification of this reliance on Jewish difference can be explicitly identified in the growing acceptance among the general population of destructive, violent antisemitic acts, as well as in films, literature, and other forms of culture with explicitly Jewish content or stereotypes. However, we can also recognize it *implicitly* in many of the constructive efforts of Jews and others to create mainstream Austrian culture after the First World War.[34] Paradoxically, those who went out of their way to avoid explicit manifestations of Jewish difference in their life and work often most sharply reveal the play between the invisible, yet tangible, boundary separating the "Jewish" from the "non-Jewish." As Michael Steinberg suggests, this sense of difference was often palpable and material, yet somehow still managed to reside just "below the threshold of articulation."[35] Indeed, the very absence of a clear-cut manifestation of the "Jewish" often signals an engagement with Jewish difference—and points to its central importance. Thus the sense of an ideal "Austrian" culture in the First Republic was often most apparent in the culture created by those who felt it most lacking in their own self-definitions, and whose cultural products reflect an engagement with that absence.

Diverse Responses

Becoming Austrian in the First Republic was complicated by the fact that most of its population—including Jews—had no desire for this new country. Unlike other European nations, Austria's First Republic was formed from the "remainder" of the break-up of a grander political entity.[36] Eric Hobsbawm, who lived in Vienna in his youth, described post-war Austria as a "smallish provincial republic of great beauty, which did not believe it ought to exist."[37] Stefan Zweig characterized it as nothing more than a gray shadow of its former self, an "artificial entity" forced into existence by the wars' victors: "A country that did not wish to be got its orders: You must exist!" [38]

Many Austrians, including later Social Democratic leader Otto Bauer, who was then foreign minister, had sought to merge with Germany—indeed, the country's official name was Deutsch-Österreich (German-Austria) until the terms of the Treaty of St. Germain forced the government to rename it the Republic of Austria in July 1919.[39] As John Boyer points out, in 1918 the Austro-Germans—those Austrians who identified with German culture and accepted its hegemony—considered themselves not the victors but rather the losers of a cultural legacy. The destabilizing, dangerous effects of the First World War were so profound that "stable political and social institutions in Austria were virtually impossible for the next thirty years."[40] Such observations suggest that a new national "Austrian" self-understanding centered on German culture developed within the bounds of an already shaky political framework that gained stability when defined in terms of Jewish difference.

Although political polarization may have been, as Modris Eksteins notes, "the hallmark of the interwar era everywhere," in Austria, the boundaries of this polarization were especially severe—and they mapped themselves intensely along the lines of Jewish difference.[41] Although many Jews self-identified as culturally German, often to a greater degree than any other ethnic group, they remained in danger of becoming shut out of a definition of Austrianness that unified its otherwise fractured political and ethnic elements under one antisemitic rubric. The oppositional relationship crystallized in 1919, during the campaign surrounding the country's first democratic election. To gain votes, Christian Socials joined German Nationalists in an attempt to use fears about a "Jewish" peril, framed as an alliance of Jews and Marxists threatening Christian Germans.[42] Jews' responses, too, were affected by this polarization, making it difficult for many Jews to reconcile their new political affiliations. Marsha L. Rozenblit aptly sums up the dilemmas for Jews struggling to redefine their place in the new republic under its newly politicized circumstances after the decline of liberal parties by noting that they found it increasingly difficult to declare themselves as Jews *or* Germans. "Adherents of German culture, they could not quite bring themselves to declare themselves German, at least not in the way that most German nationalists meant it. Thus, most of the time, they declared themselves Jews, although not in the same way that the Zionists meant it."[43]

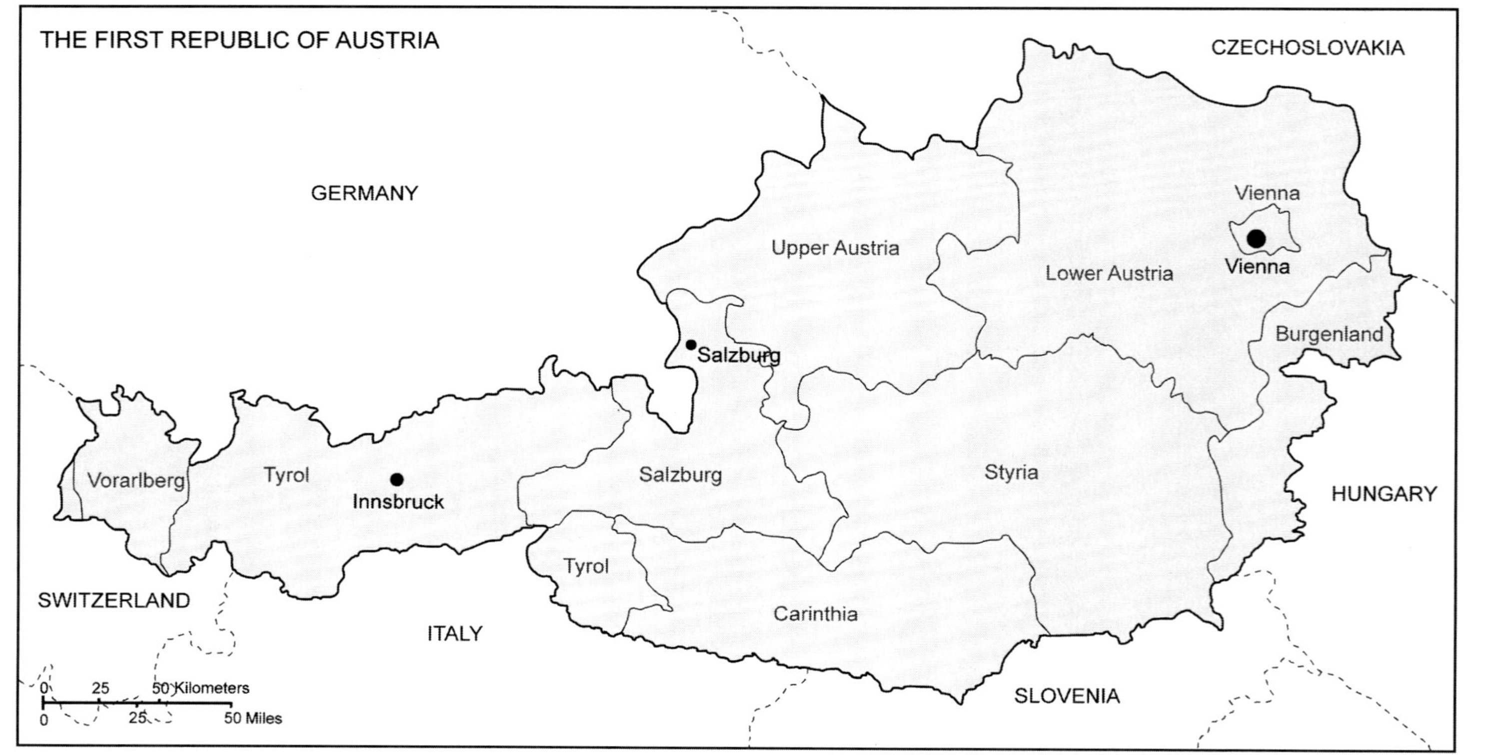

Austria's First Republic was made up of the area that remained after the other nations had been formed from the dissolved Dual Monarchy of Austria-Hungary. As French Prime Minister Georges Clemenceau remarked, "L'Autriche, c'est ce qui reste" (Austria is what remains).

Map by Emily Verch

After the end of World War I, Vienna's status as the cosmopolitan, central capital of the Austrian Empire was reduced to that of an overblown *Wasserkopf* (hydrocephalic) at the eastern end of the new, smaller state.

Map by Emily Verch

The arrival in Vienna of tens of thousands of mostly destitute Jewish refugees from Galicia and Bukovina beginning in the fall of 1914 compounded these new issues of self-identification.[44] Religious Jewish men from Eastern Europe were often easily recognizable, with their long beards and caftans, and they provided a convenient, visual target, especially when, after World War I, Jews were blamed for both the loss of the war and the nation's ensuing economic misery.[45] Antisemitic gatherings complaining about Jews attracted thousands of participants and sometimes erupted into violence.[46] "Hinaus mit den Juden!" (Out with the Jews!) was a cry heard as early as October 1919, and antisemitic rallies blaming Jews, as well as calling for the limitation on the number of Jews at universities and in public life, continued until 1923. Thus, the newcomers heightened anxieties among non-Jews and Jews alike; some Austrians turned the visible plight of the refugees into an unpleasant metaphor for their own experiences and a convenient locus onto which to displace their own frustrations.[47]

But the postwar destabilization of Austria's old social and political order also produced cultural gaps that left plenty of room for innovation and change, even as they generated concern for what—and who—would fill them.[48] Certainly, most Austrians were discouraged by the loss of the war, and the ensuing economic depression, unemployment, starvation, and social disorder hit them hard. But some felt equally intense excitement about the possibilities for reimagining and redesigning a new society. Yiddish essayist Melech Ravitsch, who lived in Vienna from 1912 to 1921, summed up that feeling of anticipation: "The year is . . . 1919—and the city is Vienna and the country is, shall we say: Don Quixote-Land, and the times are full of illusions, fantasies, and dreams."[49]

But bringing new visions to fruition first required renegotiating the terms of old orders. For one thing, the state government's decidedly Catholic tenor meant Jews could no longer so reconcile their place in the new country as seamlessly as they had in the multifaceted monarchy. Along with the imperial army and the bureaucratic system, the Roman Catholic Church had long formed the third bulwark of Austrian tradition; with 31 million Catholics out of a total population of 46 million in 1905, the monarchy formed the largest Catholic realm in Europe. But particularly in comparison to France, where Catholic intellectuals participated in socialist projects, the Austrian church was also particularly inflexible and reactionary.[50] Jesuit Ignaz Seipel, leader of the conservative Christian Socials for most of the interwar period and Austrian chancellor from 1926 to 1929, was the most visible antisemite in Central Europe. The rhetoric of his party frequently pitted Catholics against Jews, and Jews were excluded from the highest echelons of the civil service and government.[51] In the monarchy, as well as in the First Republic, Catholicism was an important way for Austrians to emphasize their difference from Germans, while still retaining their affiliation with German culture.

Jews would need to reconcile a desire to become Austrian with an increase in the importance of Catholic culture to an Austrian national self-understanding.[52]

But even in Austria-Hungary, a Jewish background had hardly precluded an attachment to or fascination with Catholic culture. In 1905, Jewish art critic and socialist functionary David Josef Bach reminisced about the Catholic influence on his childhood: "In the first place, they greatly emphasized Catholic attitudes there. . . . At that time our class was made up of about sixty students, of whom fifty were Jews, the rest Catholics; there were also some Protestants. And the Jews supported the Pope with an almost fanatical fervor."[53] Author Felix Salten recalls being the only Jewish student in his mainly Catholic class after the family moved to the Viennese district of Währing in 1876; he adapted by collecting cards with saints' pictures, singing in the church choir, and excelling in catechism.[54]

After the establishment of the First Republic, state financing of the Church continued through the 1920s. In light of the general financial, political, and social insecurities that ensued after the breakup of the monarchy, "The Catholic church was better prepared than anyone else to argue for the continuity between the old and the new, and thereby to effectively forestall a serious consideration of the separation of church and state."[55] Given its political and economic stronghold on Austrian culture, it is no surprise that the Catholic Church continued to maintain an important position as a cultural icon in the imaginations of many Austrians, including Jews, in particular for its perceived ability to maintain traditions of the old monarchy in the new republic. Elias Canetti best described the irony of this perceived sense of its receptiveness despite its hierarchical and closed structure in his seminal work *Masse und Macht* (*Crowds and Power*): "To the unbiased spectator Catholicism displays deliberation, calm, and spaciousness. Its very name contains its chief claim, which is that it has room for everyone. Its expectation is that everyone will turn to it."[56] Catholic culture became attractive to Jews precisely because it came to define the terms of exclusion of the "Jewish" from the "Austrian" as it simultaneously allowed non-Catholics to embrace it.[57]

The quest for stability amid the economic, political, and social unrest of the post–World War I period deeply affected many Europeans as they fashioned themselves into citizens in their reconfigured or newly formed nations.[58] To some extent, Austria's situation echoed the combination of political turmoil and change underway in Europe in general—and in Weimar Germany in particular, since that country also faced an intense mix of political, economic, social, and psychological upheaval. In addition to losing the war, both countries also managed to avoid full-scale revolution; the capital cities of both became postwar cultural centers in which Jews were deeply involved. But the terms of Germany's post–World War I reconstruction differed greatly in terms of its political conditions.[59]

Once the cosmopolitan capital of a vast monarchy, Vienna now found itself downgraded into a self-conscious, overblown *Wasserkopf* (hydrocephalic), like a curiously large head on the shrunken body of a beast, soon to be overtaken by Berlin as Central Europe's cosmopolitan vanguard. But while Vienna's grand old structures and buildings may have remained in place amid the rapidly declining postwar social and economic conditions, the abolishment of noble titles, the removal of imperial statues, and the renaming of streets were only surface indications of much deeper changes in the social order.[60] As Joseph Wechsberg, born in 1907 in Ostrava, Moravia, noted, "After 1918 my mother would often say that Vienna was 'finished.' I didn't understand. The big city was still there, wasn't it, the baroque palaces, the churches, the Burgtheater, the great streets? My mother shook her head . . . Vienna was only a big city then, no longer a world apart that my mother had found there. Once people had made a pilgrimage to Vienna to see the magic of the Kaiserstadt, the Imperial City. Now the magic was gone, the Kaiser was gone."[61] Even those residents of Vienna who remained where they were faced some sense of dislocation as major social and economic transitions altered their world. That the war was being fought at a distance could not quell Viennese anxieties about their physical and psychological well-being among the city's fluctuating population.[62]

Vienna had the third-largest urban Jewish population in Europe after Budapest and Warsaw, and Austrian Jews felt the effects of the collapse of the dual monarchy especially acutely.[63] Although Austria's collapse brought enormous upheaval for all Jews, their responses varied across a wide spectrum of political and social perspectives.[64] Moreover, the monarchy's collapse rendered many former citizens of Austria-Hungary foreigners, including the Jewish refugees from Galicia who had already been the target of antisemitic mistrust and hate. Although early efforts to deport these Galician Jews were not implemented, the calls for their expulsion fuelled anxiety among Vienna's Jews. As Galician-born author N. H. Tur-Sinai pointed out, although life was most difficult for refugees, Austria's new political context meant that "all Vienna's Jews turned into refugees in a sense."[65]

To some extent, the reactions of Jews to the monarchy's collapse mirrored those of other Austrians, but, indeed, the difference of opinion among Jews was much more profound, and with more radical consequences; as Bruce Pauley points out, few Christians considered leaving their homes, they had fewer (or less substantial) religious differences among them, and certainly fewer recent immigrants and unacculturated members.[66] As previously mentioned, many Austrian Jews had been loyal citizens of Austria-Hungary and simply mourned its loss. Some waxed nostalgic for the old order, and the monarchy remained a continued presence in personal items like books, photographs, and cake boxes that bore the official seal of approval from the *kaiserliche und königliche Doppelmonarchie* (Imperial and

Royal Dual Monarchy), its official name. The works of writers like Joseph Roth often poignantly reflect this sense of loss, as do the memoirs of Jews who describe how their families viewed the emperor as a representative of political and social stability.

Marie Langer, for example, describes her devastation at his death as being on par with the death of God. "I couldn't believe it: it was as if someone had told me that God had died. . . . That I . . . should have believed the Emperor to be immortal (even though nobody had told me so) indicates that for my family . . . the Empire—despite its social, political and national conflicts and contradictions—was unchangeable." Langer, who eventually became a committed Marxist and psychoanalyst, also describes a host of ensuing volatile shifts of religious and political loyalties: "Although we were rich, I was always aware of my two disadvantages: being a Jew and a woman . . . That's why joining the Left seemed to me to be the only logical solution. I was sure that Communism would put an end to this marginalization . . . When I was sixteen I had a religious crisis. At first I attempted to take up the Jewish religion but met with opposition at home. Later, during a long and painful Good Friday, I tried the Catholic religion. Afterwards I became a definite atheist and later a Communist."[67]

The events of the First World War also had a profound effect on the family of writer and Nobel laureate Elias Canetti, who was born in Bulgaria but lived in Vienna on and off during the interwar period. As with Langer, the experience of the Canetti family reveals the generational differences among Jews: those who had spent much of their lives as subjects of the monarchy frequently felt a greater sense of loss and anxiety, while younger Jews often found ways to become enthusiastic about their new situation. In his autobiography, Canetti emphasizes how his mother was drawn back to Vienna, where they had lived briefly during the war, not only because of their personal belongings, but also by strong cultural loyalties:

> There were so many reasons for going to Vienna; the chief reason was Vienna itself. We kept hearing how bad things were in Vienna. Along with all the private reasons, she felt something like an obligation to see how things stood. Austria had crumbled; the land she had thought of with a kind of bitterness so long as it had waged war, now mainly consisted of Vienna for her . . . I started to realize, albeit still unclearly, that the crumbling of her health, of her clarity and solidity, of her feelings about us, were linked to the end of the war, which end she had so passionately wished for, and to the collapse of Austria.[68]

Linking the monarchy's collapse to the deterioration of Canetti's mother's health and a renewed longing for Vienna, this passage illustrates the complicated system of self-identification and meaning engendered by the monarchy's demise, even for those Jews who had not considered themselves among its most loyal citizens. For many Jews, their new self-understandings as Austrians consisted chiefly of renewed and intensified identification not with the nation, but with the city. Many dealt with the collapse of the monarchy by shifting the terms of their divided loyalties in Austria-Hungary according to a new tripartite system. They considered themselves politically Austrian, ethnically Jewish, and—now, more than ever—"culturally" Viennese.[69] Other Jews responded to post-Habsburg doubts and confusion about their new precarious position in the nation with ardent support for socialism, not least because it appeared to provide for a more universal, inclusive political and cultural landscape.[70]

Socialist efforts thrived in many European cities, but by all accounts "Red Vienna," as the city was branded by Christian Socials and other opponents of the socialists, was the site of the most comprehensive attempts by Social Democrats to completely transform urban culture and life.[71] Modern dance, music, and literature continued to thrive, and the city became a site of unprecedented initiatives in housing, education, culture, and public works programs—of which Jews were often at the forefront. The overwhelming majority of Viennese Jews voted for the Social Democratic Party in both municipal and national elections. Jews also comprised nearly 80 percent of the movement's intellectual leadership as well as the majority of socialist student organizations and editors of socialist publications.[72]

Political movements based on a collective Jewish "ethnic" self-understanding, were another option for Austria's Jews, not all of whom believed in a renewed attachment to Vienna and its bourgeois culture. To be sure, Zionist participation increased immediately after the war, contributing to a new sense of ethnic Jewish pride and renewed support for Jewish culture; Jewish nationalists, too, were caught up in the hopeful spirit of the new era.[73] These movements found much of their support among Galician-born Jews, many of whom came to Vienna as refugees during the early years of World War I and felt alienated from the acculturated Jews who tended to resent their presence. But some native-born Viennese also promoted Jewish nationalism. A number of young interwar Austrian athletes, for example, expressed their strong sense of Jewish pride through their participation in the sports clubs Makkabi and Hakoah, which competed against other Austrian teams and won national championships.[74] Still, activities and attitudes explicitly promoting Jewish culture were far from the norm among Jewish youth. Over the course of the interwar period, the original two thousand members of Vienna's forty Jewish youth movements decreased significantly, both due to emigration to Palestine and to refugees returning home.[75]

The distribution of Jews across interwar Viennese sports teams provides insight into Jews' myriad responses to their new political status in the First Republic. It also provides an example of another theme that runs throughout this book: that the coding of groups and places as "Jewish" and "not-Jewish" played a role in whether people chose to affiliate with them, but did not necessarily correlate with the presence of actual Jews or non-Jews. Certainly the members of the Jewish nationalist teams Makkabi and Hakoah were, of course, Jews. Yet Jews also participated in other teams, whether they were coded Jewish or not. They were active members and leaders of Austria, a sports team coded as bourgeois and Jewish. But even Rapid and Admira, staunchly proletarian teams with nationalist and antisemitic reputations whose members stemmed from the working class districts, counted Jews among their members and leadership. Like the culture of the Catholic Church, such sports teams, through their very exclusion of the "Jewish," often attracted Jews seeking to distance themselves from associations with that category.[76]

The notion that the "Jewish" was increasingly excluded from the "Austrian" also formed the basis for what might seem like the opposite phenomenon, Jewish nationalism. As one former Hakoah member points out, her team pride stemmed not from a sense of Austrian patriotism but rather from a desire to counter antisemitic stereotypes about Jews. But her words indicate that she still considered the group to be a world apart: "We wanted to show them!" Her defiance rankled her father, however, who wanted his daughter to excel at swimming, but who implied he did not want her to join a Jewish team.[77] In other words, neither a feeling of shame at displaying Jewish symbols nor a determination to wear them with pride indicated that they—or anyone else—considered the "Jewish" as part of a national "Austrian" culture and an erasure of social divisions; rather, both responses actually acknowledged the continued exclusion of things coded "Jewish" (that is, weak and unfit) from the "Austrian."

The Jew as Austrian

As indicated above, Jews found many opportunities to participate in interwar Austrian culture, but in order to do so they had to navigate cultural norms about Jewish difference already in place, even as they reshaped them through their participation. Their responses ranged from completely rejecting the hierarchy of the terms of Jewish difference—as typified by Zionism—to accepting its basic tenets and repeating antisemitic tropes. Counterintuitive though it may seem, the success of Austrian Jews in creating popular Austrian culture did not indicate that society accepted them as Jews so much as it signaled their anxiety about being excluded from mainstream culture. Moreover, their passionate efforts to create cultures of inclusion often involved implicit attempts to dissociate themselves from anything coded as Jewish.[78] Author Friedrich Torberg best summed up this widespread, paradoxical coping strategy with a pithy quote that has been attributed to Dorothy Parker: "Jews are just like everybody else. Only more so."[79]

Marjorie Perloff, born Gabriele Mintz in 1931, recounts leaving Vienna as a six-year old refugee and characterizes her subsequent experiences as both culturally and psychologically upsetting. She points out that, while her assimilated family was hardly free from prejudices against Jews, they still remained loyal to Judaism as well as to German culture. Nevertheless, Perloff recalls that her mother neglected to tell her and her siblings that they were forced to leave Austria because they were Jews. Instead, she told them "Now we are no longer Austrians. Hitler has taken Austria," a statement which, according to Perloff, underscores how far many Jews went to deny self-identification as Jews. As she makes clear, culture continued to function as a kind of magic key that allowed Jews to enter European society and shake off any appearance of Jewish difference. Perloff admits that much of her fascination with the cultural, social, and artistic legacies of Vienna has to do with to what she calls the energy expended to downplay or hide "the Jewish presence that had, ironically, done so much to make Viennese culture the richly textured, complicated, and super subtle culture it was. Indeed, the *Kulturdrang*, especially of the interwar years, seems to have gone hand in hand with a collective desire for passing—passing as someone or something one could never quite be. . . . "[80]

To be sure, to some extent the same could be said about Jewish experiences before the collapse of the monarchy, and in areas outside Austria as well. Nevertheless, it was precisely their efforts to appear "not Jewish" that often made Jews stand out—even to other Jews. Viennese Jewish lawyer Franz Rudolf Bienenfeld made this point about Jews in Poland in a 1937 speech to the Jewish Association for Sociology and Anthropology:

> But whatever the cause of the distinctive peculiarities of the Jews, they undoubtedly exist . . . They preserve . . . them . . . throughout several generations even when they make considerable efforts to identify themselves with their surroundings. Frequently it is this passionate desire to adapt themselves at any cost which is a distinguishing feature . . . In Poland I knew a lawyer whose Catholic piety—he always wore a cross under his tie—and lordly behaviour struck me even in that environment where both are common. It was their exaggeration which made me and everyone else realise that he was of Jewish origin and not a genuine Pole.[81]

Bienenfeld, who was one of the drafters of the Universal Declaration of Human Rights in 1948, cared deeply about equality and human rights, but that did not stop him from recognizing the complicated vicissitudes of Jewish difference, and identifying those Jews whose struggles to efface difference paradoxically resulted in maintaining it. Nevertheless, he cannot help but repeat the terms of the system that divided "Jews" and "genuine Poles" in the first place, as both Jews and non-Jews commonly did. As historian Joan Scott has aptly noted, we cannot expect historical subjects to be aware of the terms of the larger, systemic frameworks according to which they operated at the time.[82] And as Scott Spector points out for German Jews in particular, the dialectical conditions that created this problem also delimit the terms of its articulation—an issue that he suggests historians can address by leaving room for subjectivity and Jews' various levels of self-consciousness in their studies of such frameworks.[83]

Nevertheless, the elision of the "Jewish" from an emerging sense of the interwar "Austrian" did not preclude explicit manifestations of Jewish culture during that period. Understanding and aspiring to an Austrian cultural ideal did not prohibit Jews from remaining Jewish, or living among, socializing with, and marrying other Jews. Moreover, it would be absurd to claim that Jewish topics never appeared in the literature and film of interwar Austria, or that Jewish men and women in Central Europe never participated in public life openly and proudly as Jews. However, explicitly Jewish topics and themes typically appeared under delimited conditions of "authenticity" in works involving Yiddish, Zionism, Judaism, or as narratives of Jewish social transformation turning away from traditional Jewish life.[84]

Explicit manifestations of Jewish life in Vienna were to some extent a significant part of the city's life. There were at least ten newspapers catering explicitly to the Jewish community, several of which were published in Yiddish.[85] Books on Jewish religion and customs were published in both German and Yiddish,[86] and popular Jewish and Yiddish theater performances were well-attended by non-Jews as well as Jews. Interwar Vienna may never have achieved the status of Berlin as a thriving metropolis of Yiddish culture,[87] but it nevertheless remained a place where Yiddish and even Hebrew self-expression was accepted and, in some cases, embraced.[88]

Still, publishing in Yiddish or Hebrew or writing about Jewish themes allowed access to the public sphere only on circumscribed terms. Yiddish culture was popular among certain sections of the mainstream because it appealed to the spirit of unity, authenticity, and cultural stability that so many Austrians sought amidst the political, cultural, and social instabilities of the interwar years—not because it was accepted as "Austrian" or "Viennese." This becomes clear when we see the "Jewish" performed in full force in cabaret and other underground or marginal types of theater, which by their very nature sought to maintain their status as outside mainstream culture, where one did not have to worry about the aesthetic values and expectations of "self-consciously elite" critics and audience.[89]

For some, then, Jewish topics provided an authentic ideal that was imagined in opposition to the superficial, materialistic, mimetic qualities associated with stereotypes of the "Jewish." For others, it was useful as a form of lowbrow culture to be performed on the margins of the mainstream. Nevertheless, we can see in both cases an engagement with, although not necessarily a destabilization of, the Jewish social symbolic order, and yet more evidence of the degree to which the culture of the time reflected the important role Jews played in defining and redefining its limits. But the striving for that Austrian ideal emerges most clearly when we analyze those works by Jews that specifically *lack* explicitly Jewish themes.

Whether reluctantly, nostalgically, or eagerly, Jewish and non-Jewish Austrians had to come to terms with forming a new national self-understanding, while non-Austrians who lived in the country had to find their place within it. Defining the terms of exclusion—that is, determining what was *not* "Austrian"—formed a major, if not always conscious, part of that process of national self-identification. Although the creation of a new country was accomplished easily enough within a political and legal framework, delineating how "Austrian" was different from "German" would be harder to achieve. German author and philosopher Oskar A. H. Schmitz attempted to hammer out the terms of this distinction in 1924 in his book *Der österreichische Mensch* (The Austrian man). Schmitz characterized the German as Protestant, intellectual, humanistic, bourgeois, individual, specialized and possessed of an American work ethic, while the Austrian embodied the Catholic, sensual, baroque, aristocratic, community-oriented, and graceful. Significantly, there is no room for Jews on either list.[90] But the negative characteristics of the "Jewish" would prove a more usable way to clarify and understand the "Austrian." Thus, it is no surprise that some authors most explicitly articulated the exclusion of the "Jewish"—not the German—from their newly forming conceptions of the "Austrian." Karl Paumgartten's 1924 novel *Repablick*, for example, complained that the "Austrian" had become too influenced by the Jewish and proletarian, and should be more of a "German" republic.[91]

As Benvenisti's interview with Schnitzler indicated, outbursts of antisemitic violence increased in the years immediately after the founding of the new state.[92] Immediately after the end (and loss) of the war, when Jews were convenient targets for political and economic frustration at political rallies, antisemites' efforts to run Jews out of Vienna became both increasingly vocal and public. Antisemitic outbursts of "*Saujud*" (Jew swine) increased after 1918 on places like the sports field and in the Leopoldstadt, Vienna's Jewish district.[93] According to Vilna Troupe actor Luba Kadison, the group of Yiddish actors was enthusiastically received in Vienna in 1922, but faced catcalls and jeers from the audience when they performed in the nearby town of Baden.[94] On February 4, 1923, catcalls of "*Saujud*" and "*jüdisches Schwein*" (Jewish pig) disrupted a lecture on

"Sexual Crimes" by Jewish sexologist Magnus Hirschfeld in Vienna. At the lecture, men sporting swastikas set off stink bombs, fired blanks, threw women to the ground and stomped on them, and yelled "Hirschfeld must be done away with! The guy has to be murdered!"[95]

Chava Holtzmann clearly remembers being attacked by students from the Hochschule für Bodenkultur (University of Agriculture) when she accompanied her father and Zionist activist and Jewish community leader Robert Stricker on their annual procession to Theodor Herzl's grave in the Döbling cemetery.[96] American psychoanalyst Muriel Gardiner, who studied medicine in Vienna during the late 1920s and early 1930s before joining the Austrian antifascist movement, noted that there were two divisions in different wings of the anatomy building, one attended by Jews and Socialists and the other by Christian Socials and antisemites. She recalls Jewish students being injured and even thrown out of windows.[97] By 1931, antisemites were bold enough to place a sign on the university's main entrance forbidding entrance to Jews, and by 1933, antisemitism at the university had reached new heights.[98]

The Jew in Vienna/Vienna in Austria

In the face of the postwar destabilization of both the political order and traditional gender roles, Jewishness as a social and symbolic order, with its hierarchical division between the "Jewish" and the "non-Jewish," remained stable. Amid the general sense of chaos and anxiety, these age-old codes were invigorated with new urgency as a means of understanding and interpreting people, places, and events. Austria's city/province binary was one of the most significant cultural constructs to be strengthened by the framework of Jewish difference, a fact that could not be ignored by those who shaped the new nation, whether they approved of it or not. Moreover, Jewish difference applied not only to people and groups, but also to places, and in this capacity played a major role in the development of Austrian and Viennese self-understandings along this symbolic center/periphery divide. The terms of the city/province discourse were not always explicitly based upon Jewish references, but they often relied upon references to Jewish difference to establish their meanings.[99]

When historian Friedrich Heer notes that the "Jews' place in Vienna was a perfect mirror image to Vienna's place in the country," he links the politics of interwar Vienna's urban geography to that of the Austrian nation and underscores the importance of the "Jew" as a foundational symbol in interwar Austria.[100] His observation suggests that Austrians articulated both national and urban power struggles according to the terms of Jewish difference, and indicates the fundamental role geography played in providing the basis for this axis of power. After 1918, the cultural divide between Vienna and the provinces intensified, buttressing both the foundations of Austria's unstable political frame and its new national self-understanding.[101]

In his seminal book *The Country and the City*, Raymond Williams crystallizes the function of his titular binary by showing how it operated to conceptualize social differences and articulate power in English literature over centuries. In a similar vein, Austrians invoked Jewish difference as a way to articulate and reinforce power struggles between city and province. From the viewpoint of the provinces, interwar Vienna loomed large as a dangerous "Jewish" metropolis—superficial, ugly, crass, corrupt, depraved, socialist, capitalist, materialist, decadent, modern, and immoral, depending on the demands of political or cultural expediency. In turn, the provinces functioned as the site of all that was pure, good, beautiful, respectable, and moral—values that many sought to include in a new "Austrian" sensibility. However, maintaining a perspective from Vienna remained crucial for defining this provincial ideal: Tyrolean-born Karl Schönherr, author of interwar *Heimat* literature celebrating the provinces, claimed to do his best work at the marble-topped table of a Viennese café where, he noted, "Only the big city made my homeland come alive for me artistically."[102]

The hostility between the provinces and Vienna, aggravated by the First World War, intensified after the formation of the First Republic.[103] After the war, it was by no means clear that the provinces would be able to unify themselves, let alone unite with the city whose modern urban life they already viewed with suspicion.[104] Referendums held in Vorarlberg, Tyrol, and Salzburg in the years after the war voted overwhelmingly for annexation with Switzerland and Germany, respectively; however, these political actions carried no legal weight. Vorarlberg, Austria's westernmost province, already in May 1919 voted they would rather join Switzerland than remain part of what they termed "der Wiener Judenstaat" (the Jewish state of Vienna), pointing to the conflation of Jews and Vienna as Austrians defined their place in the new nation.[105]

Politically, the city/province divide intensified further when the Social Democrats gained political control of Vienna in 1919; by 1920, Vienna had become became a lone "red" city surrounded by the "black" Christian Social provinces and federal government.[106] Antisemitic rhetoric had linked socialism and Jews well before the interwar period, but this linkage became even stronger as Jews became more involved and visible in the movement after World War I. Provincial newspapers often used the moniker "*Rotes Wien*" (Red Vienna) as a negative term that meant virtually the same thing as "Jewish Vienna."[107] Although efforts to transform the city into a socialist utopia bore few explicit traces of Jewish difference—indeed, its leaders sometimes espoused antisemitic rhetoric—the significant presence and crucial role of Jews in Vienna's socialist leadership, as well as the modern innovations they developed, helped cement the city's negative Jewish coding. Similarly, the disproportionate presence of Jews among Vienna's lawyers, philosophers, poets, doctors, psychologists, writers, and journalists, decried by vocal antisemites as contributing to the *Verjudung* (jewification) of Vienna, fuelled prejudices and stereotypes of Jews as visible defilers of the urban landscape.[108]

But within the city itself, as Friedrich Heer suggests, Vienna's Jews were to Vienna as Vienna was to Austria: a critical symbol as "Other" necessary for self-definition. Vienna had already been coded internally as "Christian," thanks to fin-de-siècle mayor Karl Lueger, whose well-known political antisemitism furthered the divide between "Jew" and "non-Jew." "In Vienna," notes Heer, "'Christian' came to signify 'Non-Jew,' largely due to opportunistic mayor Karl Lueger's skill in harnessing antisemitism to maintain power in the city."[109] Moreover, the Christian Social party stepped up its efforts to portray Vienna as a Catholic and German (in a cultural sense) city by staging overt demonstrations of Catholic culture alongside state events, like the openings of schools.[110] After the end of the war, political power struggles in the city—including Vienna's struggle with the national government over issues like censorship and taxation—were often articulated according to the terms of Jewish difference, both because many Jews were socialist leaders and because the divide between imagined Jew and Christian already held firm ground there.[111]

Most of Vienna's Jews lived in the Leopoldstadt district, nicknamed the *Mazzesinsel* (matzoh island), a portion of which had served as the city's Jewish ghetto from 1624 to 1670, when Emperor Leopold expelled the Jews from Austria. A substantial number of Jews made their homes there when they returned decades later, and during the interwar period, the Leopoldstadt still housed a third of the city's Jewish population. Most of the tens of thousands of impoverished Jewish refugees from Galicia who arrived during World War I via its main train station (Nordbahnhof) made their homes there. Although the entire district was far larger than its relatively small Jewish quarter, and its residents included more non-Jews than Jews, both its history and its concentration of Jewish life and culture assured its continued coding as Vienna's most "Jewish" district, even as Jews moved to other areas.

While Vienna's Jews often found themselves pressed to eliminate traces of the Jewish from their life and work, due to their high concentration in the city, the absence of significant numbers of Jews in the provinces only served to promote negative—and often fantastical—uses of their image. As opposed to the city, then, where their physical presence often required Jews to inscribe their absence onto the urban landscape and its culture, in the provinces, the physical absence of Jews most defines their imagined presence. This paradoxical dynamic is reflected in provincial performances, literature, and trial transcripts, in Innsbruck, Salzburg, and beyond. Only in the provinces, for example, did the murder of Christ by Jews, re-envisioned annually in passion play performances, become a significant part of local culture.

As Jews tried to find their way to "becoming" Austrians in the new republic, they stumbled along the same paths as non-Jews, but they did so with more urgency. As members of a minority with a long (and precarious) history in the region, Jews needed to fill the cultural gap left by the collapse of the monarchy with definable—yet inclusive—ways of self-identifying and creating culture. Their efforts to do so reflect the fact that the notion of the "Jewish" in Central Europe, with its traditionally negative and ubiquitous connotations, permeated the thoughts and lives of those who lived there. Jews in Austria often inscribed their desire for home just as deeply in their stories, dramas, and other works of art as did those in exile, but those desires were powerfully shaped by the fact that their homeland was at times as hostile to them as it was appealing.

This book traces Jewish difference in interwar Austrian culture as it manifested itself in both the provinces and the city, regardless of the actual presence or absence of Jews, from performances "on stage" both at trials and in the theater, to the reading, writing, and viewing of urban narratives. It also examines how Jewish difference colored the outcomes of three notorious interwar murder cases that garnered sensational international and national headlines and reveals how the dynamic relationship between Jewish and non-Jewish played out on both provincial and urban stages. Latvian Jewish student Phillipp Halsmann was twice tried and convicted of killing his father Max while hiking in the Tyrolean Alps in 1928, before eventually coming to America, where he became a renowned photographer. Despite no motive or physical evidence, Max Halsmann's death by bludgeoning was deemed an act of patricide by the trial's provincial jury. The dramatic rhetoric used to describe the bloody scene and the frequent references to the foreign demeanor and language of both father and son evoked the powerful symbols at work during centuries-old blood libel accusations, when Jews were accused of murdering Christian children to obtain their blood for religious rituals. Similar to traditional local passion plays linked to such accusations, reenactments of the events at the scene of the murder and courtroom proceedings functioned as "performances" that called upon longstanding antisemitic stereotypes in the service of maintaining community boundaries.[112]

In contrast, the murders in Vienna of author and publisher Hugo Bettauer in 1925 and philosophy professor Moritz Schlick in 1936 were then, and are even more so today, viewed as manifestations of antisemitic violence. But deeper examination reveals the trumped-up moral reasons behind Bettauer's murderer's intent, and Schlick's murderer's personal grudge; both, however, avoided heavy punishment by claiming antisemitic motives in front of juries sympathetic to their cause, with little concern for the fact that neither Bettauer nor Schlick were, technically, Jews. These trials transformed their victims into Jews by reimagining their murders as clear acts of antisemitic rage. In other words, both the violent acts and the resulting trials turn out to reflect the nature of Jewishness in their urban contexts more than they do the antisemitic intent of their murderers. In all three cases, the presence or absence of Jews made little difference to lawyers using antisemitism to legitimate violence, as both provincial and urban courtrooms became stages upon which Jewish difference functioned as a deeply engrained system used to shape contemporary interpretations of unexpected events in unstable times.

The vicissitudes of Jews' imagined place in this urban/provincial divide are also taken up in Hugo Bettauer's 1922 novel *The City without Jews*, which illuminates the presence of Jews in Vienna by asking readers to imagine their absence. Remembered today mainly as a prescient warning about the dangers of antisemitism, the book and its 1924 film version actually satirized both Jews and non-Jews, revealing them as equally complicit in perpetuating the very structures that set them apart. Stripped of its Jews, the city literally becomes the provinces. And by depicting a city literally devoid of Jews, *The City without Jews* explicitly addresses the way in which many Jews considered their presence in Vienna to be conditional upon their accepting an abstract form of their own "absence" by downplaying or eliding their Jewish self-understandings.

Yet by excluding Jewish women from its text, the book also links the presence of Jews to the effacement of Jewish women, a phenomenon not limited to interwar Austria. The implications of this gendered Jewish absence are explored via examples from the publishing industry. Publishers like Paul Zsolnay and Richard Kola provided opportunities for Jewish women like Mela Hartwig, Hilde Spiel, and others to earn a living as writers, translators, and literary agents, but only at the price of strictly limiting—and sometimes even prohibiting—their content. Viennese Jewish writer Vicki Baum was more successful in penetrating the German market when she moved to Berlin, but the rigidity with which she was marketed as a New Woman by her Jewish publishers indicates the strict limits placed upon her visibility in the public sphere. Yet those same limits allowed Austrian writers like Mela Hartwig to experiment with less mainstream writing styles and content, albeit still at the cost of Jewish visibility. Together, the lives of these women writers underscore the various ways in which literature—and its accompanying rules of consumption—framed the condition of Jewish "absence," as well as how Jewish cultural participation often came at the price of eliding both Jewish self-identification and Jewish content.

In their reading, as in their writing, lives of Vienna's Jewish residents were shaped by how they and others both imagined and described the qualities of Jewish space in the city. From the provinces, interwar Red Vienna represented a socialist—and Jewish—metropolis, but within the bounds of the city itself, a complex coding of Jewish space affected how all residents established, used, and described their city. These physical and symbolic spatial distinctions mirrored the country's larger city/province divide, but on different terms. Representative examples of space that was coded Jewish in the late nineteenth century illuminate the Leopoldstadt as a site understood as "Jewish" on a number of social and historical grounds. The persistence of the Leopoldstadt as an imagined "Jewish space" served a purpose for both Jews and non-Jews: It enabled them to envision other urban spaces they wished to design or inhabit as "non-Jewish." Just as Vienna was never more Jewish than when it was used as a way to articulate its relationship to the Catholic, conservative provinces, so did the Leopoldstadt—the majority of whose residents were not in fact Jews—emerge as most Jewish when considered in its relationship to the rest of the city. The texts set all or in part in the Leopoldstadt by authors writing in German (Veza Canetti), Yiddish (Abraham Moshe Fuchs), and Hebrew (David Vogel) both shaped and reflected the ways in which different engagements with Jewishness in Vienna were inextricably intertwined with the city's "Jewish" geography.

Theater productions in both Vienna and the provinces also demonstrate how the need for Austrian Jews to come to terms with their changed social status after World War I drove the creation of new cultural productions that provided potential answers—or, at the very least, an escape—for both Jewish and non-Jewish Austrians seeking an inclusive national cultural ideal that would combine past traditions and modern sensibilities. The theater proved to be a particularly resonant site upon which the social and political upheavals of the postwar era played themselves out, particularly in light of the fact that the previous era's censorship was reduced and then eliminated completely in 1926, a change that not only broke taboos but opened up space for antisemitic sentiment.[113] More importantly, however, this shift enabled the theater to serve as a space where competing interests could work to shape a new national self-understanding through performance. Max Reinhardt's involvement in—and passion for—both the Catholic Salzburg Festival and the Yiddish theater in Vienna points to the significant role of Austrian Jews as driving forces behind two seemingly oppositional forms of culture, which both thrived at a time of deep social crisis. The fact that Max Reinhardt and Hugo von Hofmannsthal both played major roles in creating the Salzburg Festival along traditional, conservative lines allows us to revisit the overdetermined portrayal of Jews at the forefront of modernity in all aspects of European culture. Their success, however, depended on their understanding that a theater production in the provinces had to remain devoid of Jewish associations in order to qualify as "Austrian." On the other hand, the fact that both Jews and non-Jews were avid enthusiasts of Yiddish theater in Vienna emphasizes the appeal of an explicitly Jewish form of theater to broad audiences in an urban context. Despite their differences, both forms of theater sparked intense, emotional reactions in audiences composed of Jews and non-Jews, using provincial and urban stages to reinvent mystical worlds of the past and create new ethical and cultural ideals with possibilities for future redemption.

The presence of Jewish difference as a category of analysis permeates the words of many of the figures whose narrative histories form the core of this book. Their experiences suggest possible directions for applying the lens of Jewish difference to other key interwar figures whose work lies beyond the scope of this study, in areas such as music, philosophy, and architecture. In Austria between the wars, the terms of Jewish difference played a crucial—if often unrecognized—role in the shaping of culture. The manifestations of these terms indicate that the self-understandings of Austrian Jews between the wars had as much to do with knowing when *not* to appear "Jewish" as they did with embracing traditional mainsprings of Jewish culture. Ultimately, recognizing these polarities as part of the same socially constructed order can help us understand how the intensification of Jewish difference after the monarchy's collapse reflected the significance of its imagined boundaries both for Austrian cultural creativity and for the toleration of brutal acts of injustice.

1 COURTS OF INJUSTICE

FOUR TRIALS, THREE MURDERS, TWO JEWS

The libel trial at the courtroom in Hietzing, a leafy outer district of Vienna bordering the Wienerwald, began like any other. On June 19, 1928, judge, jury, witnesses, lawyers, court guards, and secretary assumed their roles in the service of justice.[1] Jewish editor Bruno Wolf stood accused of libel for his public claim that Oskar Pöffel had blackmailed firms into advertising in the newspaper—the very firms Pöffel covered as editor of the *Neues Wiener Journal*'s financial section. But before the judge could call the first witness, Pöffel himself calmly pulled a pistol from his pocket and fired six shots. Two of them hit Wolf, two hit the wall, one hit the briefcase of Wolf's lawyer, and another brushed a table. As the judge testified seven months later at the murder trial in his new role as witness, he immediately called for the guard and rushed over to Wolf, who lay face down on the courtroom floor. "Because he moved his foot I thought he might only be hurt, so that's why I called for the ambulance." Another witness, the courtroom secretary, recalled that Pöffel shot at Wolf even after he had fallen. "I went right over there and raised Wolf's head. His blood ran over my hands."[2] Wolf died before the ambulance arrived.

The setting of the murder in the middle of a Viennese courtroom had both profound and ironic consequences. To be sure, every trial is a performance of sorts in which all involved assume roles as prosecutors, defendants, witnesses, judges, and jurors. But the trial for the murder of Bruno Wolf that began nearly seven months later turned into an unusual repeat performance that cast former judges, lawyers, and court guards from the first trial in new roles on a different stage as witnesses, in which they were compelled to revisit and reenact their earlier roles.[3] As newspaper reporters and even the state prosecutor quickly noticed, instead of focusing on the murder, the trial not only replayed the original libel case but also carried it even further. It seemed that instead of Pöffel, on trial were prominent, mainly Jewish, businessmen and publishers whose names had long been associated with shady deals in Vienna, most notably that of Jakob Lippowitz, the publisher of the *Neues Wiener Journal*. As *Das Kleine Blatt* reported on January 18, "Not yet mentioned was the murder, the horrible bloody deed in the Hietzing courtroom! Instead one got to hear well-known names: Castiglioni, Rintelen, Bosel, Ahrer, Braun-Stammfest, Lederer, Lippowitz . . . Austria is so small, that they all knew each other—financiers, finance ministers, and their editors." Ironically, the fact that Pöffel killed Wolf in a courtroom became a major factor in his acquittal instead of sealing his fate. By allowing the original libel trial to be replayed in the absence of Wolf, defense lawyers Walter Riehl and Hans Gürtler easily transformed a courtroom murderer into an impoverished, unemployed victim who sought only to honor his "contract" with the shady, wealthy publisher Lippowitz.[4] And thus Lippowitz, not Pöffel, became responsible when the jury declared Pöffel's murderous act a result of *Sinnesverwirrung* (mental confusion) as Riehl had urged and on January 19, 1929, declared him a free man.

The acquittal came as a shock to most Viennese. As correspondent Heinrich Eduard Jacob noted, "The telephone screamed through all of Vienna at one o'clock in the morning; people raised their hands to their heads in disbelief; nobody wanted to believe what the morning's news would bring. Pöffl [*sic*] was set free! So one was allowed to commit murder, then?" The release of a man who brutally murdered his former colleague was without a doubt, as Jacob lamented, nothing short of a catastrophe for the Austrian justice system.[5] But the trial's unexpected outcome also highlights the intersection of its performative nature with the codings of Jewish difference and their heightened role during the Austrian interwar period. At no time during the trial was it ever alleged that antisemitism was the murderer's motive. But the terms of Jewish difference nevertheless colored everyone's "performance," as defense lawyers played upon political tensions and prejudices between Vienna and Burgenland, home of the trial's jurors, and portrayed both Pöffel and the man he murdered as victims of a larger, more powerful force: Vienna's press network and, by implication, the Jews who ran it.[6]

The ways in which Jewish difference overlapped with interwar political tensions between city and province in this relatively little-known trial echo those of four better-known trials in interwar Austria. These legal events received much more national and international attention and became critical barometers through which to gauge the complex system of Jewish codings in Austria: the two trials of Latvian Jew Philipp Halsmann for the murder of his father, who was killed on a hiking trip in the Tyrol in 1928, and the two trials for the murders of two well-known Viennese figures, both Protestants: writer Hugo Bettauer in 1925 and philosophy professor Moritz Schlick in 1936.[7] In these four interwar trials, Austrians in both city and province sought to explain these violent murders by engaging familiar social codes of Jewish difference, assigning abstract qualities coded as "Jewish" and "not-Jewish" to victims and perpetrators in order to construct culturally plausible accounts of the crimes. But while the urban cultural contexts of the Viennese murders demanded that their victims' Jewish qualities be emphasized to render their brutal killings more palatable, Halsmann's conviction in the Tyrol was accompanied by symbols and allusions that associated its Jewish victim with a Christian martyr who suffered at the hands of his Jewish killer. Together, these three cases suggest that Jewish difference was a pliant and potent force that buttressed social and political tensions throughout the Austrian interwar period according to specific geographical contexts.

This chapter examines in detail the symbolic substance of Jewish difference in these four prominent trials and its role in their resulting subversions of justice. The reception of all three murders in the courtroom and the public sphere hinged upon spectators' and readers' interpretations of words and images that engaged deeply embedded notions of Jewishness—notions that shifted according to their provincial and urban contexts. In the Tyrol, the powerful cultural iconography and rhetoric of blood libel trials and the reinforcement of their meaning in annual passion plays combined with other longstanding antisemitic prejudices to help transform the courtroom into a stage where Philipp and his deceased father echoed the traditional roles of a Jewish murderer and his victim, the Christian martyr.[8] In Vienna, the murders of two public figures were portrayed in court as acts of antisemitic rage against men spreading dangerous "Jewish" ideas about sexual perversity and philosophy. The lawyers for their murderers may not have entirely convinced their urban audiences that their clients were heroes, but at the very least, they used the terms of Jewish difference to reframe their clients' actions as understandable and acceptable to a broad spectrum of people. In both Vienna and the Tyrol, justice was thwarted: assassins Otto Rothstock and Hans Nelböck received less than three years imprisonment and emerged unscathed, while Philipp Halsmann was wrongly imprisoned for roughly the same amount of time for a crime that remains unsolved to this day.

In each of these trials, the courtrooms became stages upon which codings of Jewish difference revealed themselves to be part of a deeply engrained system that was easily manipulated to shape contemporary interpretations of unexpected events. Scandalous trials in Europe had long played a significant role in transforming cultural life and opening up new public platforms for political and social debates, so the cultural contexts and ramifications of the Halsmann affair and the Vienna trials certainly had historic precedents. But these trials in particular underscore how they could also readily be used in the service of injustice.

Foregrounding a trial's performative aspects helps us to see how cultural forces are always at work in the courtroom, as well as to understand how Jewish difference could be used to shape the mediated space between its actors and audience both inside and outside its walls. As one recent investigation into the role of "legal performance" in law's reception and production suggests, an acknowledgment of "law's ambivalent relationship to its own theatricality" can reveal much about how trials influence the attitudes leading to both the jury's decisions and their acceptance (or rejection) by the public.[9] Similar to gender, Jewish difference requires not only performance, but also repetition, for its power. Rather than a fixed condition, Judith Butler suggests we consider gender as an "act" that requires repeated public performances in order to reinforce what we understand as "masculinity" and "femininity." In other words, gender must be continually re-experienced for the legitimization of its socially established meanings.[10]

As a socially constructed system that functioned similarly, Jewish difference also required public performances of its terms in order to perpetually legitimate the boundaries between what was coded "Jewish" and "not-Jewish." Considering the framework of repeated performance not only reveals the obvious antisemitism that led to unjust verdicts in these trials, but it also lets us see how the courtrooms served as stages upon which performances of Jewish difference served both to reinforce and redefine its boundaries, independent of whether the "actors" involved in their roles were Jews. Ultimately, these trials show that codings of Jewishness were abstract, detachable, applicable to a range of individuals, and not necessarily contingent upon the degree to which they, or others, considered themselves as Jews, if at all. Moreover, they show how Jewish difference was used as a powerful method of articulating broader political and social tensions between urban and provincial Austria that increased after the collapse of the monarchy, playing a key role in how Austrians shaped the culture of the First Republic.

A Provincial Passion Play: Starring Philipp and Max Halsmann

Renowned photographer Philipp Halsman's 1959 *Jump Book* still charms, although its images of celebrities joyfully springing into midair may strike us as gimmicky by now. In fact, Halsman poked fun at his own work at the time, accompanying the photographs with essays in which he provided tongue-in-cheek "analyses" of the jumps using a technique he refers to as "jumpology": "In a jump the subject, in a sudden burst of energy, overcomes gravity. He cannot simultaneously control his expressions, his facial and his limb muscles. The mask falls. The real self becomes visible. One has only to snap it with the camera." Typically, Halsman announces to readers who are in on the joke that such probings into the depth of the human psyche are accomplished only by the psychologist or psychoanalyst. But the photographer who captures a "jump" also rises to their level of expertise and insight.[11]

Philippe Halsman captured himself leaping into the air with Marilyn Monroe in one of his popular celebrity "jump" portraits from the 1950s. Few of his admirers knew that his passion for cameras that could capture action shots was linked to the sensational "Austrian Dreyfus Affair" of 1928–1930, in which he had been unjustly convicted of killing his father.

The belief that a photograph or painting could reveal what was not normally visible to the naked eye, like the hidden depths of a person's character, was hardly an innovative idea when Halsman's book appeared. But for all its surface triviality, *Jump Book* takes on new meaning when we consider the shocking events of Halsman's past.[12] Thirty years earlier, long before he made a name for himself as a celebrity portrait photographer, Philipp Halsmann was convicted of brutally killing his father by bashing in his head with a stone and throwing his body over a cliff while the two were on a hiking trip in the Tyrolean Alps.[13] Ironically, photographs were a central element in both the prosecution's case against Philipp and his own interpretation of his father's death, while the misuse of psychological theories played a significant role in his convictions.

When an Innsbruck jury convicted Halsmann of patricide for the first time in 1928, and again in 1929 after a subsequent trial for the same crime, Halsmann's sister Liouba worked feverishly to garner local, national, and international support. She managed to gather supporters ranging from international human rights organizations to public figures like Thomas Mann, Jakob Wassermann, and Albert Einstein. The prosecution's failure to provide either physical evidence or plausible motive led many to believe that antisemitism played a central role in his conviction.[14] As a consequence of international pressure, Austrian president Wilhelm Miklas pardoned Halsmann on September 30, 1930, under the condition that he never return to Austria.[15] Halsmann left for Paris, then moved to America in 1940.[16] As his fame as a photographer grew, few people were ever aware of his involvement in the two trials that became known as the "Austrian Dreyfus Affair" due to the role antisemitism played in them.[17]

Philipp Halsmann's first trial for the murder of his father began on the morning of November 30, 1928, in Innsbruck. Less than two months later, the jury found Philipp guilty of patricide by a vote of 8–4, and he was sentenced to ten years of hard labor.[18] However, in October 1929 the case was retried on the basis of an appeal by four Innsbruck professors who claimed that, with no apparent motive, a psychological evaluation would be needed to determine whether Halsmann could legally be determined guilty. In subsequent character evaluations by court-appointed experts, competing explanations of Halsmann's supposedly twisted psyche emerged. One lawyer for the prosecution attempted to utilize Freud's theory of the Oedipus complex as a possible motive, a contention that Freud himself later refuted in a newspaper essay.[19] Such conjecture, as well as antisemitic and sensational coverage by the press, helped the prosecutors achieve their goals, and Philipp was again convicted by the jury, although this time he was sentenced to four years of hard labor.[20]

The Halsmann affair bears the trappings of other antisemitic trials in modern Central Europe: detailed eyewitness testimony against accused Jews that mysteriously increases in the months after the murder; questionable autopsies carried out by local doctors in the service of reinforcing preconceived, antisemitic stereotypes; accusations of sexual impropriety and perversity; and local fears that outsiders might unduly influence the trial's outcome.[21] But the fact that the Halsmann affair took place during a period of relative economic and political stability in Austria highlights not only the jarring nature of this particular violent event, but also its specifically Tyrolean context.[22] When the Halsmanns set out on their alpine hike in the Zillertal in September 1928, political and social tensions between the ethnically homogenous and politically conservative Christian Social Austrian provinces and the urban, liberal, Jewish-coded Socialist capital of Vienna were running high. Although few Jews lived in the Zillertal, numerous long-standing chimerical notions associating them with blood, sexual perversity, pornography, greed, equivocation, and crime—particularly murder—were deeply embedded in the local culture.[23] In Philipp's trial, the manipulation and interpretation of police reports, witness testimonies, expert medical evaluations, and photographs according to historical antisemitic narratives became critical to upholding this particular Tyrolean brand of "antisemitism without Jews" as a way to define responses to interwar political and social change.[24]

Numerous scholars have pointed to the widespread post-1918 Austrian phenomenon of scapegoating Jews for wartime losses, but in the Tyrol, its force was exacerbated by a long history of animosity toward both the central government and Jews, as well as by a deeply embedded Catholic culture.[25] The occupation of the region by Italian troops between 1918 and 1920 and, especially, the annexation of South Tyrol by Italy intensified tensions with the central government.[26] Indeed, after the collapse of the monarchy, Tyroleans were by no means certain that they wanted to be part of the new Austria.[27] The regional government in Innsbruck even went so far as to (unsuccessfully) proclaim an independent state in the hopes of being able to keep South Tyrol, invoking its beautiful landscape and the feared rift to local identity its loss would cause.[28] Although the liberalization of politics after 1918 actually meant that the Tyrolean parliament gained more administrative control over its own workings, its members still advocated for keeping as great a distance as possible from the federal government.[29] Coding Vienna, the seat of perceived government tyranny, as Jewish points to how deeply conceptions of local identity overlapped with traditional antisemitism, and how Jewish difference was used as a way to articulate broader political struggles in the interwar period.

While it is not surprising that Austria's provinces, particularly their pristine mountains and forests, played a major role in *völkisch* nationalism, it is hardly as self-evident how these breathtaking landscapes might hold equal significance for

Jews as they found their place in the new nation.[30] The Tyrol's alpine setting, which remained a strong element of local self-identification after World War I, provided a strong basis for the local rejection not only of Jews, but of all things perceived as Jewish and therefore damaging. As early as 1920, several Alpine sports associations were among the first to include *Arierparagraphen* (regulations restricting membership to Aryans) in their bylaws, setting the stage for a more widespread exclusion of Jews; their publications from the 1920s—well before the *Anschluss*—play up Jews' foreignness as the cause.[31] That these groups were already calling for the "purification" of their associations in the 1920s, however, did not lessen the appeal of alpine hiking to the people they wanted to keep out.[32] Ironically, for some, the more these associations attempted to exclude them, the more attractive hiking in the mountains became. Ernst Ruzicka's articles on the Halsmann trials appeared regularly in the *Neue Freie Presse*; his son, Martin Ross, explains why his Jewish grandparents chose to continue vacationing in the Tyrol despite their awareness of its antisemitism and their sympathy for Halsmann's plight: "In retrospect this, too, was in character with their general attitude. Inasmuch as Tyrol was the gathering place for antisemites, it followed that by going there they felt that they dissociated themselves from the people who were the target of antisemitism."[33] Like the summer resorts around Salzburg, where provincial antisemitism was a given, the bourgeois leisure activity of mountain climbing, by virtue of being coded as "non-Jewish," attracted many Jews seeking to overcome their own disenfranchisement. Although put off enough by antisemitism to avoid traveling to the provinces' enchanting mountains, Galician-born Benno Varon nevertheless admits to having worn alpine leather shorts and loden jackets while growing up in Vienna. [34] Marjorie Perloff's autobiographical narrative, too, highlights the desire of her family to appear as anything but Jewish. To demonstrate the level to which her family endeavored to appear as "Austrian" as possible, Perloff, who was born in Vienna in 1931, includes a photograph from a family vacation in the provinces in 1934, which features her, her brother, and her mother in full Austrian folk dress, including dirndl and lederhosen. Clearly, performing Austrianness was a way to elide Jewishness.[35]

Intergroup tensions between Jews and non-Jews had long played out across the Zillertal region, ever since the Deutscher und Österreichischer Alpenverein (German and Austrian Alpine Association, or DÖAV), a prominent hiking club, had discussed excluding Jews from membership even before World War I. After a 1921 vote by the association's "Austria" branch to exclude Jews, many former members (including some non-Jews) formed their own branch, the Donauland, which then teamed with the Jewish Deutsche Alpenverein Berlin (German Alpine Association of Berlin) to build their own *Schutzhütte* (climbing hut) in the Zillertal.[36] By 1924, the Donauland had been expelled from the DÖAV. After that expulsion, almost all of the Austrian (and German) alpine associations adopted regulations excluding Jews.[37] When the Halsmanns decided to go climbing in the Zillertal for their vacation, they thus walked right into a long-simmering cultural conflict.

According to many witnesses in the courtroom, the Halsmanns had garnered suspicion from the moment they set out on their journey. Several mentioned that Philipp and his father spoke Russian or a language they "could not understand," and others commented disapprovingly on their inappropriate attire and lack of proper gear for mountain climbing.[38] One witness claimed they were "dressed in an entirely unalpine way,"[39] and another mentioned that the shoes both Halsmanns wore were not recognizable as hiking footwear.[40] The fact that Max had admitted to some of them that he was a "proper tourist" who

Philipp, Ita, Max, and Liouba Halsmann pause for a photograph on an Alpine hike around 1928. Philipp and Max's lack of proper climbing gear pegged them as foreign tourists and helped prosecutors brand the Latvian Jewish pair as outsiders.

wanted to buy himself some better equipment also marked him as a wealthy but inexperienced hiker.

Because of its breathtaking alpine scenery and resulting tourism industry, Tyrol had long been exposed to foreign customs and politics. However, the province also maintained a deeply Catholic and staunchly conservative culture with a reputation for intolerance.[41] Robert Musil even claimed that Tyrol was the most Catholic of all the Austrian provinces.[42] Of particular significance to local culture were annual performances of traditional "passion plays," reenacting the crucifixion of Jesus, which had been performed in Europe since medieval times.[43] These plays maintained a tradition of highlighting the murder of Jesus as the ultimate Jewish sin while simultaneously cementing the boundaries of the community by excluding Jews from its core.[44]

Blood libel trials, in which Jews were accused of killing Christian children for blood to be used in matzoh or other fantastical rituals, were intricately linked to passion plays. A Jew was first accused of killing a Christian boy and nailing him to a cross in Norwich, England, in the twelfth century; such allegations subsequently surfaced throughout Europe, reoccurring with renewed popularity in the late nineteenth century.[45] The initial appearance of these trials at the same time that the Fourth Lateran Council rendered transubstantiation as dogma in 1215 has led some to believe that they actually served to reinforce the ritual of the Eucharist by convincing Christians that, since Jews already used these elements in their own ritual reenactment, Christians needed to properly reappropriate them.[46] Doing so, however, required that the murdered Christian child be beatified and his status as martyr secured. Thus, the first written accounts of such trials link the brutal killings to the supposed desire of Jews to reenact the killing of Christ, and, by extension, to local passion plays.[47] Helmut Walser Smith has argued that reenactments—such as those performed in the plays—hold the key to the true power of blood libel accusations. He suggests that the traditional blood libel accusation has embedded within it an assumption that in carrying out a killing, Jews perform a ritual reenactment of the killing of Christ, but this time in order to collect blood for one of their own secret rituals. Thus, passion plays—like blood libel trial—became another social ritual in which the Christian community reiterates the exclusion of Jews and cements its own boundaries.[48]

As Hillel Kieval points out, written accounts of blood libel trials also created a deeply embedded narrative authority that instructed the community about the danger of Jewish criminals and their mysterious ways, setting the stage for their reinterpretation according to modern "needs," especially in the decades after 1880, when blood libel trials became far more popular than they had ever been centuries before.[49] Between 1867 and 1914, in Austria-Hungary alone, Jews were accused of fantastical murders about a dozen times; often, these trials are explained as a consequence of social friction, economic distress, and age-old local traditions of antisemitism.[50] Together, the tradition of performing passion plays and the reemergence of blood libel trials served to reinforce the self-definition of local communities as exclusively Christian and decidedly "non-Jewish."

Trial transcripts, court documents, and events surrounding the Halsmann trials indicate that they, too, served a similar community-reinforcing social function for interwar Tyroleans. To be sure, nobody actually suggested that Halsmann had murdered his father to use his blood for a ritual, nor do I suggest that his trials should be considered as equivalents to blood libel trials. In fact, the last literal blood libel trial in Europe took place in Russia before World War I. But throughout the interwar period in Central Europe, antisemitic legends and publications kept powerful and palpable symbols and tropes from such trials alive by claiming to unearth the evil, mysterious Jewish roots underlying seemingly "ordinary" murders.[51] By attending to the echoes of symbols of local blood libel trials repeated in the Halsmann affair, where, ironically, the death of the Jew Max Halsmann sparked an outcry among the local population to convict his murderer, we can better understand how Jewish difference functioned in this provincial context and served to falsely condemn Philipp as the murderer. I am making a claim, in other words, for the cultural afterlife of history: for the way that past events give shape and substance to—and function as an underlying driving force for—future events. The specter of blood libel trials may not have been on the minds of those individuals involved in Halsmann's trial, but it is hard to ignore the cultural associations—the kinds of resonances that cannot help but seep into and underneath awareness during such fraught moments—of Jews committing terrible crimes according to mysterious rituals.

Unfortunately for the Halsmanns, the region where they chose to hike was only six miles away from the town of Rinn, where a fabricated story about a fifteenth-century traveling band of Jewish merchants who murdered a three-year-old Christian boy named Andreas Oxner had become the foundation for a seventeenth-century cult dedicated to upholding Oxner's memory. Since then, the townspeople had regularly conducted liturgical processions to the presumed site of the murder, a stone they called the "*Judenstein*," around which an entire church had been constructed and dedicated; its ceiling displayed a fresco depicting the act.[52] There, passion plays were performed specifically in the boy's honor. In the eighteenth century, the pope officially acknowledged this "cult of Andreas," and the diocese officially honored the boy with a feast day on July 12.[53] Figurines of the boy and representations of his torture at the hands of the Jews were common throughout the area.[54]

Although hikers were occasionally murdered on mountain paths in Tyrol, local newspapers typically reported their deaths without mention of their nationalities or religions. But a gruesome murder with a Jewish suspect—and an alleged patricide to boot—offered the perfect opportunity for staging "performances" at the scene of the crime, as well as in the courtroom, that resonated with powerful tropes associated with Jewish ritual murder accusations. Although crime reenactments were not uncommon in contemporary trials, the fact that Philipp reenacted the events in an area loaded with antisemitic symbolism linked to traditional passion plays that were very important to the self-identification of the local community suggests that Halsmann would have little chance of defending himself in this symbolically overloaded arena, no matter what he did or said.

Innsbrucker Festspiel: A Command Performance

Philipp's first "performance" in the role of guilty Jewish murderer occurred at the *Lokalaugschein* (on-site investigation) in the Zillertal one day after the murder on September 11, 1928. Obliged to participate without knowing the details of what evidence had been collected at the scene, he was essentially forced to implicate himself in the crime as he relied upon his memory to reenact the events.[55] Earlier, Philipp had explained to the police how he had walked a bit ahead on the mountain trail because his father needed to relieve himself. He continued his narrative account of events at the first trial, where he described how he heard his father cry out, at which point he turned around: "My father was 4–6 meters behind me. He had his arms pressed against his chest. His body was on the edge of the path in a position as if he were going to fall. In the next second my father disappeared from my line of sight. What happened further, I cannot remember." As Philipp carefully tried to explain to the court, he had a clear image in his mind—in his own words, like a "fixed photograph"—of his father about twenty feet behind him exactly at the moment before he fell, although he did not actually see him fall. When he reached the bank of the brook, he found his father badly bruised but still alive. He then ran to get help. By the time he returned, a small crowd had already gathered around his father, by now dead from deep and fatal wounds to his head and immersed in the water.[56]

At least this is how Philipp described what had happened at the first reenactment at the scene of the crime. Everyone in the "audience" at the scene, however, knew something he didn't: that the likely murder weapon—a bloody stone with clumps of his father's hair on it—had been found nearby on the day of the murder. They also did not tell him it was likely that his father had been bashed in the head with the stone several times, and, due to the amount of blood on the ground and cliff, some of the blows must have occurred before he fell over the cliff to the brook below.

As a result of these omissions, the guesses Philipp offered both at the reenactment and later at the first trial about what had happened to his father sounded a lot like a cover-up. When Philipp described having stood in a spot that everyone else knew had been found soaked with blood, he unwittingly stepped into the exact role his audience expected him to play: the lying Jewish murderer.[57] He had no choice but to perform this role: All he knew was that his father was bruised but alive when he left him, and dead when he returned. As a consequence of this "performance" at the scene of the crime, much of the second trial would pivot on the prosecution's contention that, having insisted, both at the reenactment and throughout the first trial, that his father's death must have been the result of an accidental fall, Philipp was a liar.[58] The more Philipp acted in his own defense, the more often he returned to the scene for a reenactment determined to prove his innocence, the stronger was his transformation into the role of the lying Jewish murderer that the prosecution and community had already ascribed for him.[59]

At the trials, Philipp and his team of lawyers would prove defenseless in the face of powerful, long-standing local cultural memories and symbols linked to passion plays and blood libel trials, but the trials would also require a combination of words and images, and a perfect mountain setting, for Philipp to play his role. Unfortunately, many of his own statements, in combination with the testimony of the locals, presented him to the audience as the perfect guilty Jewish murderer. Luckily for the prosecution, Philipp fit his part before he even walked into the courtroom. His dark hair and black-rimmed glasses marked him as a foreigner and matched the image of a stereotypical Jew. The prosecutors did not have to work hard to prove that he fit other common antisemitic stereotypes as well. At one closed session in the trial, the court analyzed a number of supposedly "erotic" poems he wrote during his imprisonment for "evidence" of character flaws.[60] They also challenged him to account for phrases taken out of context from letters he had written to his father, including "white slavery" (which Philipp would later explain was in reference to a film they had both seen). Besides playing into stereotypes of sexually perverse Jews, the prosecution highlighted a request to his father for an increased allowance as evidence of his traditionally Jewish greed, which would explain his desire to murder his father for his money.[61]

As the prosecutor attempted to link Philipp with as many negative Jewish stereotypes as possible, Halsmann's defense team tried to convince the jury that he and his father were as non-Jewish as Jews could possibly be. In doing so, they revealed cultural and personal characteristics that were coded as non-Jewish: They stressed the Halsmanns' love for nature, their enjoyment of socializing, their unbridled generosity and civic-mindedness, and, above all, their noble position as successful and upstanding members of bourgeois society. Several people the Halsmanns knew from Riga were called in as character witnesses to attest to the father and son's healthy relationship.

But Philipp's defensive account of his family's lives and finances only made them appear more foreign and suspicious. Philipp's contention that his father was owner and landlord of houses in Berlin, Zurich, and Palestine, as well as three summer cabins in Riga, played into long-standing notions of Jewish cosmopolitanism and greed. When Philipp tried to explain that they didn't actually own the house in Palestine, but only held it in their name on behalf of a relative in Russia, this surely only served to make the family seem more foreign and suspicious. Likewise, his proud proclamation that his father was "one of the best and most expensive dentists in Riga," who often traveled to Berlin to obtain the best new instruments,[62] would not have endeared them to the jury as respectable bourgeois members of society, as surely he hoped, but rather evoked stereotypes about wealthy Jews who greedily preyed upon others in need of their services.

Philipp's constant interruptions of the trial with lengthy, technical explanations in his own defense ironically helped seal his fate. According to several people at the trial, his anxious, earnest testimony and awkward self-assuredness struck the jury as unsympathetic and arrogant; his insistence on offering his own interpretations of events was considered merely as Jewish or "Talmudic" argumentation. As one audience member noted, "He is more convinced of his own logic than of his actual memory. Whoever has lived in Prague knows this type of Jewish dialectician. For Tyroleans, he is an impossible figure to understand."[63] As court-appointed examiner and Innsbruck University Professor of Forensic Medicine Karl Meixner would later note in a publication about the Halsmann affair:

> I've observed many defendants at trials, and I have never seen someone at such a long trial who gives so few signs of weariness as Philipp Halsmann. One could not notice him expressing a trace of exhaustion and he never let his attention wander even for a moment. He immediately registered every word, every sound—whether to his advantage or not. . . . Above all, his urgent dogmatism and sophistry made an unfavorable impression . . . at any moment the wavering sense of the word, the meaning of a statement, could be rapidly and skillfully shifted.[64]

From the very beginning, the Innsbruck prosecutors worked hard to come up with plausible reasons to charge Philipp, although in the end, they did not succeed in evincing anything but circumstantial evidence for his role in the crime. The fact that he and his father had asked for separate rooms at the inn where they stayed the night before the murder became a cornerstone of their claim, along with the fact that Philipp's father had joked at least twice to others that his son "had a desire to succeed him," which they interpreted as a serious statement of fear.[65] The explanations of Philipp's character witnesses from Riga that Max Halsmann's references to his son as his *Naslednik* (inheritor or successor) had been spoken in jest fell on deaf ears. The indictment makes much of the fact that several witnesses perceived Philipp as sullen, silent, and strange, as did the testimony of a twelve-year-old shepherd boy who claimed to have seen them arguing, but also, admittedly, didn't understand what they were saying.

Philipp consistently tried his best to counter the prosecution's charges. He insisted, for example, that he and his father had asked for separate rooms at the inn solely because they were tired and did not want to be disturbed; he made sure to emphasize that they had also told the innkeeper they would gladly take a room together if the inn had no room for additional guests. Moreover, he tried to describe how his father loved to make jokes about his son "succeeding him" and claimed not only that he had *not* been arguing with his father when they came across the shepherd boy, but that the boy did not understand what they said to him at the time.[66] However, Philipp's rational and earnest attempts to describe the events of the day in detail proved to be little match for the fantastical tale of bloody Jewish murder woven by the local prosecutor and supported by the words and images supplied by antisemitic witnesses, lawyers, newspaper reports, and medical experts.

The efforts of Philipp and his attorney were to no avail. Their defense strategy was dismissed in some newspaper articles as nothing but the superficial prattle of Jewish lawyers from modern, decadent, Jewish Vienna. The witnesses, on the other hand, had apparently been told by at least one local authority that they should not mention anything about Jews to anyone, lest the trial be dismissed as nothing more than *Judenhetzerei* (an attack against Jews).[67] That the mood outside the courtroom was against Philipp is clear from accounts of the trials mentioned in public gatherings and at church services. At least one Innsbruck preacher, Father Wimmer of the Servite Church, used Philipp Halsmann in one of his sermons as an example of one who "lacked a conscience," since, according to Wimmer, he "had so brutally murdered his father and not admitted it."[68] In October 1929, posters advertising a Nazi gathering proclaimed, "The Halsmann trial shows everyone who wants to see the monstrous influence and strength of Judaism. The Jew is master of the German people."[69]

For the second trial, Philipp acquired new lawyers who conceded that evidence indicated that Max Halsmann had undoubtedly been murdered—but also robbed, a fact which, they claimed, made it much more likely that an unknown person, rather than Philipp, had committed the crime.[70] They better understood the power of local antisemitic biases, and made an effort to involve the federal minister of justice by informing him of their difficulties. The two new lawyers accompanied Philipp's original defender on a visit to the minister of justice in Vienna on September 25, 1929, where they asserted that new evidence indicated that Max Halsmann had been robbed, and tried to prove that local antisemitism was negatively influencing the trial. They delivered a letter from a man who claimed to have overheard a member of the jury saying, "[W]e'll surely bring down the Jews," and they also claimed that one of the supposedly neutral court experts had told the jury he thought Halsmann was guilty.[71] Internal memos from the federal ministry of justice illuminate the tensions between Vienna and the provinces by indicating their understanding of the antisemitic biases involved in the provincial courts. Nevertheless, Viennese authorities did not intervene in the trial until the Austrian president pardoned Philipp in 1930.

The fact that Philipp's new set of "Viennese Jewish lawyers" supposedly changed his story based on new evidence showing that Max had been robbed as well as murdered unfortunately only solidified local belief that Philipp was lying. The prosecutors continued to insist that Philipp's claim that he had been standing only fifteen steps away when his father fell over the cliff, and that he had seen no other person in the area, ruled out the possibility that the murder could have been carried out by a third party. Significantly, to contradict this claim, Philipp's lawyer argued during the second trial that the shock of his father's death had resulted in either a memory lapse or a "false memory" of what he had actually seen. The new team renewed the initial request of Philipp's first lawyer to obtain the expert opinions of psychologists who might be able to determine whether the trauma might have caused such a memory lapse, and therefore might account for the discrepancies between Philipp's story and the state of the crime scene. This time, the court agreed to the request for an expert opinion—but instead of psychologists, they turned to psychiatrists who, at that time, were believed to work best with "unhealthy and abnormal" people who were mentally ill. Unsurprisingly, the court experts ruled out the possibility that Philipp could have had a memory lapse, but the damage caused by associating Philipp with psychiatrists—and, therefore, deep mental illness, and Jews—cemented and even furthered negative opinions of him.[72]

In the Blood

Those familiar with Jewish history will find it no coincidence that blood served a key role in the trials' antisemitic allegations, not only in framing Philipp as the guilty ritual murderer, but also in enabling the audience to envision the victim Max Halsmann, with his bloody head, as a Christian martyr. Traditional associations of Jews with blood had been part of antisemitic rhetoric for centuries and played an important role in modern antisemitic imaginings, not only with the advent of nineteenth-century racial antisemitism, but also by linking Jews to additional fears about modernity during the twentieth century. David Biale notes that the "control" of blood gained new urgency for Jews and Christians alike with the advent of blood-based nationalism.[73] Blood became the Halsmann trials' visceral visual image, allowing audiences to imagine a scenario of gruesome patricide, replete with the familiar antisemitic trappings of the past but adapted to fit new national concerns.

The main witness to emphasize the blood at the scene of the crime was Josef Eder, a known local antisemite whose tavern was located close to the murder site. However, the first one to weave Eder's statements into a narrative with the trappings of blood libel was actually the prosecutor, who used them to construct his initial trumped-up charge against Philipp for the court, providing a preliminary authoritative narrative that Eder himself would embellish when he testified. According to the prosecutor, Eder was one of the first to arrive at the scene, where he claimed he immediately noticed the lack of blood around the body, despite heavy wounds to its head. Then he noticed his dog sniffing around a bush; upon closer inspection, he saw that the ground was soaked in blood which, when he poked it with his walking stick, revealed even more blood. He also found a bloody stone matted with hair; on the path they came across more hair that later, enlarged under a microscope, looked as if it had been pulled violently from someone's head. The prosecutor completed his initial charge by asserting that there could be no other explanation for the presence of the deceased in the brook than Philipp bashing his father with a stone, dragging him through the grass, and throwing him from the cliff to the water below.[74]

Later, when Eder addressed the court, he added many more colorful details to his account, claiming that when he first arrived on the scene, he "already knew" something was out of order. Significantly, his first witness statement includes the word "blood" or "bloody" eleven times. Eder also vividly described how the site was littered with blood specks that looked as if they had been spattered "with a paintbrush," and the grass nearby was matted as if a "bloody pig" had been pulled through it. By introducing the imagery of a pig, Eder evoked the centuries-old *Judensau* (Jews' pig), which features several Jews sucking on, probing, and having intercourse with a large pig.[75] The *Judensau* was portrayed in church carvings and wall paintings, and throughout Central Europe, it is associated with scenes depicting ritual murders like the murder of Simon of Trent in 1475.[76]

In what will strike modern audiences as profound irony, both the presence *and* the absence of blood linked this trial to tropes introduced at blood libel trials. The absence of blood on the Jewish ritual murderer or at the murder scene was a common theme of blood libel trials: Guilty Jewish murderers, it was explained, would have been careful to conserve every trace of blood for their nefarious Jewish rituals. Eder had already evoked the presence of blood at the scene, on the grass, and on certain personal items, like Philipp's backpack. But he also made sure to emphasize that, mysteriously, despite the bloody surroundings, Philipp himself bore no traces of blood on his person: "The backpack was bloody—whether it was still dripping or not, I don't know. I didn't see any drops of blood on the accused himself, neither on his face nor on his clothes."[77] To an audience predisposed to cultural memories of Jewish murderers whose lack of bloodstains only served to condemn them, such testimony had the potential to make Philipp appear more guilty than innocent.[78]

But tragically, from the beginning, in hopes of proving his innocence, Philipp's defense team also emphasized the fact that no traces of blood had been found on his torso, trousers, socks, or shoes.[79] Moreover, at least four of the witnesses who came into contact with Philipp immediately after the event noticed no blood on him. But the expert forensic report on the case requested by the court from Karl Meixner, as well as attorney Anton Werkgartner, went to great lengths to try to explain, in farcically "rational" terms, how a brutal murderer might escape bloodlessly from an extremely bloody murder.[80]

Meixner made much of the fact that Philipp, who by his own account had taken off his shirt for part of the hike in order to help clear up a skin condition, could have washed the blood off his hands and torso in the brook. Further, he added, the fact that the police report did not mention blood on Philipp's body or

On a trek in the Alps with his mother Ita around 1928, Philipp hikes without his shirt to help clear up a skin condition. At the murder trial, forensics expert Karl Meixner maintained that hiking shirtless could have allowed Philipp to wash away all traces of his father's blood from his bare torso.

Copyright 2011 by Nicole Emanuel. Used with permission

clothes could have been an oversight due to the evening twilight.[81] Werkgartner claimed that in a case from his own law office's practice, a woman who had murdered someone with an axe had also exhibited few traces of blood because the blood had simply spurted "away from the murderer." Philipp protested this account heavily in a letter he wrote after the trial. "Prof. Werkgartner's example must have made the jury think that a murderer might be able to act without traces of blood," although, Philipp pointed out, the case Werkgartner mentioned was actually not an axe-murder but rather a death caused by blows to the head with a beer glass.[82] But in an area where tales of Jewish murderers without blood had long been part of the local culture, the jury would likely have little trouble believing this fantastical tale.

Max Halsmann's Head

Portraying Philipp as a traditional Jewish murderer would prove relatively easy, but transforming a middle-aged Jewish dentist from Riga into a Christian martyr required surprisingly little effort as well—after all, Jesus, too, had been a Jew. Photographs of Max Halsmann's severed head, as well as the actual head itself, became crucial gruesome "props" in the service of the prosecutors' courtroom performances. The transformation of Max Halsmann began on the day of his death, at the very first moment Joseph Eder planted the idea that Philipp had emerged clean and unscathed from carrying out the bloody, brutal murder of his father. The process continued two days later at the autopsy, when Meixner insisted that Max's head be removed from the rest of his body. As Philipp's sister Liouba later recounted, by the time she arrived in the Zillertal, her father's body had already been disfigured: "The autopsist cut off Papa's head and put it in a jar. . . . He planned to bring the head to trial as evidence. Burying Papa whole—a Jewish burial—was now impossible." The physicians who removed the head took care to store it in a way that was visible from all sides, took dozens of photographs, and wrote pages of medical notes about it.[83]

Removing Max's head and forcing the Halsmanns to bury the mutilated body without it was not only a sign of disrespect for Jewish ritual and practice, but also a transformative cultural moment. Decapitation made forensic examinations easier, but showing it to the jury meant that the severed head could be associated with Christian symbols like the head of John the Baptist, an easily recognizable icon of Christian martyrdom. The jury saw the actual head at the second trial (at the first they just saw photographs), much to the consternation of Philipp's lawyer, who noted:

> I always asked to allow Max Halsmann's head to be buried. To view such a thing confuses the brain. It's easy to conflate the horrible wounds with the

> accused. What is gruesome does not exactly stir the finest instincts. At the first trial, the prosecutor asked if he could show the court the head, but the court rejected the request. That was humane and sensible. This time, the prosecutor did not even ask. But the court asked the jury 'Do you want to see the head of the deceased?' One called out: Yes. The others nod spontaneously . . . so they gather in the consultation chambers, without Philipp Halsmann or the public. Professor Meixner shows the head, and the substantial wounds. The stench of blood rises. In the minutes we read: "Due to the specific desire of the jury the head is shown to them."[84]

At the second trial, the jury also viewed images of the head as court expert Meixner explained the details and cause of each wound; the trial documents contain dozens of photographs taken from all sides. Some show Max Halsmann at calm, peaceful rest, but others are gory, featuring wounds and skin pulled away from the skull.

Meixner's published account of his participation in the trial includes fourteen gruesome images of Max Halsmann's skull. But its last page features a photograph of a very different nature: a snapshot of Philipp happily holding his smiling father in his arms on the beach by a lake. To most, this image would suggest that Philipp had a loving relationship with his father. But Meixner interprets it differently: Does it not, he asks his readers, indicate that Philipp actually possessed the strength to gather his father in his arms and throw him over a cliff? Significantly, Meixner's "control" over Max Halsmann's head did not end until decades later. Only in 1991, at the behest of a concerned journalist who realized that the head was still stored at the university, did the Austrian Minister of Culture insist that the university arrange for its proper burial alongside the rest of Halsmann's body at the Jewish cemetery in Innsbruck.[85]

Reporting the Crime

In his account of the Halsmann affair published in 1976, Martin Ross offers much insight into the effects of the trials on Austrian Jews. Although he was only a child at the time, he remembers how even those who tried to avoid antisemitism by not commenting on the matter found themselves forced to take sides. His schoolmates remained convinced that the entire affair was a Jewish conspiracy, and even tried to implicate Ross's own father, who had been reporting on the trials for the *Neue Freie Presse*: "I was trying so desperately to tell them that we were not the kind of Jews who were involved in 'Jewish activities'—let alone conspiracies. 'My father does not even fast on Yom Kippur' I shouted. 'Why would he be involved?'"[86]

62 Prof. Dr. Karl Meixner

eine Anzahl Treiber auf und machte sich mit ihnen auf den Weg. Ansteigend begegnete er den zwei Frauen Rauch und Ossana und fragte sie, ob der Verunglückte noch lebe. Denn er wollte wissen, ob er mehr eilen müsse, worauf ihm die Frauen erwiderten, sie wüßten es nicht. Diese Äußerung wurde von der Verteidigung als Beweis dafür betrachtet, daß Halsmann, als ihn die Frauen sahen, nicht mit dem Kopf im Wasser gelegen sein könne, daß Philipp Halsmann seinen Vater also mit dem Kopf aus dem Wasser gezogen habe. Vom Breitlahner zum Tatort geht man 1 Stunde 20 Minuten, hinunter weniger.

An Ort und Stelle angelangt, bestätigte Dr. Rainer, ein alter, erfahrener, in jener Gegend sehr geländekundiger Jäger, der nach seiner Angabe den Weg wohl 100mal zu Fuß und zu Pferd zurückgelegt hatte, die ihm von Eder gezeigten Spuren. Dr. Rainer ging zur Leiche hinab, die

Abb. 13. Fünffach vergrößerte Teilansicht des Steines mit zahlreichen durch Blut angeklebten Kopfhaaren, die mit den Haaren Mordach Max Halsmanns übereinstimmten.

man auf Weisung Eders gleich mit Stauden und Farren bedeckt hatte, besah sich, ohne an der Leiche zu rühren, die Wunden am Hinterhaupt, stellte die Blutspuren am Hang fest und schloß sich auf Grund seiner Wahrnehmung der Meinung Eders an.

Philipp Halsmann, den man zunächst abseits gehalten hatte, verlangte nun, daß die Leiche seines Vaters sogleich abgetragen werde. Das wurde ihm verweigert und ihm von Dr. Rainer und Eder erklärt, daß die Leiche liegen bleiben müsse, bis eine Gerichtskommission eingetroffen sei. Halsmann war darüber sehr entrüstet und äußerte nach Nettermanns Aussage u. a.: „Tun Sie mich vielleicht verdächtigen, daß ich meinen Vater hinabgestoßen habe?" Dr. Rainer gab den Treibern den Auftrag, „den angeblichen Sohn" nach Breitlahner mitzunehmen und bis zum Eintreffen der Gendarmerie zu bewachen. Er selbst verständigte noch um

Lehren des Halsmannprozesses 63

½6 Uhr durch Fernruf vom Breitlahner aus den Posten Mayrhofen, von wo spät abends Gendarmen beim Breitlahner eintrafen. Nettermann und Schneider ließen sich bewegen, am Tatorte zu wachen. Am nächsten Morgen nahmen die Gendarmen die Spuren auf und vernahmen die anwesenden Zeugen.

Um ½5 Uhr nachmittags traf die Gerichtskommission aus Innsbruck ein. Leider war die Tätigkeit beim Augenschein durch einen vielstündigen Gewitterregen sehr erschwert, der schon begann, ehe der Tatort erreicht war. Es regnete dann bis zum Abend in Strömen, zeitweise prasselte der

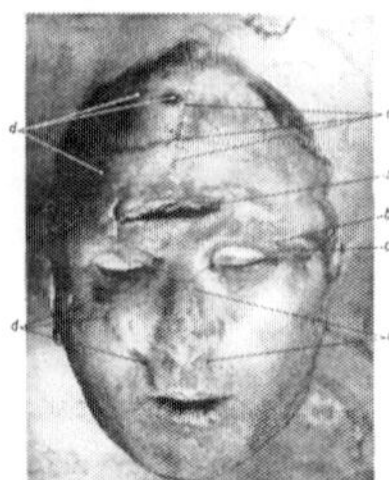

Abb. 14.

a) Durch beide Stirnhöhlen und die vorderen Schädelgruben ins Innere des Hirnschädels führende Wunde.
b) und c) Kleine, auf den oberen äußeren Rand der linken Augenhöhle führende Quetschwunden.
d) Abschürfungen.
e) Zur Untersuchung des Gesichtsschädels an dem gehärteten Kopf angelegter wiedervernähter Schnitt.

Regen herab. Die Blutspuren auf dem Boden im Bereiche des Weges hatte man bei Beginn des Regens durch Bedecken, so gut es ging, zu schützen getrachtet. Die Örtlichkeit und die Wetterunbill machen es begreiflich, daß keine genauen Aufnahmen der Schuhspuren an der blutigen Wegstelle vorliegen. Doch wurde schon beim Augenschein von diesen Spuren gesprochen. Die Leichenöffnung, die am nächsten Tag beim Breitlahner vorgenommen wurde, ergab eindeutig, daß der Vater Halsmann

64 Prof. Dr. Karl Meixner

durch zahlreiche Hiebe erschlagen worden war, worauf über Philipp Halsmann die Untersuchungshaft verhängt wurde.

Die im ersten Verfahren tätigen Sachverständigen Dr. Fritz und Dr. Vonbun haben umsichtiger Weise den Kopf des alten Halsmann, das Schädeldach, die gesamten kleinen Splitter und die harte Hirnhaut aufbewahrt, sodaß im zweiten Verfahren eine genaue Nachuntersuchung möglich war. Bei der ersten Schwurgerichtsverhandlung hat die Verteidigung das Recht zur Entnahme von Leichenteilen bestritten.

Wir lehren nicht nur in der gerichtlichen Medizin, daß man von ge-

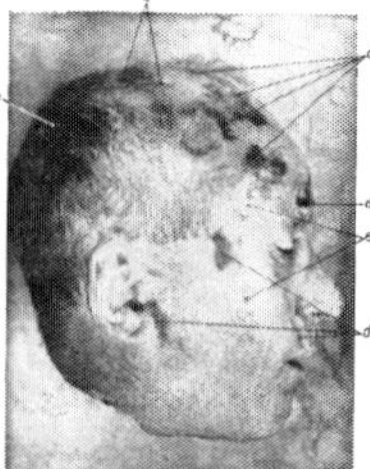

Abb. 15.

a) Stirnwunde.
b) Aus zahlreichen Einzelwunden sich zusammensetzende Gruppenwunde hinten unten vom rechten Scheitelhöcker.
c) Zwei kleine Quetschwunden.
d) Abschürfungen.
e) Zur Untersuchung des Gesichtsschädels am gehärteten Kopf angelegter, wieder vernähter Schnitt.

richtlich geöffneten Leichen Weichteil- und Knochenwunden ausschneiden und aufbewahren soll — sie sind oft die wichtigsten Grundlagen für die neuerliche Prüfung eines Gutachtens nach Bekanntwerden neuer Umstände — sondern auch die Strafprozeßordnung bietet, obwohl sie aus einer Zeit stammt, da es neben Ärzten noch Wundärzte und Geburtshelfer gab, eine genügende Grundlage.

§ 127 schreibt vor, daß „die etwa vorgefundenen, möglicherweise gebrauchten Werkzeuge mit den vorhandenen Verletzungen zu vergleichen" sind. Das geht in vielen Fällen, da man nicht weiß, was noch alles

Lehren des Halsmannprozesses 65

behauptet wird, nur dann, wenn man die verletzten Teile aufbewahrt. Auch § 131, der von der Zuziehung der Chemiker neben den Ärzten spricht, setzt die Entnahme von Leichenteilen voraus. Es gibt eine große Zahl von Verordnungen, Erlässen und Entscheidungen, die sich mit der Entnahme, der Beförderung und Untersuchung von Leichenteilen befassen. Bei der chemischen Untersuchung ausgegrabener Leichenreste muß man oft die Hauptmenge verarbeiten. Ist die Entnahme von Leichenteilen für spätere Untersuchungen überhaupt vorgeschrieben oder zulässig, so ist es ganz gleich, ob man für mikroskopische oder bakteriolo-

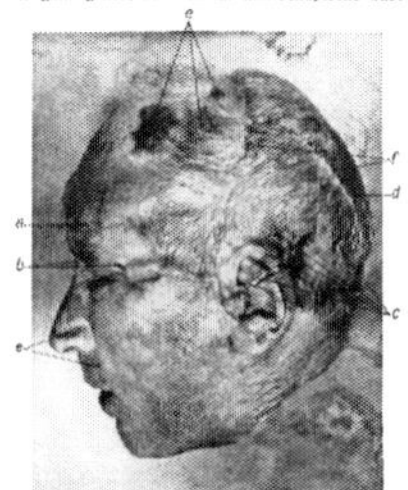

Abb. 16.

a) Stirnwunde.
b) Zwei kleinere, auf den äußeren oberen Rand der linken Augenhöhle führende Quetschwunden.
c) Gruppe von sechs Wunden im Bereiche der linken Ohrmuschel.
d) Quetschwunde in der Mitte des Hinterhauptes.
e) Abschürfungen.
f) Wieder vernähte Untersuchungsschnitte.

gische Untersuchungen kleine Mengen, für chemische Untersuchungen die ganzen Eingeweide oder für andere Untersuchungen einen Kopf zurückbehält.

Im Wesen hat die zweite Untersuchung nichts Neues ergeben, hat trotz Feststellung verschiedener Einzelheiten keine andere Deutung zugelassen. Es ist auch sachlich gar kein schwieriger Fall, vielmehr ein Schulfall.

Neben einer Anzahl von kleineren Wunden, die über den ganzen Kopf verstreut lagen, war vor allem eine große Wunde in der Mitte der

Beiträge zur gerichtlichen Medizin. X. 5

Forensics expert Karl Meixner's report on his involvement in the Halsmann trials published in 1930 features fourteen gruesome images of Max Halsmann's wounded, severed head. The jury was shown both photographs of the head and, over the protests of the defense, the head itself. *ÖNB Vienna/506.865-B.Per10*

Whether in the Tyrol, the other provinces of Austria, or the rest of the world, most people got their information about the Halsmann affair from the press. The depictions of the trials in Austrian newspapers in many ways reflect the ways all crimes involving Jews were reported in Central Europe throughout the late nineteenth and early twentieth centuries. These reports reveal how the trial's "performances" were likely received by its audience in the provincial court, as well as how the trial itself was used to reconfigure tensions underlying the urban/provincial binary and its overlap with the constructed categories of Jewish difference.

Newspaper and magazine articles about the trials reflected interwar tensions between Vienna and the provinces, as well as between Jews and non-Jews. The local press used the opportunity to complain not only about Philipp, but also about the "Jewish press" and its attempts to turn him into the "Jewish Messiah." On the other hand, many Viennese newspapers also used the occasion to poke fun at the provincial Innsbruckers for their xenophobia and opportunism. As the Social Democratic *Arbeiter-Zeitung* proclaimed, "Whoever believes that the Halsmann trial is as much a sensation for the Innsbruckers as it is for the Viennese is mistaken; they don't like to talk about the trial because there are still too many foreigners there."[87]

The so-called Jewish press—Viennese newspapers with Jewish editors and reporters like the *Neue Freie Presse*—often published articles and statements of support in favor of Halsmann. But an article in the Viennese *Der Morgen* claimed that antisemitism had nothing to do with the affair, and that "any foreigner" would have been treated the same way.[88] The fact that the editor-in-chief of the Christian Social *Tiroler Anzeiger*, Franz Baldauf, retracted his original signature on a telegram in support of Halsmann to the Austrian ministry of justice and the president, underscores this divide. In a telephone conversation with the ministry of justice, Baldauf stated that he had only signed in the first place because Halsmann's lawyer had threatened to instigate an anticlerical scandal by reporting that a local priest had spoken about the Halsmann case to his congregation.[89] When called to appear at the ministry, however, he dropped the accusation of having received threats from Halsmann's lawyer, claiming that he had signed on his own initiative in the hopes that his action would stop stories about the priest from being published.[90]

The irritation of the Innsbruck prosecutors with the Viennese and international press is evident throughout their reports to the ministry of justice in Vienna. On the surface, many of these reports aim at countering allegations about antisemitism in the trials, but they typically draw upon the same kinds of antisemitic tropes and stereotypes they were accused of in order to make the case for their defense. The Innsbruck prosecutor complained to the ministry of justice about false accusations in "foreign newspapers" that the prosecutors were "playing the race card" (*Rassenmoment*) to Halsmann's disadvantage. His language, of course, indicates that, given different circumstances, this might actually happen.[91] Blaming the press, and especially the "foreign press," for putting an antisemitic "spin" on the trial was another way the Innsbruck prosecutor also revealed his bias: "No antisemitic atmosphere was ever generated neither during the proceedings, nor currently. The entire trial was carried out in peace. On the other hand, the press is now intensifying the mood on behalf of Halsmann."[92]

Another report, this one from the local prosecutor to the upper court in Innsbruck, contained thinly veiled antisemitic references in its accounts of the "animated shouts" of those in the courtroom (including Philipp himself) who were unable to show decorum when the guilty verdict was read and resisted leaving the courtroom; he added that this "heated tumult" was instigated mostly by the relatives and friends of Halsmann.[93] Significantly, only a few lone voices in ultra–right-wing newspapers strained to convince readers that the murder of a Jew like Max Halsmann was a positive event.[94] Their failure to stir up enthusiasm about the fact that there was one less Jew in the world indicates that Max Halsmann's role as a symbolic Christian martyr was a stronger one than that of a dead Jew. For most Tyroleans, convicting a Jewish killer rendered a random act of violence understandable, and provided a powerful instance of regional self-reification in the new Republic to boot.

Philipp Halsmann took numerous photographs while hiking with his father; later, during the trial, he even mentioned that he had his camera in his hand when he ran back to the place where his father fell.[95] But only when he was finally told the facts of what was found at the scene did Philipp fully recognize the urgency of the moment he had missed. His frustration at not seeing his father's fall is apparent from his rhetoric in the accounts he gave at the trials: "The image of my father leaning backwards was completely frozen, as if captured in a photograph. I don't mean clear, I mean without movement and fixed. . . . I didn't see the fall itself." Years later, he gave what seemed like a rather mundane account of how he came to be a photographer and why he needed a specific kind of camera: "I needed a camera capable of capturing the expression of the sitter *at the same instant my eye saw it*" (emphasis mine). This account, as we can see now, was directly linked to his past.[96]

By 1959, photographers had long since begun to explore images of people in midair, capturing athletes diving into pools or leaping deliberately in sporting events. But Halsmann's jump photographs are different. His subjects are not athletes, and they rise into the air solely because he has asked them to jump. In 1928, an unforgettable "imaginary" photograph was imprinted on his mind: the devastating picture of his falling father—an image that he knew existed, but that he had not seen. Back then, Philipp missed his chance to capture that image of his

Liouba, Max, Ita, and Philipp Halsmann pose for a family photograph. During the trial, Philipp's lawyer Franz Pessler claimed that family photographs provided evidence of the strong bond between Philipp and his father. He noted, "The son had a whole series of pictures of his father always with him. Father and son photographed each other every minute."
Copyright 2011 by Nicole Emanuel. Used with permission

father. But thirty years later in his *Jump Book*, he made sure to catch each and every one of his subjects before they fell.

Urban Crimes of Passion: Hugo Bettauer and Moritz Schlick

In contrast to the Halsmann affair, the identities of the murderers of Hugo Bettauer and Moritz Schlick were always crystal clear, even if the role antisemitism played in the murders was not.[97] But for the purposes of their trials and the interpretation of their murders by the general public, engaging with Jewishness made it easier to depict their murderers as heroes who acted for the sake of bettering society or who, at the very least, they could pass off as naïve young men, confused and driven to violence by corrupt Jewish ideas. Indeed, this portrayal was relatively easy because each victim was already strongly associated with areas coded as "Jewish," like erotic literature, newspaper publishing, and positivist philosophy.

In Vienna, more immediate interwar political tensions between city and country overlapped with traditional conceptions of Jewishness to shape the nature and interpretation of crimes in the city, where coding people as Jews was an easy and expedient way to play out the struggle for control among the municipal, federal, and Catholic leaders. However, it was somewhat more difficult to portray acculturated Jews as "foreigners" in a city that was already a web of impersonal encounters among a population of people who did not necessarily know one another, rather than a tightly-knit province. Since the nineteenth century, using racial or chimerical tropes—like those found in the provinces—as the foundation of antisemitism was untenable in Vienna, as Jews became undeniable and integral parts of the economic, social, and cultural fabric of the city.[98] It would take an emphasis on other negative associations of Jews, not with blood and ritual murders, but with sexual perversion and dangerous and manipulative philosophy, to render antisemitism more usable in an urban context.

Hugo Bettauer was no stranger to scandal, even before unemployed dental technician Otto Rothstock entered his office in Vienna's eighth district in broad daylight on March 10, 1925, and shot him at close range with a pistol.[99] As editor of Vienna's first erotic lifestyle weekly, *Er und Sie: Wochenschrift für Lebenskultur und Erotik* (He and she: weekly for lifestyles and erotica), Bettauer had already become well-known in the city for breaking publishing taboos with his frank articles about sexuality and women's and gay rights.[100] By then, he had also deserted the army, traveled twice to live in the United States, been expelled from Prussia, served as editor of several newspapers, and been brought to trial for allegedly violating pornography laws. Like his childhood classmate Karl Kraus, Bettauer criticized government and social hypocrisy through satire, so he was used to—and even encouraged—outrage and criticism, particularly from the right wing, politicians, and the mainstream press.[101] By 1925, Bettauer had written over twenty popular novels featuring the "common man" and simple stories addressing issues such as alcoholism, drugs, and poverty. All of his exploits and writing would be overshadowed, however, by the events of 1925 and the presumed association of his murder with what is today his most controversial 1922 novel, *Die Stadt ohne Juden: Ein Roman von Übermorgen* (published in English in 1926 as *The City without Jews: A Novel of Our Time*) and H.K. Breslauer's 1924 film of the same name.[102]

Despite the constant criticism he faced, Bettauer had a loyal following. His willingness to deal explicitly with political and social issues regarding not only women, sexuality, prostitution, and marriage but also poverty, unemployment, and mental illness raised topics that few others dared to air publicly. Although only five issues appeared between February 14 and March 13, 1924, his magazine *Er und Sie*, devoted to questions of sex, love, and women's rights, rapidly grew in readership and contributed to his popularity.[103] Early articles by Bettauer included "The Erotic Revolution," "Sadism, Children, and Death," and

"Eros in Chains," and every issue featured a column by a psychiatrist who answered questions from readers.[104] Visits to city-run social services in related fields, such as the marriage counseling center, as well as psychoanalytic clinics, increased in number after the magazine's publication, further demonstrating its impact.

One of the most controversial aspects of the magazine, however, was its personal ads section, where both men and women advertised for dates, escorts, and partners. The first issue featured only 14 ads, but by the fifth and last, the number had climbed to 123. Ads ranged from young men looking for women and girls "free from all conventions," "modern-thinking" and "fun," to more serious men and women looking for long-term companions and marriage partners. A significant number indicated that they either had been posted by, or were looking for, Jewish or Aryan men and women.[105]

The personal ads led his enemies to charge that Bettauer and his co-editor had violated the city's code of public decency and morality by abetting prostitution; they were also charged with "pornography," since some issues reprinted nudes painted by Old Masters. None other than Austrian Chancellor Ignaz Seipel, in a 1924 speech in Vienna before an assembly of his fellow Christian Socials,

Nr. 4. **Preis 2000 Kronen.** 6. März 1924.

Aus dem Inhalt: **Unsere Novelle:** Begebenheit von Charles-Louis Philippe — **Nervenarzt Dr. med. Werner:** Über die Impotenz Jugendlicher. — **Erinnerungen einer Hebamme,** von ihr selbst erzählt. — **Der neueste Roman von Hugo Bettauer:** Die lustigen Weiber von Wien. — **Probleme des Lebens.**

Eros in Ketten.

Von Hugo Bettauer

Unheimlichstes Großstadtbild, grauenhafter Sumpf mit Geschehnissen unter dem grünlichen Schlamm, von denen die meisten Menschen nichts ahnen: Eine Wohnung, aus zwei Kammern bestehend, mit sage und schreibe acht Insassen! Vater und Mutter, ein Mädchen von vierzehn und ein Knabe von sechzehn, eine aus der Bukowina vertriebene Schwester der Frau im Alter von achtundzwanzig, ein Neffe des Familienvaters, Bankangestellter, im Alter von sechsundzwanzig Jahren, und zwei junge Mädchen, Verwandte aus Deutschböhmen, die man aufnehmen mußte, weil sie sich mit ihrem lächerlichen Kontoristinnengehalt unmöglich ein möbliertes Zimmer nehmen können.

In den zwei Kammern, von denen eine eigentlich die Küche ist, nichts als Betten, Schlafdiwans, Sofas. Zwei Waschschüsseln, die unaufhörlich belagert sind, frühmorgens ein Gewurl von halb angezogenen Menschen. Einer der Wohnungsinsassen kommt zu mir, schildert mir burleske, groteske, grauenhafte, phantastische Verwicklungen, die unter den acht Menschen entstanden sind, entstehen mußten. Wohin ein Men-

Palma Vecchio: Venus

Reprints of nude paintings, such as the one featured here on the front page of the fourth issue of *Er und Sie: Wochenschrift für Lebenskultur und Erotik,* led to charges that Bettauer and his co-publisher Rudolf Olden had violated public decency.

ÖNB Vienna/607.534-C. 1924 Neu Mag

announced to the public that the Viennese city government was enabling the publication of pornography in the city, and referred to Bettauer as a pornographer. In a city that at the turn of the century was rumored to have "invented" political antisemitism with Mayor Karl Lueger's alleged dictum "I decide who is a Jew," Chancellor Seipel understood very well that making references to a "pornographer" who was also a converted Jew was an opportune way to use antisemitism to take potshots at the Socialist city government.[106] Christian Social representative Anton Orel denounced the "Jew Bettauer" who published a "Jewish, piggish magazine" in "true Jewish fashion" at a meeting of the Vienna City Council on March 21, 1924.[107] As reported in *Der Volkssturm*, Orel also accused mayor Karl Seitz of not opposing Bettauer—a "dirty Jewish businessman" who was "ruining our children" with Jewish poison and Jewish "*Schweinerei*" (smut).[108]

Viennese newspapers lost no time in exaggerating the scandal surrounding the September, 1924 trial and castigating Bettauer's indecent behavior; the ultra–right-wing press even went so far as to call for his lynching. But Bettauer and his co-publisher Rudolf Olden were acquitted by the jury after only two days.[109] Nevertheless, this was still long enough for Bettauer to become more Jewish than ever for the purposes of the public audience. His acquittal did not de-emphasize his apparent Jewishness or indicate support for his acts; rather, in the complex matrix of Vienna's culture and politics, the city used it as a way to wrest control over censorship laws from the federal government. In this way, Bettauer's Jewishness was useful to the city in its battles for local control against the Christian Social government.

Despite his acquittal, Bettauer was forced to cease production of the magazine, although he continued running personal ads in his weekly *Bettauers Wochenschrift: Probleme des Lebens* (Bettauer's weekly: life's problems), which began publication on May 15, 1924. Although it was not an "erotic magazine" per se, the newspaper nevertheless broke social taboos: It featured articles about "independent women," fashion, and American culture; published "gender-bending" photographs of women sporting the *Bubikopf* (short haircut), wearing pants, and smoking, and it advocated the legalization of abortion.[110] By the time of his death, Bettauer was receiving 200–300 letters per day from readers asking for advice and commenting on his articles.[111]

The confluence in interwar Vienna of sex scandals, Jewishness, literature, and political conflict was not unique to Bettauer's pornography trial. The 1921 premiere of Arthur Schnitzer's *Reigen* (published in English translation as both *Hands Around* and *La Ronde*), first published in 1903 to antisemitic cries of immorality and featuring scenes that merely implied that acts of intercourse followed, had already crystallized tensions between the municipal and federal government. The play was not performed until Max Reinhardt requested to stage it in Berlin in 1918; when it was brought to Vienna in 1921, it became an early interwar opportunity for a public power struggle between the Christian Social government and "Red Vienna." The liberal press feared the play's sexuality and moral uncertainty, although they acknowledged its high artistic quality; denunciations of Schnitzler by the Christian Social, Catholic, and right-wing press referred to it as pornography and "Jewish literature." Its performance caused disturbances in Munich on February 5, 1921, and, three days later, Nazi youths stormed the Vienna theater and tried to interrupt the performances by yelling antisemitic and other insults and throwing stink bombs—despite the fact that the performance had already run peacefully for several evenings. More stink bombs were set off a week later, causing panic and unrest in the audience.[112] These events and the political tensions surrounding them helped create the context for Bettauer's prosecution and, eventually, the release of his murderer.

The fact that Bettauer, a convert to Protestantism from Judaism, was killed one year after the release of the film version of Bettauer's satirical novel *The City without Jews* by a disgruntled man who had been a member of the Nazi party, has led most to simply interpret his murder as an act of antisemitic rage. For years, not only had Jews been linked to criminality, but press reports on crimes and trials often searched for links to Jews in order to make the crimes seem worse and the stories more sensational.[113] Obviously, the fact that Bettauer had been born a Jew, and that Rothstock was an antisemite, played an important role in the murder. Nevertheless, it was the intense focus on Bettauer's Jewishness *after* the murder that reveals the degree to which he was more or less "transformed" into a Jew by the context of the crime committed against him. In his case, sexual indecency and immorality were not deployed as superficial pretexts for killing a Jew; rather, these functioned as a way to buttress acceptance of the killer's crime and to make his act both explicable and politically "useful."

Predictably, newspapers reacted to the shooting according to their political agendas, each blaming another party for fostering the conditions that allowed the murder to happen. But portraying its victim as a Jew made it easier for the public to accept his murderer as a valiant, if confused, crusader against sexual perversity without explicitly condoning the act. As a result, Bettauer's status as a Jew, first emphasized at his trial for public indecency, only increased after his death. Coding Bettauer as Jewish by associating him with pornography, prostitution, and sexual perversity helped the Viennese envision Rothstock as a hero and allow him only light punishment for the murder. Although sexual deviance, crime, and Jews had long been linked in Central European culture, in this urban context of politically useful antisemitism, Bettauer's Jewishness was more significant to the audience needing a "rational" reason for accepting his brutal murder than it had likely been for Rothstock, who needed few excuses to justify killing him.[114]

The news that a journalist had been shot in broad daylight might have made headlines regardless of who he was, but playing up Bettauer's status as a Jew was an advantage to all. Most newspapers found it useful to level some of the blame on Bettauer himself, a theme especially common when Jews were victims of violent crimes.[115] In doing so, they mirrored the even stronger defense tactic of Rothstock's lawyer, Walter Riehl. In court, Rothstock outright admitted that he had planned to harm Bettauer, and that he cancelled his membership in the Nazi party not because he disagreed with its ideals, but because he sought to distance himself formally from the party to spare its reputation and make sure his acts were "taken seriously." Rothstock would later rejoin the party, indicating that party and its members continued to influence him both before and after the trial.

Rothstock's lawyer did all he could to ensure that his act would be sympathetically received by the jury. Not only did Riehl arrange for his client to plead *Sinnesverwirrung* (mental confusion), he also emphasized, in the courtroom and to reporters, that Rothstock's precarious mental state resulted from "exposure" to

Hugo Bettauer's co-publisher Rudolf Olden featured a portrait of Bettauer on the cover of *Bettauers Wochenschrift* during the week that Otto Rothstock stood trial for his murder. Olden, who attended the trial, complained bitterly that the entire first day focused on Bettauer, Jews, and the "immoral" media instead of on his murderer.

ÖNB Vienna/608.078-C.Neu Per 1925/2

the "smut" published by the "pornographer" Bettauer.[116] Bettauer's wife Helene did her best to bring her husband's murderer to justice by hiring Walther Rode, a prominent polemical Jewish attorney, originally from Czernowitz, known for speaking and publishing in defense of erotic literature.[117] But their efforts could do little in the face of strong public sympathy for a patriotic young murderer confused by the sexual perversity of a "Jewish" pornographer; the jury of twelve unanimously found him guilty of committing the deed, but were divided six to six on whether he was insane, so he was automatically acquitted. After spending nineteen months at two different mental hospitals, Rothstock was released.[118]

Rothstock himself expressed a curious ambivalence toward Jews. In his first statements to the police immediately after the murder on March 13, 1925, he claimed his hatred of Bettauer stemmed from Bettauer's newspaper *Er und Sie*; he found its erotic texts confusing and disturbing and felt they "were only intended to whip up and arouse lust, which I experienced myself from reading this publication." From reading these works, he told the police, youth are "led astray from the proper path, and that is where the danger of these writings lies in my view." He made no mention of *The City without Jews*, Bettauer's Jewish background, or Jews. Three months after his attack, in a statement clearly prepared by his lawyers, he dubiously revealed himself as a voracious consumer of Bettauer's works horrified by their depraved erotic content: "I've read many of Bettauer's novels, including *Die Freudlose Gasse*, *Die Stadt ohne Juden*, and *Das entfesselte Wien*, as well as many issues of *Bettauers Wochenschrift*. I saw *Die Stadt ohne Juden* first in the cinema and then borrowed the book. All these books scandalized me, and I was enraged at the description of the love lives of many of the characters."[119] In prison, Rothstock continued his crusade against the corruption of Viennese youth through sexual immorality by writing letters to the judge claiming that Bettauer's films and writings had deleterious effects on young people, including himself.

Speculation about Rothstock's antisemitic views and possible support from the Nazi party garnered much attention, from the police as well as the press, and indicate how Jewishness functioned to shape the reception of Bettauer's murder. Witness statements to the police reveal how many actively sought to ascribe antisemitism as Rothstock's sole motive. One man, for example, reported to police that he had overheard a group of men on a train voice threats toward Bettauer and make comments about doing violence to a Jew. It soon became clear, however, that Rothstock was not part of the group, and the man later had to admit that there was no evidence of his being acquainted with them at all. By contrast, Rothstock's close friend from the Nazi party and fellow dental technician Ferdinand Dittenberger claimed that his friend wasn't "truly" antisemitic. According to Dittenberger and another friend, Burkhardt Schlindegger, Rothstock had complained about *Schundliteratur* (smut), but never specifically about Bettauer: "I had the impression that he was not a National Socialist at heart, despite the fact that he was in the party, because even though he knew the party had antisemitic tendencies, he often claimed that the Jew did not bear the guilt of the circumstances alone, but rather the state, which tolerated the damaging actions of the Jews. . . ." But the persistent (if deliberately misguided) efforts of Rothstock's Nazi cronies to help distance him from antisemitic and Nazi party-driven motives only underscore the degree to which the general public believed in—and accepted—those motives.[120]

The police also continued to investigate for possible antisemitic connections, but the results of their efforts remained ambiguous. A report from March 10, 1925, describes their visit to a café located not far from Rothstock's previous place of employment, where he claimed to have waited on the day of the shooting until Bettauer came back to his office. The report notes that "The Café Kronprinz at Wiedner Hauptstrasse 78 is an elegant coffeehouse frequented mainly by Jewish guests. The staff did not recognize Rothstock's name or photograph." Rothstock's former employer, dentist Rudolf Eisler, told police that he had fired Rothstock only a few weeks previously for poor performance, but not any other reasons. He claimed Rothstock had an agreeable personality, although he was shy with women.[121] In response to police questions about Rothstock's political orientation, Eisler said that although he had once asked his former employee not to wear a swastika or other party symbols to work, Rothstock's attitude toward religion nevertheless remained tolerant and open, and suggested that the motivating factor in his behavior was likely not "in this direction." Eisler's assistant, on the other hand, claimed Rothstock was a real *Hakenkreuzler* (Nazi) who was constantly dissatisfied and complaining about his work.[122]

Although the police report notes that Eisler was Protestant, his remark about Rothstock's "tolerant" attitude toward religion and his continued relationship with Rothstock raise a number of questions. Eisler was born in 1872 and may well have converted to Protestantism from Judaism, as suggested by one of the confused and contradictory comments Rothstock made about his former employer during the trial:[123] "I remained working for Eisler because I was happy to have found a job at all, and incidentally I was working for a Jew whom I admired greatly. But Eisler was still a son of lies and of Satan, and I just had to stay there."[124] Regardless of whether Eisler had converted from Judaism, what is clear is that at the trial Rothstock played up how important antisemitism had been to him, in order to make himself look like a hero. However, Rothstock would continue his relationship with Eisler by writing him a lengthy letter from his confinement and, later in life, continue to maintain his ambiguous relationship to Jews by simultaneously downplaying and admitting the role of antisemitism in the killing. In the truest sense of Viennese political antisemitism, both Bettauer and Eisler became Jews for the purposes of acquitting Rothstock.

Rothstock did not publicly emphasize antisemitism as his motive until his trial, when, at the encouragement of Riehl, he employed antisemitic rhetoric in order to explain his violent act and figure himself as a new messiah and martyr, claiming Bettauer ridiculed all that was Christian and German:

> Two thousand years ago—just a few moments of heavenly time—the son of God came into the world to lead the struggle against Jewish writers and teachers, because they are the sons of lies and of Satan. I came into the world in order to continue this struggle. That which I have done was no assassination, but rather a warning shot for all the peoples of the world so they could free themselves from the sons of Satan . . . He ridiculed everything that could be called German and Christian.[125]

Conceptions of Bettauer as a Jew and his links to erotic publishing made it easier to justify the killing to the broader public, who interpreted the event according to a pre-existing structure of Jewishness and Jewish crimes that had been set in motion by Schnitzler's *Reigen* scandal in 1921 and Bettauer's pornography trial in 1924. The press in Vienna remained true to form, just as they had in those scandals. To the extreme right wing, Rothstock was a hero; but to more moderate conservatives and even liberal newspapers, which did not necessarily promote liberal attitudes toward sexuality, Bettauer had brought his misery upon himself.[126]

Whatever his "true" motivation, most important is the role of the trial in providing the necessary stage upon which Rothstock performed his role as a dutiful Austrian serving the interests of society by killing a filthy, perverted Jewish purveyor of smut. That Bettauer became more Jewish for the purposes of the trial suggests that, just as in the trial for the murder of Max Halsmann, codings of "Jewish" stemmed from, but were not equal to, actual Jews and could be transferred to any person as needed. In the case of Halsmann, the victim's Jewishness was at times downplayed for the jury in order to prosecute the accused Jewish murderer, but the victim of this urban crime needed to be as Jewish as possible in order for his murderer to fit the paradigm of a hero. The circumstances surrounding both Rothstock's trial and his mild sentence underscore the abstract nature of Jewish codings and their ability to be applied to particular people and situations for political expediency. Rothstock was free on the basis of his contention that, in carrying out the murder, he had been entirely robbed of his senses due to the confusing nature of Bettauer's erotic publications and films—an excuse that he later admitted had been a lie.[127] Rothstock was undoubtedly an antisemite, but he also knew that emphasizing the Jewishness of one's victim was clearly how to get away with murder in Vienna in 1925.[128]

"We'll find a Rothstock for you, too"[129]

In 1925, Hugo Bettauer's status as a converted Jew and the subject matter of his publications shaped the nature of the support for his killer. But by 1936, mere associations with dangerous "Jewish"-coded philosophy were enough to make the reasons for a random act of violence palatable. Compared to the Jewish-born Hugo Bettauer, Moritz Schlick, professor of philosophy at the University of Vienna and descendant of a long line of prestigious Prussian nobility, was an unlikely victim of an antisemitic attack. On June 22, 1936, Schlick's former student, Hans Nelböck, shot and killed him on the stairs inside the university while he was on his way to lecture. Nelböck had been threatening to harm him for over five years, ever since his disturbed and paranoid mind had envisioned his professor involved in an unlikely love affair with Sylvia Borowicka, a fellow philosophy student and unrequited love interest. One witness to the tragic events at the university that day claimed she heard Nelböck utter, "Now you'll get it, you damned dog!" before pulling the trigger.[130]

Despite his romantic delusions, however, Nelböck was "sane" enough, both at his trial and in his later appeals for pardon, to play up Schlick's association with corrupt, Jewish ideologies to garner sympathy with the jury. His urban audience was only too eager to use familiar prejudices against Jews to ascribe meaning to his violent act, once again illustrating the pliancy and potency of the symbolic substance of the "Jewish" in Central Europe—and of the violent consequences to which it could lead. The transformation of Schlick into a *Mussjude* (Jew by circumstance) intensified long after his trial.[131] As in the case of Bettauer, whose murder and its aftermath Schlick's evoked, envisioned images of Jews and non-Jews along with the power to apply them independently of the Jewish self-identification of the actual person allowed the defense to deploy antisemitism when it was politically expedient.

Schlick, who helped found the Vienna Circle (*Wiener Kreis*) school of philosophy in 1924, was among the first to explore the philosophical implications of Einstein's theory of relativity.[132] The fact that eight of the fourteen members of the Vienna Circle were Jews, along with its generally liberal ideology and modern, anti-speculative philosophy, secured its firm coding as "Jewish." Schlick's visible support of Jewish students also fostered this association.[133] By the time he was appointed chair of philosophy at the University of Vienna in 1922, antisemitism had become an increasingly powerful way to express opposition in universities. When Schlick was under consideration for the chair, the committee inquired whether he was of Jewish descent before making their decision.[134] For the members of the university committee, adherence to certain philosophical principles was enough to raise suspicions that he was a Jew, just as Bettauer's involvement in and sympathy for open attitudes to sexuality linked him to stereotypes about Jewish perversion.

In 1931, Moritz Schlick filed a police complaint stating that Nelböck and Sylvia Borowicka had threatened to shoot him. As a result of these charges, Nelböck was committed to the Steinhof psychiatric institution for three months, while Borowicka was deemed a victim of his mental illness. After a second confrontation in 1932, at which Nelböck accused Schlick of having an intimate relationship with Borowicka and threatened him with a revolver, Schlick filed yet another complaint which resulted in Nelböck's nine-day detention at another psychiatric hospital. After his release, Nelböck maintained close contacts with other philosophy professors at the university, including Leo Gabriel, another of Schlick's former students who later distanced himself from the philosopher.[135]

According to the Vienna prosecutor's report dated April 12, 1937, Nelböck said that he had bought a pistol and ammunition in 1935 with the intention of killing Schlick and then killing himself, but that he had lost the nerve to kill himself at the last moment. In impassioned detail, he explained that although five years earlier he had threatened Schlick with harm on account of Borowicka, neither the situation with Borowicka nor Schlick's philosophical world view had anything to do with his motive for the shooting, which was based, instead, on a "personal conflict" with the professor. He believed Schlick was responsible for his losing his job as a lecturer at Ottakring's Volksheim (adult education center). Nelböck claimed that a philosophy teacher at the center, Leo Gabriel, a strongly conservative Catholic who would later become known for his support for the Austrofascist regime, and who lectured on the "Jewish Question" under the rubric "Race" at a teacher training series, had told him that Schlick had threatened the director of the school's philosophy section, Viktor Matejka, that if Nelböck were rehired, he would publicly expose the fact that he had been at Steinhof.

In fact, even this supposedly "personal" conflict had a political context in which antisemitism played a pivotal role. In Vienna, the university had long been the site of political tensions, as well as early open expressions of antisemitic violence. In the interwar years, the university rapidly lost its atmosphere of change and liberal belief; by 1933, there was speculation about a new set of chairs at the university. Even though the Nazi party was outlawed, conservative and German nationalist professors and students mobilized to drive Socialist professors out of their jobs. Thus Leo Gabriel finally obtained a position, after which he secured academic employment for Nelböck, including lectures in philosophy at the Volksheim Brigittenau in 1934, and a lecture in the philosophische Hochschule Ottakring entitled "Critique of Positivism."[136]

In 1934, the Volksheim Ottakring fired philosophy lecturers Edgar Zilsel and Friedrich Waismann, both Jews and logical positivists, while Leo Gabriel and Viktor Matejka, a Catholic socialist, remained locked in a power struggle for control over the philosophy department. In an attempt to reinstate the fired lecturers, Matejka blocked the appointment of Nelböck.[137] During his trial, Nelböck explained at length his frustration about his lectureship not being renewed in Ottakring and intimated that Schlick had written a defamatory letter about him to the head of the institute and tried instead to get the job for Waismann, one of his advisees.[138] Leo Gabriel had clearly played a significant role in firing up this rumor, which was at least in part based on antisemitism.

Despite his initial contention that a personal conflict was the cause of the murder, Nelböck ultimately, like Rothstock, later offered increasingly confused and contradictory reasons for killing his victim. At the trial in 1937, he claimed that in addition to Borowicka rejecting him due to her relationship with the professor, Schlick's philosophical teachings and close associations with dangerous, Jewish world views had called his own Christian religious beliefs into question. Nelböck likely emphasized the latter in order to gain favor with the Catholic-authoritarian Austrian regime, which had come to power only a few months before the shooting.[139] While he did not label Schlick as a Jew outright in his testimony, he likely knew that associating Schlick with Jews through his philosophy would make him "Jewish enough" to convince the jury that he had done a good deed by killing him.[140] Although he was convicted and sentenced to ten years imprisonment, he served only two before being freed six months after Austria's annexation by Nazi Germany. By 1941, while in the process of trying to revive his failed doctorate, he had already openly declared his loyalty to the Nazis by claiming he had done the regime a great service by getting rid of a professor who was spreading "Jewish, foreign, and damaging teachings."[141] But in May of 1941, the Nazi authorities, who wanted him pardoned, were careful to cover their tracks, making sure in their papers that it did not look as though they were giving him special treatment. They noted that he was not a Nazi party member and his neighbors described him as a quiet man with a good reputation.[142]

Regardless of Nelböck's own testimony, the immediate effect of Schlick's murder in the public sphere indicates that its audience interpreted it according to the framework of Jewish difference—despite the absence of an actual Jewish victim. Schlick's intellectual preoccupations and the company he kept were enough for him to be branded not only a leftist but also Jewish, and for his death to be re-envisioned in the popular imagination as an act of antisemitic rage. According to a number of sources, his death led to a "massive antisemitic and anti-positivist defamation and hate campaign," as most newspapers spread propaganda against an "Austro-Marxist" professor they linked with "Jewish logical positivism," or simply labeled him a Jew outright, even though they surely were familiar with his aristocratic heritage.[143] In the influential and popular Catholic weekly *Schönere Zukunft*, a writer under the pseudonym "Austriacus" proclaimed that Schlick embodied the Jewish characteristics associated with the anti-metaphysical philosophical movement to the highest degree, and expressed hope that his murder would result in a peaceful settlement of the "Jewish Question."[144] Noted writer and emigrant Hilde Spiel, whose eulogy of her beloved former professor appeared in the *Neue Freie Presse* on June 24, 1936, recalls the widespread labeling of Schlick as a Jew by the Austrian press.[145]

Not long after philosophy professor Moritz Schlick arrived in Vienna in 1922, his antagonistic university colleagues erroneously suspected him of having Jewish roots. During his trial for the murder, Hans Nelböck associated Schlick with Jews and the "Jewish" philosophy of the Vienna Circle, which helped Nelböck garner sympathy for his murderous deed.
ÖNB Vienna/NB 508.706-B

Aware of such potential associations, Schlick had tried to distance himself from leftist ideals and their Jewish connotations years before the murder. On February 23, 1934, after the Vienna Circle had been disbanded by the *Ständestaat* (corporate state) because of its alleged involvement with the Social Democratic Party, Schlick lodged an unsuccessful appeal against the decision. In doing so, he stressed the apolitical character of the group in general, and his distaste for the Social Democrats in particular. He even went so far as to join the *Vaterländische Front* (Fatherland's Front), the political organization all state employees needed to join to have any hope of advancing their careers under the Austrofascists.[146] Even if he did so only for opportunistic reasons, his very act indicated a defensive attempt to disassociate himself from Jews, for whom this option was not available.

The interpretation of Schlick's death as an antisemitic act also indicates that the framework Jewish difference was strong enough to preoccupy even those who may have decried its effects. In other words, antisemitism was an easy way for society to interpret this disruptive event—the murder of a professor by a former student—regardless of whether those doing the interpreting were active antisemites.[147] While it is nothing new to recognize the labeling of individuals as Jewish merely for their associations with particular individuals and ideologies, Schlick's case reveals how extremists made antisemitism an acceptable part of public discourse and how willing the wider public had become to believe that the murderer not of a Jew, but of someone just "Jewish enough," should not face harsh punishment. The more Schlick was envisioned as Jewish, the less guilty and more heroic became Nelböck. Bettauer was killed for his willingness to break social taboos, just as Schlick paid the price for his willingness to espouse the philosophy he believed in and act against a crazy man whose work he did not respect, but Jewish difference was used to articulate both cases and to justify the acts of their killers in the public eye.

This chapter has told the story of three murders that were framed at once as acts of antisemitic rage or as consequences of Jewish deviance: Halsmann embodied the foreign, greedy, manipulative, lying Jewish murderer; Bettauer was a symbol of Jewish sexual deviance; and Schlick stood for dangerous Jewish philosophical ideals. Keeping in mind Robert Cover's contention that, ironic though it may seem, violence actually forms the foundation of the system set up to do justice for its victims, we can better understand how trials could do violence to Jews or justify criminal acts against them. Helmut Walser Smith identifies two patterns that begin with the celebration of the Eucharist (ritual reenactment), proceed with Christian claims that Jews have re-enacted the killing of Christ (symbolically, with blood and victims), and end (before beginning again) with an act of violence against Jews or, at the very least, a denigration of them.[148] Imprisoning Philipp Halsmann as a murderer and releasing Nelböck and Rothstock as innocent "victims" of Jewish sexual deviance and dangerous philosophical ideas echo this trilogy of social reenactments during the Austrian interwar period, beginning with antisemitic meetings, statements, and acts, followed by accusations that Jews are ruining society, and then, finally, reinforcing the boundaries of community by denigrating or killing the Jew—or, in the absence of a Jew, someone who came close enough.

2 STADT OHNE JÜDINNEN

ABSENT JEWS AND INVISIBLE WOMEN IN *THE CITY WITHOUT JEWS*

In 1890, Ella Zwieback, a young piano student at the Vienna Conservatory, fell in love with fellow student Franz Schmidt. They wanted to marry, but their match was unthinkable: she was the daughter of Ludwig Zwieback, the prominent Hungarian Jewish founder of one the city's noblest department stores, and he was merely a poor, unknown Christian music student recently arrived from Pressburg (Bratislava). Pressured by her family to find a more suitable marriage partner, in 1899 she wed the son of the Imperial court jeweler, Alexander Zirner, a man fifteen years her senior, with whom she would have little in common apart from their two children.[1] Although Schmidt married another woman that same year, he and Zwieback continued to play piano together at her grand apartment on the Kärntnerring next to the Hotel Bristol, fostering their love of music along with their clandestine relationship. In 1904, he dedicated an opera entitled *Notre Dame* to her. When she gave birth to her third child, Ludwig, in 1906, the news that Schmidt was the father spread around the city, although Ludwig would not learn that his music teacher was really his father until decades later.[2]

Despite the ensuing scandal, Zwieback's career flourished. Although she became a prize-winning pianist, after her father died in 1906 she inherited Zwieback & Brothers, the grandiose eight-story luxury department store centrally located across from St. Stephen's Cathedral. By then, Schmidt was already on the path toward a stellar career as a composer.[3] Although the two still met and played piano together, their lives drifted apart and then diverged radically in 1938 when, forced to sell the store due to Nazi Aryanization laws, Zwieback fled to the United States with her son Ludwig.[4] Schmidt stayed on in Vienna, working on *Deutsche Auferstehung* (The German Resurrection), a piece commissioned by the Nazis that remained incomplete when he died in 1939.[5] Despite the National Socialist taint attached to his last composition, Franz Schmidt is celebrated today as one of Austria's most important modern composers. Ella Zwieback's dubious legacy, however, appears as the only figure satirized by her real name in Hugo Bettauer's well-known 1922 novel, *Die Stadt ohne Juden: Ein Roman von Übermorgen* (The novel was translated into English in 1926 as *The City without Jews: A Novel for Our Time*).[6]

The divergent histories of this interfaith pair of Viennese lovers provides an excellent starting point to examine the intersections of Jewishness and gender in interwar Austrian culture. After World War I, despite the ensuing economic crisis, Jewish men took advantage of a flurry of new career opportunities in publishing, film, commerce, and politics—to name only a few fields. Their success in these endeavors, coupled with the era's loosening of gender norms, in turn helped Jewish women enter new careers in greater numbers than ever before as lawyers, doctors, writers, painters, dancers, teachers, administrators, business owners, and even parliamentary delegates.[7] At the same time, however, Jewish women, like Jewish men, could not escape the gendered terms of Jewish difference. Zwieback's family's rejection of the unknown, non-Jewish Schmidt surely had to do with

After Ludwig Zwieback died in 1906, his daughter Ella inherited his department store in the center of Vienna, which she ran successfully from her tastefully decorated salon-style office. Her son recalls having to wait all day long outside her office before being allowed to speak to her because she was so preoccupied with business.
ÖNB Vienna/A 244

their concerns about their social standing as Hungarian Jewish parvenus fashioning themselves into bourgeois Austrians.

Likewise, Bettauer's text's inclusion of Zwieback as the only female Jew in his book reveals the anxieties of Jewish men about a Jewish woman who reverses the terms of the Jewish man's fantasy by achieving success both in business as well as in her amorous pursuit of a Christian. Ironically, Hugo Bettauer was one of few men in Vienna who made a point of publicly opposing misogyny and championing the rights of women in various contexts. In light of this sympathetic attitude, the fact that the only person he mocks by name in a novel that critiques antisemitism is a Jewish woman requires an understanding of the powerfully gendered nature of Jewish difference, and the price Jewish women paid for destabilizing its terms.

This chapter explores how the interwar publishing industry and much of its literature highlighted a drive to suppress certain Jewish-coded themes and topics, suggesting a belief that successful participation in mainstream Austrian culture often required expunging traces of the "Jewish" from artistic work and behavior. Doing so, of course, did not prohibit artists and others from remaining religious Jews, or living among, socializing with, and marrying other Jews. Regardless of whether and to what degree, if at all, they openly self-identified as Jews, actors, writers, filmmakers, and publishers often maintained affiliations with Jewish social networks that proved crucial to their careers. Moreover, it would be absurd to claim that Jewish topics never appeared in popular literature and film in interwar Austria, or that Jewish men and women in Central Europe never participated in public life openly as Jews. Explicit expressions of Jewish culture certainly appeared in works involving Zionism or Judaism, or as part of narratives of Jewish social transformation. But the marked absence of the "Jewish" in so many of the works of Austrians running the gamut of Jewish self-identification—from openly asserting to converted—suggests a deliberate attempt to bracket its engagement as part of the process of becoming Austrians.

To reveal how an absence of explicit topics related to Jews can actually mark the presence of an engagement with Jewish difference, however, requires the use of multiple strategies of critical analysis, especially when considering the implications of its gendered structure. Jewish men were undeniably instrumental in supporting the entry of Jewish women into professional networks during the interwar years. However, at the same time, they also displaced their own anxieties about the coding of male Jews as feminine in a range of responses including marketing and capitalizing upon tropes of Jewish women as seductive consumers and sexually mysterious figures, or by mocking or simply ignoring Jewish women and idealizing Christians in their works. Jewish women's careers often progressed in the service of men's desires—which often meant suppressing or subordinating their own. In order to fully understand the implications of the gendered absence of the "Jewish" from these works, this chapter traces the careers of several Jewish women to show how the limitations placed on their active participation in film and writing affected what they produced as they addressed their conflicting desire to make visible the call for their own disappearance.

The chapter begins with an analysis of the plot of Hugo Bettauer's *The City without Jews*, which serves as a trenchant critique of the social and symbolic orders that underlie and perpetuate antisemitism. The novel parodies an earlier antisemitic text that appeared in Austria in 1900: Joseph Scheicher's *Aus dem Jahre 1920: Ein Traum vom Landtags- und Reichratsabgeordneten Dr. Joseph Scheicher* (From the year 1920: a dream of the state and national representative Dr. Joseph Scheicher), which envisions the expulsion of Jews from Vienna leading to a utopian state.[8] Using the terms of its predecessor, but rendering their result an absolute dystopia, *The City without Jews* thematizes the suppression of the "Jewish" in the cultural sphere, and brings to light the boundaries of Jewish difference that remain present, albeit unarticulated, in fiction written for mainstream audiences. By mocking every imaginable Jewish and non-Jewish stereotype, Bettauer parodies not only those who put antisemitic acts into practice, but also Viennese Jews who, in their attempts to achieve elite status as Austrians, perpetuated the very same hierarchical divisions between the "Jewish" and "non-Jewish" that they often claimed to lament. Moreover, the novel envisions this process spatially. When the expulsion of the Jews removes every trace of the cosmopolitan culture for which Vienna had become famous, the division between city and province effectively collapses: without Jews, Vienna essentially becomes the provinces. In depicting the crumbling of this physical boundary in terms of culture, *The City without Jews* mocks the terms of an idealized Austrianness that glorifies the provinces to the detriment of the modern city, and criticizes the use of Jewish difference as a way to articulate that idealization at the same time.

What Bettauer's novel fails to critique, however, is the gendered nature of Jewish difference. Regardless of whether critics laud Bettauer's book as prescient or decry it as antisemitic, they overlook its complete lack of female Jewish characters. Yet the invisibility of Jewish women in this text rests at the heart of the book's engagement with interwar Austrian discourses about Jewish difference. Although many of the characters correspond to real people, the novel mentions only one person by her proper name.[9] Ella Zwieback is, in fact, not a character, but a discursive figure, referred to in her absence by a non-Jewish male store owner who conjures her ambiguous appearance as an emblematic figure of the consumption of luxury items, as well as a figure of authority. As an editor and journalist, Bettauer overtly supported women's rights like abortion

Artist and illustrator Martha von Wagner-Schidrowitz, wife of Gloriette-Verlag publisher Leo Schidrowitz, designed the covers for all of Hugo Bettauer's novels published by the firm, including *Die Stadt ohne Juden*. Both Bettauer and Schidrowitz were accused of corrupting morals by writing and publishing pornography.

Author's collection

and fought against double standards in the workforce.[10] In the face of his extensive support for women's rights, the fact he used a *real* Jewish woman to epitomize the fictional stereotype of Jewish commercialism underscores the disadvantages successful Jewish women like Zwieback faced, but also provokes deeper thinking about the gendered implications of suppressing the "Jewish" in mainstream culture.

However, Jewish women do appear as characters and actors in H.K. Breslauer's 1924 film adaptation of Bettauer's novel, which the second section of this chapter examines. The film *Die Stadt ohne Juden* introduces the character of Kathi, a clingy, comical, portly Christian cook played by the popular and unmistakably Jewish cabaret and stage actress Gisela Werbezirk. Although Kathi is Christian, her exaggerated gestures and overall "Jewish" affect mark her as a thinly disguised "Yiddishe Mama," a popular character type in early twentieth-century stage and film productions. However, her inclusion in the film suggests not a covert attempt to reincorporate Jewish women into a story that lacks their presence, but rather an effort to reassure audiences that Jewish women could not really "pass" as non-Jews.[11] As an actress from Galicia on the Jewish stage, Werbezirk was widely accepted—even lauded—by Viennese audiences and critics as a purveyor of "authentic" Jewish culture, although the actual roles she played on stage were broader. Ironically, however, this film reveals the limits of her acting career by forcing her literally to act out her inability to pass as a Christian. The film thus not only falls short of the book's critique of the underlying social order that perpetuates antisemitism, but also reinforces that structure's misogyny.[12]

The gendered nature of Jewish difference is precisely the reason that Jewish women in the interwar period could not engage with issues of Jewish absence as explicitly as Bettauer, even though their careers and work often more deeply reflected its consequences. Because its plot focuses directly on the absence of Jews, *The City without Jews* lends itself to standard narratological analysis in this context. But in order to understand the lack of the "Jewish" in the works of Jewish women writers, we need to contextualize those works within the limits of their participation in the public sphere. Although Jewish women were active in publishing and entertainment during this period thanks to the Jews men active in these fields, they nevertheless often remained limited in roles addressing primarily Jewish men's concerns. The final section of this chapter examines Jewish women writers' experiences in publishing, illuminating how men's anxieties about their own roles as visible creators and marketers of mainstream culture affected the careers of the Jewish women writers they published.

As a student at the Vienna Conservatory, Ella Zwieback might have crossed paths with another young prodigy, Vicki Baum, who began studying harp there in 1896 when she was only eight years old.[13] Unlike Zwieback, Baum achieved her dream of a professional musical career, playing for the Vienna Concertverein and at churches and synagogues. On the side, she wrote short stories, submitted them to magazines, and sometimes even won prizes. Ironically, she would eventually make her name not as a musician, but as the best-known Austrian woman writer of the early twentieth century, although only after she left Vienna for Germany in the 1920s. Baum gained access to publishing with the help of Jewish men who supported her work, but also limited its scope and content. Tracing the exceptional contours of her role as the German publisher Ullstein's most successfully marketed New Woman writer helps frame her contrasting position with most other Jewish women writers of the time. The lesser-known Austrian author Mela Hartwig, for instance, was the first woman to be published by the esteemed Viennese publisher Zsolnay, but remained much less visible in the public sphere. Her novels' focus on women's lack of agency and the negative spaces they occupy reflect her own career as a writer, in which she remained largely hidden from view. That Baum and Hartwig dealt directly with the subject of gender yet avoided explicitly referring to any of their main characters as Jews in their most popular texts cannot be separated from the conditions of their own employment. Their narrative histories, like their texts, reveal the terms of their limitations in the public sphere as both Jews and women.[14]

A City without Jews

By the time he published *The City without Jews*, Hugo Bettauer was already a professional taboo-breaker. The five issues of his weekly *Er und Sie: Wochenschrift für Lebenskultur und Erotik* (He and she: weekly for lifestyles and erotica), with its frank discussions about sex, love, and women's rights, and its personals section, "People seeking people," where both men and women advertised for dates, escorts, and partners, led to enormous popularity—and much criticism. Bettauer and his co-editor were accused of violating the city's code of public decency and morality by abetting prostitution through the magazine's personal ads; they were also charged with pornography because some issues reprinted nudes painted by Old Masters.[15] As one so frequently and intensely exposed to public intolerance surrounding explicit manifestations of sexuality, Bettauer recognized better than anyone the injustices of misogyny and antisemitism, as well as the social structures that kept them in place.

The City without Jews is commonly hailed as the most prescient of his novels, not least because of its title.[16] The book's satirical depiction of Vienna's economic and cultural decline after its Jews are expelled caused a sensation, and it became one of the year's best sellers, even though Bettauer ironically referred to it as nothing more than "playful" musings on what might happen if Vienna's Jews followed what he termed the "polite" invitation of the government to leave.[17] Today critics laud *The City without Jews* for foreshadowing the expulsion and murder of Austria's roughly 200,000 Jews that began in 1938.

Scholars also read Bettauer's stinging portrayal of the cultural and economic decline of Vienna without its Jews, along with the astonished and pathetic reactions of its remaining Austrians, as castigating the absurdity of antisemitism.[18] Bettauer's assassination, only three years after the book's publication, by a man who claimed to be on a mission from Christ to "lead the fight against Jewish writers and scholars," has only cemented his current reputation as a martyr to the cause of greater tolerance toward Jews. However, in the aftermath of the Holocaust, it has become almost impossible for us to accept Bettauer's novel for what it actually accomplished at the time of its publication: a critique of everyone for perpetuating the underlying conditions of society that create antisemitism.[19] *The City without Jews* mocks all Austrians who continue to accept the socially constructed terms of Jewish difference. The focus on the book as a plea for tolerance thus obscures its effectiveness as a satirical critique of all of society, including Jews.[20]

The story begins when Christian Social chancellor Dr. Karl Schwertfeger issues a decree, passed by parliament, expelling all Jews in order to alleviate Austria's economic misery. He is perplexed, however, that Jewish newspapers perceive him as their great enemy, since he has nothing but praise for their "autochthonous Jewish virtue, extraordinary intelligence, striving for improvement, exemplary sense of family, cosmopolitanism, and their ability to blend in to any environment" (*CwJ*, 9). The Austrian *Volk*, on the other hand, he characterizes as naïve, sincere mountain people who are perhaps unlucky and unable to realize their goals, but who nonetheless remain "fond of music and calm contemplation of nature, upright and pious, thoughtful and good" (*CwJ*, 11). The irony of the Chancellor's words is unmistakable: although Schwertfeger claims to deeply admire Jews, he insists that they oppress the "Aryans" who, lacking their qualities, simply cannot compete with them (even though the Jews are the minority); therefore the Jews must leave, with no exception, or face death.

After celebrating the departure of the Jews with fireworks, the novel depicts the Viennese enjoying a few weeks of prosperity. Newly-emptied Jewish apartments alleviate a housing crisis. Business competition dissolves, and theater tickets become easy to come by. But the negative effects of the Jews' absence reveal themselves soon enough. Currency rates fall, and inflation rises, followed by bankruptcy, unemployment, starvation, failing newspapers, and a general malaise that permeates all classes. Provincial dress styles, *Heimat*-literature, and superficial cultural activities replace cosmopolitan fashion, intellectual pursuits, and sophisticated theater productions. Fashionable cafés are replaced by lowbrow taverns whose customers seek drunken revelry rather than intellectual conversation. Without Jews as a convenient minority and scapegoat, politics becomes "even more stupid and boring" (*CwJ*, 110). Viennese women lament the loss of Jewish boyfriends who treated them to fancy dinners, abstained from drink, and "knew how to treat a lady," unlike the boorish, drunken, selfish Aryan men who remain. Prostitutes also miss their wealthy, chivalrous Jewish customers who were never as demanding as Aryan men who "want a lot of loving at no expense" (*CwJ*, 36). It becomes painfully apparent that—true to the stereotype—Jews supplied everything that made Vienna a city: theater, romance, politics, fashion, luxury, beauty, taste and the drive for competition.

The narrative hinges on an interfaith couple, the Jewish Leo Strakosch and his fiancée, the sweet and innocent Lotte Spineder, sister of Strakosch's deceased Christian army comrade. As dissatisfaction and unrest rise among the population, Leo—who is described as "slender, dark-haired, and smooth-shaven, with sparkling brown eyes that flashed forth wit and humor"—emerges as the hero of the story (*CwJ*, 52). After his expulsion, he becomes a successful artist in Paris and secretly returns to the city by cleverly disguising himself as Frenchman Henry Dufresne.[21] Through his own self-professed "Jewish impudence," and at the expense of the Aryan-Austrians' "trusting" nature, Leo gets the law repealed, and the Jews are welcomed back into the country.

Although *The City without Jews* is frequently understood to foreshadow the actual expulsion of Austria's Jews in 1938, at the time of its writing the text looked back upon the history of their expulsions in the fifteenth and seventeenth centuries, as well as more contemporary attempts of both Socialists and Christian Democrats to expel the 20,000–25,000 Eastern European Jewish refugees who had not yet returned to their homes in Eastern Europe after the war.[22] The book's narrative also reflects the fact that, throughout European history, Jews were often asked or allowed to return to their original countries of residence, but for reasons of political or economic expediency, not because antisemitism had been overcome. In fact, antisemitic sentiment often grew in their absence. The novel highlights—and mocks—this pattern of expulsion and return when, at the end of the novel, the Jews return to Vienna at the government's request. The book's crowning satirical moment occurs at its conclusion, when Leo Strakosch returns to a jubilant crowd and is greeted with the opportunistic mayor's proclamation "My dear Jew!," echoing the chancellor's salutation "My dear Christians!" at the start of the novel. Leo's return implies that the Jews are returning, eagerly, to a country that is just as antisemitic as they left it, beginning another round of the historical cycle.

The literal absence of Jews from the city and its consequences as a plot expose and critique the socially constructed order of Jewishness according to which antisemitism operates. By satirizing both Jews and non-Jews, *The City without Jews* calls into question and therefore destabilizes that underlying social structure. The novel depicts Christians as bumbling fools. Mayor Karl Maria Laberl is a thinly veiled reference to Karl Lueger, Vienna's mayor from 1897 to 1910. Lueger was known for his alleged infamous proclamation "Wer Jude ist, bestimme ich!" (I decide who is a Jew!), which represented his political, opportunistic style of antisemitism that allowed him to publicly profess antisemitic ideologies yet socialize with Jews and employ them as close confidants. Vienna's mayor is assisted by his right hand man Kallop, who avoids expulsion only because his Jewish grandfather converted.[23] This opportunism reveals itself in the reversal of his name: Pollak, a common Jewish name as well as a derogatory term for a Pole. Kallop, in the stereotypical role of the evil Jewish advisor, is responsible for enabling the mayor to depose the chancellor and invite the Jews back to the city. But Kallop's goal remains political and personal gain: His hushed cry of *Mazel tov* upon hearing that he has succeeded reveals both his glee at the return of his wealthy Jewish mistress (mentioned only in her absence, like all the novel's Jewish women), since his finances are faring poorly, as well as his underlying "Jewishness" despite his conversion. Nevertheless, this "Jewish" assistant is as opportunistic as the Christian mayor.

Bettauer spares virtually no one from his satirical whip. Along with his negative portrayals of the naïve Aryans remaining in Vienna, he includes overdetermined stereotypical images of all kinds of Jews, from assimilated bourgeois Jewish intellectuals to supposedly indigent Orthodox refugees from the East. When the expulsion law is passed, a lone Zionist representative claims to welcome it since it "falls in line" with his party's goals and tendencies, and he makes sure to let the chancellor know that the supposed "curse" of this law is actually a "blessing." In another scene, a caftan-clad Galician Jewish refugee from the 1918 pogrom in Lemberg (Lvov) begs for money in a cafe.[24] When rich Jewish patrons ask him what he plans to do about this latest expulsion, he remarks coolly, "If I could get out of the burning Lemberg ghetto and reach Vienna, I guess I'll find some place to go from Vienna. It's all the same to me whether I *schnorr* in Vienna, or Berlin, or Paris. Only I won't talk about the pogrom any more, but I'll tell 'em how they threw out an old Jew like me. —Tell me, Herrleben, do you think it's good to buy Siemens before the Exchange closes?" (*CwJ*, 29) By mocking Jews alongside Aryans, Bettauer foregrounds the imagined boundaries between the socially constructed Jew and non-Jew and reveals them to be equally ridiculous.

The novel depicts Jewish men of all classes as both the most sophisticated and the most crass, the most loyal and most likely to betray, the most upstanding and the most degenerate, the most generous and the greediest. Taken together, their range of attributes reveals the logical impossibility of antisemitism as well as its illusory—yet powerful—"reality" in Austria. Yet, not one character in the book—including Aryans sympathetic to some Jews, like Lotte and her father, and the Jews themselves—ever questions the hierarchical categorization of the constructed social order of Jewishness according to which antisemitism functions. The novel's "happy ending" thus implicitly mocks both the antisemitic Aryans when they invite back expelled Jews, as well as the Jews who willingly return under the same antisemitic conditions. Bettauer's book critiques the terms of antisemitism by exposing and destabilizing them, but it hardly offers a plea for tolerance or a utopian vision for a better world. *The City without Jews* suggests no possibility for a break in European history's unending cycle of Jewish expulsion and return.

Satirizing Scheicher

Bettauer's fame for predicting the future expulsion of the Jews obscures how his book actually parodies a text from the past. In 1900, a notoriously antisemitic priest and parliamentary representative named Joseph Scheicher articulated his dream of a Jew-free Austria in the book *Aus dem Jahre 1920: Ein Traum vom Landtags—und Reichsratsabgeordneten Dr. Joseph Scheicher*.[25] The complaints in Scheicher's narrative bear more than a passing similarity to the ones Bettauer mocks: He accuses Jews of controlling literature, drama, cultural criticism, the press, banks, stocks, and insurance, and he laments how they have taken over summer resorts, theaters, concert halls, and evening balls, as well as how they disrespect Christianity—especially Catholicism—and prey upon the naïveté of simple Christian craftsmen, farmers, and workers. The text utilizes common derogatory stereotypes for Jews, describing them as a "plattfüssige, körperlich misgestaltete Nation der Einwanderer" (nation of flat-footed, physically misshapen immigrants), referring to their "Krummnasen" (hooked noses), and describing their speech as "mauscheln" (a derogatory term used for a "Judaicized" German or Yiddish).[26] This section is replete with compound words that are a hallmark of antisemitic German discourse, such as "Judensoci" (Jew socialist) "Judenwunsch" (Jew wish), "Judenzeitungen" (Jew newspapers), "Judengift" (Jew poison), "Judenwein" (Jew wine), and "Judenkalbe" (Jew calf).

Scheicher's dream begins with the return, in 1920, of a missing Austrian airship soldier named André previously believed to have been lost at the North Pole. In his absence, Vienna has become the capital of the *Ostmark*, the Austrian section of a new federation called the "United Eastern States" modeled on Switzerland and the United States, a political configuration that Scheicher also sketches out in his autobiography. The Leopoldstadt is renamed "Lueger-Stadt" and each Austrian province has become its own state. The newly-elected head of the Ostmark, none other than the former Viennese mayor Karl Lueger, tells André how they "cleaned" out the city: in a single day: They hanged three hundred Jews and twenty Aryans on suspicion of plotting a stock market crash; later, they hanged thousands of Jews who procured prostitutes. Lueger explains to André that Jews "worse than the plague" had overrun Vienna, spreading syphilis and other diseases. They had taken all the positions in literature, the press, banks, stock markets, and as theater directors, doctors, lawyers, and army officers: "In short, Vienna was a New Samaria or New Jerusalem. The Jews were the masters and the original residents, the Helots." To rid the city of this scourge, 100,000 Christians boycott Jewish stores, inflicting such economic misery that the Jews emigrate to Budapest. Both the dream—and his book—end with "Hail the unified Eastern states! Hail the rebirth of the Christian people!"[27]

Framing this story as a dream underscores Scheicher's desire to tout it as a prophecy. But Bettauer's book turns Scheicher's dream on its head by deploying its same codings, but rendering the city dystopian rather than utopian as a result of the Jews' expulsion. Moreover, he transforms the melodramatic terms of prophecy into a mock tale of political intrigue and romance. The imagined Vienna of Bettauer's novel is in many ways identical to its real counterpart, down to its political parties, municipal buildings, cafes, notorious antisemitic mayors, and scandalous Jewish bankers. But when Bettauer removes the dream frame of the story and refashions it as a simple satirical novel, as emphasized by the German subtitle, *Ein Roman von Übermorgen* (A novel from the day after tomorrow), he effectively exposes Scheicher's prophetic vision as a ridiculous fable and places it squarely in the realm of his obviously authentic, conscious jealousy and greed. Bettauer's parody thus points directly to the reality of antisemitic visions and the societies that enable their existence suggested by Scheicher's text.

Some Jewish critics who reviewed Bettauer's novel shortly after its publication failed to recognize the power of parody as social critique. They accused Bettauer of antisemitism and Jewish self-hatred,[28] just as they did his contemporary and former schoolmate Karl Kraus, also a convert from Judaism.[29] But Paul Reitter's analysis of Kraus's mimetic project can help illuminate the effect of Bettauer's satirical style. Reitter claims that Kraus acted out the roles of both Jew and antisemite through performance and rhetoric. Never intending for readers to take him literally, he used contradictory and illogical statements and satire as a method of self-stylization to move beyond the bounded categories of the "Jewish" and the "not-Jewish."[30] As Judith Butler has pointed out, the power of parody lies not only in the repetition of a performance of the constructed social orders, but also depends on the performance's context, time, and audience in order to have meaning. Socially constructed orders are performed everywhere, but parody is the one form of performance that destabilizes these implicitly assumed categories at the same time as they are performed, instead of reconfirming them.[31] As a parody of Scheicher's text, *The City without Jews* thus destabilizes and reveals the inherent contradictions of the hierarchical, socially constructed categories of Jewish difference. It illuminates the fact that there is no "real" Jewish or Austrian culture beyond the constructions envisioned by the minds from which they emerge. In fact, the more true to the quintessential stereotypes of Jews and Aryans the text remains, the more power it gains as a critical destabilizer of the very system that created those stereotypes.

Bettauer's parody functions, then, by leveling critique not only at antisemites, but also at those who uphold the constructed categories upon which antisemitism is based—including Jews themselves. In their attempts to assimilate and become part of the city's elite bourgeois culture, he accuses them of ignoring the past and perpetuating the divisions between the "Jewish" and "non-Jewish" by striving for an impossible goal: losing their "Jewish" characteristics to become ideal "non-Jews." In parodying both strudel-eating, dirndl-wearing, beer-drinking naïve Aryans along with their wealthy, conniving, talented, cosmopolitan, clever Jewish counterparts, Bettauer turns the hierarchical structure on its head instead of reifying its conditions. In his book, Jews do not merely represent all that is urban and cosmopolitan, but, in attempting to shape and achieve their own version of the ideal "Austrian," they become negative placeholders for its terms. A crucial segment of Bettauer's parody lies, then, in poking fun at Jews' efforts to pass as "Aryans," even as "Aryans" do all they can to keep them at bay. Each group is thus shown as irrevocably dependent on each other in an ultimate dysfunctional relationship.

The locations of these performances matter. It is no surprise that, along with Jewish and Aryan stereotypes, Bettauer also parodies the territorial bounds of Austrian national self-fashioning. In his dream, Scheicher outlines his vision of a "United States" of the East, in which Austria is comprised of provinces recast as semiautonomous states, each with its own ethnic population. Bettauer mocks both the premises of Scheicher's plan, as well as those who worried about the *Verdorfung* (provincialization) of cosmopolitan Vienna after the monarchy's collapse, by having the absence of Jews result in the erasure of the boundary between city and province.[32] When Leo returns to Vienna disguised as Henry Dufresne, the consumers of unsophisticated *Heimat*-literature and theater and the proliferation of Alpine clothing and dirndls he encounters make him believe he has not arrived in the city, but in the provinces. Parliament's Jewish representatives have been replaced by men with full beards crying "Heil!" Leo notes, "With a slightly different background he could have supposed himself at an assembly of Tyrolean farmers in the days of Andreas Hofer" (*CwJ*, 139).[33] Vienna has not become a provincial city; rather, the boundary between city and province has collapsed, and Vienna's former image has dissolved. In this strange new province-city hybrid,

Leo may pass as an Aryan to most, but he nevertheless still feels uncomfortable beneath the wary gaze of a peasant girl suspicious of his (Jewish-coded) dark blue suit, patent leather shoes, and costly silk tie (*CwJ*, 115). The space between city and province may have collapsed, but the distance between the Jew and non-Jew is upheld in her gaze.

With its satirical focus on the consequences of the physical absence of Jews from Vienna, the novel also pokes fun at those Jews who played significant roles in the city's social, artistic, and economic development and culture while striving to remain as least "Jewish" as possible. Thus, it highlights the irony of the "Aryan" accusation that the best Austrian summer resorts had become the "Jews' playgrounds" (*CwJ*, 118) because many Jews in Austria actually *did* summer in provincial resorts with the most beautiful views, in part because they envisioned them to be the ideal Austrian (i.e., non-"Jewish" coded) vacation areas.[34] Bettauer's work thus underscores how Jews' desires to achieve unattainable, "Austrian" ideals of beauty, culture, fashion, and wealth was fed by their perception of being excluded from its definition. This perception, Bettauer's satire reveals, was based on associating the category of the "non-Jewish" with the ideal "Austrian." In participating in the acceptance of this coding system, the "Aryans" and "Jews" in the novel are actually not separate, but rather indistinguishable.

The Power of Purchasing

Though *The City without Jews* offers a trenchant critique of social constructions, and although Bettauer championed women's rights in real life, the novel's lack of Jewish women characters is noticeable even before the expulsion of the Jews. Whenever Jewish men trace the line of descent in their families, they refer only to their fathers and grandfathers. None of the women in the novel's myriad interfaith couples are Jewish.[35] Unlike their female Christian counterparts, Jewish women appear in the text only as discursive creations: absent figures we learn about only through men's memories, dreams, and conversations.[36] And even these few brief passages promote only one stereotype—that of Jewish women as wealthy, demanding consumers. But curiously, amidst this marked absence, Bettauer evokes the presence of one lone Jewish woman, the novel's only real-life figure represented by her proper name: Ella Zwieback. In making Zwieback the only "real" target of his satire, Bettauer to some extent echoes other interwar writers who either ignore Jewish women or tend to give them more than their share of blame for society's ills. Thus, the special attention accorded her status alone—and, in particular, Zwieback's appearance in a man's dream as a figure of authority—suggests that her place in the novel is more ambiguous than mere denigration.

The absence of Jewish women from the novel's interfaith couples is particularly striking. These couples range from bourgeois to working class to prostitutes, yet each one features a Jewish man and a non-Jewish woman. "A composer's wife" who is having an affair with a Jewish playwright (*CwJ*, 32) is a thinly-veiled reference to Alma Mahler-Werfel, the notorious non-Jewish widow of Gustav Mahler who married novelist and playwright Franz Werfel in 1929. Christian girls and prostitutes lament the loss of their Jewish lovers and customers. The Jewish-looking Herr Pinkus explains that he is exempt from expulsion because his father and grandfather married "Christian girls" (*CwJ*, 33). One chapter even begins with the observation that having a Jewish "sweetheart" has been a "tradition" among Viennese middle-class girls for the past half century (*CwJ*, 105). This emphasis on Christian women as the object of Jewish male desire—and vice versa—satirizes Jewish male anxieties about sexual prowess and their efforts to overcome it by dating Christian women. Jewish women, it seems, have no place in their fantasies—only in their nightmares.[37]

Gender studies scholars have written extensively about woman's constructed role as primal Other to man as the ideal subject, and the ways in which this construction negatively affects women's lives. Likewise, Jewish studies scholars have long recognized the similar role of Jews as the Other to the idealized member of European culture. Clarifying how these two Others overlapped shows how both worked to delimit the bounds of both Jewish men and women's experiences. The Jewish Other incorporates the constructed categories of gender in two ways: On one level, it mimics gender by taking the man as its main subject. The imagined "Jew" is first and foremost a Jewish man. However, it also posits that the "Jew" is subordinate to the "non-Jew," and thus this main subject, the Jewish man, is subordinate, ergo lacking in masculinity. Thus, the primal Jewish Other is a feminized male Jew.[38] The Jewish woman is thus doubly Other, based on Jewishness and gender. Trying to overcome the links between the "Jewish" and the "feminine," Jewish men often engaged in misogyny, displacing their anxieties about their own supposed lack of masculinity onto Jewish women through their words and deeds.[39] This helps account for novel's prevalence of interfaith relationships in which Jewish men can affirm their masculinity via non-Jewish women, but it also shapes the way it represents—or rather, suppresses out—Jewish women.

But Bettauer's novel moves a step further by reinserting them, not as characters, but as figments of the imaginations of Jewish and non-Jewish men. *The City without Jews* mentions Jewish women exactly four times, ascribing to them few qualities besides materialism, greed, and wealth. In one brief scene, Kallop, the mayor's opportunistic right-hand man, finds he is losing money on his investments and laments the absence of his "twice-divorced," wealthy Jewish mistress who is now living in Prague (*CwJ*, 147). Two other scenes portray Jewish women as wealthy, insatiable department store customers in the minds of the men who imagine them. When business falters, Wilhelm Habietnik, the Aryan owner of the formerly Jewish-owned Zwieback department store recalls a dream in which he imagines himself rendered helpless before the wealth, fashion sense, and demands of Jewish women:

> I dreamt that all of a sudden only Jews and Jewesses start to come to my store. Every last one of 'em's dressed in the latest style, and carries piles of bank-notes, and there's a big rush. The girls can't bring the furs and cloth and cloaks and suits fast enough for 'em, and all the ready-made clothing department's filled with silks and velvets and laces and embroideries. But nothing's good enough for 'em, and one Jewish lady, dressed in very good and stylish clothes, keeps on crying: "That's nothing! We're coming from Paris and Palestine, where everything's in the latest style. Show me the best you've got!" Then without warning, my salesgirl brings out a pair of cotton bloomers and says: 'But my dear Jewish lady, this is the newest thing from Paris!' Then everybody laughs so terrible much that I wake up (*CwJ*, 135).

While the text mocks Habietnik as a fearful man, emasculated in his inability to satisfy the desire of the much wealthier, cosmopolitan Jewish women, it also satirizes Aryan women by portraying them as unfashionable, passive consumers. Although Aryan women used to consume French fashion, the novel suggests they had worn it only to compete with Jewish women, and in any case, their Jewish lovers bought it for them. The novel indicates that Aryan women are still avid consumers of both clothing and literature—just no longer discriminating ones. They may be parodied, but these non-Jewish women still figure in the text as characters—we hear their views and attitudes in their own words—while the book's Jewish women exist solely as descriptions by men, their multiple levels of displacement undoubtedly exemplifying their double Othering as Jews and as women.

The novel's participation in this doubled Othering, however, is rendered somewhat ambivalent in a conversation between Habietnik and his manager about the department store's poor sales. When the manager suggests to Habietnik the unlikely business strategy of trying to convince their Christian customers that the cheap durable cotton, wool, and flannel garments they prefer are actually the latest fashionable items from Paris, Habietnik roars with laughter at the thought: "See here, if Frau Ella Zwieback, who's living in Brussels now, ever hears of this, she'll think we've all gone crazy in Vienna!" (*CwJ*, 74–75). The Jewish-owned Gerngross department store on the Mariahilfestrasse in the seventh district may have been the first modern department store in Vienna, but "Ludwig

Zwieback & Bruder Co." was known for its luxury items and opulent setting in the city center.[40] Ludwig Zwieback's daughter Ella inherited his property and the business upon his death in 1906, and became a known figure in Viennese society.[41] Evoked only in her absence, the novel depicts her as a demanding, derisive "competitor" and consumer who bore the responsibility for luring Christian women into buying stylish, expensive wares, but who mainly mocks the men who perceive her that way. Habietnik and his manager are rendered impotent in their ability to make sales compared to her "seductive" power and authority, another common stereotype of the Jewish woman. By presenting the ultimate Jewish woman consumer as a *person*—not merely a discursive figure—the novel does not necessarily cast her as an object of derision. She is also a figure to be reckoned with. Moreover, her presentation by Habietnik in this way links the two as yet another imaginary interfaith couple—though for once featuring a Jewish woman and an Aryan man—in which the Jewish woman exists only in her absence. Ironically, her "real" figure breaks out of the narrative's fictional frame, but is still confined to the terms of Habietnik's laughter. Rather than merely satirizing both her and her detractors equally, as the novel does with other parallel sets of Jews and Aryans in the novel, her presence as an absent "real" woman subtly accords her a powerful place in the male imagination.[42]

With the advent of consumer culture in the nineteenth century, department stores throughout Western and Central Europe came to be associated with all that was Jewish and modern, not least because many of them were Jewish-owned, largely because Jews had long been active in the garment industry. In a number of cities, Jews were often the engines behind the construction of grandiose stores created to attract customers with their opulence and luxury items.[43] As the department store became the symbolic and actual site of modern consumerism, it developed into a particularly charged site of Jewish codings; similarly, mass consumption also came to be coded as "Jewish." According to Paul Lerner, many Central Europeans imagined department stores as dens of iniquity upon which they overlaid their fears about modernity, consumption, and, especially, what were viewed as "female" (i.e., Jewish) pathologies like hysteria and kleptomania, itself an overdetermined embodiment of the desire to consume.[44]

The Viennese public was well aware that Jews remained at the forefront of many, although not all, large department stores; like other areas of cultural production, these stores, too, were coded accorded to the constructed terms of the "Jewish" and "non-Jewish." A 1932 dissertation submitted to the University of Vienna by Friedrich Tannenbaum, a student of the notoriously antisemitic economics professor Othmar Spann, neatly sums up the terms of this division. Tannenbaum complains that Jews founded the largest department stores for "racial"

Ella Zwieback posed several times for portraits by celebrity fashion photographer Madame d'Ora (Dora Kallmus) during the 1920s. Zwieback's extravagant ideas regarding *haute couture* and innovative fashion concepts inspired numerous designs and products.
ÖNB Vienna/204.396-D

rather than "religious" reasons.[45] He divides stores in Vienna along the lines of Jewish difference, concluding that Jews are particularly likely to manage successful large department stores, while specialty grocery stores, like the well-known *Meinl*, tended to be owned by non-Jews. Moreover, he notes, the Jewish department stores in and around the city center, like Gerngroß and Zwieback, catered to the bourgeois population by supplying luxury items, while department stores in the working-class districts, like Wodicka in Floridsdorf and Leopold Dichter in Ottakring, were "not Jewish" and cared for the needs of the working class. This analysis clearly codes Jews and their stores according to class, but also casts "Jewish" department stores as useless forces of frivolity.

Satirizing the Zwieback store, typified as a Jewish woman consumer's ideal since a Jewish woman inherited it from her wealthy father, exposes the combined negative effects of misogyny and antisemitism: Jewish women are not only wealthy, demanding consumers, but they did not even work for their wealth. As Belinda Davis reminds us, women first gained a public role as "consumers," as well as the space to publicly express these desires - the department store - during World

War I. However, she also notes that the war made this image increasingly negative, with the female consumer posed as a potential traitor: Conspicuous consumption of luxury items in times of scarcity implied the sacrifice of the needs of the group for one's own selfish desires. After World War I, with the rise of advertising, the associations between women and consumers grew even stronger, but became no more positive.[46]

Jewish women consumers thus often bore the brunt of responsibility for the marketing and consuming of luxury items. Even the 1926 *Handbook of Viennese Society* noted that the reason the "most Parisian department store in the world" could be found in Vienna was largely due to Ella Zwieback; a backhanded compliment since Paris not only evoked the height of fashion, but also the pinnacle of superficial urban frivolity.[47] As Darcy Buerkle has pointed out, it is no coincidence that advertising in 1920s Weimar used Jewish-coded women as marketing tools. Cover art and advertisements often showed figures who were marked as just "Jewish enough"—with dark or curly hair, for example—to engage codings that would generate consumer desire.[48] Such images, predicated on negatively casting Jewish women as the "ultimate" consumers, would either entice Jewish women who saw themselves in the images, or lure other women who would choose the item based on the Jewish woman's mark of approval.

To some extent, these attitudes toward Jewish women, whether expressed by Bettauer or others, echoed the general misogyny of Austrian society. Although Austrian women gained the right to vote in 1919, their full social participation remained an open question as gender divisions intensified during the interwar period.[49] Maureen Healy argues that gender was fundamental to Austrian women's experiences as citizens in the early years of the First Republic, not least because women were more likely than men to be suspected of not having the proper *Gesinnung* (disposition) to become true "Austrians."[50] In a place like Austria, which was hardly known for its fair treatment of women, it makes sense that the notion of women as consumers, rather than professional or political actors, should become so prominent.[51]

Nevertheless, Jewish women like those in Bettauer's text—who are present as powerful and demanding consumers in its male characters' dreams, even from the distance of their comfortable perches in Prague and Brussels—remained the standard-bearers for the transgression of conspicuous consumption, as they did even before World War I, when Jewish writers already blamed them for fulfilling popular antisemitic stereotypes of materialism, cosmopolitanism, and superficiality. The following satirical piece from Karl Kraus's *Die Fackel* details these qualities in their turn-of-the-century Central European context and reveals this bias against Jewish women as part of a literary tradition:

Quiz:

a lady sits on an Olbrich sofa—Darmstadt,
wears a Van de Velde dress—Brussels,
Lalique earrings—Paris,
an Ashbee brooch—London,
drinks from a Kolo Moser glass—Vienna,
reads from a book published by "Insel"—Munich,
printed with Otto Eckman letters—Berlin,
written by Hofmannsthal—Vienna.
To which religion does the lady belong?[52]

Unlike Bettauer's book, Kraus's "quiz" does not name any specific woman, but it sarcastically foregrounds the stereotype of Jewish women—of the upper class, presumably, if they are able to afford such expensive items—of being derivative followers of the latest fashion and art trends, of superficially ornamenting themselves with trinkets, of striving for cosmopolitanism, and of being obsessed with "decadent" writers of the Young Vienna circle, whom Kraus also mocked.[53]

While Kraus and Bettauer, through their satirical writing styles, level serious critiques at the social forces underlying antisemitism, whether these efforts extended to a destabilization of its gendered nature is far less clear. A corollary of the criticism of Jewish women as the ultimate consumers and seducers for consumption highlights that ambiguity. Joseph Roth, a contemporary of Kraus, accused Jewish women of seducing Jewish men away from their "authentic" Eastern European roots. "The assimilation of a people always begins with the women" laments Roth in *The Wandering Jews*,[54] his sympathetic portrayal of Eastern European Jews in Berlin, Paris, Vienna, Russia, and America.[55] This comment appears in a scene where he vividly depicts the indecorous behavior of Eastern European Jews at a Yiddish theater performance in Paris in the 1920s. The house is crammed with people, and umbrellas and strollers block the aisles. Patrons pick up their seats and move them for a better view. Mothers cradle babies. People eat oranges, leaving a fragrant scent in the air. Roth's skillful description generates a community of such vibrancy and warmth that one almost wishes to be part of it. But his tone changes when he turns to a small group of women. "The young Jewish women spoke only French. They were as elegant as Parisiennes. They were beautiful. One might have taken them for women from Marseilles. They have Parisian gifts. They are cool and flirtatious. They are gay and matter-of-fact. They are as faithful as Parisian women. The assimilation of a people always begins with the women."[56] By sarcastically equating Jewish women's faithfulness to their culture with the morals of stereotypically louche women and suggesting that they might pass as non-Jewish French women, Roth actually underscores his attempt to defend the authentic world of Eastern European Jewry against the encroachment of superficial Western culture.[57] In so doing, he paints young Eastern European Jewish women as seductresses who lure men into renouncing the Jewish culture of the *shtetl* for a superficial, immoral, urban life. He suggests it is an inevitable condition of their gender that Jewish women will prove themselves to be unfaithful to their husbands, not by taking lovers, but by renouncing Jewish "authenticity." This passage is the only one in his entire text that describes women in detail. Apart from brief mentions of the wives, mothers, and daughters of the Jewish men he renders meticulously, Jewish women otherwise remain invisible.[58]

That Jewish men were the sources of some of the harshest criticism lobbed against Jewish women is neither uncommon nor limited to Central Europe during this period; scholars have documented how this phenomenon reflected the anxieties of Jewish men struggling to rid themselves of the stigma of being seen as "feminine" as they entered mainstream culture.[59] What is significant in this case, however, is that Bettauer chose to present Ella Zwieback within the expanded—though still limited—terms of the "real." He could have picked any number of public figures who were driving forces behind various social welfare, journalistic, pedagogical, and cultural projects in Vienna. In fact, although he did not do so in the "quiz" above, his contemporary Karl Kraus did indeed mock some of them by name—particularly those active in the public sphere as supporters of the war effort and/or bourgeois culture, like Eugenie Schwarzwald, Alice Schalek, and Berta Zuckerkandl. But given the context of the "Jewish" department store, and the Jewish woman as the ultimate consumer/purveyor of its luxury goods and seductress of its allure (as well as the seductress of a Christian man), Ella Zwieback stands out as the ultimate symbol of Jewish men's transgressive desire.

Bettauer was against neither urban consumption, nor department stores in general. A brief article he wrote for his newspaper *Bettauers Wochenschrift* in 1925 illuminates his position on consumer culture. In it, he reviews the opening of the new modern, large American-style department store in Vienna, praising it for offering the best of American stores: the lowest prices, a pressure-free environment for customers, and tasteful arrangement of a broad variety of goods. "All of this finally comes together in 'Stafa'" declares Bettauer, who is pleased that the store operates as a cooperative so profits go not to private capitalists or anonymous stockholders, but rather to members. The advertising, he notes, is groundbreaking according to Vienna's standards, as it demonstrates an ability to revive the desire of ordinary people to buy and thus help overcome crisis at a time of economic stagnation. He notes, "It appears that finally, after so many years of mistakes, the right men are at the helm of 'Stafa' and have brought it to the top of

Vienna's department stores."[60] Because she achieved the Jewish male fantasies of coupling with a Christian and bringing her own luxury department store to the top Bettauer may have been more ambivalent about Ella Zwieback's participation in Viennese cultural life.

H.K. Breslauer's *Die Stadt ohne Juden* (1924)

Ironically, although H.K. Breslauer's 1924 silent film adaptation of Bettauer's novel pays more attention to Jewish women than the original text does, it reinforces to an even greater degree the gendered nature of Jewish difference.[61] In one scene that does not appear in the book, a policeman visits the home of an impoverished family of Eastern European Jews after the chancellor has issued the expulsion decree. When the kerchief-clad mother faints at the news of the expulsion, the police officer pulls her up roughly by the arm. Her young son moves to strike him, but holds back at the last minute. The Jewish woman is little more than a prop used to highlight the Jewish boy's failure to stand up to the policemen, and, by extension, the idea of the "feminine" inability of Jews to resist.

In another brief scene, a group of wealthy Jews leaving the city chat happily with one another other as they walk to the train station, their servants carrying their fancy trunks. One fur-clad woman toting a child and accompanied by her husband greets an older, well-dressed woman who carries her own small suitcase. They look as if they could be on their way to a fancy soiree, hardly disturbed, although the scene foregrounds the automobile and home they nonchalantly leave behind. In contrast, the scene cuts quickly to another impoverished Eastern European Jewish woman in a kerchief, who collapses with anguish on the train station platform. Neither of these scenes appears in the book, but the Jewish women depicted in the film appear only for a few seconds, have no lines, and play no active role in furthering the narrative. Poor Jewish women are unhappy to leave, and rich Jewish women are not bothered in the least, but both serve as mere reflections of their male Jewish counterparts, like a rich speculator at the beginning of the film, or a group of Orthodox men lamenting their fate, who, in contrast, have fleshed-out characters and lines of dialogue.

However, women *do* have significance when it comes to the film's casting of Jewish and non-Jewish actors—especially in the portrayal of interfaith couples—and their presence reveals much about the film's distortion of the novel's original critical message regarding antisemitism, as well as its reinforcement of its gendered terms. In the years after the end of the war, despite the poor economic situation, Vienna was on its way to becoming an important film center, a development in which Jews played a central role.[62] At its interwar peak, the film industry showed much evidence of cooperation between Jews and non-Jews; as S.S. Prawer points out, even the most famous films from this period featured both Jewish and non-Jewish actors. *Die Stadt ohne Juden* is no different. The film features both Jewish and non-Jewish film, theater, and cabaret stars. But the parts in which these actors were cast reveal how the film reinforced rather than destabilized the constructed social categories of Jewishness.

True to Bettauer's description in the book, Jewish protagonist Leo Strakosch appears as a dark-haired, handsome, bourgeois gentleman. But the fact that he is played by the well-known non-Jewish actor Johannes Riemann, and his lover Lotte is played by Anna Milety, a non-Jewish actress who had previously starred in Breslauer's films (and later became his wife), substantially diffuses the satire.[63] The "ideal" interfaith couple mocked in Bettauer's book is thus not mocked at all in the film; rather, it is portrayed via a Christian couple on the basis of the "real" Christians who play the parts. Significantly, the film also adds another interfaith couple as a comic counterpart to Leo and Lotte: Kathi, the corpulent Christian cook of the antisemitic parliamentarian Bernart, and her equally fat Jewish lover, the salesman Isidor, played by Jewish actors Gisela Werbezirk and Armin Berg, both well-known for their comedic appearances in Jewish theater.[64] Kathi and Isidor are working class, simple-minded, comical, and, although they play an interfaith couple, are nevertheless thoroughly coded as "Jewish" in both appearance and affect. When Isidor has to leave Vienna, Kathi is so upset that she announces her intention to follow him to Palestine, laying the ultimate Jewish guilt trip on her boss, Bernart, who had eagerly supported the expulsion: "If I commit suicide, then it's your fault!"[65] The humor, of course, is that Isidor can't wait to be freed from her clutches. Simple Kathi is easily dissuaded and sees Isidor off on the train with a basket of sausages, asking only that he send her a postcard "from Zion." When he arrives in the desert of Palestine, Isidor strikes a ridiculous figure in his urban suit among the uniformed soldiers and "natives" wearing caftans. Yet we see him adapt with ease as he brokers a deal, settles in to play cards, and eats a big matzoh. By casting Christians in the roles of the ideal mixed couple and Jews in their parodic counterpart, the film achieved its intended humorous effect. However, it does not destabilize the hierarchical binary, but rather fully affirms the superiority of the "non-Jewish" over the "Jewish."

By the time *Die Stadt ohne Juden* opened, Gisela Werbezirk was already an established actress in the Jewish theaters in the Leopoldstadt, where she played in comedies that typically featured her as a strong widow from a petty-bourgeois Jewish milieu.[66] Originally from Pressburg, Werbezirk often played roles that were similar to what has been characterized as the American "Yiddishe mama"—the stereotypical corpulent, attention-demanding yet big-hearted mother who plies her sons with food and tries to control them—in German-language films

Christian actors Anna Milety and Johannes Riemann portray the ideal, bourgeois interfaith couple of Leo Strakosch (a.k.a. Henry Dufresne) and Lotte Spineder (above), but Jewish stage actors Armin Berg and Gisela Werbezirk star as their comedic, lower-class counterparts Isidor and Kathi (below) in H. K. Breslauer's 1924 film *Die Stadt ohne Juden*. Werbezirk plays a Christian cook but remains unmistakably Jewish in appearance and affect.
Filmarchiv Austria

and Jewish theater productions.[67] She had completed one her most successful roles just one year earlier in *Frau Breier aus Gaya*, a stage production that began its run on October 2, 1923, starring as Sali Breier, a successful poultry saleswoman from the town of Gaya in Moravia and prototypical *baleboste* (Yiddish for an efficient Jewish housewife). Sali leaves the town for Vienna, where she helps vindicate her son David, who is an apprentice to his uncle and has been falsely accused of stealing money. While there, she has words with her brother, the successful banker Maurice Kron-Korn married to a Christian woman, whom she reminds of his origins in Moravian town and of his real name, Mottche Kohn. In both cases, Werbezirk plays a woman who controls her men and holds them back from assimilating and achieving independence: the flip side of the stereotype of the demanding and seductive Jewish female consumer.[68]

Werbezirk was one of many Jewish women who came to Vienna from Eastern Europe specifically to become stage actresses, although most of them came as part of traveling Yiddish theater troupes. Ironically, their presence on the Yiddish stage highlighted their relative absence from the rest of the theater world. In contrast to mainstream German-language theater in Vienna, where it was not uncommon for women to found their own ensembles, Jewish women rarely led their own theater groups or became directors, managers, or playwrights.[69] Critics often praised Werbezirk for her acting abilities and humor, although not without making their share of backhanded compliments about her ungainly appearance. Dedicating an entire *feuilleton* in her honor, but with a title both honoring her stature and mocking her size—"Bezirk der Werbezirk" (Werbezirk District)—writer Anton Kuh noted "That is the entire Frau Werbezirk, this improbable faux pas of a creature, this jargon miracle of body, soul, and voice!"[70] Friedrich Torberg lauded her timing, magnetism, and acting prowess, but was more critical of both her appearance and her stage persona: "She had an extremely monstrous stage presence that she established by her mere appearance, through the grotesque conquering power of her looks."[71]

Though these Jewish male critics clearly respected her work, their words, along with her stage and film roles, reveal the limits Werbezirk faced as an unattractive, Jewish female actor who could not "pass" for a non-Jew as easily as others. As the cook Kathi in Breslauer's film, Werbezirk played a Christian in a humorous role that would obviously come across to the audience as one similar to those she played on stage. Her character further suggests that the lower-class, unacculturated, Jew from Eastern Europe figures as yet another Other to their wealthier counterparts in Western and Central Europe who strive to become its opposite: bourgeois, non-Yiddish speaking, and secular. In each case, the imagined Other serves as a repository for the members of the group doing the Othering to displace their own responsibility and blame for the negative qualities they fear others see in themselves.[72] Such limitations indicate that Jewish women from Eastern Europe (or, like Werbezirk, could easily play that role) faced yet a *third* Othering as the opposite of the ideal acculturated, decorous non-Yiddish-speaking Jewish ladies.

This is not to say that Jewish women only played the role of Yiddishe mama in the film. *Die Stadt ohne Juden* features at least two other Jewish actresses and was even co-written by Hungarian Jewish screenwriter Ida Jenbach.[73] But, tellingly, the two Jewish actresses also play Christian women, albeit in another highly "Jewish" coded context: the department store. Salcia Weinberg, a popular actress of the Yiddish stage, plays a comical role as a corpulent customer rejecting the fashions on offer at the "Aryanized" department store: "Nowadays thank God it isn't necessary to keep up with all the stupid fashions. I'm going to have all the old things made again."[74] Weinberg was also known for her personification of a particular Jewish manner; as Nathan Birnbaum noted of her performances in Vienna, "in her entrance and her movements she embodies in an interesting way the definition of Jewish *Cheen* [charm]—as opposed to the grace of the French woman and the delightfulness of the German Gretchen."[75] By utilizing Jewish actresses from the Yiddish and Jewish theaters whose affect and appearance marks them as stereotypical Eastern European Jewish women, the film reveals the limitations of women's participation in the public sphere.[76]

Besides that of Kathi and Isidor, at least two other mixed marriages in the film serve as parallels to Lotte and Leo, but only in scenes where unnamed, dark-haired, Jewish-coded men like Leo are forced to leave their non-Jewish wives after the expulsion decree. Moreover, the character of Alois Carroni (né Cohn), the Jewish-born, converted husband of the antisemitic parliamentarian Bernart's daughter, is also played by a non-Jewish actor. The film does not reflect the reality of post–World War I interfaith couples in these depictions, according to which the percentage of Jewish women in interfaith marriages was on the rise.[77] But even if Jewish women like Ella Zwieback did not marry their Christian lovers as often as did Jewish men, they still had relationships with them, as she did, and, at least in her case, had children with them, too. By completely eliding the configuration of the Jewish woman and the non-Jewish man as a possibility, the film underscores the boundaries of acceptable, respectable roles for Jewish women in the interwar Austrian public sphere.

Though it lacked the novel's satirical power, the film was nevertheless a great success; it opened in Vienna in July 1924 to sold-out performances in six theaters, one of which, the Zirkus-Busch-Kino in the Leopoldstadt—the largest cinema in the city—had 1,767 seats.[78] Sold out showings turned into extended runs,[79] and the movie continued to show in Vienna theaters throughout the fall.[80] But despite its respectable cast, well-known director, and box office popularity, most critics attacked the film as poorly conceived and awkwardly directed.[81] Even Bettauer himself was disappointed in the outcome.[82] And the movie even sparked violent antisemitic outbursts: in Wiener Neustadt, a group of fifty Nazis entered a theater as the film was playing and threw stink bombs, and some audiences in Berlin protested at its premiere there in 1926.

In addition to its failure to destabilize the gendered nature of Jewishness, several other aspects of the film compromised the book's cutting critique as part of its intention to render the narrative less political and incendiary. The film is not set in Vienna, but instead takes place in a deliberately ambiguous "Utopia," although some scenes show unmistakably Viennese locations. Other scenes depicting crowds of Eastern European Jews streaming out of the city on foot hardly approach satire, with their focus on the departure of bearded men wearing prayer shawls and phylacteries in poor, decrepit surroundings (one scene takes place in a synagogue never mentioned in the book); we are simply supposed to sympathize with the plight of this mass of poor Jews. In stark contrast to the book, antisemitism remains relatively muted up until the actual decision to exclude the Jews, and the film makes every effort to suggest that it is economics, not antisemitism, that is ultimately to blame for the expulsion decree. A crowd at the beginning of the novel cries, "Down with the Jews!" on the first page, but the film's opening scene depicts protestors carrying signs that read, WE WANT TO WORK, and text screens carefully point out that people are starving and THE DOLLAR IS STEADILY RISING, then cut to a ballroom where wealthy partiers celebrate with dancing, streamers, and champagne. Even the chancellor, portrayed in the film as almost benevolent, struggles with the notion of the expulsion as though it poses a serious ethical dilemma.[83]

Unfortunately, not all of Breslauer's film survives.[84] The last scene of what has been reconstructed, however, veers significantly away from the plot of the book and reveals most clearly the weakness of the film in contrast to Bettauer's trenchant social critique. In that scene, the antisemitic parliamentarian Bernart finds himself in a sanatorium to which he has been committed after Leo, still disguised as Frenchman Henry Dufresne, has incited him to a night of heavy drinking. The room is decorated as a nightmare in Expressionist style, replete with angled walls and ceilings, harsh wooden chairs, and angular Jewish stars built into the wood. The scene in the room includes two doctors discussing Bernart's case, and the text that appears reads: "An interesting case of delirium, my dear colleague: the man believes he is a Zionist."

Although the recovered scenes of the film end there, the film's final scenes have been reconstructed from critics' accounts of the plot that were published when the film was released. They suggest that the conversation in the sanatorium is later revealed as a figment of the antisemitic parliamentarian Bernart's unconscious mind, as he has lapsed into a drunken sleep after a night spent trying to convince his fellow drinkers to support the chancellor in expelling the Jews and wakes up in the tavern. Ironically, then, the film shoves the story back into a dream frame reminiscent of Scheicher's story: The effects of the law have all been Bernart's dream, and his final words are "Thank God this stupid dream is over. We're all human and don't want to hate. We want to live peacefully, side by side." This ending is as ineffectual as it is illogical; it is hard to see why Bernart's dream would render his original hatred of Jews groundless. While this may have been the sceenwriters' intent, the film in the end disturbs no social orders, although the theme itself obviously provided enough of an excuse for Nazis and others to decry its "subversive" content.

Vienna's "Invisible" Jewish Women

The rocky career paths of Viennese Jewish women with far fewer economic advantages than Zwieback and much less renown than Werbezirk indicate that the challenges these well-known figures faced were widespread, as Jewish women struggled with their own visibility as well as their modes of creative expression. The invisible Jewish women of Bettauer's novel and Breslauer's film echo the realities of Jewish women's literary careers in interwar Vienna—realities in turn reflected in much Austrian Jewish women's writing, albeit often implicitly. Examining the contexts within which these women wrote and published helps reveal their engagement with Jewish difference, even when that engagement was not explicitly visible.[85]

After the war, employment and professional opportunities opened up for many women. Numerous Austrian Jewish women worked in offices or, with the support of their families, opened their own businesses. In Vienna, in particular, Jewish women ran their own dance, gym, and photography studios, operated schools, served as piano teachers, and even took over the directorships of family businesses.[86] Many chose fields in which advancement did not require an advanced degree, such as journalism, library science, and social work.[87] For a number of women, such activities would not have been possible without the support of their families, but for others, entering the public sphere served as their only means of income. This was particularly true for writers and translators.

Jewish women writers in interwar Austria both benefited from and were limited by the increasing numbers of Jewish men at the helm of newspapers and publishing houses.[88] Regardless of their degree of Jewish self-identification, Jewish publishers and filmmakers often supported Jewish women, although they also circumscribed the content and scope of their work.[89] These limitations make it clear that we must rely upon different, more interpretive, methodological approaches in order to illuminate how Jewishness functioned in these women's lives and works, since their texts, performances, and other forms of culture they created often reflected Jewish "absence" only implicitly. Considering Jewish women's texts not only for their content, but also as a many-faceted social process encompassing production, consumption, and marketing, reveals the particular ways in which their narrative histories engaged both Jewish difference and gender.

Like many other Central European Jewish women, Vicki Baum owed the start of her successful writing career to ambivalent support from Jewish men.[90] Baum began her professional career ghostwriting for her husband, Viennese journalist Max Prels, who introduced her to the city's intellectual world of coffeehouses, culture, and literature after they married in 1909. She relished the invigorating intellectual atmosphere of the coffeehouse and happily soaked up its camaraderie even if, as she noted, her husband was the one most at home there: "I don't remember a ladies' room in the *Kaffeehaus*," she wrote flippantly in her memoirs.[91] When Max faced a severe bout of writer's block in the face of a six-article contract for the German magazine *Monatshefte*, Baum stepped in so he wouldn't have to pawn his gold watch:

> It was a remarkable evening . . . I rooted out a couple of stories, not good enough to please me, not bad enough to be thrown away. Hesitant and embarrassed, I carried them in to Max . . . 'I'm sorry,' I said timidly . . . Max changed two commas to semicolons, put a title on the head of an untitled manuscript, signed it with a surprisingly unashamed 'by Max Prels,' and carried it personally to the nearest mailbox.

After that, she continued to support them by writing articles under his name, as well as playing harp in the symphony orchestra, churches, and synagogues.[92]

Though Baum divorced Prels in 1913, he continued to play a crucial role in her writing career, as did other Jewish men. After she moved to Darmstadt for a position as an orchestra harpist, her friend Armin Wassermann, an actor and the half brother of writer Jakob Wassermann, sent one of her manuscripts to the German Jewish publisher Erich Reiss. Reiss offered to publish what would become her first novel, *Frühe Schatten: Das Ende einer Kindheit* (Early shadows: the end of a childhood), on the condition that she "translate" it from the Austrian vernacular into standard German. Reiss published two more of her books, but only to moderate sales. Meanwhile, her second husband, conductor Richard Lert (Löw), whom she married in 1916, was not earning a large income either.

Around this time, Prels, by now remarried and an editor with the Jewish-owned Berlin publisher Ullstein, wrote to ask for a loan. When Baum told him she had money troubles of her own, he encouraged her to send him one of the manuscripts of her novels, which he could help get published as part of a new series of cheap paperbacks. As Baum recalls, he made the offer not entirely out of concern for her well-being: "Of course, the Little Ullstein Books are not literature but they sell like hot cakes, and I'd see to it you'd get a neat handful of cash and then you can pull me out of this momentary jam." Whatever his motive, Prels initiated Baum's lucrative relationship with Ullstein, who published her best-selling 1920 novel *Eingang zur Bühne* (translated as *Once in Vienna*). By 1926, Baum had moved to Berlin, where she negotiated her way into a position with Ullstein as an editor and exclusive author, first serializing books in its various publications, including *Die Dame, Uhu*, and the *Berliner Illustrirte Zeitung*, and then publishing five of her novels between 1926 and 1932, including her most well-known work *Menschen im Hotel* (*Grand Hotel*). By the time *Menschen im Hotel* became a success, critics were more concerned with her image and activities than with her work. These years were, in her own words, the happiest and most fruitful of her life.[93]

Nevertheless, Baum's career as "seductress" luring other women into consuming literature was structured according to the needs and desires of the publishing industry and the Jewish men who stood at its helm—regardless of whether she was happy to fulfill them. As Lynda King notes, Baum's successful career was intimately connected to the success of Ullstein, which by 1929 had become the largest publisher in Europe, not least because of its innovative marketing strategies and advertising based on serializing its books in its periodicals. According to Baum, Hermann Ullstein suggested that she write a novel about "an efficient girl," an idea she turned into the best-seller *Stud. chem. Helene Willfüer*. Helene, a chemistry student in love with her married professor, bears an illegitimate child with another man. Helene is not explicitly Jewish, although Jewish women were overrepresented at universities and often the first to pursue degrees after restrictions were lifted.[94] When the father of her child dies, she is implicated in his death and unjustly jailed. Upon being freed, she completes her chemistry studies and invents a "youth potion" which the chemistry professor, now divorced, takes. He then finds her again, and they marry. Although the novel's conventional ending drew criticism from some circles, it also assured the book's popularity among mainstream audiences.[95]

Ullstein not only shaped the content of Baum's novels, but also marketed her image as a prototypical New Woman—albeit one who did not completely rock the boat—by featuring her picture on book jackets and representing her in advertisements as modern, independent, and capable, yet, in the end, wedded to traditional values and ideals.[96] As King points out, unlike other best-selling Ullstein authors, like Erich Maria Remarque, Baum's success was the result of deliberate long-range publishing and marketing plans. Only the articles and reviews that correlated with her New Woman image bore her name and featured her photograph when they appeared in Ullstein periodicals; the rest remained unsigned. In *Die Dame*, the publication for upper-class women, her stories appeared with her name but not her picture: instead, they were illustrated with pictures of society women and actresses, and advertisements for chic products. Since the novel *Stud. chem. Helene Willfüer* featured the invention of a "youth potion," *Uhu*, a magazine geared toward middle-class women more like Baum, published it alongside an article on rejuvenation potions and the announcement that Baum had "put at the disposal of *Uhu* the studies she had to make during work on a new novel about the problem of rejuvenation." The article was accompanied by a photograph of Baum which took up a third of the page, showing her dressed in a chic coat with a fur collar, long earrings, and a determined look.[97]

By publishing in Berlin instead of Vienna, Baum may have escaped the confines of stereotypes that cast Jewish women as either Yiddish mamas or luxury consumers, but she did so, ironically, at the cost of being locked into a newer role: the modern, independent New Woman. On one hand, as the most visible representative of contemporary gender destabilization, this figure challenged conventional notions of femininity and sexuality by appearing in public with short hair, trousers, and an abundance of intellectual and sexual curiosity. On the other hand, the New Woman was also a figure implicitly associated with Jews in a way that often served marketing interests. Atina Grossmann has observed how rhetoric about the New Woman as a danger to society linked her to Jewishness via her sexuality, consumerism, and financial greed.[98] And Hugo Bettauer's periodicals often featured articles and advertisements with positive representations of independent New Women who, as Darcy Buerkle notes, are often coded in Weimar-era publications as just "Jewish enough" to

The broad appeal of Vicki Baum's interwar works stemmed in part from her publisher's ability to simultaneously market her as both a New Woman who valued her independence and a more traditional woman who upheld conservative values. The photo's German caption reads "Vicki Baum became world famous with her play *Grand Hotel.* As opposed to the first generation of feminists, her works stress women's duty to be graceful and charming." *ÖNB Vienna/NB 523.690-B*

evoke the desired effect on potential consumers. Bettauer's support for the New Woman can be seen as the flip side of his disdain for the "other" symbolic role of Jewish women as consumers and suppliers of luxury. For publishers like Ullstein, however, who sought to capitalize on her image, the New Woman, coded as just "Jewish enough," was just another marketing strategy, one that trapped writers like Baum, even as it enabled her professional and financial success. It is no wonder, then, that the protagonist of Baum's first novel for Ullstein is explicitly not Jewish, but as an independent chemistry student likewise just "Jewish enough" to evoke the ideal of the New Woman to satisfy its marketing strategy.[99]

In Vienna, where the publishing business operated on a much smaller scale and publishers were often reliant on the German market, Jewish women had fewer opportunities to position themselves as authors, even for marketing purposes. The career of Mela Hartwig, the first Austrian woman published by Vienna's successful publisher Zsolnay, illustrates in vivid detail how the publishing world both supported and delimited Jewish women's activity in the public sphere.[100] In 1895, two years after Hartwig was born in Vienna, her father, Theodor Herzl (a teacher and writer who became the chairman of the international proletarian Freidenker (Freethinker) movement in 1925; not related to the well-known Zionist of the same name), converted from Judaism to Catholicism and changed the family name to Hartwig.[101]

Like Baum, Hartwig pursued another career before becoming a writer, beginning a course of study in acting at the Vienna Conservatory in 1917. She acted at theaters in Baden, Vienna, Olomouc (Olmütz), and Berlin until 1921, when she married lawyer Robert Spira and moved to Graz.[102] At that point she gave up acting, but she remained active in the public sphere as a freelance journalist, author, and translator. Although her career as a writer advanced mainly after her marriage, Hartwig had begun to publish when she was still an actress, although in a letter to her publisher Zsolnay, she described her literary attempts before 1923 as "very poetic and inaccessible."[103] Like Baum, she first published short pieces in German periodicals: In 1918, her poem "Erkenntnis" appeared in the Munich-based magazine *Jugend*, and the *Arbeiter-Zeitung* published an article of hers in 1924 and a poem in 1927.[104] Hartwig submitted her novella *Das Verbrechen* (the crime) to a literature contest for the magazine *Die literarische Welt* in 1927 and was selected as the only woman among the nine winners. One of the judges was Alfred Döblin, who lauded her work's strong engagement with psychoanalysis (Stefan Zweig also supported her work long before she was a published author). The Psychoanalytischer Verlag in Vienna referred her to the Zsolnay Verlag on the basis of her winning novella.[105]

After the collapse of the monarchy, a number of Jewish men used the opportunity to found new literary publishing houses.[106] For Paul Zsolnay, who came from a wealthy family, publishing served not as a way to earn money, but rather as a means to actively reshape the boundaries of Austrian culture.[107] His interest in Austrian intellectual culture developed at salons hosted by his mother Amanda Wallerstein, which he attended beginning at a very young age. Guests included cultural luminaries like Franz Werfel, Arthur Schnitzler, Alma Mahler, Felix Salten, and Gerhart Hauptmann.[108] Both Zsolnay and his editorial director, Felix Costa, were of mixed Jewish background.[109]

By 1924, Zsolnay had become the largest publisher of belletristic texts in Austria, yet before issuing Hartwig's book *Ekstasen* (ecstasies) in 1928, the firm had published texts by only two other women, both translations.[110] In 1929, Zsolnay published Hartwig's second book, *Das Weib ist ein Nichts* (Woman is nothing) to great critical acclaim.[111] The publisher also supported other Austrian and Jewish women writers, such as Lili Grün and Hilde Spiel, as well as the German writer Victoria Wolf. Robert Neumann, a key figure in the Jewish literary scene in Vienna, recommended both Hilde Spiel and Lili Grün to Zsolnay, indicating the importance of Jewish men and their networks in the careers of women writers.[112] But although

Mela Hartwig Spira relaxes in the garden behind the house she and husband Robert Spira owned in Gösting, a district of Graz, in August 1931. Both this property and a house they bought in the mountain village of Tauplitz were "Aryanized" after they fled Austria in 1938.

Greta Hartwig Manschinger and Kurt (Ashley Vernon) Manschinger Papers, M.E. Grenander Department of Special Collections and Archives, University at Albany Libraries

Zsolnay published Hilde Spiel's first novel *Kati auf der Brücke* (Kati on the bridge) on March 30, 1933, they rejected her second novel, *Der Sonderzug* (The special train) in 1935, claiming that her work suffered from, as Costa explained, an "excess of emotion."[113] Costa's comment suggests that, for authors like Spiel, gender was a limiting factor in their ability to publish.[114]

Despite the fact that none of Hartwig's stories before 1936 dealt explicitly with Jews or Jewish themes, many of her female characters—like Baum's Helene—were implicitly coded as Jewish by virtue of their associations with fields like psychoanalysis and their engagement in activities of the New Woman, like holding office jobs, becoming sexually liberated, drinking, smoking cigars, and so on. Hartwig's texts from the late 1920s and early 1930s also engage the theme of the New Woman as they address modern women confronted with unsatisfying careers, fleeting relationships with egotistical men who treat them badly, and controversial social issues such as abortion.[115] But her female characters notably lack any sense of stable self-identification; they often literally become the men who shape their lives. The titles of two of her novels—*Bin ich ein überflüssiger Mensch? (Am I a Redundant Human Being?)* and *Das Weib ist ein Nichts*—point to the effacement its protagonists' experiences. Hartwig plays with language to achieve these effects; in *Das Weib ist ein Nichts*, protagonist Bibiana's declaration to her lover, who describes her as a figurine who has come to life, "ich liebe dich" (I love you) is quickly transformed into "ich lebe dich" (I live you) showcasing the ease with which the love relationship effaces her own. The relational sense of a couple's intertwined lives is lost in Bibiana's construction: not "I live *through* you," but simply "I live you." In the latter novel, "I think I would stop living if I lost you, not die, no, stop living, do you understand that? I don't live myself, I live—I think, I live you." Her life is not eclipsed by her lover, but is fully effaced.[116]

Hartwig's first book, *Ekstasen*, a collection of four novellas, includes *Das Verbrechen* (The crime), a story much admired for its originality by Alfred Döblin and Stefan Zweig, and one of the first works of fiction to criticize Freud's theories on the basis of gender. The story concerns the troubled relationship between a young woman who refuses to eat or drink, and her father, a psychoanalyst, who insists that she marry a man he has chosen for her. She resists because she is in love with her father, who in turn finds this form of 'oedipal' desire exceptionally interesting, although he claims to have no intention of indulging her incestuous fantasy. His abominable, cold behavior toward his daughter, disguised as "treatment," eventually turns into physical abuse when she dares to visit the home of his lover; in the end, the father cruelly smiles and laughs at his daughter's pain and illness. In the novel's final melodramatic scene, the daughter shoots and kills her father with a revolver he gave her.[117] Only after he is dead does she feel liberated, proclaiming, "Now my life begins."[118] Hartwig's novella critiques psychoanalytic treatment as manipulative abuse and the origins of psychoanalytic theory as misogynist, according to which women cannot exist unless men are absent. By turning the tables and making the daughter, not the son, murder the father, Hartwig questions the fin-de-siècle male identity crisis often portrayed by other writers and critiques psychoanalysis as an instrument of male power.[119]

Unlike Ullstein's campaign for Vicki Baum, Zsolnay and Costa had no specific marketing plan in place for Hartwig. Yet her "Jewish" sensibility was clearly evident to the reading public, which became a problem for Zsolnay after 1933. As one editor explained to her, "You know, my dear madam, that the world view of the German reading public and the German woman in particular is currently different from the view of life that comes out of your works."[120] In the early 1930s, Zsolnay rejected two of Hartwig's texts, *Bin ich ein überflüssiger Mensch?* and the story collection *Quer durch die Krise* (Straight through the crisis), due to concern that the German reading public had become more conservative since the Nazi rise to power. Her "esoteric" novel, they noted, would surely fail with the public, and they suggested she try to publish it as a newspaper serial. However, *Arbeiter-Zeitung* editor David Joseph Bach claimed that the newspaper could not afford to publish a book "catering only to women," although he did tell her, "If we had a women's supplement with a section for novels, I would acquire your novel immediately."[121] Their rejection indicates just how important the persona of their author was to book sales, even in Vienna; apparently, the reading public would not accept a Jewish feminist writer writing about the independent, Jewish-coded New Woman.[122] As a result, Hartwig offered to efface herself in order to publish: "I would also be willing, if you are of the opinion it would be necessary and if you think my name would not be able to bring it success, to allow the book to appear without my name."[123]

After 1934, however, Zsolnay's dependence upon its large German market ultimately led him to cease publication of works by Jewish authors, including Hartwig.[124] But Zsolnay continued to try to help Jewish writers as antisemitism became an increasing problem. In 1934 he attempted to help Elias Canetti obtain a Turkish passport and wrote a letter on his behalf to the Swiss consulate.[125] Costa also tried to assist a number of Jewish authors whose work he was forced to reject. In 1935, when Lili Grün was quite ill and in urgent need of funds, he wrote letters on her behalf asking for aid, as well as letters of introduction to the largest Vienna newspapers, asking them to publish her articles in order for her to gain a source of income. He succeeded in persuading the newspaper *Der Wiener Tag* to publish her novel, *Loni in der Kleinstadt* (Loni in the small town) and he also obtained small grants for her from the PEN club and the Concordia organizations.[126]

There is evidence that Hartwig's stories interested an audience outside of Austria, and that she might have become an internationally known writer, had her career not been curtailed by the Nazi ban on authors of Jewish descent. In 1928, the Berlin monthly periodical *Velhagen & Klasings Monatshefte* asked Zsolnay for the opportunity to test Hartwig on its readers. Unfortunately, the German publisher found the material in Hartwig's story "Schauspielerin" (Actress) so "extraordinarily agonizing and unpleasant" that they refused to accept it, although they recognized that the work contained evidence of Hartwig's talent.[127]

Both Baum and Hartwig rarely refer to Jewish characters in their interwar stories, although their texts both engage Jewish difference implicitly by figuring New Women or women whose self-understandings are effaced. Both remained limited from openly articulating any double outsider position in their art.[128] Significantly, Baum did write stories with Jewish themes before World War I. One of these, published in the Jewish periodical *Ost und West*, titled "Im alten Haus" (In the old house) appeared in its January 1910 issue, while "Rafael Gutmann" appeared in early 1911. Both feature European Jewish men attempting but unable to escape literal and metaphorical ghettos and are replete with common negative stereotypes about Eastern European Jews as decrepit, ugly, impoverished, greedy, effeminate, and sexually deviant.[129]

It is only after her first major successes, however, and the worsening political situation in Germany that Hartwig turns to explicitly Jewish themes, and writes about Jewish characters. Her novella *Das Wunder von Ulm* (The miracle of Ulm), which she wrote in 1933, is a melodramatic story about a Jewish man and his daughter set in the Middle Ages. She referred to this story as a political *Streitschrift* (polemical essay) adding that she found the debate between "Judentum und Deutschland" to be of great importance, recommending that it first be published in a different language "to gain the attention of international Jewry."[130] However, *Das Wunder von Ulm* was not published until 1936, and then only in Paris, by the Phoenix Verlag.

The lack of explicit Jewish characters and themes in Baum and Hartwig's interwar texts attests to the persistence of the unarticulated boundaries of Jewishness in interwar Austria, since they implicitly parallel the condition of Jewish "absence" that Bettauer rendered explicit in *The City without Jews*. Hartwig's Expressionist, avant-garde stories thematize women's absence by foregrounding female characters who renounce their own identities for the sake of their husbands, bosses, and fathers, and who lack strong female role models, including mothers. They call into question the possibility for women to retain the distinction between Self and Other by collapsing those boundaries—her women lose any sense of self and literally become the Other. Although done much more traditionally, Baum's narratives also push the limits of the gendered social order. Regardless of their differences in style, the fiction and careers of both of these Austrian women indicate just how deeply gendered the constructed Jewish social order remained, and show that, ironically, those whose lives most deeply reflected its consequences—Jewish women—could least afford to render them explicit. A number of women who wanted to participate successfully in mainstream Austrian culture apparently either found it necessary, or *thought* it was necessary, to write themselves out of that world in order to inscribe themselves within it.[131]

Vicki Baum emigrated from Germany to the United States in 1932, settling in Los Angeles where she built a successful career as a screenwriter. Hartwig would not be as fortunate in her career. In 1938, she emigrated with her husband to London.[132] There she met Virginia Woolf, who would prove an instrumental source of help to the émigré couple, particularly when Robert was interned on the Isle of Man as a "suspicious person" on account of his Austrian background. However, in England, her networks of Viennese Jewish publishers were of little use.[133] Hartwig published only a few more texts, including an essay on Virginia Woolf and her few explicitly Jewish stories, before she died in London in 1967. Her husband committed suicide shortly after her death.

Ultimately, the lives and works of Baum, Bettauer, Zwieback, and Hartwig indicate that although Jewish men and women were similarly positioned to take advantage of new career opportunities after the end of World War I, they faced different challenges. While Jewish men faced their own limitations, the ways in which Jewish difference echoed the patriarchy inherent in established gender divisions meant that Jewish women were often doubly disadvantaged, particularly if they transgressed prescribed gender roles as women and as Jews. And if they were Jewish women from Eastern Europe, they might face yet a third disadvantage, particularly if their looks and affect pinned them as representative of what was considered an unpalatable form of visible Jewish culture. The paths of these men's and women's lives may have diverged, but they all reflect the terms of the constructed social order of Jewish difference and of its inherently gendered nature, which meant that even those sympathetic to the injustices of its application often could not avoid its implications.

3 VIENNA'S JEWISH GEOGRAPHY

THE LEOPOLDSTADT IN INTERWAR LITERATURE

The city is not a spatial entity with sociological consequences, but a sociological entity that is formed spatially.[1]

—GEORG SIMMEL, *The Metropolis and Mental Life* (1903)

Vienna had more prestigious addresses, but growing up in the interwar period on the border between the Neubau and Ottakring districts suited Helen Blank just fine. As she told an interviewer in March 2001, "It was a very nice area, just across the street from Ottakring. I liked it. In front of the house there was an *allee* with benches—we played there all the time."[2] Although her father ran a delicatessen on Klosterneuburger Strasse on the other side of the city, he was one of a growing number of Jews who, in the decades before 1900, had chosen to raise their families outside the bounds of the Leopoldstadt, the district that had once served as the Jewish ghetto, where the highest population of Jews of all classes continued to reside.[3] For the first ten years of her life, Helen enjoyed a middle-class childhood typical of Vienna's acculturated Jews. Encouraged by her parents, she excelled at school, spent summers in the country, and enjoyed learning to play her violin, a treasured gift from her father.

But Helen's life changed dramatically in 1927, when her father ran off to Bulgaria with another woman, leaving her mother struggling to support Helen and her younger sister. As the family's financial situation declined, so did her mother's mental health. Helen began to identify with her working-class friends in Ottakring, although she maintained some middle-class cultural practices like playing the violin. By the time she received a scholarship to the *Bundeserziehungsanstalt*, a state-sponsored *Gymnasium* (high school) attended mostly by the daughters of high-ranking civil servants, she was accustomed to being the only Jew among her peers.[4] Meanwhile, she became increasingly politically active with the Socialist youth movement *Rote Falken* (Red Falcons) in Ottakring. She played piano at their film screenings and secretly ferried messages in her violin case to party functionaries in the city's outer districts. She proudly recalls how her classmates at the *Gymnasium* confided in her about their brothers' clandestine activities as members of the Nazi Party. They had no idea of her "double life," as she termed it, as a Socialist activist.[5]

Despite its apparent contradictions, Helen Blank's life was not, in fact, particularly uncommon for a middle-class Jew in interwar Austria.[6] What was unusual about Helen was not her diligence about her studies and music nor her passion for socialism, but the fact that she went about her life in city districts where relatively few Jews resided.[7] This meant that her self-understanding was shaped less by being part of a real or perceived Jewish community than it was by understanding the diverse social codings of the spaces she inhabited and by adapting herself to their parameters. Helen was aware that she was Jewish, but this knowledge did not form part of her conscious daily life. Instead, who she was quite literally depended on where she was. Her life experiences thus clearly symbolize those of many of Vienna's interwar Jews, for whom the social and physical landscape of the city's geography would become closely entwined with redefining their place in the new nation. As her statement about playing on the street's benches instead of in a playground indicates, Blank learned at an early age to manipulate her environment in order to suit her needs, to use her imagination to create a world she could enjoy. As Kevin Lynch points out, children derive most satisfaction in playing when they can do exactly that.[8] But as this chapter suggests, Vienna's Jews were often the ones who most intensively maneuvered along the fine line between shaping the city to suit one's needs, and allowing oneself to be shaped by it.[9]

Further reflecting on her childhood, Blank explained how Vienna's public spaces provided the basis for her feelings of comfort and easily achieved orientation: "[Vienna] is a metropolis, yet small enough to get to know intimately. Especially because of its star-like formation, the center of the city is within easy reach. Perhaps that is why we felt at home in the entire city. That is, in the streets, in the many public parks, museums, and other places open to the public. Private life was a different matter."[10] Her words echo those of many Austrian Jews, whose richly detailed descriptions of Vienna reveal the powerful emotional effects of its spaces and signal not only the city's legibility, but also how deeply the urban environment affected their experiences.[11] But Blank's intimacy with the city, as opposed to her discomfort with her life at home, is no mere reversal of the norms of public and private urban spaces. Living "on the boundary"—both literally and metaphorically—between two city districts, one working-class and the other up-and-coming middle class, Blank adopted various self-identifications based on her personal background as an acculturated Jew from a broken family in financial decline and her awareness of the collective knowledge and experiences that shaped the social codings of the districts she inhabited. Her successful navigation of the physical boundaries of interwar Vienna's districts required an intimate, if implicit and unarticulated, knowledge of its imagined social boundaries.

Helen Blank's reflections suggest how Jews and others navigated Vienna's social codings as a way to make sense of themselves and the world they inhabited. To many interwar Austrians in the provinces, the entire city of Vienna was imagined as a site of dangerous "Red" and "Jewish" elements.[12] Jews, like the built environment of the city itself, remained the ultimate construction in opposition to those who inhabited the natural landscapes of the provinces. But within the city limits, issues of class, ethnicity, and religion took on various localized and specific meanings at different locations. Vienna's actual inhabitants implicitly understood those codings of urban space, regardless of their reactions to the collapse of the empire and their visions for the city's future. As Robert Musil makes clear in his seminal interwar work *Mann ohne Eigenschaften* (*The Man without Qualities*), the question "Where am I?" often replaced "Who am I?" for those at a loss as to how to reposition themselves during the decline of the monarchy. Knowing exactly where they stood was a particularly crucial part of the interwar experience for the many Jews whose relatively stable self-understandings had been thrown into disarray by recent events. It indicates a growing awareness that orienting oneself in relation to others accompanied a deeper need to engage with the city's physical environment and to use it as the locus for shaping and achieving one's imagined desires. The instability of the interwar years made the power of place that much more apparent.

This chapter examines how interwar Viennese engaged Jewish difference as they navigated both the physical spaces and the metaphorical codings of their city. It begins by using history and geography to trace how Jews reacted to and inhabited the urban spaces in which they lived. While practically no Jews lived in the city in 1850, by World War I, their numbers had grown to almost 200,000, and by 1910 they made up 8.6 percent of the city's population.[13] Although that growth paralleled an increase in the general population, for a variety of reasons Jews remained a distinct group in the city, a fact that had significant geographic and cultural ramifications.[14] While the Leopoldstadt's history as the city's "quasi" ghetto and its continued vibrant Jewish population and cultural scene assured its continued coding as a Jewish district, other spaces in Vienna could be described as contested sites of Jewish difference, even if their boundaries were not as clearly rendered.

After establishing the complex and often vexed contours of Jewish Vienna, the chapter turns to three fictional representations of the Leopoldstadt that

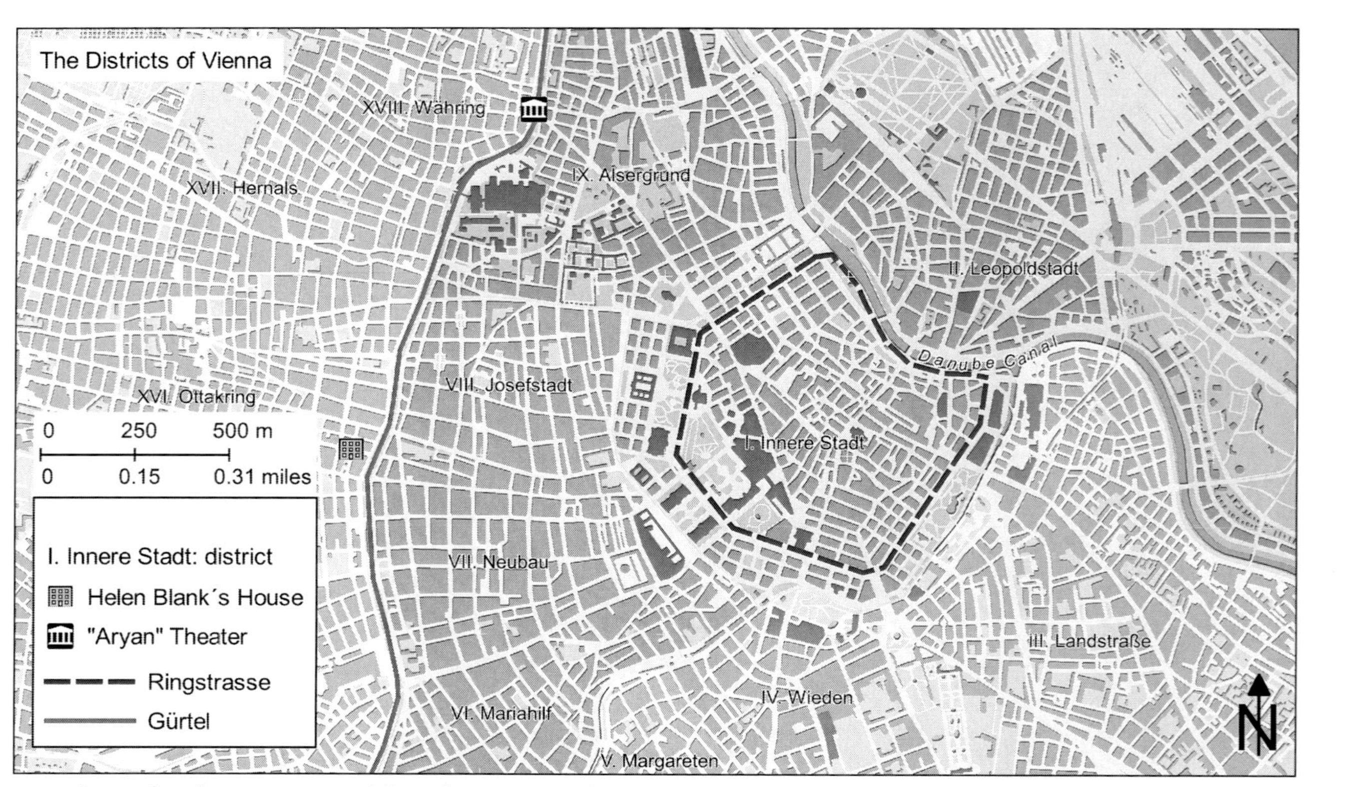

Vienna's core first district is separated from districts IV–IX by the Ringstrasse, which in turn is separated from the mostly proletarian districts outside the Gürtel. This map also shows the location of the former "Aryan" theater located between the districts of Alsergrund and Währing, as well as the approximate location of Helen Blank's home on the border between Ottakring and Neubau.

Map copyright Jobstmedia

simultaneously make legible and complicate its role as Vienna's quintessential Jewish space. This turn to literature rests on the conviction that works of fiction do not emerge in a sphere divorced from historical circumstances. Rather, in the spirit of historiography as a creative and constructed undertaking, fiction can serve to document historical circumstances, attitudes, and emotions—and in the process, can address most powerfully the wider experiences of individuals caught in the collective pressures of community, city, and nation. When the matter at hand concerns symbolic meaning and culture, as it does here, fiction becomes all the more relevant, driven as it is to figure and refigure the subtle symbolic forces at work in a culture and a country, rendering visible that which the physical world cannot offer.

David Vogel's novel *Hayyei nissu'im* (*Married Life*) first published in Palestine in 1929–1930, follows Galician Jew Rudolf Gurdweill as he traverses the Vienna's districts over the course of several years following the end of World War I. By tracing his wanderings and his orientation techniques, the novel illuminates the Leopoldstadt as a Jewish space that was both integral to and yet still isolated from the rest of the city. Abraham Moshe Fuchs's 1924 Yiddish novel *Unter der brik: un andere dersteylungen* (Under the bridge: and other stories), first published in Warsaw, delivers a shocking depiction of the district as a site of Jewish pimps, prostitutes, criminals, and disfigured war veterans who live in a distorted version of the world outside its bounds. By pushing antisemitic stereotypes about Jewish degeneracy to their limits, the text forces Jewish readers to come to terms with their own worst imagined fears about the Leopoldstadt. Fuchs's dark Jewish netherworld contrasts starkly with the neighborhood described in Veza Canetti's *Die gelbe Strasse* (*Yellow Street*), parts of which first appeared in Vienna's *Arbeiter-Zeitung* in the early 1930s. With no explicit mention of the district's Jews, Canetti's discursive Leopoldstadt—focused on a single street, rather than an area of the district or the entire city—emerges as an impossible *Zwischenort*, or "in-between" space, where Jews are paradoxically both present and absent. The abuse, misogyny, and murder that take place there thus remain detached from any specific Jewish foundation, and their meanings become more universally applicable. What emerges from these readings are the integral links between the form of the city and the values and needs of its residents, as well as the fact that the processes of exclusion in the home, the neighborhood, and at the national level are not discrete issues. Illuminated through these texts is how the relationship between the Jewish and non-Jewish-coded spaces of the city operated as part of a broader system of sensory cues utilized by all residents to make their city legible as they reinvent and situate themselves within its shifting interwar boundaries.[15]

Vienna's Jewish Geography

Thinking about Jewish space immediately conjures up images of sites intended explicitly for the practice of Jewish religious customs, such a synagogue or *eruv*.[16] Residential areas with relatively high concentrations of Jews, especially those, like the Leopoldstadt, with a thriving religious and cultural Jewish life, are also easily understood as Jewish spaces. But even such incontrovertibly Jewish areas generate important symbolic meanings that extend far beyond their physical realities.[17] Meanwhile, spaces that lack visible evidence of Jews or Jewish culture can nevertheless be perceived—or coded—as Jewish for a variety of social, economical, and historical reasons.

For seminal thinkers on space like Henri Lefebvre and Georg Simmel, constructed social orders are crucial to how we think about physical space, to the point that they actually become more important constitutive elements of space than the material world. As Lefebvre reminds us, all spaces consist of both the material space in which human interaction takes place—streets, buildings, houses—and the abstract notions of what those spaces represent.[18] In other words, physical environments do not exist independent of the people who utilize them, since it is only through people's consciousness, actions, and interactions—that is, their engagements with the constructed social orders that shape the space—that the material world acquires meaning.[19] Thus, a combination of the material, political, and ideological conditions according to which individuals construct the material world, along with what they imagine that material world to be, forms the basis of the spaces people inhabit.

Setha Low suggests that we consider how two complementary processes work in tandem to give meaning to space: social production (the economic and sociological factors that result in the creation of the material setting) and social construction (the symbolic system that conveys the meaning of that material setting when people interact with it).[20] This dichotomy helps us to see more clearly how each individual's personal background, values, and ideals combine with the sociological processes that form—and continue to inform—a specific site to shape urban experiences.[21] However, such thinking also immediately gives rise to the question of authorship. Who, exactly, has the power and authority to define space and determine its social meaning? Whose space is it? The spaces that most clearly reveal the contested nature of spatial authorship are those that generate visible and verbal manifestations of disputes about social boundaries, both physical and metaphorical, real and imagined.

One of Vienna's first and most clearly delineated Jewish spaces was its *Judenviertel* (Jews' quarter), an area bounded by walls and gates, near the center of the city.[22] Jews lived there until 1420, when they were expelled from Austria.

They did not return to the city in significant numbers for another 150 years, when they populated a marshy section outside the city walls known as the *Unteren Werd.* This area became the site of the *Judenstadt* (Jews' city), or ghetto, until the second expulsion of the estimated 3,000 Jews in 1669–1670 under Emperor Leopold I.[23] The city crystalized the expulsion by renaming the entire district Leopoldstadt and replacing its main synagogue with the *Leopoldskirche* (Leopold's church). Ironically, the Leopoldstadt later became synonymous with "Jewish district" in the nineteenth century, after Jews returned to Vienna in significant numbers and repopulated the district.[24]

Practically, the significant involvement of Jews in the material production of space in Vienna outside the bounds of the former *Judenviertel* and *Judenstadt* only became possible when the exclusionary laws that bound them to live in those areas were removed. Still, their choices of what to build and where to build it, as well as the reactions their construction engendered, reveal the contours of the sociological boundaries that persisted in the city.[25] Dell Upton notes that it is the relationship between the seen and the unseen, the disjunction between the physical order and social space, that shapes the meanings of the spaces people inhabit.[26] In a Viennese context, constructing buildings and residences did not automatically give Jews the power to determine the meanings of their homes, workplaces, and neighborhoods. In the nineteenth century in particular, when Jews gained more freedom to build in some of the choicest areas of the city, these sites often became contested areas of authorship as the efforts of Jews to change their social status clashed with the antisemitic prejudices of others.

The persistence of social boundaries that divided Jews from non-Jews, even in the absence of physical boundaries, comes to the fore just before the turn of the twentieth century, when Jews became involved in the massive construction project for the city's majestic and centrally-located Ringstrasse. Over the centuries, as the city's geographical boundaries expanded, Vienna's urban landscape grew in a roughly circular fashion. New districts radiated out from the original city in the center, as adjacent villages, towns, and undeveloped land were incorporated into Vienna. The fundamental division between the inner city and the newer districts, long marked by a wall constructed for defensive purposes, was made official with the construction of the Ringstrasse in the 1860s and cemented decades later with the completion of its development into a showy thoroughfare.[27]

In his seminal work *Fin-de-siècle Vienna: Culture and Politics*, Carl E. Schorske examines the Ringstrasse's original construction in the nineteenth century, emphasizing the attempts at "cultural self-projection" on the part of its liberal, bourgeois planners who designed buildings and structures to represent various historical periods that represented their ideals.[28] Those ideals centered on the best of European high culture. In this spirit, the Corinthian columns of the Parliament building evoke the birth of democracy in ancient Greece, while the neo-Renaissance university harks back to the beginning of universities in Italy, and so on. What Schorske does not mention, however, are the parallel "cultural self-projections" reflected in the construction of the private residences that adjoin these public buildings, many of whose owners were Jews.[29] After restrictions on owning real estate on the Ringstrasse were lifted, a number of well-to-do Jews built stately residences for their families and grandiose *Mietspaläste* (rental apartment "palaces") in prime locations there. The brothers Eduard and Moritz Todesco, Jews born and raised in the Leopoldstadt, were among the first to commission a monumental private residence on the Ringstrasse, located on the corner of the street's prominent Kärntnerstrasse crossing.[30] Significantly, the Todesco brothers and other early developers took meticulous care to construct their private residences in the Historicist neo-Renaissance style as a signal of their successful entry into Viennese society.[31]

Jews sought and—to some extent—also acquired cultural capital through owning, building, and residing on the Ringstrasse. In reality, however, the social equation is complicated by the fact that very few members of the (non-Jewish) aristocracy actually lived there at that point. Jews thus were not acculturating into a pre-existing ideal Austrian nobility, but into one that they only imagined did—or should—exist.[32] Living up to what Pierre Bourdieu suggests is the principle behind the performative magic of all acts of institution—"becoming what you are"—these wealthy Austrian Jews moved to the most noble of Viennese districts in order to further the process of becoming noble Austrians. Their opulent residences on the Ring signify not only the material reality of the city's wealthy denizens, but the imagined social ideal they sought in that material reality.[33]

The visible efforts of the Todesco brothers and others to blend in to this ideal of nobility by constructing buildings that matched the opulence of their surroundings did not go unnoticed by the general population, especially after 1873 when the stock market crashed and many held Jewish financiers responsible. The efforts of Jews to become aristocrats was publicly highlighted and mocked for turning the Ringstrasse into a freshly-minted "Jewish" space, precisely the opposite of what these "Jewish aristocrats" had wanted to do. One 1873 city guide sarcastically described the Ring as "Zion Street of New Jerusalem . . . the most splendid street of the Imperial city. The palaces adorning it nearly all belong to millionaires of the 'chosen people'; only a few belong to Christian intruders."[34] In 1888, Friedrich Uhl, editor and drama critic of the *Wiener Zeitung*, described the competitively opulent Jewish buildings on the Ring as attempts at gaining attention.[35] These prejudices also revealed themselves in music, as in this stanza from an early alternate version of the lyrics to Vienna's signature "Blue Danube" melody by Johann Strauss:

> Whoever hasn't seen
> Our city of Vienna in quite a while
> Will find nary a house;
> Since wherever you look stands a palace!
> The Ring is a jewel, all of Israel lives there,
> In ten years they'll have built
> Themselves a nice New Jerusalem there.[36]

Ironically, in attempting to become nobles by leaving the Jewish district of the Leopoldstadt for the center of the city, the Todescos and their peers re-enacted in the minds of their detractors an imagined Jewish narrative of return to a homeland, their "Jerusalem."

Clearly, the turn-of-the century Ringstrasse was a site of struggle over the authority to define social meaning, but it was far from the only area outside the Leopoldstadt where the real or imagined presence of Jews elicited contests over space. In his writings, Joseph Scheicher, the antisemitic Catholic prelate from Styria, lamented the powerful role of Jews in governing Vienna's fourth district of Wieden.[37] Although Wieden was never home to a significant numbers of Jews—in 1910, they totaled just 6 percent of the population—the prominence of those who did live there and their involvement in the leadership of the district inflated their presence.[38] In the working-class district of Favoriten, the Suschitzky brothers, owners of the first and only socialist bookstore in the district, faced a constant stream of attacks by accusers who deployed common antisemitic tropes of Jews as dangerous deviants and purveyors of pornography. The location of a socialist bookstore in a working-class district was in itself hardly controversial, but a socialist bookstore owned by Jews in a decidedly non-Jewish-coded district proved an isolated, and therefore highly vulnerable, Jewish space.[39]

Districts with more substantial Jewish populations also became sites of contested authority. Marsha Rozenblit's research on the pre-1914 residences of Jewish community members indicates that, although many Jews had become less observant by this time, most retained some form of secular Jewish self-identification and sense of community, since they tended to live largely amongst themselves, belong to Jewish organizations, and socialize with and marry other Jews. Even the poorest Jews chose to live with middle-class Jews over non-Jews of their own class; regardless of their reasons, writes Rozenblit, "the Jews of Vienna chose housing mainly with their Jewishness in mind." By World War I, the segregation of Jews from non-Jews had become significant, and their residential concentration remained constant, despite acculturation, social mobility, and the arrival of new immigrants. Although Jews made up only 9 percent of Vienna's population, they were one third of the population of the Leopoldstadt and one fifth of the inner city and Alsergrund districts.[40]

While many Jews of all classes continued to live in the Leopoldstadt throughout the interwar period, a significant number moved to the inner city and the Alsergrund; while the percentage of Jews living in the first and second districts remained relatively stable, the Jewish population in the Alsergrund doubled from 10 percent to 20 percent between 1870 and 1910. The Alsergrund was directly adjacent to the Leopoldstadt and particularly attracted white-collar Jews, including business employees and professionals, to the point that it became "the proper address for a new breed of urban Jew" seeking cultural cachet.[41] Benno Weiser Varon, for instance, recalls that he and his brother Max moved out of the Leopoldstadt as soon as they made enough money, even though they were still in *Gymnasium*. They lived in a furnished apartment with a bath in the "much more classy Ninth District," although they "never missed a meal" back at their parents' home in the Leopoldstadt.[42]

Though many Jews who moved to the Alsergrund clearly sought to leave the Jewish Leopoldstadt behind, the unintended result of their collective migration was the creation of another Jewish space, a development that did not go unnoticed by vocal antisemites. In 1898, Adam Müller-Guttenbrunn, a zealous German nationalist who would later become editor of the feuilleton section of the *Deutsche Zeitung*, indicated his discontent with these population shifts when he led the call for the establishment of Vienna's Kaiserjubiläums Stadtheater (the Emperor's Jubilee City Theater) in the eighteenth district. From the beginning, the new establishment was intended as—and indeed became—Vienna's first "Aryan" theater. Its location on the northern border of Alsergrund, separated from Währing by the Gürtel, had symbolic significance.[43]

The locations and intended audiences of theaters had been a major issue in Vienna since the middle of the century, when the demolition of the old city walls first made possible the construction of new buildings on the Ring.[44] While the Ring's Burgtheater, constructed in 1870, was run by and served the city's aristocracy and wealthy bourgeoisie, theater and music were important elements of acculturation for Jews, many of whom were deeply involved in the cultural life on the Ring, as producers and creators, and as audiences.[45] Jews were also visible theatergoers in other districts, including, of course, the Leopoldstadt, that featured Jewish-themed and Yiddish-language dramas.[46] The substantial presence of Jews in theaters throughout the city—as audiences, actors, playwrights, and critics—made antisemites particularly wary of their involvement.

Müller-Guttenbrunn and the other founding members of the board of the Emperor's Jubilee Theater made it clear that, although the official purpose of the theater's founding was to celebrate the emperor, its underlying goal was the

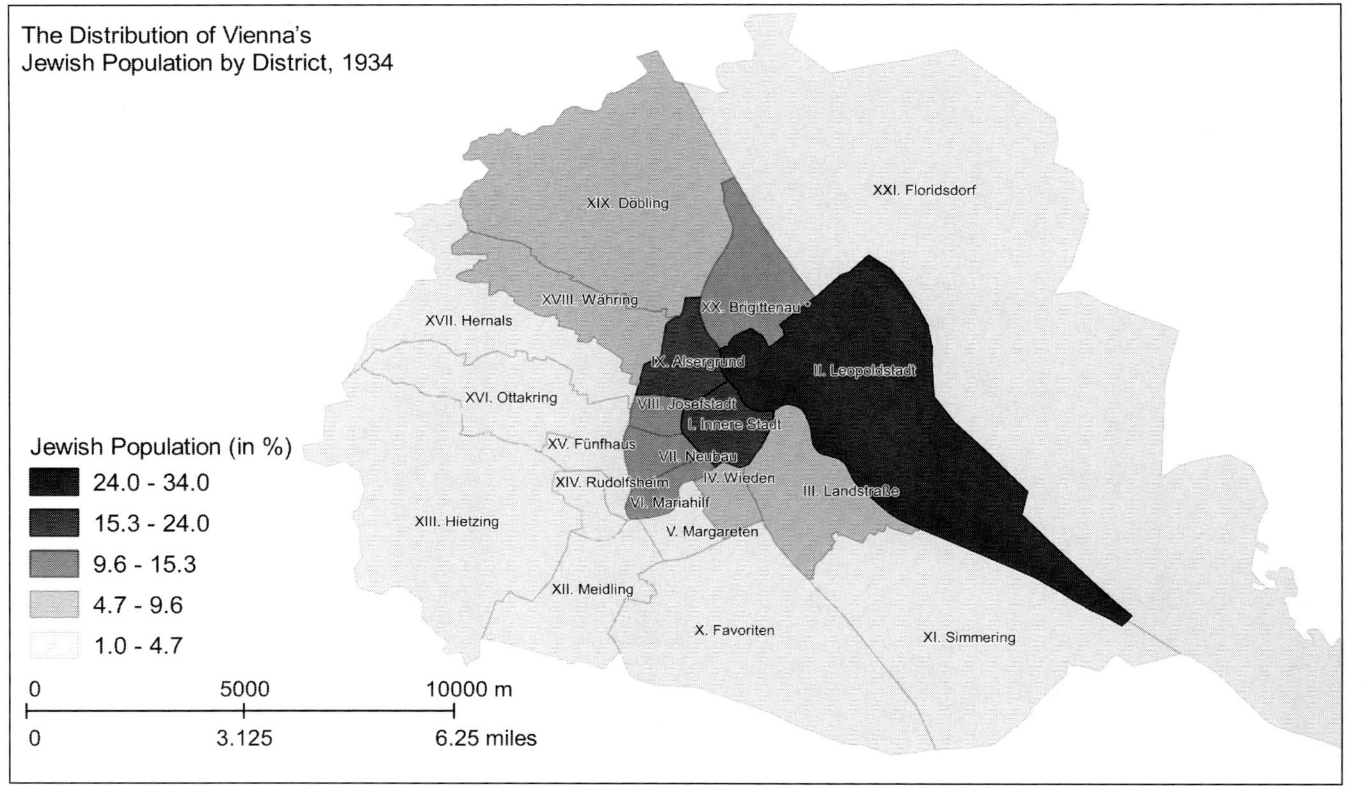

With a population that was at least 30 percent Jewish, the Leopoldstadt remained Vienna's premier Jewish district during the interwar period. The inner city and Alsergrund followed with Jewish populations of just under 25 percent.

Map copyright Jobstmedia

exclusion of Jewish playwrights, actors, and audiences.[47] In addition to proclaiming the need to construct theaters free of characteristics like "showy boxes," typically ascribed to Jewish parvenus, Müller-Guttenbrunn stressed the importance of locating the theater on the border between the districts of Währing and Alsergrund, a site of increasing Jewish population in the decades before World War I. At the same time that his insistence belies his implicit perception of these areas as Jewish space, it indicates that the theater was to serve as a symbolic physical buttress against a growing Jewish population.[48] The link between the theater's underlying purpose and its location is supported by his reflections on his childhood apartment which was located on the same street. In his memoirs, he nostalgically recalls the *ländlichen* (rural) roots (i.e. coded as non-Jewish) of the district before it transformed into a *städtlichen* (urban) area (i.e., Jewish coded). In its untainted state during his youth, he laments, it was bucolic and innocent, replete with grazing sheep and children's playgrounds. He sourly complains that an editor from the *Neue Freie Presse*, whom he refers to as a "real estate speculator" (i.e., a Jew), bought the houses next to the children's playground and planned to build a theater there.[49] By expressing his desire for urban spaces imbued with the slow-paced, pure, innocent nature of the romanticized provinces, and by associating Jews with the destructive forces of modernity and culture, Müller-Guttenbrunn reveals the emerging boundaries of Jewish space in the ninth district.[50]

In light of such antisemitic efforts, a 1909 study by the Historical Commission of the Jewish Community of Vienna takes on new meaning. *Das Wiener Ghetto: Seine Häuser und Seine Bewohner* (The Vienna Ghetto: Its Houses and Its Residents) was part of a series on Jewish history, but served a different purpose from the other volumes in the series.[51] Its publication represented an attempt by the Jewish community to reclaim Vienna's Jewish spaces, historically and symbolically, by reconstructing detailed maps outlining where Jews had lived in the *Judenviertel* and *Judenstadt* before the destruction of their communities and expropriation of their property in 1421 and 1670, respectively. The 314-page study contains detailed lists of the Jewish owners of each house, the amounts for which the properties were sold after they were expropriated, the names of their new (non-Jewish) owners, and the physical layout of each house in question, including number of rooms, their sizes, and so on.[52] This study is all the more remarkable because the *Judengrundbücher* (Jewish property registers) in which transactions involving Jewish property were recorded were missing for both areas, which meant that these Jewish-owned properties were literally erased from official city history. But author Ignaz Schwarz painstakingly reconstructed the details through official city records of the property transactions that immediately followed the expulsion of the Jews, when their property was confiscated by the state and sold to non-Jews.

This first attempt by the Jewish community to reconstruct a topographical view of Jewish space, writes Schwarz in the preface to the study, expressed their desire not for the history of the destroyed communities, but to know "the nature of the space they inhabited."[53] Schwarz's work is part of the Jewish community's broader impulse to document its past and prove its legitimacy as part of the city's history.[54] But the study also stands as an important corrective to other nineteenth-century historical accounts that focus on the destruction of Vienna's Jewish spaces by celebrating the expulsion and murder of the Jews and the expropriation of their property.[55] By in effect negatively reconstructing Jewish spaces from records of postexpulsion transactions, the study not only fills important gaps in the city's urban history, but also stresses the social *destruction* (not production) of Jewish spaces signaling the collapse of physical boundaries that separated non-Jews from Jews by virtue of their murder and expulsion.

At the same time, the study highlights the relationship between past and present physical and social geographies by including both maps with numbers corresponding to the exact houses in which the Jews lived and smaller inset maps pinpointing the location of each area in present-day Vienna. The 1909 study, by highlighting the physical boundaries that no longer separated Jews from non-Jews, addressed the social boundaries that not only persisted, but were, in fact, growing in importance as fin-de-siècle Jews created "Jewish spaces" in other parts of the city. More than just merely responding to perceived antisemitic threats as they became "visible" residents of other areas of the city, like the Ring or the ninth district, these maps provided a "spectral image" of the Jewish past, one that allowed Jews to orient themselves as to where they stood in the present.

By the time these studies appeared, Vienna's space was clearly coded according to a relatively strict class system: the inner core and Ring were marked not only as the seat of the emperor, but also constituted the space of the wealthy and cultured; most of the districts immediately surrounding the Ring were up-and-coming or bourgeois; and working-class districts were located outside the Gürtel.[56] Schorske recounts how, when the Ringstrasse was reconstructed, its broad horizontal band created a circular flow that cut off the inner districts from the rest of the city. He contends that, instead of linking the outlying districts—and the lower classes who lived there—to the city center and exposing them to the vibrant heart of the metropolis, the Ring formed a "sociological isolation belt" that kept undesirable members of the population from penetrating the center.[57]

In Vienna, more than in other European cities, both physical and symbolic district boundaries thus provided an imagined line of defense between the "potentially dangerous" working class districts and the elite, wealthy residents of the city center's luxury housing.[58] To be sure, these simple codings did not strictly

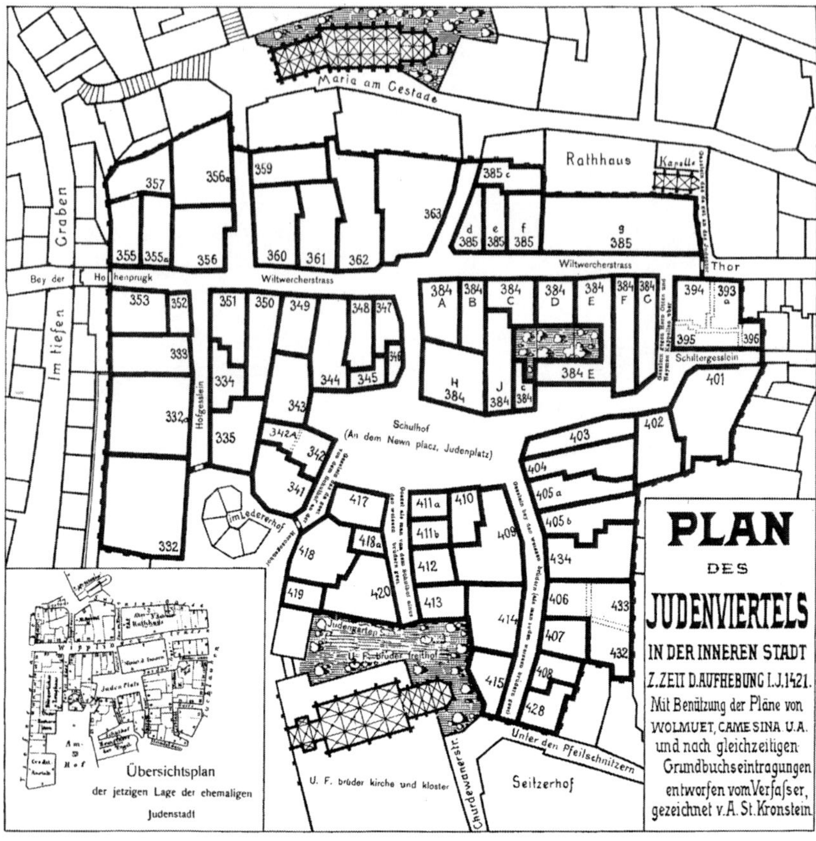

Around 1900, Vienna's Jewish community commissioned maps of the *Judenviertel* (Jews' quarter), abolished in 1421, and the *Judenstadt* (Jews' city), abolished in 1670. The numbers on each map correspond to a detailed description of each house's physical layout, former Jewish owner, new, non-Jewish owner, and sales price.
Promedia Verlag/Wienbibliothek

conform to reality: Members of the working class lived inside the Gürtel, impoverished Viennese lived in the city center, and the well-to-do often owned villas in the outer districts. As interwar property registers, memoirs, and other sources make clear, Jews made their homes in virtually every district of the city.[59] Jewish space could physically overlap working-class or aristocratic space or be at odds with it; the real or imagined presence of Jews was often intertwined with spatial codings of class, ethnicity, and religion. For example, a 1927 essay from the *Illustriertes Sportblatt* delineates the city's sports teams not only along the lines of Jewish difference, but associates that difference in particular sections of the city. Thus it notes, "The healthy, unconsumed suburbs lead physically, morally, and

Zu Schwarz: Das Wiener Ghetto. II. Teil.

Wien und Leipzig. Verlag von Wilhelm Braumüller.

materially," and would produce teams that would without a doubt conquer the "sticky coffeehouse air" associated with the Jewish clubs.[60] But the powerful implications of Vienna's imagined, class-based district configurations inevitably affected how Jews and other Viennese lived their lives.

The collapse of the monarchy radically destabilized such geographical codings in interwar Vienna, both politically and symbolically. City residents found their economic ties severed and their political power greatly reduced in the face of worldwide economic, social, and political shifts.[61] Post–World War I shifts in the physical boundaries of Austria and Vienna also changed how the Viennese perceived their city. On January 1, 1922, the city became an independent *Land* (state), which gave it more financial independence and autonomy, but also isolated it even further from the rest of the country.[62] Reaction to these changes among the Viennese were mixed. During the first two decades of the interwar period, many longed for "Alt-Wien" (old Vienna), a city comprised of untainted rural villages that they imagined to have existed before the expansion and urbanization of the *fin de siècle*.[63] For Jews, however, this vision had little appeal, given that it did not include them.[64]

In contrast, many Jews did, however, identify with Vienna's past as the former imperial capital that typified the high culture of the fin-de-siècle, in which they had actively participated. Indeed, Jews who were born or grew up in Vienna after the First World War often note in their memoirs that they identified more closely with Vienna, both culturally and geographically, than with Austria as a whole. For Weiser Varon, the events following 1938 may have made him unwilling to self-identify as Austrian, "But I never stopped being a Viennese. Vienna has formed me."[65]

Despite such nostalgic reminiscences, competing notions of an imagined future Vienna arose after the collapse of the monarchy as well: One envisioned a city "redefined" via provincial codings, while another sought to maintain and further develop a cosmopolitan urbanity. Both Jews and non-Jews participated in shaping the latter vision. Jewish writers, however, recognized and articulated the terms of the struggle over the contested imagined space of the new Vienna. Journalist Anton Kuh, for example, sarcastically noted that, as the capital of the Austro-Hungarian Monarchy, Vienna had been known as the city "on the Danube," but now it had become "Vienna by the Mountains."[66] "Graz from the south, Linz from the west, creep closer and closer . . . Politics carries in air from the mountains and pastures, wooden barn breezes . . . Vienna is an alpine capital—we others, with the slaves to the industry, are carrying out a defensive struggle together. The mountains are looming—soon 'by the mountains' instead of 'on the Danube' will be inscribed in books." [67]

A year later, Kuh reiterated his fears about a "*gemütsumdämmerndes Bergland*" (mountain land surrounding the mind with shadows) around Vienna in an article he wrote in the *Prager Tagblatt* in response to provincial groups parading on the Ring in *Tracht* (traditional Austrian dress), as part of the celebrations on *Allgemeiner österreichischer Katholikentag* (Austrian Catholics' Day). He further details the stakes of what he views as a topographical encroachment of culture that was attempting to bring "authentic" provincial Austrianness to the city. Articulating a fear that Hugo Bettauer also alluded to in *The City without Jews*, Kuh clearly outlines the terms of this urban/rural divide, linking the authority over the space of the city to that of the country: "The representative Austrians were made up of Germans, Jews, Europeans. But the gentlemen from Graz, Mödling, Salzburg give themselves the title 'New Austrians.' And maybe they really deserve it. Because since the end of the war, it has become even clearer that 'Vienna' and 'Austria' are two almost diametrically opposed terms. . . ."[68] He ironically reverses the traditional fear of the city taking over the country with decadence, filth, and decay, complaining that the city has been taken over by forces that oppose the cosmopolitanism of its earlier heyday, bringing with them an "unter sich" (among themselves) mentality that excludes the participants in its earlier cultural glory. His words illuminate the intensity of the struggle between province and city to define the new nation as the contested space of a new, imagined Vienna, and they echo the competing visions of a new Austria, both of which were frequently—and powerfully—articulated in terms of Jewish difference.

Discursive Leopoldstadts

If Vienna served as the definitively coded Jewish space for Austria, the Leopoldstadt often played this role for Vienna. Popular interwar author Leo Perutz frames the Leopoldstadt of the urban imagination in one of his brief sketches about Jewish life. In "Skizzen aus der Ukraine" (Sketches from the Ukraine) two Jewish men on a train ride strike up a conversation about Odessa, their destination. One man tells the other that he has visited Galicia, Stanislau, Lemberg, Tarnow, and Vienna, but none can compare to Odessa: "Such a life! . . . The glitter! The riches! The toilets!" Pulling back his lips to reveal his toothless mouth, he continues: "And the cafes! The hotels! The theater." The narrative continues: "And the well-traveled and world experienced man searches in vain for something similar, one memory after another, what could render the splendor of Odessa visible before our eyes. And now he has it. It finally occurs to him. 'Just like your Taborstrasse in Vienna' he says with a romanticized smile of illuminated memory."[69] As the man ascribes the height of sophisticated cosmopolitan culture to this marginalized, lowbrow section of the city, Perutz underscores—and mocks—the "dream" of Vienna held by many emigrant Eastern European Jews.[70] While the sketch pokes fun at Jewish life in Odessa and Vienna, it also reveals the Leopoldstadt not as the antithesis, but rather as a central distorted reflection of their fast-paced, modern, urban life and culture.[71]

Regardless of how interwar Jews may have envisioned Vienna's future urban landscape, the Leopoldstadt remained Vienna's Jewish "home," both metaphorically and, for a large percentage of the population, actually, up until the end of the interwar period. Yet Jewish actor Leon Askin (born Leon Aschkenasy), who grew up in interwar Vienna, dismissed any illusion of the Leopoldstadt as a unified whole. "When you talk about the Leopoldstadt, you have to talk about six Leopoldstadts," he said in an interview, dividing its territory into separate residential and garden quarters, along with the Prater, the city's renowned entertainment and leisure park.[72] Librettist and writer Peter Herz's description of the lively Jewish life in and around the Praterstrasse, the district's grand boulevard, also maps the district's divisions: "The closer you got to the Praterstern, the lower the level

With their black caftans, hats, and long beards, these traditionally dressed orthodox Jews on the Leopoldstadt's Karmeliterplatz typify most interwar depictions of *Ostjuden*. *ÖNB Vienna/PCH 17953-A(B)*

of the restaurants and pubs. There, for example, was the Café Madrid, a place with priority on the list of places the police searched when looking for a defrauder. They hung out in these and similar eateries, the cardsharps, petty thieves, pimps and their 'ladies' . . . that, too, belonged to this boisterous street."[73] These eyewitness perspectives suggest a reality that later was often subsumed by the imagined Leopoldstadt: while the entire district came to be coded as Vienna's paradigmatic Jewish space, in fact only one section served as the city's ghetto, and the whole district had both Jewish and non-Jewish residents.[74] In other words, the part would come to stand for the whole.

In *Die Mazzesinsel*, her book on the history of the Leopoldstadt, Ruth Beckermann notes that although the Leopoldstadt was connected to the city, it was a world apart from the rest of Vienna. This historic state of affairs was exacerbated during the nineteenth and early twentieth centuries as Jewish emigrants and refugees from the East arrived in Vienna and contributed to the Leopoldstadt's growing Jewish population. The thousands of poor Jewish refugees from the East who arrived in the Leopoldstadt via the *Nordbahnhof* during World War I typically remained in the district, ensuring that Jewish life continued to thrive there, with Yiddish and other newspapers, theaters, cafés, and synagogues. Although two thirds of Vienna's interwar Jews lived outside the Leopoldstadt, the district retained its image as a sort of homeland, evoking shtetl life and in effect turning the rest of the city into a microcosm of the Diaspora. Indeed, it is precisely this ambiguous relationship to the rest of the city which allowed the Leopoldstadt to maintain its status as Jewish space.

Discursive descriptions of the district reveal the complexity of its relationship to the rest of the city. In order to properly describe the atmosphere of the Praterstrasse, Peter Herz briefly narrates its history, describing it as a site of Jewish acculturation. Austrian aristocrats first built palaces adjacent to the Prater when it served as the emperor's hunting grounds. Prosperous Jews followed, constructing their own beautiful buildings. Eventually, many considered the street too bourgeois, and the wealthy moved on, at which point Jewish musicians, artists, scholars, and doctors repopulated the street and enlivened its vibrant theater and café scene.[75] Eva Brueck, who grew up in a neighboring district, observed:

> I remember that area, mainly populated by Jews, as a place with coffeehouses, theaters, cinemas, with people speaking Yiddish, Polish, Russian, Roumanian, German with a foreign accent, Jews whose outer appearance characterized them as Rabbis, with their black hats, their beards, young boys with side-locks . . . Many of my class-mates at school had lived in this area, where I had often been invited for a "Seder" or Khanukka celebration. It was an area full of vitality, with a varied cultural life enriched by the influence of the traditions of many countries.[76]

Herz's and Brueck's rosy depictions notwithstanding, most Viennese Jews describe the Leopoldstadt with ambivalence, as in the case of Ernst Epler, a Jewish émigré raised there, who characterized the efforts of Orthodox Jews to stay separated from the rest of the district's population as producing a ghetto with "invisible walls."[77]

Lotte Hümbelin, who grew up in the Leopoldstadt, noted the sharp distinctions between its Jewish and "working-class" residents, along with the effects of those distinctions on those Jews who were in reality (if not nominally) part of the proletariat: "The poor Jews of the Leopoldstadt, the small handworkers, craftsmen, shoemakers, tailors, belonged in reality to Vienna's proletariat. They differed only in the fact that, wherever possible, life was worse for them. In our section of the district there were few real men and women workers, only many poor Jews and also poor Christians. Our existence was uncertain, the organized workers didn't take notice of us . . . if one got sick, one was left to live or die."

Hümbelin's memoir stresses the financial and cultural values that separated her own family not only from the non-Jewish working class, but also from the poor Jews of the Leopoldstadt, who, despite living close by, remained a group apart. Although her family had little money, they were cultured: Her parents gave her books as presents, including Grimm's *Fairy Tales* and works by Goethe, Schiller, and Heine, and families like hers tried to send their children to the schools of the wealthier classes, which would have been unthinkable for non-Jewish families of the same social background.[78]

For Stella Klein-Löw, whose family emigrated to Vienna from Galicia soon after she was born, the Leopoldstadt remained integrally tied to her emotional response to the city. She devotes an entire chapter of her memoir to the district, not because it was where she was most comfortable, but because, as an acculturated, middle-class Jew, she felt *least* at home in the *Judenbezirk* (Jews' district, the term she used). The chapter outlines the gamut of her ambivalence. She admits to being fascinated as a small child by the Prater's leisure-time offerings, an excitement focused on both the Ferris wheel and the area's proletarian "half-world" of athletes and prostitutes. When she started to work in the district on a daily basis, however, she developed more negative feelings: "There I didn't like it, the Leopoldstadt. It smelled bad, the streets were dirty, the people strange.. . ." Not until she began to teach there did she develop a certain pride in the Orthodox Jews who stood out because of their clothes and their "disdaining, hate-filled rejection of the antisemitic 'Urwieners' [true Viennese]." When she witnesses the post-Kristallnacht outbursts of hatred from non-Jewish residents, she notes, "Then I began to hate the Leopoldstadt." [79]

Sonia Wachstein grew up in the western part of the city where there were few Jews, and she recalls antisemitic taunts but claims to have been even more frightened by a statue of Jesus: "A life size statue of Jesus, often prominent on a street corner, as there were many in Catholic Austria, was so frightening to me that every time I passed the spot by myself, I would cover my eyes and recite the 'Shemah.'"[80] She nevertheless felt more at home in her neighborhood than among the refugees and poverty of the Leopoldstadt. A visit to Russian relatives living in a tenement on the Taborstrasse reveals her alienation:

> The building was bursting at its seams; a mass of humanity lived, fought, loved and argued in a narrow space. It was all so different and foreign to me. When Sunday afternoon came I could not wait to get home. As I came into the coolness of our house on the hill, into the spacious isolation of our rooms, into the silent fragrant garden, I could not understand how

> people could bear to live in the crowded atmosphere and the noisy streets.[81]

In contrast, many of the Jews who called it home felt attached to the Leopoldstadt. For writer and musicologist Otto Erich Deutsch, who, according to his daughter Gitta Deutsch, converted to Protestantism "without ever disowning his Jewish origin," the district was a site of fond family memories. After his death in 1967, she found a *Heimatbuch* on the Leopoldstadt published in Vienna in 1937, in which he had written "prohibited in 1938" and underneath "bought in 1939," registering his act of defiance in the face of Nazism.[82] Benno Weiser Varon may have moved to a more upscale district, but he also defended the Leopoldstadt, despite its reputation as a squalid, repulsive ghetto, claiming that it was the one space in Vienna where a Jew could feel that Christians were in the minority.[83]

Clearly class—along with class aspirations—and politics played a role in the range of Jewish responses to the district. But whether they viewed it positively or negatively, most Jews remember the Leopoldstadt as a Jewish space that was separate from the rest of the city, but played an important role in defining it. Jews' contemporary reports on its conditions, on the other hand, tended to emphasize its mixed nature. Interwar journalists like Bruno Frei, Else Feldmann, and Joseph Roth tried to balance accurate reporting on the area's poverty with an emphasis on the dignity of impoverished Jews who were resilient and willing to work. In so doing, they hoped to counteract the district's negative reputation—in the eyes of Jews as well as non-Jews—as a site of Jewish homelessness, overcrowding, and poor hygiene. Still, although Frei claims that "Das jüdische Elend ist nicht anders als das nichtjüdische" (Jewish misery is no different from non-Jewish misery), his defensive insistence on their similarity indicates the persistence of an imagined social order that coded them differently. Similarly, Joseph Roth's description of the area as a "voluntary ghetto," which emphasizes the bridges connecting it to other districts, actually highlights just how separate a space it was, and just how much its isolated status depended on its relationship to the rest of the city.[84] In other words, the imagined otherness of the Leopoldstadt was inescapable.

In interwar fiction, however, we find a complex way of addressing this imagined Leopoldstadt and its relationship to the rest of the city that at once reveals the district's otherness and often seeks to challenge it. As Michel de Certeau suggests, like a walker in a city, the reader of a text also combines the fragments of what he or she experiences and—regardless of what the author (or the architect) intended—makes sense of what follows. "To read is to wander through an imposed system (that of the text, analogous to the constructed order of a city or a supermarket)."[85] David Vogel, Abraham Moshe Fuchs, and Veza Canetti all lead their readers through Vienna, and mine the Leopoldstadt for their narratives, depicting its marginal residents, the harsh violence accompanying their lives, and its physical distance from the other districts of the city. By portraying childless couples, abusive marriages, petty thievery, and characters with grotesque bodies and flawed faces who lead pathetic or criminal lives, each of these authors challenges typical depictions of the Leopoldstadt and the ambivalences they generate.[86] But instead of portraying the district as a fixed site of Jewishness, their writing calls into question its very definition as a "Jewish" space; the act of reading the story itself offers a multiplicity of meanings. There is rarely a moment in these novels when their protagonists do not know exactly where they are. Less clear, however, is where they belong, for these narratives reveal the Jews' impossible situation of being attached to, yet fundamentally excluded from, their city, a situation in which the Leopoldstadt plays a crucial role.

A Wandering Jew

Though Rudolf Gurdweill, protagonist of David Vogel's 1929 novel *Married Life*, begins and ends his daily journeys in the Leopoldstadt, the novel's readers must map his urban meanderings outside its bounds to understand the district's importance to his character. An impoverished Jewish writer from Galicia, Gurdweill spends most days wandering Vienna's streets, eating and drinking in its cafes, and trying to *schnorr* (beg for) money from acquaintances for food, drink, and cigarettes. In the novel's opening scene, the sound of rushing water from the communal tap in the hallway awakens him in his rented apartment: "In the passage the tap woke up with a roar. In an instant the noise filled all the space around, penetrating the rooms, which were still steeped in the half-light of dawn, and invading the sleeping body of Rudolf Gurdweill" (*ML*, 3). That the tap awakens before Gurdweill underscores his character's role as a vessel to be filled; this oft-repeated trope highlights not only his passivity, but his lack of subjectivity, and the very impossibility of his existence independent of the material world of the city around him.[87]

Gurdweill's emotional state changes drastically when he meets and falls helplessly in love with the Baroness Dorothea von Takow, Thea for short, a sadistic Viennese woman who eagerly converts to Judaism for the express purpose of marriage and, as the reader soon finds out, torture.[88] Although she berates him, denigrates him, and orders him about, he remains inexplicably drawn to her, and his friends, although they are aware of the dysfunctional relationship, remain unable to wrest him away. The narrative arc of the story revolves around their marriage and its subsequent disintegration. Thea gives birth to a son, but indicates that there is no chance Gurdweill could be the father—until the baby falls ill and dies, after which she does all she can to emphasize his paternity. Even when Lotte

Bondheim, a Jewish woman who is in love with Gurdweill (a fact to which he remains blind), accuses Thea of sleeping with her boss and his friends, Gurdweill cannot be persuaded to leave her.

Yet even as this relationship forms the skeleton of the novel, the text itself focuses more on the intimate details of Gurdweill's walks than on the couple's daily life and degrading interactions. The narrative traces his daily journeys from his rented apartment in the Leopoldstadt throughout the city. Names of streets, districts, and landmarks punctuate the text: St. Stephen's Cathedral, the Hofburg, Parliament, Schottentor, Franz Josef's Kai, Urania, Zentralfriedhof, Prater, Volksgarten, the Ring, the Lerchenfelderstrasse, and so forth. At times he goes even further, to the city's outlying areas, including the Steinhof sanatorium, Klosterneuberg, and Nussdorf, but he never ventures far from the city limits and is always eager to return. Every sensation he feels as he traverses its streets and sites combines with his memories of past experiences on those paths only hours or days before to form a richer experience of connection to the city.

Gurdweill's wanderings situate him in a long and winding history of literary walkers, a lineage that sheds light on the implications of his inverted subjectivity. In the early Romantic period, walkers solidified and strengthened their characters by getting closer to nature, and perhaps to God. But by 1900, the role of the walker had been transformed from this notion of an individual on a spiritual, character-shaping mission to the modern and detached flâneur, a figure crystallized in Baudelaire's "The Painter of Modern Life" (1863). The flâneur is an urban, solitary walker who serves as the paradigm of a consciousness that observes and illuminates the details of the rapidly-changing modern world, but remains unchanged by these observations. Yet if walking does not affect the flâneur's sense of self, then Gurdweill turns this paradigm on its head. His subjectivity is inverted: He does not observe the material world; rather, his material world defines him. Thus, the text does not detail what Gurdweill sees as he wanders the city, but instead describes in painstaking detail exactly where he is. The flâneur loses himself in the city; Gurdweill, in sharp contrast, *finds* himself there, and is always and ever oriented within its precise coordinates. Gurdweill's own need to know exactly where he is before he thinks, speaks, or acts signals the total collapse of the boundaries between city and self, and space thus becomes the single most important defining characteristic of his subjectivity. Rudolf Gurdweill, a Jew born in Galicia, may not be *from* Vienna, but by the end of the novel, no character is more *of* Vienna.

Michel de Certeau suggests that "The walker individuates and makes ambiguous the 'legible' order given to cities by planners, a little like the way waking life is displaced and ambiguated by dreaming."[89] He stresses that it is not merely being present in a particular place, but walking according to one's own rhetoric, or logic, that generates the dynamic interaction between one's awareness of the material world's interaction with one's sense of self and thus enables the metaphorical city to come to life. Moreover, such wanderings represent a "tactic" of rendering the city legible, in that it is a way one can resist the city's exclusion of oneself by walking it and mapping it according to one's own inner logic.[90] And this is precisely what Gurdweill does, even if he is not aware of it. But unlike the wandering military officer in Arthur Schnitzler's 1900 novella *Leutnant Gustl*, Gurdweill's meanderings do not elucidate the suppressed subjectivity of a character at odds with the changing world around him, helping him to define who he is.[91] We only rarely hear from Gurdweill in the first person, and when he speaks to other characters, he often whispers or retreats into his own thoughts. Unlike Ulrich, the rather passive protagonist of Robert Musil's *The Man without Qualities*, he does not take on the morals and values of the world around him: Gurweill literally *is* the world around him—if the city is his partner, he has subsumed himself within it.[92]

The significance of walking for Gurdweill includes crossing physical boundaries, since such crossings also highlight the persistence of metaphorical divides between Jews and Christians. At home one evening, he reflects upon the moment when he first learned about the boundaries that separate Jews from Christians, back home in the Galician shtetl of his youth, and he recounts his earliest consciousness of his simultaneous fear and fascination with this difference:

> All this once had an attraction for me that was both fascinating and terrifying. Everything, I mean, that took place on the other side of the boundary between Jews and Christians . . . The women passing me on their way to church on Sundays and holidays for some reason attracted me. And the church itself, which was situated not far from our house, gave me no peace. People seemed to be divided into two separate species, utterly different from each other, as different as cats and dogs . . . The boundaries are well-defined. Jews are Jews and Christians are Christians. You can't possibly confuse the two. Especially in the little settlements of Galicia and Poland. My parents weren't Orthodox but nevertheless they had nothing to do with Christians. In short: the Christians fascinated me with their strangeness (*ML*, 221).

Unlike Galicia, however, where the established boundaries of the shtetl clearly define Jews according to where they are, Vienna allows for the blurring of that epistemological distinction, as Gurdweill's visions of the city show. It is thus not just the city that holds an attraction for Gurdweill, but the possibilities it offers for those longed-for "border crossings." Vienna seduces him with the possibility of breaking free from a tautology—"Jews are Jews and Christians are Christians"— that presumably appears to crumble as one walks Vienna's more porous cityscape.

Yet while Gurdweill's walks constantly remind him that Vienna offers countless opportunities to cross the physical boundaries between districts, the socially constructed boundaries between Jews and Christians nevertheless remain clearly intact. When Gurdweill, Lotte, and their Jewish friend Dr. Astel ride the tram back from an outing to Cobenzl, a charming spot on the outskirts of town, their pleasurable excursion is interrupted by a man with a thick, coarse Viennese accent who "outs" them as Jews and foreigners: "Three Poles, you can't get away from them!" he bellows to his wife, followed by an accusatory "Why are you staring at me? I mean Jews! You're Jews aren't you?" (*ML*, 313). As easy as it is for these three Viennese Jews to traverse the city, the sociological boundaries that divide the city and distinguish Jews from "true Viennese" still hold true. The flush of excitement that comes from crossing boundaries and of being invisible turns out to be fleeting and illusory; even here, it seems, "Jews are Jews and Christians are Christians."

Gurdweill's intimate relationship to the city is less a matter of detail, it seems, than of a pervading, inarticulate sensibility that fuses him to it. In a powerful realization, "it came to him that he, Gurdweill, now lived not at this or that address, but in the city of Vienna as a whole: in the literal sense of the words, he lived in Vienna. For some reason this struck him as amusing, and he smiled" (*ML*, 429). But his amusement, which stems, presumably, from his having finally overcome his dependence on the city's precise coordinates for the constitution of his very self, will soon become overrun by the negative consequences of this transformation. The most telling indication of the total collapse between city and self comes at the end of the novel, upon Gurdweill's final return to his home in the Leopoldstadt. Lotte issues a final plea for him to accept her offer of love which is also contingent upon their leaving the city: It is no accident that she asks him to leave Thea at the same time she asks him to leave Vienna. "I can't go . . . go away," he replies, stammering, "Even if my life depended on it."

"It's impossible, I can't leave her," he continues, "I haven't got the strength," and leaves it ambiguous as to whether he is speaking of Thea or the city. This vagueness persists in his response when Lotte asks if he loves Thea: "I don't know. Maybe I love her and maybe I don't. But I'm incapable of leaving her. I'll never be able to leave her. Never" (*ML*, 454).

Lotte commits suicide soon thereafter, and Gurdweill, distraught at her death, quarrels with Thea, then spends several nights wandering in and around the city. As he realizes that his world is slowly beginning to unravel, Gurdweill's state of emotional insecurity is echoed by his confusion about where he is. For the first time, he walks down strange streets and gets lost: "Afterward Gurdweill found himself alone in one of the ancient, winding alleys in the city center . . . He stood still and looked fearfully around him. The alley was ill lit, and there were no shops in it. It was a short, deserted side alley with very old buildings, into which people seldom strayed. Suddenly alarmed by the desolation, Gurdweill began to hurry" (*ML*, 458). He becomes concerned with locating where he is: "How could he find out where he was?" (*ML*, 495).

It is this final state of desperation that empowers him to engage in what he describes as a preordained action: He gives himself over to a prevailing sense that something is going to happen, rather than actively deciding upon what he should do. But as Gurdweill unravels, Leopoldstadt remains at his unarticulated, subconscious core. Not the shtetl of his past nor the liberating unbounded urban space, Leopoldstadt's symbolic meaning as a reference point for Gurdweill—the "Jewish" side of the boundary that he crosses each and every day to live out his fascination with the "Other"—renders it his spiritual, as well as physical, home. The district frames not only his daily life, as the place where he begins and ends his walks, but also the novel, from its very beginning when he first awakens, to its startling, violent conclusion when he murders Thea in their bed. His final state of desperation empowers him to engage in what he describes as a preordained action; he senses something is going to happen, but never actively decides to act.

As the novel careens toward its final twist, Gurdweill returns to his apartment in the Leopoldstadt, where he finds Thea asleep in bed with his friend Heidelberger. He murders her with a knife, an action he nevertheless renders passive in the last line of the book when he tells his friend Ulrich not that he killed her, but that she is dead, as if by some unseen hand: "Thea died last night" (*ML*, 501). With this statement, the novel ends by returning Gurdweill to the purest form of his subjectivity: No longer dependent on his "better half," Thea, he fully and completely returns to his true partner, Vienna.

David Vogel's life paralleled his protagonist's in more ways than one, not least of which is his admittedly inexplicable attraction to the city. He was born in Satanov, Podolia, in 1891. Upon moving to Vienna initially in 1909 and then, after a time in Lemberg and Galicia, returning in 1912, he tried unsuccessfully to enroll at the university and to become a Hebrew teacher. He wrote in his diary of being cold, homeless, and hungry, and of seeking money from friends and acquaintances just to eke out a day-to-day existence.[93] Sometimes he stayed overnight with friends or in the synagogue, but after a month he still had no teaching position. "Loneliness and hunger, hunger and loneliness. And I change apartments often," he wrote. By October 1913, his frustration had increased along with his restlessness: "The big city brands you. One is not allowed to be here without an income. Now for example my monthly salary is higher than in Vilna, but I'm still poorer here." Even in 1914, two years after his arrival, he wrote, "This Vienna . . . At the moment an acceptable city, I like it. But something is missing. Something unknown and without a name. Missing."[94]

As a Galician Jew in Vienna, Vogel's position as "Other" was clear, but his experiences in wartime further underscored his exceptional status and pushed Gurdweill's story to an even more tragic extreme.[95] In August 1914, he was interned in Schloss Karlstein, Lower Austria, as an enemy alien. After the war, Vogel married his first wife Ilka in Vienna in 1919, and the couple had a baby, who subsequently died. By his own admission, Vogel's relationship with his wife was ambivalent, paralleling his feelings about Vienna. As Robert Alter notes, Vogel's feelings of self-estrangement are clear from the language of his diaries; in particular, he uses Hebrew in a unique fashion to make sense of his inner turmoil. Alter suggests that he may even have coined the term "the self" in Hebrew (the first person pronoun "ani" with a definite article): In an entry from 1912 he writes, "I am not I," and as an internee on June 1, 1915, "I don't know myself. Fogel has lost Fogel."[96]

Like Gurdweill, Vogel seems never to have found a place where he felt at home: He moved to Paris in 1925, then Palestine in 1929, stayed briefly in Berlin in 1930, and then moved back to Paris in 1932. He was detained in France in 1942 and deported to a concentration camp, where he died, in 1944. It is only recently that the depth of his significance to modernist Hebrew writing has been recognized—and only even more recently its specific Viennese context. Although the peregrinations of Gurdweill do not extend as far as his author's, they nevertheless similarly reveal how place—distinct, city, country, continent—could become a longed-for substitute for the self. But for the alienated Jewish subject making his or her way amid rapidly changing national and cultural imaginings of the majority, that substitute could never fully satisfy that desire. Even the Leopoldstadt, arguably the most Jewish of Vienna's interwar spaces, will eventually overtake its subject.

A Distorted World

As a Hebrew novelist in Vienna, Vogel likely had contact with the city's Yiddish writers from Eastern Europe, as these groups collaborated closely.[97] But the Leopoldstadt of Abraham Moshe Fuchs's novel *Unter der brik* (Under the bridge) contrasts starkly with Vogel's. Fuchs creates a twisted and perverse territory that typifies Expressionist fiction, which creates alternative worlds by rendering the familiar unrecognizable. In fact, if one didn't know that its author was Jewish, the novel's merciless description of the Jewish underworld would read like an antisemite's dream. But the novel specifically aims to address the position of Jews in

Vienna from the perspective of its underclass, a group that did actually exist, but nevertheless remained even more sharply defined for what it was imagined to be.

By the last decade of the nineteenth century, the arrival of Jews from the East was transforming the Jewish image of the Leopoldstadt as a "Jewish ghetto."[98] But the increase in Eastern European Jewish refugees as a result of World War I, and the tendency of those refugees to remain in the district surrounding the Nordbahnhof where they first arrived, further intensified that reputation. That part of the Leopoldstadt actually *was* dirty and decrepit, but by making it entirely nightmarish, *Unter der brik* addresses the clear, yet unarticulated, boundaries that still persisted between the "real" and the "imagined" city, exposing their construction on the basis of prejudices, predispositions, and fears.

The novel's first chapter details the tone, atmosphere, and aura of the district, beginning with a description of the railway station and, most significantly, its heavy, black, rusted old bridge which when in use affords the visual image of a cross: "When the red tramway wagons bound together drive down below through the cool, arched hole, and at the same time the train runs through up above, it looks like a running, thundering cross" (*UdB*, 5). By opening with the railway station, the point of entry for most of the Eastern European Jewish refugees to Vienna during World War I, the novel from the start engages with the physical boundaries of the area, borders that may be permeable, allowing people to come in and out, but nevertheless remain incontrovertibly fixed, keeping it metaphorically sealed off from the rest of the city. As Certeau suggests, in stories a "bridge" serves as both a central and ambivalent character—a figure that both transgresses the limits of space while it allows for the alterity to emerge, which had been hidden inside the limits. In other words, it is the bridge alone that can provide the subject with the knowledge of that space's otherness.[99]

The description soon turns from the poor, stinking, garbage-filled alleys behind the train station to the Prater, the city's premier area for colorful fun and entertainment. Although typically packed with festive leisure-seeking Viennese, Fuchs's Prater is empty and deserted. The chapter concludes by portraying its iconic Ferris wheel, the *Riesenrad*, but instead of carrying joyful occupants, it has stopped turning. The empty, unmoving Ferris wheel—a sort of distorted train with "cars" hung separately on a circular "track" that circles endlessly but leads nowhere—contrasts with the opening image of the train station's thundering cross. As this chapter describes it, even the Prater can be described as dirty, decrepit, bleak, and, most of all, an unchanging world apart.

Still, several moments emphasize the simultaneous permeability and persistence of the districts' borders. Both a plane and a balloon fly overhead and quickly disappear. A newspaper boy carrying hot-off-the-press editions "smelling like burned, fresh out of the oven matzoh" mistakenly wanders into the Leopoldstadt, notices he is in the wrong place, and just as quickly runs out again, yelling, "Extra! Extra! Newspaper! War!" without leaving a single paper behind (*UdB*, 9). The only trace that remains of the boy and his announcement of war is a green, nearly featherless parrot, who mimics his words (*UdB*, 14–15), emphasizing the fact that, although a "total war" may have been taking place in Vienna, its effects in the Leopoldstadt rendered it a world apart.[100] Fuchs drops hints that other areas of the city are foreign and strange: "From here, from the Vorstadt behind the railway bridge, one saw how at the end of the streets over there in the city, flags waved over the houses, a whole sea of flags" (*UdB*, 8). Underscoring this isolation, he describes the Leopoldstadt's streets as empty and forgotten by those outside its bounds (*UdB*, 14).

The novel's protagonist could not be more pathetic: a disabled, fat Viennese Jewish pimp named Maxl, he feels most at home, and most powerful, when he shares space under the bridge with other impoverished pimps and prostitutes with missing fingers, glass eyes, and wooden legs. There, he imagines himself King of the Underworld. Maxl is married to one of his "ladies," Mizzi, and he procures customers for her to take home to their apartment where her mother sits by the window and waits while Mizzi conducts her business in the bedroom. In this alternate world, the power relationship between husband and wife—and pimp and prostitute—are turned upside down. This becomes clear when Mizzi at first rejects his sexual advances and then demands payment for them. Maxl can be a fearless leader, but only in situations where his defects are an advantage. Aware that his missing thumb and glass eye will lead him to be rejected as a soldier, Maxl enlists, knowing that in a lineup of men less than eager to face the war, he will gain his chance to lord his "power" over the other candidates as the lucky one who doesn't have to go, even if just for a few moments. He stands "naked, fat, round, and heavy like a stuck pig, covered only by a small cap on his yellow, greasy, shaven, shiny round head—a sign, that he had no fear" (*UdB*, 19). He hops about authoritatively, looking mockingly at the other prospective recruits, scared and shivering, until those in charge, with hardly a glance at him, declare him unfit for service.[101]

Through the reflections of Mizzi's mother, we learn that, as a girl, Mizzi worked as a salesperson at a store; her boss, a German, presented her with her first pair of stockings, after which she spent an hour in a hotel with him. From there, it was a short step to the streets: "As soon as she was almost grown, she walked the Kärntnerstrasse by herself—just as all the other pretty girls there, with painted red lips" (*UdB*, 86). She would stay out all night in coffeehouses, perched on a red sofa in the corner, drinking wine with a gentleman, coming home only in the early gray morning, against the traffic of workers leaving the suburbs for work in the city, in a kind of "reverse commute" to the Leopoldstadt. The downtrodden space of the Leopoldstadt they inhabit renders Maxl and Mizzi a perfect couple, inverted counterpoints to the bourgeois Jews who have escaped its bounds and are living their lives "respectably" in other districts.

Although the novel's descriptions and plot may shock with their extremely derogatory depictions of Jews and liberal use of antisemitic stereotypes, the text is in fact not an antisemitic novel at all, but rather a story that seeks to dredge up and expose the worst imagined fears Viennese Jews have of each other. One of the clearest ways it demonstrates this is through its largely satirical depiction of Maxl's own attitude toward the Orthodox Jews in the district. Maxl misreads *Ostjuden* as poor, holy men who speak an incomprehensible language, which allows them to communicate directly with the "terrible" Jewish god, yet to whom he remains nevertheless connected through their shared experience of antisemitism: "and he feels the heavy burden he has in common weighing upon him" (*UdB*, 31). His reaction echoes other rosier literary meetings between Eastern and Western Jews, in which the initial sense of unfamiliarity with the "Other" eventually leads the Western Jew to reclaim an inner sense of Jewish authenticity.[102] Yet the text distorts this convention by representing Maxl's combination of respect and fear for *Ostjuden* as pathetic and misguided, since they view him with similar fright but no such respect. At one point, Maxl, overcome with sympathy, approaches a Jew dressed in a ripped caftan and presses a bit of bread and a small amount of money in his hand. The Jew, however, is hardly destitute—we learn that he left a business and four houses in the East—and pretends not to understand the charitable gesture. Once out of sight of Maxl, he spits on the ground (*UdB*, 31). Reversed in this upside down world, too, then, is the relationship between the supposedly assimilated, wealthy Western Jew and the impoverished *Ostjude*, for in fact the majority of the Eastern European Jewish refugees in Vienna were indeed impoverished; in Fuchs's novel, however, they are not so easily recognized and the effort to treat them charitably is, in consequence, ironic.[103]

The meaning of Judaism as a religion is also turned upside down. Maxl and Mizzi were married in the synagogue, we learn, because "Mizzi only wanted to marry in the temple—and nowhere else. She knew that any other wedding was not valid" (*UdB*, 35). The irony of a Jewish prostitute and her pimp expressing concern for the validity of their union according to Jewish law is underscored in the scene immediately following the ceremony. After the rabbi blesses their marriage and they take their vows "to remain together forever" in joy and life with happiness and blessings (*UdB*, 37), Mizzi heads for the doctor's office, conveniently located near the temple, to get an abortion, and Maxl steals a gold watch from a wealthy, better-dressed groom. For Maxl, the central Jewish community is the place to get matzoh for Passover, to marry and to die, ritual undertakings that Maxl believes (correctly) link him to the heavy burden other Jews face (*UdB*, 31).

With the city's men gone to war, the whores under the bridge have little to occupy their time; the one remaining customer is an Orthodox Jew who visits the one non-Jewish prostitute; as his bent figure says Jewish prayers in "Talmudsingsang," the prostitute's room momentarily resembles a prayer room (*UdB*, 47).

Most Austrian interwar writers, unlike their German counterparts, chose not to focus on the war despite its prime role in determining subsequent political events. Fuchs addresses this phenomenon both directly and indirectly. The war may be taking place outside the Leopoldstadt, but its broader effects in Vienna are distorted within its bounds. The narrative explains that the war took care to "camouflage itself" on the streets: Fuchs describes people walking with their empty shirt sleeves rolled up due to lost limbs, people in wheelchairs ignored by passersby, people who decide not to talk about it. Yet, the absent war also leads to increased violence on the home front: Soldiers abuse their newfound status by sticking swords in the stomachs of those who disrespect them; a brother murders his sister, and a mother her daughter; and a crowd of people encourage the beating of a lame horse (*UdB*, 38–39). While "home-front" violence during the war was indeed a common phenomenon among men in Vienna who had not been drafted, in Fuchs's Leopoldstadt we find that soldiers are the city's most violent actors.[104]

This context of increased violence sets the stage for Maxl's own final act of violent, distorted "heroism." His enemy and counterpart throughout the novel is Karl, a slim "goy" who represents, as the novel clearly tells us, "an old, unwelcome animosity" (*UdB*, 22) between goy and Jew. Karl was once engaged to Mizzi and in effect becomes her fiancé again toward the end of the novel, in an impromptu ceremony at their local café. Unlike Maxl, Karl has gone to war and returned home a "hero" who regales the café crowd with tales of his "adventures," such as raping a Galician rabbi's "beautiful wife" and cutting off the finger of a dead soldier he killed, which he shows to the crowd, along with the ring it still sports. Mizzi, in awe, asks for the ring, and struggles to remove it from the dismembered finger. Maxl comes to the table when he hears the commotion, and shows how much he hates it when she lends her attention to other men when she is not "in service." He punches Karl, but Mizzi taunts him, even as he yells and hits her. As a result of his blows, Mizzi's health steadily deteriorates; after lying sick in bed for weeks, she finally dies. In a final religious charade, Maxl attempts to pray for his dead wife, but cannot remember the prayer. By the end of the novel, Maxl realizes he is powerless before God, and, in response, attempts to kill his mother-in-law.

Unter der brik takes places almost exclusively, as its title suggests, under the bridge, a commentary, perhaps, on the symbolism of the actual "bridges" that link the district to the rest of the city that, in theory, represents the ability to pass from the Leopoldstadt to other districts (and to "pass" in them as well), actually symbolizes Jews' inability to do so. Unlike Gurdweill and the other Jews in *Married*

Life, the characters in this novel cannot move around anonymously, nor do they have the illusion that they can. They remain fixed in this nonspace, beneath the symbol of crossing from one part of the city to the other. By presenting Jewish life in the Leopoldstadt in its worst light, in its worst manner, the novel questions the area's designation—and indeed, the designation of Jewish culture and religion in general—as emblematic of a positive historical reality for the Jews.[105] As Allison Schachter notes, the shtetl continues to dominate the literary landscape of Yiddish literature during the interwar period even in the works of modernist writers who sought to move beyond it. It remained wide open as an imagined world that continued (and continues) to captivate writers and audiences.[106] Successful Yiddish writers, like Sholem Asch, whose translated works garnered the support of mainstream authors, including Franz Werfel and Stefan Zweig, as well as publishers like the Zsolnay Verlag, focused on the shtetl.[107] Asch's 1919 novel *Kiddush ha-Shem* (Sanctification of the divine name) for example, lauded as one of the earliest historical novels in modern Yiddish literature, retells a story of Jewish martyrdom during the notorious Chmelnitsky pogrom in Ukraine in the seventeenth century. Indeed, he is lauded as the first Yiddish writer to enjoy international acclaim for bridging the world of the shtetl in which he was born, yet also speak to the modern world. That Asch's works fulfilled such mainstream demands is clear from a speech in which Franz Werfel lauds him as a prophet, a seer of reality, and a writer able to escape the bounds of his Eastern-Jewish origins.[108] That others resented this particular brand of Yiddish literature is apparent from Joseph Roth, who criticized the fact that his works were easily translatable to the German stage, noting: "That Shalom Asch could be played on the German stage almost without change or concession seemed to me a proof of the decline of the Yiddish theater, not its rise, as was proclaimed."[109]

Though Fuchs's Jewish underworld presents a distorted mirror version of these celebrated works of Yiddish literature, he did not go completely unnoticed as a writer; Isaac Bashevis Singer later hailed him as the best of Vienna's Yiddish literature.[110] However, Fuchs never gained the notoriety of writers like Asch. Born in 1870 in East Galicia, Fuchs received a traditional orthodox Jewish education before leaving home at age fifteen for Tarnopol and Lemberg, where he became a member of the Jewish labor group, the Bund. After renouncing his political affiliations in 1911, he published his first story in the Galician weekly newspaper *folks-fraind*, and soon was publishing regularly in some of the best known Yiddish publications in Galicia. His first book, *einsame* (Lonesome) was published in Lemberg in 1912; soon after, he left for America. In 1914, he returned to Europe with his wife Sonya Paltun, whom he met in America, and they continued to live in Vienna until 1938.[111] Unlike more popular Yiddish writers praised for bringing their Jewish characters out of the ghetto, Fuchs's text explores how, in reality, they remained anchored there in the popular imagination. In that sense, his fictional Leopoldstadt under the bridge comes closest to illuminating the relationship between the district's real and imagined versions, and to illustrating the paradox that, by powerfully defining what the rest of Vienna isn't, the Leopoldstadt remains necessarily linked to the city's own self-definition.

A Leopoldstadt without Jews

Unlike Vogel and Fuchs, Viennese "outsiders" from Podolia and Galicia who wrote in Hebrew and Yiddish, Vienna-born author Veza Canetti had the luxury of broader audiences because she wrote and published in German. Yet, she also faced the pressure of conforming to mainstream market standards and the limitations of being a woman writer. Moreover, her Sephardic Jewish heritage rendered her an outsider to mainstream Jewish culture in yet another way.[112] Born Venetiana Taubner-Calderon in 1897, Canetti was raised in the Leopoldstadt by her mother, Rachel Calderon, a Sephardic Jew from Belgrade, and her stepfather.[113] Veza's Hungarian-born father, Hermann Taubner, who died in 1904, was likely Ashkenazi. In 1910, her mother married a wealthy Sephardic widower from Bosnia, Menachem Alkaley, who, according to a number of sources, physically abused both Veza and her mother. Her childhood experiences, including domestic abuse and the general mistreatment of women, loom large in her texts.

Canetti's novel *Yellow Street* consists of five biting vignettes of life in the private apartments and public storefronts on a fictional street: Yellow Street. Each story takes place in different locations: an employment agency for young girls, a café, a grocer's shop, the *Trafik* (tobacconist), the soap shop, a children's home, and the apartment of a miserable couple with an abused wife.[114] But unlike Vogel's obsessive tracing of his Jewish protagonist's wanderings around Vienna's urban landscape, and Fuchs's portrayal of a Jewish underworld around the Nordbahnhof, Canetti's characters are explicitly not Jews, and are very deliberately marked as such through their names: Sister Leopoldine, Meta von Ders, Hedwig Adenberger, Emilie Jaksch, Anna Kozil, Anna Fasching, Mizzi Schadn, and so on. Only the leather merchant, Herr Koppstein, could be considered a Jew by name and occupation.[115] Later readers have associated the young writer Knut Tell, who appears in several of the stories, with Canetti's husband, writer Elias Canetti. But even if these characters may be modeled on Jews, the reader only knows so obliquely, for the book seldom mentions Jews, explicitly or implicitly, and when it does, it is in relation to their religious or (perceived) murderous roles, not in terms of a specific character. In one scene, for instance, the meticulous, inscrutable bachelor Pilatus Vlk and a clergyman discuss a passage in the Old Testament, and the unnamed grocer speculates that Jews are likely responsible for the disappearance of little Helli Wunderer, saying, "The Jews've butchered her" (YS, 134).

Canetti's stories typically lack both explicitly Jewish characters and themes.[116] Before 1938, few of her works highlighted Jewish characters, and those that did often reflected antisemitic stereotypes, such as Herr Topf, the Jewish businessman in her short story "Der Sieger" (The Victor), whose unsophisticated speech, replete with a heavy Yiddish accent, contributes to his overall portrayal as an unsavory character, bereft of tact and unable to speak proper German.[117] But Canetti is only one of numerous German-language Jewish writers who only began to write directly about Jews after emigration. Since most of her stories were first published in the *Arbeiter-Zeitung* in the early 1930s under pseudonyms like Veza Magd, Veronika Knecht, and Martha and Martina Murner, it makes sense that *Yellow Street* is devoid of Jewish themes; the socialist aversion to appearing sympathetic to Jews and their own often thinly-veiled antisemitism is well-documented. As Canetti herself noted, editor Otto Koenig forbade her to

Vienna's Taborstrasse served as a main thoroughfare in a section of the Leopoldstadt heavily populated by Jews. Veza Canetti's *Yellow Street* stories are based on the nearby Ferdinandstrasse, on which she lived.

ÖNB Vienna/29.154-B

use her own name, not wanting her byline to reflect badly on the newspaper and its Socialist efforts. He told her that publishing too many stories by a Jewish woman in such an antisemitic atmosphere would not be possible, although hers were "unfortunately" the best.[118]

Nevertheless, we learn from Elias Canetti, in his introduction to the version of *Yellow Street* he published after her death, that both the characters and the street they live on were based upon her experiences living in the Ferdinandstrasse, a street in the Leopoldstadt known both for leather merchants like Herr Koppstein and for Sephardic Jews. Canetti claims that although the characters in the book appear to have been invented, they are actually based on people they knew from the Ferdinandstrasse. As he notes, "When I dip into *Die gelbe Strasse*, I can visualize the model for every single one of them, yet I would have forgotten them all if she had not invented them in her acute, vital way."[119] Veza's choice to situate stories without Jews in the most Jewish-coded area of the city thus requires further investigation.[120]

Historical accounts indicate that many Jews lived in the Ferdinandstrasse during the interwar period, and indeed it was situated at the heart of the Leopoldstadt's vibrant Jewish life.[121] Some even refer to the area around the Ferdinandstrasse as having been a Sephardic "colony" of sorts and take it as a given that Veza Canetti's *Yellow Street* describes the Jewish world of the Leopoldstadt.[122] We do know of at least a few deep connections between Veza and the area's Sephardic heritage. She lived not far from the Leopoldstadt temple at the corner of Ferdinandstrasse and Tempelgasse, and near the Zirkusgasse, the location of the Sephardic temple, built by her maternal grandfather, where she and Elias were married. According to unpublished material in the Canetti archive in Zurich, this temple, which was destroyed in November 1938, along with all the others in the Leopoldstadt, bore two plaques honoring the founder and his wife, Veza's grandmother and namesake, Veneziana.[123]

As we have seen, Jews never made up the entirety of the population of the Leopoldstadt, even in those neighborhoods where they were most predominant. Ernst Epler, who grew up only a few blocks away from the Ferdinandstrasse, noted the mix of Jews and non-Jews even in his building: "Our street, the Blumauergasse, was 'mixed.' The building's cooper was a Christian, the locksmith a Jew, the hairdresser a Christian, the milliner Jewish and so forth."[124] Interestingly, while Canetti's novel highlights the occupations of its residents—the grocer, the tobacconist, the shopkeeper—she rarely notes their religion except, in a few cases, where she references pious Christians like Herr Vlk; she never explicitly mentions Jews or Jewish difference. As a result, rather than presenting the Leopoldstadt as "Jewish space," the novel suppresses its identification as such altogether; ironically, this suppression highlights the presence of Jews in the Leopoldstadt by making them markedly absent from the one place where her Viennese readers know they ought to be, and thus attesting to the persistence of the unarticulated boundaries of Jewishness that continue to define its space. As though alluding to this issue, one of Yellow Street's residents muses that even Jesus Christ was from a Jewish space: "'Nevertheless, our Lord Jesus Christ was born in the Jewish province of Bethlehem,' notes Herr Vlk, crossing himself" (*YS*, 9).[125] Whether Veza would have made her characters less explicitly non-Jewish without the restrictions of the *Arbeiter-Zeitung* is less important than this effect of underscoring the absence of the "Jewish" from her stories, an absence echoed in much of mainstream Austrian interwar writing.[126]

Although *Yellow Street* features fictional characters on an invented street, it thus actually reveals truths about interwar Jewish experiences that straightforward reporting cannot access. By detaching the district's harsh conditions and miserable lives from any specific group, the novel universalizes the supposed flaws of its characters and implicitly critiques the notion that the Leopoldstadt is a separate Jewish world bounded by either physical or sociological borders. The district may be full of marginal inhabitants, but their experiences are universally recognized: "It's a remarkable street, Yellow Street. All sorts of people live there, cripples, somnambulists, lunatics, the desperate and the smug. The normal passer-by doesn't particularly notice them" (*YS*, 9). This is a world of "shop-girls, serving-maids, ordinary folk" (*YS*, 10), social outcasts, lonely people, single parents, and aging men and women, some with children, some without. Their universal personal relationships stress parental misery and contractually-arranged unhappy marriages.[127] In its willingness to confront the misogynistic and often violent relationships in the Leopoldstadt without marking its denizens as Jews, the novel exposes the contours of Jewishness as they apply not only to people, but also to the space of the "imagined" Leopoldstadt as a site of Jewish difference that is based upon, but not equivalent to, the physical space it occupies. At the same time, its universalizing tendencies point to the limitations of the continued reinforcement of that difference.[128]

Veza Canetti's husband Elias makes it clear that, even if she was not an observant Jew, her Sephardic background still played a role in her life. He notes that they spoke Ladino together, and mentions how different she appeared to others:

> Everyone found Veza exotic. She drew attention wherever she went. An Andalusian who had never been in Seville, but spoke about it as though she had grown up there. You had encountered her in "The Arabian Nights," the very first time you'd read any of the tales. She was a familiar figure in Persian miniatures. But despite this Oriental omnipresence, she was no dream personage; your conception of her was very definite; her

> image never melted, it never dissolved; it retained its sharp outline and its radiance.[129]

By drawing attention to her "Spanish" heritage without explicitly mentioning her particular Spanish-*Jewish* connection, he too recasts her background as one with which any German reader could identify, whether Jewish or not. In other words, by referencing her Sephardic heritage through the *Arabian Nights* and Persian figurines—that is, with details of anything but Jewish cultural history—Elias Canetti uses the cultural references he and Veza shared with their German readers to reconfigure Sephardic Jewish identity as simultaneously exotic, admirable, and palatable for those readers. As scholars have noted, Canetti's work often reveals his efforts to link antisemitism to larger issues, such as the failure of humanism.[130] Since we know now from the meticulous work of Julian Preece that the two influenced each other greatly as writers, it makes sense that they would approach depictions of Jews and antisemitism similarly—and obliquely.

Veza Canetti continued to publish in newspapers as late as 1937, even after the *Arbeiter-Zeitung* had been closed down. Although she was born in Vienna, she was threatened with deportation in 1934 because of her stories for the *Arbeiter-Zeitung*, and because she had a Yugoslavian passport; in October 1938, she and Elias fled, first to Paris and then, in January 1939, to London.[131] There she began work on her novel *Die Schildkröten* (The Tortoises), which focuses on Jews living under the Nazis and is her only work concerned explicitly with Jewish themes. However, this topic made it difficult for her to find a publisher, and she spent most of her time in England handling the correspondence of her by then well-known husband. Only after the rediscovery of her work in the 1990s, did Veza Canetti become recognized as an important Austrian writer. Unfortunately, she never wrote again during her exile in England; *Die Schildkröten* was her last known work until her death in 1963. England, unlike Vienna, never became her space.

The novels foregrounding the Leopoldstadt by Vogel, Fuchs, and Canetti indicate that, for Jews in particular, to position Vienna's role in the new republic required that one first understand where one stood in Vienna. The fictionalized characters of these works know who they are only because they know where they are in the city. Like Helen Blank, they implicitly navigate the social boundaries of the city as they traverse its physical ones. If for Jews this navigation of identity and geography pertained specifically to their own contested status in post-imperial Austria, it also had wider symbolic implications. The Leopoldstadt may have been physically cut off from the city, accessible only by bridges, yet it remained the heart of Jewish life, even as the nature of that life, both real and imagined, continued to shift. As such, these fictional representations of the district allowed readers to question not only the isolated yet connected, individual yet universalized status of the Jews and the Leopoldstadt, but also the role of Vienna as an opposing force to the provinces, and, for that matter, Austria as a separate entity located between Eastern and Western Europe. Despite their radically differing descriptions of the Leopoldstadt, the texts of each of these three authors calls into question, and asks us to reconsider, what it really means to think of the Leopoldstadt as Jewish space—and what it really means to think about the Jews, Austria, and the Jews in Austria.

4 SEARCHING FOR REDEMPTION

THE SALZBURG FESTIVAL MEETS YIDDISH THEATER

One late October evening in 1922, an expectant audience at Vienna's Roland Theater eagerly awaited a performance of S. An-sky's *Der Dybbuk* by the Vilna Troupe. The internationally-renowned troupe of Yiddish actors had been invited to perform by the *Freie Jüdische Volksbühne* (Free Jewish People's Theater), one of the successful Yiddish theater organizations that flourished in Vienna, as the popularity of Yiddish theater grew after the end of World War I. Although a number of non–Yiddish speaking cultural luminaries sometimes attended the performances of the Vilna Troupe, including writers Arnold Zweig, Arthur Schnitzler, and Richard Beer-Hofmann, the audience member whose presence caused the greatest stir that evening was the distinguished theater director Max Reinhardt. In her memoirs, Vilna Troupe actor Luba Kadison wrote, "In Vienna, the great director Max Reinhardt came backstage, kissed each actor and exclaimed, 'This is not playacting! It is a religious rite!'"[1]

Reinhardt's ecstatic reaction echoed the enthusiasm for "authentic" Jewish culture, which rose among German-speaking Jews in the twentieth century as one response to anxieties about the perceived decline of modern civilization and the Jewish condition. This enthusiasm had its roots in the nineteenth century but gained currency after World War I. A renewed interest in Eastern European Jewish culture, sparked in particular by German-Jewish soldiers who served on the front during World War I, contributed to the general enthusiasm for what they, and others, characterized as a "pure" Jewish culture, untainted by the modern world. Works like *Das ostjüdische Antlitz* by Arnold Zweig and Hermann Struck, published in Berlin in 1920, typified this glorification of Eastern Jewish culture. However, as this chapter will show, the symbolic elevation of East European Jews and their way of life as representative of a "pure" culture untainted by modern civilization was a function not only of German Jewish culture, but of Austrian culture during this time, albeit in a different context.[2] We can situate Max Reinhardt's reaction to this particular Yiddish performance in a uniquely "Austrian" dynamic, when we consider that only a few months prior, for the third year in a row, he had successfully staged his adaptation of *Jedermann* (*Everyman*) for the Salzburg Festival on the steps of Salzburg's Catholic cathedral. This event underscored the way many Austrian Jews idealized Catholicism as a parallel authentic "spiritual" response to the crises of their contemporary condition. Not the tenets of Catholicism *per se*, but rather the spiritual, dramatic gestures toward redemption and salvation it appeared to offer, which was put into the service of forming a new, inclusive Austrian national culture. In both cases, these imagined ideals of the Catholic and the Yiddish served to anchor and define the space of the new nation both literally—one in the provinces and one in the city—and figuratively as a space of national imagining.

Reinhardt's grandiose staging of the festival's performances, featuring high German, famous actors and both classical and contemporary music, contrasted sharply with the modest, low-budget, and extremely low-tech Yiddish folk

Lea (Hanna Rovina) and the rabbi (Baruch Chemerinski) of the visiting Moscow theater troupe Habima feature in a 1926 performance of S. An-sky's *Der Dybbuk* at Vienna's Carltheater. The stage and set exemplify the dilapidated conditions in which Yiddish theater performances typically took place.
Österreichisches Theatermuseum, Vienna

dramas produced in shabby Viennese theaters. Theater productions like *Der Dybbuk* typified the simultaneously repulsive and compelling anti-aesthetic of expressionism: They were alienating performances in an unfamiliar language, put on in small, dark spaces by actors, representing antiheroes, with wide-open eyes and grotesque, angular faces. In contrast, Reinhardt's baroque performances of *Jedermann* engaged audiences not through tactics of alienation, but by inspiring awe: Outdoor evening performances on the steps of the Salzburger Dom played against a backdrop of beautiful, majestic mountains; stentorian voices personified the fatal forces of life and death and combined with a musical chorus emanating from inside the cathedral; and the night's climax featured the dramatic release of birds against a background of pealing church bells. It might seem, then, that the performances at the Salzburg Festival, established for the purpose of shaping a new Austrian national culture to rival that of Bayreuth in Germany, had little in common with the urban, low-brow entertainment that thrived in interwar Vienna.[3]

But despite their fundamental differences in aesthetics, content, and location, the Salzburg Festival—explicitly Catholic, performed in the provinces, and thus stripped of any traces of "Jewish" coding—and Yiddish theater performances in Vienna—emphatically and "authentically" Jewish—were both deployed by Jewish theater artists to spark intense, emotional reactions in their

The premiere of Hugo von Hofmannsthal's *Jedermann* directed by Max Reinhardt, at the first Salzburg Festival in 1920, took place in front of the Salzburg Cathedral. As part of its grandiose staging, church bells rang and birds were released at the moment of redemption. *ÖNB Vienna/NB 613.730-B*

audiences of Jews and non-Jews. Using the stage to reinvent mystical worlds of the past and create new ethical and cultural ideals with possibilities of future salvation, these artists tapped into a desire for messianic redemption that appealed to both Jewish and non-Jewish Austrians looking for order in a chaotic, postwar world.[4] Both types of theater addressed their audiences' need for spiritual depth through a combination of a past mystical culture and a projected future world on stage—one through a perceived Jewish spirituality and one through the Catholic baroque. Reinhardt's enthusiasm for and involvement in both forms of theater illuminates the function of Jewishness in the staging and successful reception of these performances: Whether foregrounded or occluded, Jewishness was thus crucial to the constructions of Austrian national culture in post-war theater.

The fact that founders Max Reinhardt and Hugo von Hofmannsthal insisted that this national cultural festival take place in the provinces, not Vienna, and that both theme and content needed to be perceived undoubtedly as "Catholic" attested to the sensitivity of its founders to long-standing codings of both the theater in general, and Vienna in particular as "Jewish." On the other hand, Yiddish theater served the purpose of satisfying an urban theater population seeking escape via a Jewish world that was supposedly more authentic, mystical, and spiritual than the one coded as modern, superficial, and rooted in the drive for material gain. Nobody sought to create a new national "Austrian" culture with Yiddish theater, but its broader appeal was based upon its contribution to interwar aesthetics and spiritual aspirations that mirrored those of the Salzburg Festival.

Reinhardt's enthusiasm for and involvement in both forms of theater illuminates how the constructed social order of Jewish difference functioned in the staging and successful reception of these performances. Just as law serves as a way for present society to embody the dream of a perfect future world, so too did the visions of the world created by the festival and Yiddish theater tap into the desire of their audiences to use the past to construct a perfect, restorative future. In one sense, festival productions reveal the mixing of both "Jewish" and "Catholic" views of redemption used in the service of envisioning a new national culture. For some Jews, giving up Jewish ritual traditions did not automatically indicate letting go of the idea of a Messiah. Manès Sperber, for example, envisioned his belief in the redemptive qualities of socialism on par with Messianic Judaism. "I had long given up obeying the countless laws that govern the everyday life of pious Jews. But my faith in the Messiah was still as powerful as ever. Our Messianic equivalent was revolutionary activity."[5] For others, theater provided the stage upon which Messianic redemption could be performed.

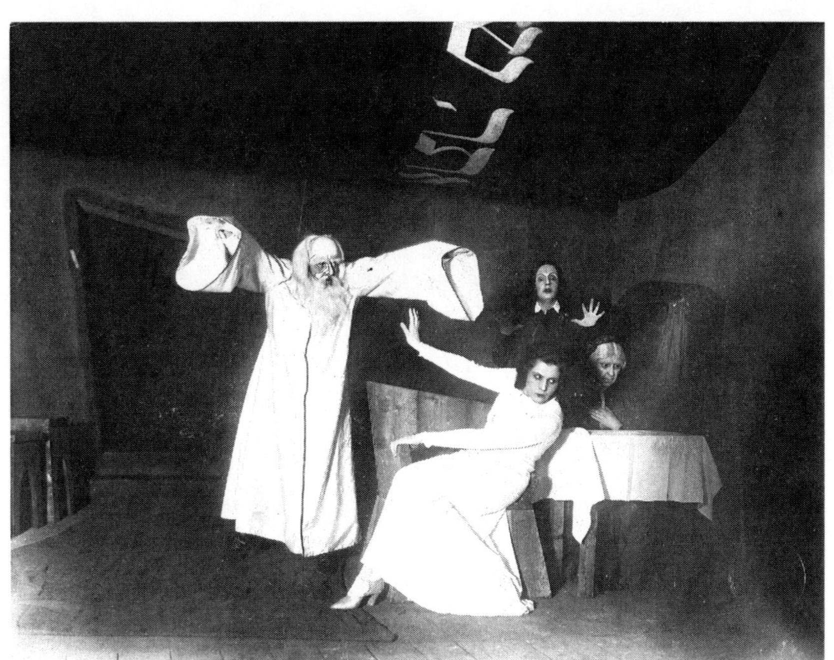

Lea (Magda Sonja) wards off the rabbi (Friedrich Feher) in a performance of *Der Dybbuk* at Vienna's Rolandtheater in 1925, and Everyman (Alexander Moissi) confronts Death (Werner Krauss) in an undated photo from a performance of *Jedermann* in Salzburg. Despite their fundamental differences, both performances utilized expressionism's simultaneously repulsive and compelling antiaesthetic, with grotesque and angular figures and wide-eyed expressions.

Österreichisches Theatermuseum, Vienna

Regardless of any conscious desire to redeem Austrians, both Reinhardt and Hofmannsthal were well aware of how Jewish difference functioned as a hierarchical code that operated independently of actual Jews and non-Jews. Their preparations for the festival reveal an anxiety that their work would be perceived as Jewish and, therefore, not Austrian—of crucial importance to their project of trying to shape a new, national Austrian cultural festival. By the same token, Yiddish theater presented a different form of the Jewish, one that seemed to address the Jewish as spiritual, mystical, and authentic—the very same values that Reinhardt and Hofmannsthal strove to produce. Both forms provided their audiences what they craved in the interwar period—intense, emotional reactions in audiences consisting of Jews and non-Jews, using the stage to reinvent mystical worlds of the past and create new ethical and cultural ideals containing possibilities for future redemption. The presence of Jews, not only as creators but also as patrons and consumers, remained a significant element in the creation and perpetuation of *both* Yiddish productions and the Salzburg Festival. But the success of these theaters relied upon their successful combination of elements of messianic redemption from the past to promise a new, inclusive future for *all* Austrians.

Theater engaged Jewish codings differently than did text-based culture. Performance allowed actors and audience alike to visually reconceptualize the categories as they were acted out. What happened belied not a disappearance or erasure of boundaries between the "Jewish" and the "non-Jewish," but a reliance upon them to entertain its audiences and communicate its ends. From socialism to Zionism, nostalgia for the stability of the old empire to future-looking avant-garde culture, Austrian Jews' responses to the political and social crises of the post–World War I years encompassed a wide spectrum between full embracement and total abnegation of their self-understandings as Jews. The need to come to terms with their changing status in the postwar First Republic drove many to create and participate in shaping culture in a way that addressed what it meant to be Austrian. These cultural creations provided answers, or even escape, for both Jewish and non-Jewish Austrians seeking inclusive cultural ideals combining past traditions with current sensibilities. The popularity of such contradictory forms of theater from such vastly different cultures makes sense when we return to envisioning the constructed social order of Jewishness as one that can entail either repressing and vilifying or idealizing the Other. In the case of the Salzburg Festival, the Jewish was repressed through a festival that relied upon an ideal, utopian vision of Catholicism at its most universal in order to make sense out of a new national culture. In the case of Yiddish theater, the Jewish was often idealized as an authentic form of culture, one that could provide a higher and purer source of salvation and redemption for a nation seeking its self-understanding. Jews were instrumental in fostering both, because as in many other aspects of culture and social life, they strove more than others to make sure these cultures could include them.

More lowbrow forms of theater, like cabaret, sought to expose—and therefore, critique—the boundaries of the social order.[6] But Max Reinhardt and Hugo von Hofmannsthal's laborious efforts to establish a national cultural festival, one that was deliberately far removed from the urban spaces of Vienna, sought a different goal: the transportation of its audiences to emotional heights and a sense of redemption, which reveals, in its reliance on Catholic spiritual imagery and ideals, an intense awareness of and engagement with society's negative conceptions of what was Jewish. On the surface, Reinhardt and Hofmannsthal were constructing a national cultural festival that would anchor Austria's status as a state and help put it on the map as a locus of culture to rival Germany's Bayreuth. But, in order to do so, they needed to construct this platform for the performance of Austrian national culture far from the *Grossstadt* and the modern—in other words, on a decidedly and definitively non-Jewish stage in the provinces.

Yiddish theater, on the other hand, fared well as a more "authentic" ideal of the Jewish—though, in the case of *Der Dybbuk*, it was repackaged to appeal to modern sensibilities. Yiddish theater had been increasing in popularity even before the war, but in Vienna it was reinvigorated by refugees from Galicia and other areas in the East. In interwar literature and theater, a renewed interest in Yiddish culture in Central Europe after World War I typically reflected the more general idealization of the "authentic Jew" that arose as a response to anxieties about the perceived decline of modern European civilization and the Jewish condition. But this was not the only reaction—indeed, a renewed use and idealization of *Catholicism* as a parallel response to the same crises also colored the works of Austrian Jews—in theater, literature, and other areas. This fascination with Catholicism on the part of Jews did not originate in the interwar period; as early as 1893, for example, would-be Zionist leader Theodor Herzl fantasized that an imaginary "pact" with the Vatican might solve the Jewish question: In exchange for the Church's help battling antisemites, Jews would convert to Christianity in a mass ceremony on the steps of St. Stephen's Cathedral. Moreover, Gershom Scholem claimed that, unlike the Christian concept of redemption, an event that takes place in the unseen and private world of the soul, Judaism conceptualizes redemption as a public, communal event.[7] Herzl's mass conversion combines elements of the visible redemption as well as the internal; so did the Salzburg Festival.

Yiddish Theater in Vienna

Theater in particular served a traditional role in Vienna as a means to establish its cultural presence on the map of Europe. For most of the nineteenth century it was Vienna—not Berlin—that served as the *Theaterstadt* (theatrical city) where theatrical life might reach the achievements of Paris or London.[8] But it was not until 1900 that the city saw the emergence of a variety of small Jewish stages and cabarets where Jewish actors performed regularly in Yiddish and German. The success of these performance spaces led to the establishment of theaters in hotels and other venues on the main streets of the Leopoldstadt, Vienna's Jewish neighborhood. From their earliest beginnings, these performances attracted audiences beyond the district in which they were performed; between 1890 and 1899, Arthur Schnitzler attended at least thirteen productions, sometimes in the company of Hugo von Hofmannsthal, Hermann Bahr, Felix Salten, and Richard Beer-Hofmann.[9] Vienna was well-suited for the development of Yiddish theater. It was home to a myriad of performers and audience members from Austria-Hungary's eastern provinces, especially after the outbreak of World War I, when tens of thousands of Eastern European Jewish refugees, driven from their homes, emigrated to Vienna.[10] These Yiddish speakers created a substantial audience for Yiddish theater, whose popularity continued even after most of them returned home after the end of the war.

Early Yiddish theater performances consisted of short variety sketches and folk tales in heavily accented dialogue, performed by small roaming troupes with primitive props and poor lighting. Some audiences found these productions lacking in sophistication and style. Many referred to Yiddish theater as *Schundtheater* (garbage or worthless theater) and sought to elevate it to a higher level, in part to counter antisemitic stereotypes of backward, unrefined Eastern European Jews.[11] A number of Viennese Jews believed that Yiddish theater needed to be transformed into a *Nationaltheater* (national theater) worthy of a people. In order to raise performance standards and offer modern Yiddish drama in sophisticated, artistic German performances, four Viennese Jews founded the Freie Jüdische Volksbühne (Free Jewish People's Theater) in 1919. By 1921, the association had grown to two thousand members and had begun to perform for broader audiences in mainstream theaters far beyond the second Jewish district.[12]

Yiddish author Melech Ravitsch may have lamented that "the hungry, postwar Vienna had no place for Jewish life in Yiddish,"[13] but within a few years, Yiddish culture reasserted itself. Yiddish theater gained popularity with Jewish audiences in Central Europe for a variety of reasons, including its willingness to deal frankly with political themes such as Zionism, assimilation, and the breakdown of the traditional Jewish family. But non-Jews and non-Yiddish speakers were also frequent audience members at performances hosted by the Freie Jüdische Volksbühne. Joseph Buloff noted that in Vienna, to audiences made up of "half German Jews" and "gentile Austrians," from whom they garnered more respect.[14] Non–Yiddish speaking cultural luminaries who were enthusiastic about Yiddish theater performances in Vienna included Friedrich Torberg, Robert Musil, and Oskar Kokoschka, who attended with Karl Kraus and Adolf Loos.

Kokoschka described the performances as "unforgettable," original and imaginative, despite his lack of Yiddish knowledge.[15] In a 1921 diary entry, Arthur Schnitzler wrote that he had enjoyed a very good performance at the Jüdische Volksbühne despite the rundown venue but had understood little because of the jargon.[16]

Clearly, audiences did not find their lack of linguistic comprehension an obstacle to their enjoyment of the performance; indeed, their *inability* to understand was often exactly what drew them in: The unfamiliarity of the language allowed them to appreciate its more "spiritual" or "irrational" qualities. This phenomenon appeared perhaps most famously in Franz Kafka's address to a Prague audience of non-Yiddish speakers.[17] The intensity of the action and the passion of the actors strongly affected Kafka; others, such as Arnold Zweig, wrote glowingly of their "spiritual" qualities.[18] For non–native speakers like Kafka, Yiddish is the authentic language for the authentic Jew.[19] Vilna Troupe actor Joseph Buloff confirms this attitude when he noted that audiences in Vienna seemed to care little about the meager surroundings or their lack of Yiddish comprehension.[20] And Joseph Roth commented sardonically on the popularity of Yiddish theater among Western European Jews noting, "It's become almost more of an institution of the Western ghetto than the East."[21]

Schnitzler was not always enthusiastic about the Yiddish theater—his diary describes a performance by the Vilna troupe at the Rolandbühne of *Schwer zu sein ein Jud* by Sholem Aleichem in 1922 as "*leidlich*" (passable).[22] However, their guest appearances from October 10, 1922, through January 31, 1923, at the Rolandbühne, after which they moved to the Lustspieltheater, indicates that they were very well-received in Vienna.[23] In addition, Schnitzler met personally with Yiddish playwrights Ossip Dymov and David Pinski, when he saw their works *Schma Yisroel* and *Eisik Scheftel* performed in Vienna in 1921 and 1922.[24] He also attended performances by the Budapester Orpheumsgesellschaft, a Jewish theater troupe that performed a variety program of dialogues, folk songs, and the like around the second district.[25]

Cultural luminaries were not the only ones charmed by the Yiddish theater. Minna Lachs, who came with her family to Vienna from Galicia during World War I, claims that the Vilna Troupe transformed her father's perception of Yiddish. After attending *The Dybbuk*, her parents became faithful audience members at the Yiddish theater, which had been accepted into the mainstream—even by non-Jews—as a legitimate form of culture.[26] Manès Sperber, who had never been hostile toward Yiddish culture, noted that his visits there only strengthened his already solid tie to his own Jewish self-understanding.[27]

Although enthusiastic reviews of Yiddish theater were also published simultaneously in Berlin, London, Paris, and New York, interwar Vienna produced some of the most loyal audiences, and Yiddish culture seems to have played an even more intense role in Vienna than it did in other cities.[28] In the confusion of post–World War I Central Europe, all Austrians—and especially Jewish Austrians—were anxious and unsure about their status as members of the new nation. As a result, Jews often became the driving forces behind the creation of new cultures of inclusion, like the Freie Jüdische Volksbühne that reinvented Yiddish theater as an art form combining the sophistication of traditional German drama with "authentic" folkloristic Jewish culture.

But the effects of the war also generated a significant impetus toward a deeper, spiritual release from social and political turmoil. In this context, Yiddish theater proved an attractive outlet not only for Jews who sought attachment to what they perceived as "authentic" Jewish culture, but also for many, including non-Jews, who found in expressionist, modern Yiddish performances an escape to an "exotic" world both familiar and strange.[29] This helps explain the reactions of Viennese audiences who were often reverent about what they saw as the "mystical" qualities of performances by "true" representatives of Judaism. As Joseph Buloff noted, "In Vienna, we [actors] are reputed as rabbis and Talmudic scholars."[30] As such, they offered spiritual succor to Jewish and non-Jewish Austrians alike.

Combining Past and Future: An-sky's *Der Dybbuk*

If a need for redemption and the search for a usable spiritual past drove both Jewish and non-Jewish Austrians to the Yiddish theater, *The Dybbuk* was the drama with the most potential for doing just that.[31] Soon after its publication in Yiddish in 1919, An-sky's mystical, magical tale became one of the most popular and controversial Yiddish dramas ever performed. Although An-sky had already begun work on *Tsvishn tsvey veltn (der dybuk)* (Between two worlds (the dybbuk)) as it was originally called in Yiddish, before 1914, the effects of World War I certainly influenced its final development. To collect "authentic" material related to Jewish folklore, An-sky visited Jewish communities in the Pale of Settlement starting in 1912.[32] And from the start, he planned to present the material in a new cultural context so that it could serve a higher, redemptive function.[33]

Der Dybbuk relates the story of two lovers, Khonen — a yeshiva student, and Leah — who rebel against the bourgeois marriage choices their parents have made for them. When Khonen dies soon after invoking the forces of the Kabbalah, he is transformed into a *dybbuk*—according to folklore, the spirit of a

Joseph Buloff (top center) and Luba Kadison (front row, second from left) in an ensemble photograph of the Vilna Troupe in 1920/1921.

Österreichisches Theatermuseum, Vienna

deceased person who inhabits the body of a living person. An-sky's original drama differed from other versions of the *dybbuk* story by featuring a *dybbuk* who falls in love with the woman whose body he possesses. His drama was also unique in its presentation of a folkloric past using modern methods.[34] The expressionist, avant-garde style of the play may have seemed to Jews to mirror their own experiences of marginalization, loss of orientation, and social isolation.[35] Many Jewish expressionist artists who distanced themselves from religious Judaism found its mystical elements an acceptable "spiritual" channel. The spiritual appeal of *Der Dybbuk* was thus not so much its ability to make religious Judaism palatable to secular audiences, but rather its concern with accessing spirituality and redemption through the lens of Jewish folk traditions. Moreover, in expressionist works one often finds both Christian and Jewish traditions of messianism, another factor that likely contributed to the play's broad appeal.[36]

For most Austrian Jews, not only the play's religious framework, but also the sounds of Yiddish were both foreign and familiar. The highly-stylized drama and the cadenced nature of the spoken Yiddish appealed to many who did not understand the language, as did the authentic Jewish songs and ritual items such as candles and embroidered arks—all of which dazzled a public eager for a glimpse of mythical past worlds.[37] From the reactions of both audience and critics, it is apparent that the play's narrative, aesthetic appeal, and language successfully transformed the stage into a platform upon which they could project the ideals they sought: a Jewish culture with an eye to the past, expressed in modern terms, and with modern—and inclusive—sensibilities. It should not be surprising, then, that performances of the play received an overwhelming reception in Vienna. In 1922, *Komödie: Wochenrevue für Bühne und Film*, a theater and film magazine, published a special issue on the Vilna Troupe on the occasion of their performance of *The Dybbuk*, emphasizing the play's mystical hold over the public: "*The Dybbuk* found the Vilnaers, and the Vilnaers found *The Dybbuk*; it was kismet, they were made for each other, and together they drew themselves into the history of Jewish literature . . . The Vilnaers do not act. As I experience *The Dybbuk*, so do they; this is no longer a show, this is religious contemplation."[38]

An-sky's own conflicted background also contributed to the play's resonance with postwar audiences not so far removed from their Eastern European roots. Born Shloyme-Zanvl ben Aaron Hacohen Rappoport in Vitebsk in 1863, An-sky was a Talmud prodigy who lost his faith by age seventeen. After living and working among Russian peasants whose folk culture he greatly admired, and after experiencing eight years of the diversity and intellectual life in Paris. He regained his interest in the "lost world" of the Jews and Jewish nationalism and returned to writing in Yiddish. An-sky only published the play after he visited Jewish communities in Galicia as a folklorist in 1915 and 1916.[39]

As scholars note—and as *Der Dybbuk* makes clear— the appeal of Jewish folklore to An-sky was its potential for unearthing values that would make meaning in the present, rather than its reflection of past, unrecoverable traditions. This potential spoke to audiences in Vienna, Jewish and not, who were themselves in the process of creating a new, progressive future based upon the illustrious past of the city and empire. In other words, this manifestation of Jewish culture appealed to audiences in Vienna precisely *because of* its mysterious and "foreign" elements and their social and cultural potential. As An-sky stated, "Throughout the play there is a battle between the individual and the collective—more precisely, between the individual's striving for happiness and the survival of the nation. Khonen and Leah struggle for their personal happiness, while the *tsaddik's* (righteous man) only worry is that 'a living branch will wither on the eternal tree of the people of Israel.' Which side is right?"[40]

The enthusiasm with which Viennese audiences responded to a drama that highlights the tension between collective and individual interests attests to its relevance in post–World War I Austrian self-fashioning. The fact that non-Jewish members of the audience often attended together with Jews provides even stronger evidence that Yiddish theater in Vienna was successful not only because it redefined authentic Jewishness for a small number of Jews, but because it also tapped into broader national and cultural concerns.

To be sure, for many in the audience the portrayal of "authentic" Jewish culture only became an attractive option once the form in which it was presented was raised to the levels of bourgeois standards. Vienna theater critic Otto Abeles commented on the issue of Jewish audience attendance by satirizing bourgeois Jews who were, ironically, as concerned with proper comportment at the Yiddish theater as they were at the Burgtheater since there were "Aryans" in the audience:

> The more interesting show this time took place on the floor. It would be very funny to sketch an amusing portrait of the confusion and embarrassment of the Jews "on the ground" (we mean the Eastern-Jew-weary, "rooted" Jews). They had been lured by a long-delayed but well-meaning rave review in the *Neue Freie Presse*, attended in great numbers, were very surprised to meet a larger percentage of art-appreciating Aryan visitors in the hall than at many premières of the Burgtheater, sat still as mice, with the sort of respect and dumb admiration typically shown when a Jew and city merchant is together with an Eastern Jew.[41]

Abeles' estimation of the numbers of non-Jews in attendance embedded within this critique of bourgeois Jews may be exaggerated, but his words nevertheless suggest that Yiddish theater held a special position in the minds of Jewish and non-Jewish Austrians alike. And as Felix Salten wrote in an equally satirical description of the non-Jews in attendance:

> Aryans and Semites, Christians and Jews made up the audience in equal parts, there were even evenings during which Christians by far outnumbered Jews . . . Once, as I went over to the small orchestra to ask where one could buy these songs, it turned out that the conductor was a racially pure Aryan and music critic for an angry antisemitic newspaper. He addressed me almost warmly as "Herr Kollege." How strange was this city of Vienna, where hostile views mixed with each other so peacefully, where no one took political programs seriously, where enemies were just as ready to embrace each other as they were to smash each other's skulls.[42]

Although there was a subset of Yiddish theater growing devoted to Zionism, or committed to spreading the Zionist message, there was another aspect of it that appealed to wider audiences: Jews and non-Jews alike could meet their spiritual and religious needs in Yiddish theater. Some Yiddish theater performances provided a redemptive message framed in terms of a lost, spiritual, mystical past with which both Jews and Christians could identify. Robert Musil summed up the potential for Yiddish theater to appeal to Catholics at this time of existential crisis when he noted in response to one Yiddish theater performance that, if he were the Archbishop of Vienna, he would support the Jüdische Volksbühne.[43]

Musil's acknowledgement of the power of both Catholic and Jewish spiritual messages at a time of political and social upheaval becomes even more salient when considered alongside another cultural response to these same crises during the interwar period: the efforts by Jews to produce and support the Salzburg Festival. Salzburg Festival productions such as *Jedermann* appealed to large audiences in Austria, including many Jews, because of their grounding in what was seen as the most spiritual, mystical part of Catholic culture—the baroque. That both Salzburg and Yiddish theater audiences found depth, redemption, and spirituality in these productions helps us to understand why Jews in interwar Austria could be so passionate about either or, at least in the case of Max Reinhardt, *both* forms.

Catholic Culture through a Jewish Lens

In the Habsburg Empire, having a Jewish background hardly precluded one being influenced by Catholic culture. Along with the Imperial Army and the government bureaucracy, the Roman Catholic Church formed the third bulwark of institutional tradition; with thirty-one million Catholics out of a total population of forty-six million in 1905, the Habsburg Empire was the largest Catholic realm in Europe. Even after the establishment of the First Republic, state financing of the church continued through the 1920s, despite the general financial, political, and social insecurities that ensued after the breakup of the empire. As Helmut Gruber notes, "The Catholic church was better prepared than anyone else to argue for the continuity between the old and the new, and thereby to effectively forestall a serious consideration of the separation of church and state."[44]

Reinhardt and Hofmannsthal were not the only ones to turn to the church as an example of how to plan festivals and celebrations. More than a few Austrian Jews recall being dazzled by the pomp and pageantry of the Church, especially when it was linked to state processionals. Even socialist leader Julius Braunthal remembers in vivid detail the processional of *Fronleichnam* (Corpus Christi Day), which celebrated the alliance between Church and state, indicating the deep impression the parade made on him as a young boy.[45] Writer

Friedrich Torberg mentions the "colorful splendor and magnificent carriages" of the Corpus Christi parade in his essay "A Sentimental Preface" which appeared as an appendix to the original *Tante Jolesch*.[46] Jewish art patron Hermine Gallia was so enthusiastic about the Corpus Christi procession that she wished her daughter Annelore could participate by "carrying one of the pillows with a crown on it."[47]

Given its political and economic stronghold on Austrian culture, it is no surprise that the Catholic Church continued to maintain an important position as a national cultural icon in the imaginations of many Austrians, including Jews, in particular for its perceived ability to maintain traditions of the old empire in the new republic. Many Austrian Jews had been patriotic citizens and strongly mourned its loss at the end of the war.[48] Like others concerned about maintaining stability, they looked to the Catholic Church and its baroque, dramatic pomp and pageantry, both to uphold the traditions of the empire and to find a spirit of redemption similar to that which others had found in Yiddish theater.

The texts of a range of Central European writers reveal a fascination with Catholicism's mystical elements, as well as its aesthetics. Celebrated author Joseph Roth sympathized openly with Catholicism, and Mela Hartwig, Veza Canetti, and Käthe Braun-Prager used Catholic imagery in their texts.[49] Prague-born Franz Werfel also included significant Catholic religious imagery in his novels, although he maintained personal loyalties to both Judaism and Catholicism throughout his career.[50] Despite his enthusiasm for Catholicism, and its frequent appearance in his work, Werfel by his own admission also remained fascinated by the mystical elements of Judaism, such as the ceremony of dressing the Torah, wrapping and kissing the tallis (the traditional prayer shawl), and what he referred to as the strange cadences of the cantor and the shofar.[51] However, critics interpreted this "Jewish" aspect of Werfel's Catholicism in various ways. Max Brod insisted that Werfel's fascination for Catholicism belied a love for Judaism in disguise; he claimed that Werfel's "Christian mission" was at base a "Jewish" one, and that the basis of his ideas such as the "Gedanke der Heiligung des ganzen Daseins" (thought of the sanctification of the entire being) or the *werttätigkeit* (worthy activity) in the sense of *Kiddush Ha-Shem* could only have been influenced by his Jewish origin.[52] Brod was hardly the only one to see in Werfel's work an element of the "Jewish." After meeting him in 1913, Rainer Maria Rilke writes in a letter to Hugo von Hofmannsthal of his disappointment at what he called a "durchaus jüdische Einstellung" (thoroughly Jewish attitude) to writing poetry.[53] In this nexus of interests and influences, then, we see the complex interconnections of Catholicism and Jewishness; the associations linked to either could be used to articulate the meaning of the other.

Psychoanalyst Helene Deutsch's fictionalized journal took the form of the diary of a Catholic girl who grew up in Vienna.[54] That Deutsch chose to tell her life story from this perspective without disavowing her Jewish background indicates that for her—as for many—Catholicism represented a way to fashion oneself as an Austrian insider. These authors' use of Catholicism thus marks a different kind of engagement with Jewish difference not a religious rejection. Rather than indicating the limits of the roles Jews and Jewishness could play in the years after World War I, as some scholars have suggested, the Catholic imaginings of these Austrian Jews actually serve to broaden our understanding of what constituted "Jewish" responses to the crises of the new Republic.[55] While certainly not every Jew in Vienna looked upon Catholicism favorably, for many it served as a way to imagine themselves included in a new Austrian culture.[56]

Interwar Theater and Politics

The reflection of Jews' affinity for Catholicism as a potential totalizing cultural ideal of Austrianness is best understood in the broader context of the development of Austrian theater amidst interwar political and cultural change. Up until the late eighteenth century, theater performances and other public celebrations and festivals had long been tightly controled by the government; only the lessees of the two existing court theaters had been allowed to offer any public entertainment. But in 1776 Emperor Joseph lifted the state's stranglehold, allowing new playhouses to be built outside the walled city. As a result, police permission became all one required to stage a performance. Combined with the 1781 Edict of Toleration, Jews were now able to become driving forces in establishing theater. But because censorship remained tight, official theater did not become a venue for social critique; controversial ideas tended to be performed in smaller theaters and cabarets. In one form or another, censorship remained in force in the court theaters until 1918, and even longer in the commercial ones;[57] the interwar period represented a turning point after which those in theater had new possibilities.

This development helps explain why, as Michael Steinberg has pointed out, a seemingly trivial leadership crisis in the Burgtheater received almost daily coverage in the *Neue Freie Presse* alongside articles on the restructuring of Europe during the summer of 1918, as fighting escalated, indicated its growing importance as a site of national cultural meaning.[58] After the war, when censorship restrictions had been lifted, the scandal caused by Schnitzler's sexually provocative *Reigen* on February 17, 1921, as well as Ernst Krenek's *Johnny spielt auf* on December 31, 1927, also raised awareness of the connections between Jews and the theater as growing elements of subversion. At the same time, more lowbrow performances associated with Jews, such as vaudeville acts and circus performances, also gained in popularity.[59] Scandals and lowbrow theater did little to raise the reputation of Jews among certain circles. Already in the nineteenth century, antisemites blamed them for degrading the reputation of Vienna as a city of theater into a showcase of superficial operettas and other un-German fare and attempted to wrest it away from what they termed "Jewish influence."

In German Nationalist Party candidate Adam Müller-Guttenbrunn's 1885 pamphlet *Wien war eine Theaterstadt*, we see early traces of the exclusion of Jews from an "ideal" of Viennese theater. Müller-Guttenbrunn proclaims German theater as a "world in itself" with Vienna as its focal point, but constantly refers to its "sick" state. He complains that the traditional, cultured Viennese theater has been ruined by operettas, which he calls the "bastard of art, spawned of a stock market speculator and a Parisian coquette" set up for profit.[60] It is no wonder, then, that in 1898 he led the drive to establish the Kaiserjubiläums Stadtheater (the Emperor's Jubilee City Theater) as Vienna's first "Aryan" theater, although he did not press for the full exclusion of Jews from its ranks. Müller-Guttenbrunn's attempts to convince his colleagues that it would be prudent not to exclude all Jews from the board in order to avoid being labeled as an antisemitic theater indicates the extent to which even the makeup of theater boards was considered a highly political, contested structure. "It was unthinkable to me to create a cultural institution in Vienna that excluded Jews as co-founders, authors, actors, and audience and, as a result, would have the Jewish critics against it."[61] By the end of the nineteenth century, theater had already become the stage upon which the divisions between Jews and non-Jews were played out very clearly.

Provincial Visions

One of the most striking manifestations of the Jewish promotion of Catholic baroque culture was the creation of the Salzburg Festival, which today remains one of Austria's most prominent cultural events.[62] From its origins, the Salzburg Festival was intended to symbolize Austrian "summoning of spiritual strength," combining an Austrian nationalist and Pan-European perspective with redemptive Catholicism.[63] The Festival's first official performance in 1920 was Max Reinhardt's staging of Hugo von Hofmannsthal's drama *Jedermann* on the steps of Salzburg's majestic, baroque cathedral.[64] Hofmannsthal had adapted this piece from the medieval English morality play *The Summoning of Everyman*, which included the recitation of the Lord's Prayer. Although Hofmannsthal and Reinhardt ensured the decidedly Catholic tone of the performance, their drive to create this national, Catholic festival reveals an intense engagement with the terms of Jewish difference.

The idea of a festival in Salzburg emerged in the late nineteenth century as a way to honor the birthplace of Austria's premier cultural icon, Wolfgang Amadeus Mozart. However, the lack of an adequate theater, professional orchestra, amenable local population, and funding made the city's attempts to stage the festival an impossibility.[65] Discussions between writer Hermann Bahr and Max Reinhardt in 1903 and 1908 about staging theater festivals in Salzburg were also never realized due to lack of funds, although Reinhardt began to direct some performances in the city. In 1917, motivated in part by a desire to limit Reinhardt's increasing artistic activity, a local merchant and Viennese music critic helped establish the Salzburger Festspielhaus-Gemeinde (Society for the Salzburg Festival Hall) to build and run a festival hall for the city. Journalist Heinrich Damisch published a call for its support in the Viennese music journal *Der Merker*, appealing to those who feared that the wrong elements were about to construct a building for a festival in Salzburg.[66] In a thinly veiled dig at Reinhardt's intentions, which he characterized as "superficial" and "material," coding for Jewish, Damisch noted:

> Only if the interest of art remains the sole driving force, disconnected from all commercial considerations and original financial difficulties and obligations, can the festival house become a cultural factor of lasting, great significance. However, for many reasons it is to be feared that the idea for the festival house after the end of the World War, when the commercial and entrepreneurial urge will expand all too luxuriously, will be taken up from a side that views the realization of this idea mainly for material reasons and carries it out only with the help of speculative art patrons.[67]

It soon became clear, however, that proceeding without Reinhardt would be impossible.[68] The Society reluctantly appointed Reinhardt to its *Kunstrat* (artistic board) in 1918; Hofmannsthal was appointed in 1919.[69] Plans for the establishment of a festival theater were underway by 1919, spurred by the formation of the First Republic of Austria after the end of World War I.

From its inception, the Salzburg Festival was integrally tied to Catholic culture, not least due to its location in the provinces. Like Tyrol, the province of Salzburg was deeply Catholic, a place where antisemitism underscored a mistrust not only of the small, local Jewish community, but of Red Vienna and the control of central government, both of which were coded as "Jewish."[70] Popular sayings of the day indicate that antisemitism against "Viennese Jews" played an important role in Salzburg's political culture after the war: "Chase away the Jews and their accomplices" and ". . . We don't want the Viennese Jew to rule over us. Salzburg should be left to the people of Salzburg."[71]

But it is precisely the fact that the provinces were coded as "non-Jewish"—and, therefore, "Austrian" that drove Reinhardt and Hofmannsthal to establish a national cultural festival there. It is no coincidence that the Salzburg Festival was founded only two years after the collapse of the monarchy, since one of its aims was to function as a "cultural" bridge between the monarchy and the new Austrian republic.[72] Reinhardt's original idea had been to produce a modern version of the traditional nativity play as a way to create a Volksschauspiel (folk performance) imbued with spirit.[73] In the end, he and Hofmannsthal chose *Jedermann*, a medieval morality play which Hofmannsthal had translated from English and reworked for Reinhardt to stage in Berlin in 1911. *Jedermann*'s story concerns a callous rich man named Everyman who is visited by Death and warned that he will die and be condemned to hell. Everyman begs without success for time; however, once enlightened by Faith and Good Works, he falls to his knees, recites the Lord's Prayer and reaches heaven.

The play's dramatic staging at Salzburg made it an instant success: the voice of Death emerged from the nearby imposing medieval fortress, an organ and chorus emanated from inside the cathedral, and at the very moment Everyman was redeemed, birds were released and the church bells tolled. Hilde Albers-Frank, a German Jewish actress who had studied with Reinhardt and who performed at the festival, noted that Reinhardt even co-opted the pigeons in the square for full effect:

> For the performance of *Everyman*, on the square in Salzburg Reinhardt took into account the glare and shadows of the passing sun and used a signal to have the bells of the castle on the mountain far above the town toll at the appropriate time. Pigeons, I guess, are on every square. Reinhardt took advantage of them. He had people stationed all over the square, and at a certain moment, those who were near the pigeons were directed to chase them over the stage to great effect.[74]

Jews made up a significant proportion of the Salzburg Festival audience.[75] While it is difficult to estimate the exact number who attended, festival programs and posters include timetables for trains to and from Bad Ischl, Bad Gastein, and other lake resorts in the area: the traditional Jewish *Sommerfrische* (summer resorts) in the Salzkammergut.[76] Antisemitic newspapers in Salzburg also complained about the "Leopoldstädter"—as they termed Jews—who came to Salzburg from St. Gilgen, St. Wolfgang, and "Ischeles" and made fools of themselves by wearing dirndls.[77] Noting the draw of Reinhardt and his theater, Stefan Zweig claimed "There is no Jew who is not now in Salzburg, and since Reinhardt has been there the people gather like black flies."[78] Even Hugo Bettauer's satire of a Vienna without Jews had to mention their simultaneous "disappearance" from the Salzkammgergut, Semmering, and "even more modernized sections of the Tyrol" that had become a veritable "playground of the Jews."[79]

According to Michael Steinberg, the Festival organizers succeeded in their attempt to combine traditional conservatism with a new, dynamic representation of Austrian national identity—a theater of Catholic pageantry imbued with a more progressive, enlightened nationalism of inclusion, which he terms "nationalist cosmopolitanism." The aim of the neobaroque style of the Salzburg productions was "to reconstitute and represent the present . . . in the image of a golden past."[80] For Hofmannsthal and Reinhardt—as well as for many Jewish members of the audience—a passion for Catholic baroque theater thus may have represented not a lack of interest in their Jewish backgrounds, but rather an attempt to distance themselves from that aspect of their identities, to find a universalizing, totalizing experience through theater, and to create a measure of inclusivity in this new Austrian cultural identity.

Reinhardt and Hofmannsthal

Although the idea of a Salzburg festival had been raised before Reinhardt and Hofmannsthal became involved, in the end Reinhardt was most responsible for bringing the idea to fruition. Born Max Goldmann in 1873 in Baden bei Wien, Reinhardt changed his name at an early age, when he first began performing, to avoid antisemitic backlash. While acting in Salzburg in 1893, he was discovered and invited to Berlin by theater director Otto Brahm. In 1901, Reinhardt's cabaret *Schall und Rauch* opened at the Berliner Künstlerhaus; it featured a large number of Jewish actors, as well as guest performers, in parodies and satires, along with some serious literary pieces. In 1905, Reinhardt took over as director of Brahm's theater and soon became one of the most innovative and well-known directors of the German-speaking stage.

Throughout his career, Reinhardt remained committed to innovative performances that were viewed as the ultimate in modern progress. However, his deep desire to become director of Austria's Burgtheater preoccupied him in the 1920s. Reinhardt was supposed to come to the Burgtheater as guest director with his ensemble from Berlin; however, Burgtheater director Anton Wildgans feared that he would be a danger to both the actors and the institution of the theater itself. Antisemitism likely played a role in Wildgans's negative attitude; he was notoriously suspicious of the leading circles of Viennese art, literature, and theater and once referred to Reinhardt as "the crafty window dresser from Pressburg." Rebuffed, Reinhardt returned to Vienna and, in 1924, transformed the smaller Theater in der Josefstadt into a successful venue, at a time when the Burgtheater still struggled to obtain funding from the state.[81]

Although it would have been easier to accomplish in a number of other more accessible cities, Reinhardt was passionately committed to staging the festival in Salzburg, a city with which he had been enamored ever since he first acted there in his youth. In fact, he had maintained his deep allegiance to Austria throughout his years in Germany. As his wife Helene Thimig noted, "In Germany he became 'der Reinhardt' but he remained Austrian. I remember how he always breathed a sigh when he crossed the border, when he stepped onto Austrian soil again for the first time, or when he heard the Austrian language. He was an Austrian, 100 percent Austrian—not only according to his passport."[82] In 1917, Reinhardt returned to the country of his birth and purchased Schloss Leopoldskron (Leopoldskron Castle) in Salzburg, which soon became a central meeting point for prominent figures in society, politics, and art.

Reinhardt's deep connection to Austria is evident in a letter he wrote to the Society upon his acceptance of their offer to be cultural director:

> I wish, nonetheless, as an Austrian, passionately, that the extraordinary artistic, cultural and also economic gain of a business of that sort should go to my Fatherland . . . To reach this proud height again, to regain the flag of leadership and to plant it in Salzburg, is an equally enticing and undoubtedly solvable task. With beauty, spirit and cheerfulness, above all with deep belief in this mission, with enthusiastic joy is the world to be conquered and bound in brotherhood. And whom would this victory and this peace better suit than the old multilingual empire?[83]

He clearly regarded his role in the construction of Austrian interwar theater not only as a culmination of all his previous endeavors, but as a mission to maintain the influence of Austrian culture. He viewed the festival as both a personal achievement and a representative victory for the old empire, linking plans for a new culture with nostalgia for the multilingual past, and using ultranationalistic language to cover any suspicions of his intent to bring in "foreign" (i.e., international or "Jewish") elements.

A number of Austrian Jews shared Reinhardt's patriotism and awareness that, as Jews, they were in danger of being shut out of the Austrian ideal. In 1922, Heinrich Eduard Jacob, the Austrian correspondent for the *Berliner Tageblatt*, noted that Reinhardt—and other Austrian Jewish writers—had been forced to go to Germany for their successes before they gained fame in Austria.[84] Jacob's text indicates that the simultaneous recognition of Jewish difference and the desire to include oneself as a member of the Austrian *Volk* was not uncommon among Jews in the interwar period.

Reinhardt was well aware of the disadvantages of being a Jew in the new Austrian nation. He knew that as a Jew he could not be director of the Burgtheater or president of the Salzburg Festival Society, and his son Gottfried notes that the status of his first wife, actor Else Heims, as "Aryan" made her an attractive partner for him.[85] Reinhardt's second wife, Helene Thimig, describes his relationship to Catholic culture as deeply bound with his love for Austria and the theater, although it did not impede his adherence to Jewish traditions. As she recounted, "He observed a few Jewish holidays out of piety for the religion of his parents, but let himself be inspired mainly by the history of the Catholic church, which, with its ornamented style and richness of dramatic material, obviously had much more to offer him, the theater man."[86] As Thimig suggests, it was the drama of Catholic culture that most appealed to him. To Reinhardt, holiness was on par with theatricality, and he separated his own personal religious beliefs from this love of Catholic drama. As his son noted, "Papa didn't love Protestant churches. They were too cool, dry, and untheatrical—as he understood the word theatrical: As something holy . . . but as a place of performance, he preferred Catholic churches to synagogues, although he remained a believing Jew."[87]

From the start, Reinhardt tried to make the festival serve a "quasi-religious" function, as a site to which people would make pilgrimages, where they could find "redemption in art," in particular after the horrors of the war.[88] As Thimig notes, Reinhardt did not really care what he produced at the first Salzburg Festival—as long as it was "something Christian."[89] For him, the drama of the Catholic baroque was the essence of what was "Austrian." Both Reinhardt's desire to remain loyal to the sensibilities of the old empire and his love of dramatic Catholic culture reveal a negative engagement with Jewish difference (as opposed to the practice of Jewish religion); in order to realize the possibilities of each, he needed to do more to establish himself—and his theater—as worthy of description as "national" and "Austrian."

Reinhardt's artistic partner, Hugo von Hofmannsthal, whom antisemites enjoyed referring to as a *Berufskatholik* (career Catholic), had a much more directly negative attitude toward Jews and Judaism based upon the complexities of his own Jewish roots. He had been raised Catholic, but was well aware that his paternal grandfather, Isaak Löw Hofmann, ennobled in 1835, had converted from Judaism. But as Abigail Gillman has pointed out, Hofmannsthal's Jewish sensibilities developed long before his involvement with the Salzburg Festival.[90] By tracing the development of his ballet-pantomime *Der Schüler* (The Student, 1901), based upon an original Jewish tale that Hofmannsthal attempted to "cleanse" of its original Jewish characters, she shows how Jewish difference influenced Hofmannsthal's artistic sensibilities even at that early stage.[91]

His later involvement in the Salzburg Festival and the intensity with which he drove it to engage Catholicism indicates the strength of the invisible, but palpable divisions between the "Jewish" and the "non-Jewish," which forced him to confront this background and contributed to his own negative visions of Jews, as well as his attempts to respond to those visions in his art.[92] As early as 1903, for example, the magazine *Kikiriki* included him along with Schnitzler as one of a group of Jewish playwrights who were responsible for the decline in success of Aryan writers.[93] Like Reinhardt, Hofmannsthal also experienced difficulties convincing the public that he was a loyal Austrian.

Judith Beniston points out that from 1918 on, Hofmannsthal became fascinated with Josef Nadler's "ethnographic approach" to literary history; this is where he was able to try to frame his own creativity in terms of a "myth of cultural continuity tied in with the unchanging Alpine landscape" and to see the Salzburg Festival as "the real idea of art generated from Bavarian-Austrian stock"[94] His central role in delineating the boundary between Austrian and German literature, along with his engagement of the cultural ideal of the new Austria, indicates his own efforts in trying to transform it into a purely Austrian national theater that is nevertheless accessible (and appealing) to all Austrians, including Jews.[95] Catholic promotional material and plays are the ultimate way to elide the construction of the "Jew" while allowing Jews (at least those who want to escape trappings of the Jewish) to become part of the experience.

W. E. Yates claims the use of a romantic myth of the homogenous *Volk* appealed to Hofmannsthal, who found it useful in his attempts to oppose the cultural fragmentation of German-speaking Europe. "Even when writing *Jedermann* he had been consciously attempting to adapt timeless material to recreate the effect of myth. His earliest notes for the play are headed: 'Jedermann. A liturgical play.' As an epigraph, the passage from the Hebbel-Uechtritz correspondence: 'I have used the Christian myth like any other.'" The fact that the play was not successful in Berlin in 1906 only confirms its appeal to post–World War I audiences in Vienna in search of national cultural solidarity.[96]

Hofmannsthal's works, however, had long been viewed with suspicion by antisemites.[97] In 1921, the Burgtheater rejected Hofmannsthal's drama *Der Schwierige* (The Difficult Man); the premiere took place in Munich, and the play opened three weeks later in Berlin to a hostile press response. The piece was not performed in Vienna until 1924, after Reinhardt had taken over the Theater in der Josefstadt. But if anyone was as patriotic and loyally Austrian as Reinhardt, it was Hofmannsthal, who had been deeply affected by the fall of the monarchy, which he viewed as nothing short of apocalyptic.[98] In his essay "Die österreichische Idee," which appeared in the *Neue Zürcher Zeitung* on December 2, 1917, he lays out what he deems the most essential elements of the new concept of Austria will be: "reconciliation, synthesis, and a bridge linking the incompatible."[99] Before the end of the war, he lectured on the positive aspects of Austrian culture and poetry, putting forth Romantic ideals with the aim of justifying Austrian cultural identity. These lectures formed the basis for his essays "Deutsche Festspiele zu Salzburg" (German festival at Salzburg) and "Die Salzburger Festspiele" (The Salzburg Festival), which he drafted in the form of a catechism, after being elected to the Festival's *Kunstrat* in 1919.[100]

Although his involvement in the *Kunstrat* postdated Reinhardt's, once involved he became the Festival's central ideological engine in putting these ideas into practice. Between 1918 and 1922, Hofmannsthal wrote a number of essays making the case for the Festival's cultural basis in the Catholic baroque; he emphasized the Austrian roots of the festival and promoted its artistic cosmopolitanism, which he insisted made it all the more "Austrian," while at the same time carefully making sure to refer to Reinhardt's Austrian citizenship. Hofmannsthal also self-consciously—and rather defensively—stressed that both his and Reinhardt's motivation in establishing the festival stemmed not from a wish to fulfill personal desires, but rather from the higher goal of carrying on the spirit of the Austrian Empire in the new republic through culture and art.[101]

The growing association of modernism with Jewishness and the attempts of Jews to supposedly undermine German culture had long affected Hofmannsthal personally; in 1906, critics had derided his drama *Oedipus und die Sphinx* for being written in a "Jewish German" way. In 1919, Hofmannsthal insisted to Hermann Bahr that being Jewish "has never penetrated my inner being, neither in my youth nor later."[102] But in a 1922 letter to literary critic Willy Haas, he admits both his connection to Judaism and his conflicted attitude toward it, as well as its effect on his career: "My position as an artist in the contemporary world is infinitely precarious. One can view my entire oeuvre as a difficult, strange self-affirmation."[103] Various other events and documents reveal his ambivalent engagement with Jewishness, from his marriage to Gerty Schlesinger, daughter of the Jewish president of the Anglo-Austrian Bank, to a diary entry in which he anxiously poses the question: "What if the sum total of my inner developments and struggles were nothing more than agitations of my inherited blood, rebellions of the Jewish blood-drops . . . against the Germanic and Romanic, and reactions against these rebellions?"[104]

In Vienna, the association of modernism with the "Jewish" and its attempts to undermine "Austrian" culture certainly affected Hofmannsthal, and Reinhardt proved instrumental in supporting him.[105] With the festival, Reinhardt continued the trend of his theater in Berlin to provide Jewish actors with opportunities. As Hilde Albers-Frank, who played in *Jedermann* at the Festival noted:

> For me it was heaven to be on his stage in the proximity of so many top actors and actresses of Germany, especially Alexander Moissi, whom I adored, and who even let me accompany him to rehearsal one time and take his picture. Some of the others took me along on excursions, and I prize the photos I have of them swimming and mountain climbing. I also possess a printed ribbon, commemorating a solo performance I gave with some famous musicians at an inn in a neighboring village.[106]

But Hofmannsthal would be less ecstatic about coming into contact with other Jews. Unlike Joseph Roth and the other writers who became fascinated with Eastern European Jewish culture, Hofmannsthal found Galicia, where he did his military service in 1894–1895, "ugly, muddy and infinitely depressing." Recently, scholars have unearthed a number of instances in which he made antisemitic statements.[107] Since Hofmannsthal, like many other Austrians, understood the "Jewish" as "divisive," "unoriginal," "rational" and "modern," it is no wonder that the development of his increasingly reactionary understanding of culture accompanied his increasingly distanced attitude toward his Jewish background.[108] The absence of Jewish themes and characters from most of his work—as well as the foregrounding of a Catholic sensibility in many of his major pieces—thus can be seen to represent an engagement with the constructed order of Jewish difference.[109]

Long before the festival officially opened, Hofmannsthal voiced concern that the *Kunstrat*, which included Reinhardt, needed to maintain a unified front in the face of the rest of the Festspielhaus-Gemeinde.[110] To that end, his "catechism" program also served to quell the potential anxieties of the members of the committee from Salzburg. In addition, his careful construction of a support group for the festival reveals his awareness of the perception that "Jewishness" played a problematic role in the festival's founding, as well as how that awareness shaped his aesthetic and administrative decisions. Hofmannsthal's own perceptions of Jewishness helped drive his desire to construct a Salzburg Festival free of Jewish overtones, even as he recognized that his connections to and familiarity with Jewish patrons could ensure that Festival's success.

Antisemitic criticism—framed as complaints that he was not a "true" Catholic—continued to haunt Hofmannsthal at the Salzburg Festival; even some laudatory reviews of *Jedermann* accused him of opportunism.[111] But his decisions about how to organize the Salzburg Festival and his attempts to control how it was perceived not only reveal concerns about antisemitism, but also highlight his awareness of the extent to which his and Reinhardt's Jewish backgrounds played a role in Festival politics. In 1922, when president Count Alexander von Thurn und Taxis resigned, the Festspielhaus-Gemeinde chose Richard Strauss as his successor instead of Reinhardt. When Strauss hesitated, Hofmannsthal urged him to accept, revealing both his belief that the Festspielhaus-Gemeinde remained firmly antisemitic and his sympathy for Reinhardt: "And now to Salzburg: I wired you and now repeat the *urgent* plea: take the purely pro forma position that will in no way require activity . . . These philistines will never accept Reinhardt as president: they hate him, they hate him three- and four-fold, as a Jew, as a castle-owner, as an artist, and as a solitary person whom they don't understand."[112]

When the Salzburg Festival ran into financial trouble, however, not long after it began, its founders were forced to seek funding outside Austria. After the collapse of the monarchy, Reinhardt had been able to procure private funding from, among others, Camillo Castiglioni, a Jewish financier, originally from Trieste,[113] who had helped to support Reinhardt's Theater in der Josefstadt. Reinhardt courted Castiglioni by appealing to their shared sense of being outsiders in Austrian society, while at the same time linking this sensibility to the most powerful forces in Austrian history. He claimed that the two of them were "the only ones who can do what in antiquity the state, in the medieval times the church and in our times princes and kings have done: prepare a worthy home for the most powerful, most popular and most immediate art."[114] Reinhardt's son notes that Castiglioni, Reinhardt, and Hofmannsthal later tried to save the Salzburg Festival with an infusion of private capital, but failed because the board viewed them as "outsiders" with too much power; he also notes that Hofmannsthal viewed Castiglioni as a distasteful figure throughout.

Hofmannsthal turned to an international base of donors for support only when he realized the festival could not otherwise continue.[115] He created a group known as the Friends of the Salzburg Festival, which included one hundred prominent and wealthy Europeans and Americans, and turned to Paul Zifferer, a Jewish novelist, former feuilleton editor of the *Neue Freie Presse*, and Austrian cultural attaché in Paris, to find suitable French donors. Hofmannsthal's correspondence with Zifferer provides evidence of his anxiety regarding the perceived Jewishness of the Salzburg Festival and reveals the subtle nature of its effects on him.[116] Although he recognized that an international funding base of Jews would cause difficulties with the Festspielhaus-Gemeinde, Hofmannsthal nevertheless did not hesitate to include Jewish members—as long as they did not raise other potential problems. Thus, while he vetoed some of Zifferer's suggested Jewish candidates, he included many more.[117] As a result, the sixty-eight names on the 1926 membership list for the "Friends of the Salzburg Festival" reveals a carefully structured mix of well-known individuals from Vienna, London, Paris, New York, and other cities. The Jews on the list included Iphigenie Castiglioni, Serena Lederer, Professor Joseph Redlich, Louis Rothschild, Andy von Zsolnay, and, from New York, Morris Gest and Otto Kahn.[118]

Hofmannsthal clearly recognized the importance of Jews for forming a base of support that would maintain the Salzburg Festival as a national cultural icon. Funding theatrical and other cultural events had long been a way for urban European Jews to demonstrate their assimilation to the majority culture. Unlike other forms of entertainment, which could be enjoyed in private, theater and concert performances represented important spaces in which Jews could publicly display their commitment to Austrian culture; theater, in particular, played a significant role as a symbol of cultural assimilation for Austrian Jews. As Leon Botstein notes,

> The Jews who immigrated to Vienna embraced the Viennese tradition of music, Mozart, Schubert, Haydn, as no other part of western culture, because it was a way to put themselves on an equal level, not only privately but also in the public sphere . . . In concert and theater life, what is especially important as a means of assimilation is the fact that, in the concert hall and the theater, witnesses could be co-opted, to confirm the reality of this equality.[119]

Botstein also points out that the proximity of the homes of many Viennese Jews to the innermost district of the city, where concerts, theater and opera took place, contributed substantially to their high participation in these forms of culture.[120]

But the Jews' support for culture, along with Reinhardt and Hofmannsthal's inescapable associations with the "Jewish," meant that the Salzburg Festival, despite all efforts to frame it as a provincial, Catholic, Austrian national event, nevertheless continued to be coded as "Jewish." From the start, local newspapers labeled the festival a Jewish project—no surprise in a city that, since 1918, had supported the fight against the "Wiener Judenblätter" and the "jüdische Presse." The *Salzburger Chronik*, the Christian Social newspaper, published frequent antisemitic articles well before the 1920 founding of the festival, complaining about Jewish businessmen invading Salzburg with "modern" theater and damaging Austrian and German cultural traditions.[121] Other newspapers focused on the Jewish roots of "Max Goldmann-Reinhardt," "Bruno Walter-Schlesinger" and Hugo von Hofmannsthal. The right-wing *Eiserne Besen* campaigned to prevent Reinhardt from presenting *Das Salzburger grosse Welttheater* in the Kollegien Church in 1923, and advocated expunging its "Jewish elements."[122]

In addition to objecting to the "false use" of Catholic ritual, local newspapers also complained bitterly about the audience of strangers the festival was perceived to attract and the prohibitively high ticket prices.[123] Because the festival had been designed to reach an international, elite audience, it immediately drew suspicions about its "Jewish" character. Local and Viennese newspapers reported in alarmist tones on the number of strangers streaming into the city, although the government actually relaxed its passport regulations on the German border just for the events. One Viennese newspaper noted that Salzburg expected a crowd of foreigners, and that one could come without a passport from Bavaria, although only for the festival.[124] Another journalist claimed that Reinhardt had let loose a "devil" in the city that needed to be exorcized.[125]

Antisemitic criticism of the Festival did not come only from right-wing newspapers. In 1923, less than a year after Hofmannsthal's production, the official Catholic *Kunststelle* (government art association) in Vienna staged its own production of the Salzburg Festival's *Das Salzburger grosse Welttheater* in an attempt to 'reclaim' the play for the Catholic community.[126] The *Kunststelle's* journal *Der Kunstgarten* criticized the festival, noting in a review of *Jedermann* the inconsistency of Hofmannsthal's allegorical figures, who spoke in a strange "cultured idiom," although the drama was supposed to be a "genuine folk play."[127] Clearly, many saw Hofmannsthal's use of Catholicism as disingenuous.

Even some of the festival's original enthusiastic supporters changed their views as antisemitic attitudes increased. Art historian and critic Joseph August Lux, an active early supporter of the festival, glowingly reviewed the first performance of *Jedermann* in 1920.[128] Yet, he rapidly became disenchanted with the festival, blaming the influx of foreigners as "damaging" and expressing fears that Reinhardt would take over the entire production. By 1921 he had become one of the festival's fiercest critics, concerned mainly with the cultural profile created by Hofmannsthal and the effect of Reinhardt's taste on the repertoire, both of which he regarded as insufficiently Austrian.[129] Discussing architect Hans Poelzig's plans for the new *Festspielhaus*, Lux derided the "German spoken with an Eastern taint" of Jewish art critic Paul Westheim, associating both the "rococo" and "expressionist" tastes typified by Reinhardt with "speculators" rather than artists.[130] That Poelzig had completed a three thousand–seat auditorium in Berlin for Reinhardt did not aid his case with Lux, who in 1921 wrote, in the National Socialist *Volksruf*, that Reinhardt had, with the "semitic Gods" Hofmannthal, Bruno Walter, and Moissi, staged a money-losing "circus" in Salzburg.[131] Although actor Alexander Moissi was not Jewish, many assumed he was because of his name and association with the festival; newspapers often compared him to Yiddish actors Alexander Asro and Yaakov Levi. Reinhardt, who had been the subject of antisemitic critique in Salzburger newspapers ever since he first acted there in 1893, was referred to as an "Oriental" and a "new Messiah."[132]

The antisemitic reactions to the Festival did not go unnoticed by Jewish journalists in Vienna, although they tended to criticize both provincial antisemitism and what they viewed as the pointless attempts of the festival's founders to overcome these attitudes through art. In 1922, Alfred Polgar noted that the city of

Salzburg remained staunchly antisemitic—since they associated all things foreign with Jews—despite the positive financial aspects of the festival:

> On the one hand the acquisition of the world and money satisfies them; on the other, they cannot stand the customs with which these are associated. To that is added a brusque humorlessness . . . and a decisive aversion to the Jews, a term under which the Salzburgers—just as the Greeks with the term "barbarian"—subsume everything foreign . . . "Festival" in the land of the dying economy is something as unwise and awkward as a painting exhibition in a home for the blind. The people of Salzburg sense what is tactless about the event. In their idiom it is then called 'Down with the Jews!'[133]

Karl Kraus also satirized Reinhardt, Hofmannsthal, and Moissi in the pages of *Die Fackel*. In an essay entitled "Die Handschrift des Magiers" (The magician's handwriting), Kraus attacked Reinhardt's ostentatious lifestyle and artistic barrenness, paralleling his rise in popularity to that of the populist Hitler.[134] One account mocked the "unifying" aims that the festival was trying to achieve by drawing attention to the continued divisions among the audience:

> The Christian and the other Socialism were moved to embrace one another, *Reichspost* and *Arbeiter-Zeitung* wept with joy, and dissolved in propitious delight, the souls of the Salzburg people, together with the souls of those from Ischl and the spa patients from Gastein, ascended solemnly towards the pure, sublime evening sky beyond all faiths. A portion of the audience attempted to applaud, but I don't know which result a plebiscite in this area at this moment would have brought.[135]

Despite its ironic tone, however, this report suggests that the festival may have succeeded in unifying Jewish and non-Jewish audience members in one cultural experience.

Indeed, in some cases we know that Reinhardt and Hofmannsthal managed to succeed in their goal.[136] Erwin Bonyhadi, born in 1906, remembers Salzburg as antisemitic in the interwar period; he recalls as a Jew being shut out of gymnastic organizations, sports clubs, and youth groups. Although the Jewish community was small, his parents had only Jewish friends, belonged to Jewish dance groups, and visited the cafés, but only with other Jews; "In Café Bazar there were almost only Jews, a lot of Jews." During World War I, his mother was very active in the Red Cross and aided Jewish refugees from Galicia and the Bukovina. As was the case for many Austro-Hungarian Jews, his father had been a great patriot of the monarchy and wept when Franz Joseph died. "We lived according to Jewish tradition, but were not as religious as other Jews in other areas, since it was difficult to be religious in Salzburg." In school, he and brother were the only two Jewish students.[137]

Nevertheless, Erwin and his brothers were deeply involved in Salzburg's cultural life. He and his brother Ernst were among the first students to enroll at Salzburg's music school, the *Mozarteum*, and one of them worked as an extra at the Salzburg Festival.[138] Bonyhadi even attended the first performance of *Jedermann*, and remembers the great impression made by the voice of God from the Cathedral as he viewed Reinhardt's first production:

> The biggest sensation of all was the opening performance of *Jedermann* directed by Max Reinhardt in 1920. I attended the first performance. It impressed me unbelievably when I heard God's voice calling down from the cathedral. . . . Many of the actors were Jews. Max Reinhardt and others, for example, they were Jews . . . The festival and especially *Jedermann* lent Salzburg another face, as many people came from out of town in order to experience the performances.[139]

Bonyhadi's statement indicates that the festival succeeded in speaking to a broad audience composed of Catholic and non-Catholic members. Reinhardt and Hofmannsthal set out to shape a festival that could, through high culture, provide a sense of inclusive national consciousness. In order to do so, they needed to exclude from their endeavors not Jews themselves, but any traces of the Jewish—a feat best served by a Catholic baroque aesthetic in a provincial setting. Yet Bonyhadi's memoir and the enthusiastic attendance of other Austrian Jews attest to the successful result of this elite, yet inclusive, performance of national culture. Even Alfred Polgar, whose critiques of Reinhardt's productions were usually highly skeptical, observed that Festival performances created a sense of inclusive community, noting that "somehow the seated individual feels his individuality reduced. Just by being there he becomes part of a community."[140]

While the Salzburg Festival represented an attempt to construct a new Austrian national culture from "true Austrian" baroque and Catholic sources, Yiddish drama attempted to keep alive an "authentic" ideal of Eastern European Jewish cultural heritage. Although the Salzburg Festival at times made use of innovative musical techniques, and Yiddish drama was often associated with expressionism and the avant-garde, both forms of theater ultimately looked to the past for their dramatic appeal. Their modern interpretations of spiritual cultures of the past—whether evocative of Yiddish or of the Catholic baroque—allowed for dynamic new cultural forms that fulfilled audiences' desires for an emotional experience that could bind them to the ideals of a stable cultural heritage. The appeal of both theaters derived from their ability to use evocative religious imagery and language to invoke what their audiences believed was a deep, spiritual, and above all "redemptive" experience, allowing them to release themselves from the burden of the losses of World War I—individual loved ones, and collective national identities—in order to construct new ways of reconciling their places within the new Austria, whether the means of that construction was Zionist-socialist-Yiddish or Austrian-Catholic-baroque. Both the baroque Catholic theatricality of the national Salzburg Festival and the mystical Judaism of Yiddish theater finally spoke to broader issues of national and cultural self-identification. That Jewish Austrians—or Austrians engaged with Jewishness—led the drive to create and support *both* forms of theater illuminates the crucial role its binary played in the development of culture after the collapse of the empire.

CONCLUSION

AUSTRIA'S JEWISH PAST AND THE FUTURE

It is a historical fact that Jews were a significant presence in Austrian culture and life before 1938, just as they were largely absent after 1945. Even before the *Anschluss*, however, the presence of Jews in Austria was already carefully circumscribed by absence. In the face of the political and social destabilization wrought by the collapse of the monarchy, Austrians continued to order their world according to the invisible framework of Jewish difference.[1] Anyone immersed in interwar public life had to be aware of the significance of this social and symbolic order, as coding people, places, and events as Jewish or non-Jewish took on new urgency amid the general sense of chaos and anxiety. In a new nation whose people were redefining what it meant to be Austrian, Jewish difference served as a crucial interpretive lens. But by 1938, those same elements of post–World War I confusion that had driven the transformation of Vienna into a center of vibrant political, social, and intellectual exchange completely excluded the very Jews who had helped bring about that transformation.

By the mid-1930s, political changes in Austria were bringing to an end the involvement of Jews in Austrian culture.[2] In February 1934, thousands of Austrian workers rose up against the Austrofascist Dolfuss regime; the subsequent proscription of the Social Democratic Party brought radical changes for Vienna's roughly 170,000 Jews who found their activities and ways of life severely curtailed.[3] The government banned the Socialist newspapers and cultural associations in which many of them had been involved, and the atmosphere at events like the Salzburg Festival became increasingly and openly antisemitic.[4]

In the days immediately preceding and following the *Anschluss* on March 12, 1938, Jews faced sudden violent and public antisemitic persecution. Thousands were arrested, many had their property confiscated, and others were forced to wash the streets with brushes as onlookers cheered. The Nazis "Aryanized" Max Reinhardt's castle

Schloss Leopoldskron in Salzburg and removed Reinhardt and Hofmannsthal's names from busts and nameplates.[5] The festival itself continued, but without its Jewish founders, participants, and audience members. The *Anschluss* also put an end to Yiddish theater in Vienna, as most of its actors, theater owners, critics, and audience were forced to flee, or were murdered; for many years, the very fact that it had even existed was forgotten—or denied.

Under the new regime, Austrians found themselves defined as Jewish not according to invisible categories, but by Nazi racial policies. Faced with a choice between emigration and persecution—and a third option for many: suicide—Austria's Jews largely disappeared. A number of the figures included in this study were able to flee to the United States, England, and elsewhere. Philipp Halsmann, banished from Austria long before 1938, made a name for himself as a photographer in France, and later in the United States. The identity of his father's murderer remains unknown to this day, but the events in the Tyrol left a lasting impression on his work. Mela Hartwig and Veza Canetti both fled to England, but, unfortunately, neither of them continued to write. Abraham Moshe Fuchs eventually settled in Israel, where he wrote short stories and became a journalist. Ella Zwieback and Max Reinhardt established new homes in the United States, where Vicki Baum had already achieved success as a novelist and writer of screenplays. Zwieback longed to return to Vienna, but her son Ludwig, with whom she had fled, rejected the possibility, so they remained in the United States. Wherever they went, however, these writers and artists continued to live with their experiences of Jewishness in Vienna and Austria between the Wars

The Austrian Example of Jewishness

Steven Beller has repeatedly pointed out that the project of distinguishing Jews from non-Jews began long before the Nazis came to power and was not restricted to antisemites.[6] This distinction was a deeply embedded, inescapable part of Central European culture that became particularly acute during the fraught interwar period. At the beginning of the First World War, Arthur Schnitzler wrote in his autobiography that "It was not possible, particularly for a Jew in the public eye, to avoid being seen as a Jew, since the others did not do it, not the Christians and the Jews even less."[7] Eric Hobsbawm later described his family's experiences in interwar Vienna similarly: "Though entirely unobservant, we nevertheless knew that we were, and could not get away from being, Jews."[8]

The lives and works of Austrians engaged this awareness in a variety of ways. For instance, although the interwar power struggles between Vienna and the provinces often had nothing to do with Jews, Austrians relied upon the terms of

Jewish difference to articulate their meaning. Like all binary processes according to which meaning is constructed, the terms of Jewish difference often remained unarticulated in Austrian culture, but this very "invisibility" could be its most powerful quality. We thus can better understand why, regardless of their degree of Jewish self-identification and their explicit intentions, Austrians seemed unable to escape repeating its terms. Even if they supported Jews, individually or as a group, their (often unwitting) investment in the idea of Jewish difference maintained the terms of the system that excluded Jews and their difference.

The implications of this approach to understanding Jewish difference can lead to a more nuanced—and ultimately more thorough—exploration of Jewishness in the lives and works of Austrians and others. It allows us to move beyond the common phenomenon of labeling Jews who express antisemitic sentiments as self-hating, and focus instead on how they used the terms of Jewishness to shape and inform their lives works. As Georg Stefan Troller notes, the admiration of many of Vienna's Jews for what they perceived as an unattainable, "Aryan" ideal did not render them parasitic followers of a foreign culture, but rather served as the driving force according to which they made that culture their own.[9]

It also helps us understand how those who were sympathetic to Jews could repeat the terms of their exclusion. This phenomenon can be found quite explicitly in the work of Robert Musil, who specifically understood the necessities—and dangers—of relying on symbolic orders in times of crisis.[10] In his fiction, Musil recognized the dangerous potency of contemporary ideologies.[11] But even as he attempted to refute antisemitic claims of Jewish predominance in Central European culture, he could not escape the bounds of the terms according to which the problem was structured. In an unpublished essay from 1933, he takes antisemites to task for accusing "men of intellect" like himself of being "so corrupted by Jewishness that we no longer heard or saw anything that had not been passed through a Jewish filter."[12] To refute this accusation, he tallies up the most influential publishers, writers, and other sources of contemporary German culture he can think of, producing a list of "twenty-three Aryans, eleven Jews, and two half-Jews." He concludes that, although Jewish authors dominate in the theater, the same cannot be said when it comes to novels in contemporary Germany, and he ends his calculations triumphant at having proven the antisemitic claim false. Yet Musil remains blind to the fact that his very arithmetic hardly destabilizes the basis of antisemitism.[13] Rather, his attempt to disprove antisemitic claims reveals just how deeply these hierarchical codings of Jewish difference were embedded in interwar Central Europe's cultural matrix.

This broadened approach also allows us to move beyond searching for explicit expressions of Jewishness in order to determine whether and how a person's life or work engaged the terms of Jewish difference. Cultural luminaries like Sigmund

Freud, Arthur Schnitzler, and Karl Kraus have been the subject of deep and thoughtful inquiries about the degree to which their Jewish self-understandings may or may not have affected their work.[14] Given that these figures explicitly engage with Jewish subject matter (in works like Freud's *Moses and Monotheism* and Schnitzler's *The Road into the Open*), it has made intellectual sense to interrogate their relationships to Jewishness. But culture that rarely—or never—addresses Jewish subject matter, created by artists and thinkers with a range of Jewish self-identifications, can also reveal much about the nature of Jewish difference. To be sure, there are built-in obstacles to such inquiries. A number of prominent scholars and advocates argue that highlighting the Jewishness of acculturated, secular Jews who rejected that definition recapitulates the essentialist logic of Nazism.[15] But such statements of rejection or denial themselves call for attention and analysis—especially in the case of Austrian Jews, and others like them, who faced enormous pressures. Otherwise, we end up naturalizing the divisions between Jews and non-Jews as "self-evident" when these divisions are precisely what require our critical examination.

As Joan Scott reminds us, effective scholarship ends when historians allow the subjects they study to define the terms in which they can be understood.[16] Scott acknowledges the temptation to consider eyewitness reports as the pinnacle of truth: "What could be truer than the subject's own account of what he or she has lived through?"[17] But she points out that by doing so, we lose the distance necessary to examine the framework that set them up to be excluded in the first place. Quite simply, good history cannot allow the evidence of experience to naturalize, rather than document, the forces of the past, no matter how painful it may be to subject the testimony of those most negatively affected by society to the same distanced scrutiny typically reserved for their tormentors. Throughout this book, I have tried to remain mindful of this fact, while at the same time respecting the insights of those who personally experienced interwar Austria. As Leora Auslander notes, "Part of the scholar's job is, in fact, to determine how gender, race or Jewishness may have mattered even when the subjects of research thought that it didn't."[18]

On the Margins

Marking the parameters of Jewish difference when those parameters are not self-evident requires both critical distance and careful consideration of the cultural circumstances within which that difference functioned. Scholars have begun to use this lens to extend their inquiries into interwar Austrian culture, and their work has the potential to further develop our understanding of how the lives and works of some major figures of the period engaged with the terms of

Jewish difference. In turn, these explorations can serve as a model for a new form of Jewish studies that could be deployed to understand other times and places.

Music is a particularly rich area for such exploration, not least because of its distance from the methods of signification and representation in texts and images.[19] This methodological complexity makes the writing of interwar Austrian composers a good place to start to consider their unarticulated yet palpable engagements with Jewish difference. Scholars have already begun to probe the connections between their writings and music.[20] For example, Heinrich Schenker's seminal work *Der Tonwille* (1921–1923) proclaims the superiority of German music in its opening essay, "The Mission of German Genius."[21] Schenker, a Jew from Galicia, considered himself an outsider in the professional world of Vienna, and most of his patrons were indeed Jews.[22] Leon Botstein recognizes Schenker's use of codings of Jewish difference in his writings, but Nicholas Cook digs deeper, linking Schenker's musical preoccupation with surface and depth to Freud's archeological metaphors, and suggesting that their mutual concern with probing hidden depths was a way to address accusations of Jewish "superficiality."[23] Beyond describing this phenomenon as a response to antisemitism, however, Cook claims that Schenker's theory translates social values into musical terms by showing how instrumental music can express "mutual abrasion or reconciliation between individual interests, or between the interests of individual and state."[24]

Recent studies of Arnold Schoenberg also indicate that his compositions that do not explicitly deal with Jewish themes may nevertheless provide deep insight into the role of Jewish difference on his life and work. Though Schoenberg became a supporter of Jewish unity and a Jewish state after being forced to leave Austria in 1933, his earlier nationalist proclamations about the superiority of German music are well-known. In an interesting new vein, Klára Móricz argues that, with his invention of twelve-tone music, Schoenberg, by his own admission, hoped to further German music by creating a new musical system completely free of anything foreign—a project which had everything to do with his rejection of his own Jewish self-identification.[25] In 1919, he even went so far as to propose to the Austrian Ministry of Culture that their musical policy affirm the superiority of the German nation.[26] This very effort, she suggests, indicates his system's engagement with Jewish difference.

Philosophy was another area where ideas were often coded according to the terms of Jewish difference. Chapter 2 showed how the coding of the Vienna Circle and logical positivism as "Jewish" played a significant role in both the death of Moritz Schlick and the release of his murderer. Yet, the nonessentialist nature of these categories is evident when Malachi Hacohen notes that Karl Popper's critique of logical positivism can also be viewed as an engagement with the terms of Jewishness. Hacohen attributes Popper's "relentless hostility toward any nationalism (Zionism was his favorite example), his rejection of any and all religion (Judaism more than Christianity), his belief in an international legal order (rare among a generation witnessing the League of Nations failure), his passionate defense of the Enlightenment," as well as what he coined the "Open Society," to his experiences as a Jew in interwar Vienna. Popper rejected both German and Jewish nationalism in favor of "uncompromising cosmopolitanism"—a universalist vision that had everything to do with an engagement with Jewish difference.[27]

Other potentially fruitful subjects of investigation include the lives and works of Hans Kelsen, drafter of the Austrian constitution in 1920 and professor of law at the University of Vienna, and his contemporary Ludwig von Mises, the economist who served as Privatdozent at the University of Vienna and as economic advisor at the Austrian Chamber of Commerce. Kelsen was born in Prague and Mises in Lemberg (Galicia) in 1881; both moved with their families to Vienna in the 1890s, where they attended the Akademisches Gymnaisum.[28] Since both engaged deeply with the relationship between Vienna and the provinces in the First Republic, examining how the terms of Jewish difference inflected their legal and economic philosophies might give us greater insight into how and why Jewishness mattered in their lives and works, beyond simply mentioning their family backgrounds or their reactions to antisemitism.[29]

These examples from music, philosophy, law, and economics are hardly exhaustive. Widening the scope of inquiry to include a broad range of subjects can reveal how Austrians responded to the terms of Jewish difference that were becoming increasingly important during the interwar period, even as they often remained invisible. They also represent potentially new directions in the study of Jews, Jewish difference, and their role in the creation of Central European culture in general. It may be impossible to understand Jewish experiences in Central Europe between the World Wars—the past *before* the past—without allowing the devastating events that followed—the Holocaust—to influence our understanding. But that influence can also drive us to recognize and attempt to articulate the integral role Jews and Jewish difference played in the formation of Austrian cultural history.

NOTES

Introduction

1. Arthur Schnitzler's novel *Der Weg ins Freie* was originally published in 1908; Horace Samuel's English translation appeared in 1923 as *The Road to the Open*. The only other explicit thematization of Jews and antisemitism in Schnitzler's fiction occurs in his 1912 play *Professor Bernhardi: Komödie in fünf Akten*, although he deals with Jewish issues more obliquely in a number of his other works. See Abigail Gillman, *Viennese Jewish Modernism: Freud, Hofmannsthal, Beer-Hofmann and Schnitzler* (University Park: Penn State University Press, 2009), 101–26; Bettina Riedmann, *"Ich bin Jude, Österreicher, Deutscher." Judentum in Arthur Schnitzlers Tagebüchern und Briefen* (Tübingen: Niemeyer, 2002); Bettina Riedmann, "Arthur Schnitzler. Facetten einer jüdisch-österreichisch-deutschen Identität," in *Wien und die jüdische Erfahrung: Akkulturation—Antisemitismus—Zionismus*, ed. Frank Stern and Barbara Eichinger (Vienna: Böhlau, 2009); and Nikolaj Beier, *"Vor allem bin ich ich—": Judentum, Akkulturation und Antisemitismus in Arthur Schnitzlers Leben und Werk* (Göttingen: Wallstein, 2008).
2. J. L. Benvenisti, "Arthur Schnitzler Foretells Jewish Renaissance. An Exclusive Interview with the Eminent Littérateur," *American Hebrew*, February 29, 1924, 460, 474.
3. Considering that Schnitzler's politically contentious 1912 play *Professor Bernhardi* could only be performed in Austria after the lifting of censorship laws in 1918, it makes sense that he expressed hope for Jews' cultural future. And although antisemitic disturbances had accompanied the production of his controversial play *Reigen* in Vienna in February, 1921, performances nevertheless continued through June, 1922—sometimes twice a day due to high demand. On Schnitzler's ambivalent relationship to Jews and Viennese cultural politics during the interwar period, see Judith Beniston, "Schnitzler in Red Vienna," in *Arthur*

Schnitzler: Zeitgenossenschaften/Contemporaneities, ed. Ian Foster and Florian Krobb (Bern: Peter Lang, 2002), 217.

4. The city's amusement and entertainment sectors, in which Jews participated significantly, flourished until the mid-1920s. The Austrian film industry peaked in 1923, but due to decreased funding, high interest rates, and the growing impossibility of keeping film production companies afloat, the number of films produced sank to fifteen in 1924 and to only four in 1925. Armin Loacker, "Werkstätten der Seh(n)sucht: Produktionsgeschichte und Produktionsstrukturen des monumentalen Antikfilms in Österreich," in *Imaginierte Antike. Österreichische Monumental-Stummfilme, Historienbilder und Geschichtskonstruktion in Sodom und Gomorrha, Samson und Delila, Die Sklavenkönigen und Salammbô*, ed. Armin Loacker and Ines Steiner (Vienna: Filmarchiv Austria, 2002). By 1919, many of Vienna's 150 cinemas ranked among the most technologically advanced in the world; Jews owned a number of them. For an extensive list see Stefan Templ and Tina Walzer, *Unser Wien: "Arisierung" auf österreichisch* (Berlin: Aufbau, 2001). On the high percentage of Jewish-owned cinemas in Vienna, see Werner Michael Schwarz, *Kino und Kinos in Wien: Eine Entwicklungsgeschichte bis 1934* (Vienna: Turia & Kant, 1992), 173–74. Austrian Jews also participated in the film industry as writers, directors, and producers. As Robert von Dassanowky points out, cameraman Jakob Julius Fleck, who was Jewish, was one of the first Austrians to produce feature films at the turn of the century, together with Louise Veltée and her husband Anton Kolm. Later, Veltée divorced Kolm and married Fleck. The couple continued to make films together in Vienna until 1922, when they moved to Berlin; they returned to Vienna in 1933 after Hitler's takeover. Others include Kurt Gerron, Otto Wallburg, Fritz Grünbaum, Ida Jenbach, Rudolf Meinert, Robert Dorsey, Paul Morgan, Joachim Gottschalk, Alfred Deutsch-German, Siegfried Lembach, and Max Ehrlich. Robert von Dassanowsky, *Austrian Cinema: A History* (Jefferson, NC: McFarland, 2005), 8–9, 16, 34, 270. Interwar Austrian films with Jewish themes included *Ost und West* (1923) and *Jiskor* (1924) (both directed by Austrian-American Sidney M. Goldin), *Theodor Herzl-der Bannerträger des jüdischen Volkes* (1921), *Der Jude von Granada* (1923), *Die Stadt ohne Juden* (1924), and *Der Fluch* (1924). Brigitte Dalinger, "Popular Jewish Drama in Vienna in the 1920s," in *Jewish Theatre: A Global View*, ed. Edna Nahshon (Leiden: Brill, 2009), 175; and Irene Stratenwerth and Hermann Simon, eds., *Pioniere in Celluloid: Juden in der frühen Filmwelt* (Berlin: Henschel, 2004), 223. German-language dramas with Jewish themes that were performed in Vienna but never published included *Der getaufte Enkel* by Beda [Fritz Löhner, pseud.], performed in 1914, and Else Feldmann's *Der Schrei, den Niemand Hört: Trauerspiel aus dem Ghetto*, performed in 1916. See Dalinger, "Popular Jewish Drama," 178–79. On Feldmann see Lisa Silverman, "*Zwischenzeit* and *Zwischenort*: Veza Canetti, Else Feldmann, and Jewish Writing in Interwar Vienna," *Prooftexts: A Journal of Jewish Literary History* 26, nos. 1–2 (2006): 42–46.

5. On the brief but intense period of Hebrew modernism in Vienna, see Shachar M. Pinsker, *Literary Passports: The Making of Modernist Hebrew Fiction in Europe* (Stanford: Stanford University Press, 2011), 90, 93.
6. Luba Kadison and Joseph Buloff, *On Stage, Off Stage: Memories of a Lifetime in the Yiddish Theater* (Cambridge: Harvard University Library Press, 1992), 42–43.
7. Bruce F. Pauley, *From Prejudice to Persecution: A History of Austrian Anti-Semitism* (Chapel Hill: University of North Carolina Press, 1992), 81–83, 116, 194–95. For a discussion of antisemitism in Austria immediately following the end of World War I, see Pauley, "Political Antisemitism in Interwar Vienna," in *Jews, Antisemitism, and Culture in Vienna*, ed. Ivar Oxaal, Michael Pollak, and Gerhard Botz (London: Routledge, 1987), 153–157. Antisemitic rallies and demonstrations held in 1919, 1920, and one of the largest, attended by 40,000, in 1921, ebbed by 1922. However, they peaked again in the first three months of 1923, when a newly formed antisemitic committee organized a rally attended by up to 100,000 people. Pauley, *From Prejudice to Persecution*, 81. Moreover, in May 1923, on the occasion of the first World Congress of Jewish Women, antisemitic posters were distributed widely in the city. See Dieter J. Hecht, "Die Weltkongresse jüdischer Frauen in der Zwischenkriegszeit, Wien 1923, Hamburg 1929," in *Geschlecht, Religion und Engagement: Die jüdische Frauenbewegung im deutschsprachigen Raum*, ed. Margarete Grandner and Edith Saurer (Vienna: Böhlau, 2005), 132–33. Albert Lichtblau also claims that antisemitic violence ebbed between 1923 and the early 1930s. See "Partizipation und Isolation. Juden in Österreich in den 'langen' 1920er Jahren," *Archiv für Sozialgeschichte* 37 (1997): 249. Yet, sporadic attacks continued, some with grave consequences. In August, 1925, 106 people were arrested and twenty-one hurt at antisemitic demonstrations on the Ringstrasse against the Zionist World Congress. See "Schwere Hakenkreuzlerexzesse: Blutige Zusammenstöße mit der Wache auf dem Freiheitsplatz, Ausschreitungen in verschiedenen Bezirken der Stadt: 106 Verhaftungen und 21 Verletzte," *Neues Wiener Journal*, August 18, 1925, 1, 3. Robert Lawrence recalls that in 1929, when he was a student at the University of Vienna, he saw an especially brutal poster in the hall depicting a large, swastika-shaped tank rolling over the bodies of Jews and Marxists. See "Mein Leben in Oesterreich vor und nach Hitlers Occupation," unpublished manuscript, Houghton Library, Harvard University, bMS Ger 91, 8. For an overview of these sporadic attacks, see Lichtblau, "Das fragile Korsett der Koexistenz: Zum Verhältnis von jüdischer und nichtjüdischer Bevölkerung in Österreich 1918 bis 1938," in *Zwischen großen Erwartungen und bösem Erwachen: Juden, Politik und Antisemitismus in Ost- und Südeuropa, 1918-1945*, ed. Dittmar Dahlmann and Anke Hilbrenner (Paderborn: Ferdinand Schöningh, 2010), 37–39.
8. Albert Lichtblau makes a similar argument that, while the terms of antisemitism had been set long before the collapse of the dual monarchy, what changed during the interwar period was its ideological significance to political parties and the

intensified ways in which it was expressed, including signs on public places proclaiming "Juden raus" and attacks on individuals coded as "Jewish." See "Das fragile Korsett," 32, 37. See also Peter G. J. Pulzer's seminal study, *The Rise of Political Antisemitism in Germany and Austria* (London: Halban, 1988).

9. Carl Schorske, *Fin-de-Siècle Vienna: Politics and Culture* (New York: Vintage, 1981); Allan Janik and Stephan Toulmin, *Wittgenstein's Vienna* (New York: Simon and Schuster, 1973); and Steven Beller, ed., *Rethinking Vienna 1900* (New York: Berghahn, 2001). Steven Beller, however, has produced pioneering research on the role of acculturated Jews in shaping modern Austrian culture, and does cover the period up to 1938 in a number of his studies. His discussion of Jewish cultural creativity in Austria has helped me develop many of the ideas in this book. See *Vienna and the Jews, 1867–1938: A Cultural History* (New York: Cambridge University Press, 1989); and *Was nicht im Baedeker steht: Juden und andere Österreicher im Wien der Zwischenkriegszeit* (Vienna: Picus, 2008).
10. On this phenomenon see Deborah Holmes and Lisa Silverman, eds., *Interwar Vienna: Culture between Tradition and Modernity* (Rochester, NY: Camden House, 2009).
11. Georg Stefan Troller, who was born in Vienna in 1921, captures the tension between the flowering of Jewish creativity amidst widespread antisemitic sentiment when he describes this so-called Silver Age as the "last great gasp of primarily Jewish creativity in central Europe." *Das fidele Grab an der Donau: Mein Wien 1918–1938* (Düsseldorf: Artemis & Winkler, 2004), 13. Further, Edward Timms suggests that the intellectual climate experienced a dramatic radicalization in the interwar period. See "School for Socialism: Karl Seitz and the Cultural Politics of Vienna," *Austrian Studies 14: Culture and Politics in Red Vienna* (2006): 46 and "Cultural Parameters between the Wars: A Reassessment of the Vienna Circles," in Holmes and Silverman, *Interwar Vienna*, 26.
12. Lisa Silverman, "The Transformation of Jewish Identity in Vienna, 1918–1938" (Ph.D. diss., Yale University, 2005).
13. Jews made up a disproportionally large percentage of Austrian bankers, landlords, and merchants, and were hardest hit by financial crises after the war. For example, ten of the twelve banks that went bankrupt in the early 1920s were Jewish-owned. Pauley, *From Prejudice to Persecution*, 80.
14. Here, I use the term "social boundaries" in the sense Fredrik Barth used to describe the units of analysis in social systems. A focus on boundaries rather than the content of what is bounded by any particular group signals the awareness that the group under study is constructed, fluid, and often contested. In describing the situation of Jews in Austria-Hungary, Marsha L. Rozenblit indicates the usefulness of Barth's term of "ethnic boundaries" in helping to demonstrate the subjectivity of constructed Jewish ethnic self-understandings, as well as the perception that nonreligious Jews still formed a distinct group despite their acculturation to the larger society. See Marsha L. Rozenblit, *Reconstructing a National Identity:*

The Jews of Habsburg Austria during World War I (New York: Oxford University Press, 2001), 7–8; and Fredrik Barth, ed., *Ethnic Groups and Boundaries: The Social Organization of Cultural Difference* (Boston: Little, Brown, 1969).

15. The terms of antisemitism and its effects in Austria were certainly not new; what shifted was the political context. What changed most was not the relationship of the "Jewish" and "not-Jewish" to each other, but rather the importance of that relationship in the context of the Austrian interwar period's destabilized political, social, and economic structures. As Malachi Hacohen makes clear in his study of Karl Popper and the complex relationship between his assimilationism and his drive for an imagined, cosmopolitan community, "Contrary to their aspirations, neither assimilated nor acculturated Viennese Jews became Austrian-Germans. Much like their predecessors in nineteenth-century Germany, they constituted a German Jewish community of their own, united by ethnic origins, social class, German education, the Enlightenment's ethos, liberal politics, and, of course, the anti-Semites' malice." *Karl Popper—the Formative Years, 1902–1945: Politics and Philosophy in Interwar Vienna*, (Cambridge: Cambridge University Press, 2000), 32–33. See also Steven Beller, "Patriotism and the National Identity of Habsburg Jewry, 1860–1914," *Leo Baeck Institute Year-Book* 41(1996); and Marsha L. Rozenblit, "Sustaining Austrian 'National' Identity in Crisis: The Dilemma of the Jews in Habsburg Austria, 1914–1919," in *Constructing Nationalities in East Central Europe*, ed. Pieter M. Judson and Marsha L. Rozenblit (New York: Berghahn, 2005). Steven Beller notes that, while most Austrians accepted the fact that Jews were an integral part of shaping culture during the interwar period, many of them still did not consider Jews to be "genuine" or "native" Austrians. See "Was *nicht* im Baedeker steht: Juden und andere Österreicher im Wien der Zwischenkriegszeit," in *Wien und die jüdische Erfahrung 1900–1938: Akkulturation—Antisemitismus—Zionismus*, ed. Frank Stern and Barbara Eichinger (Vienna: Böhlau, 2009), 12.
16. Marsha L. Rozenblit, "The Crisis of Identity in the Austrian Republic: Jewish Ethnicity in a New Nation-State," in *In Search of Jewish Community: Jewish Identities in Germany and Austria, 1918–1933*, ed. Michael Brenner and Derek Jonathan Penslar (Bloomington: Indiana University Press, 1998), 135. The works of dramatists Abisch Meisels and Leon Weissberg also reflect this point of view. Even if they are reluctant to go to war, their protagonists remain loyal to the idea of Austria-Hungary. See Dalinger, "Popular Jewish Drama," 180.
17. In using the terms "dual monarchy," "Austria-Hungary," and "Habsburg monarchy," I refer to the "kaiserliche und königliche (k. u. k.) Doppelmonarchie" (Imperial and Royal Dual Monarchy), the official name of the two sovereign halves into which the Austrian Empire was divided in 1867. As István Deák points out, although there was no official capital of the dual monarchy, Vienna continued to be regarded as such, and after 1867, the term "Austrian Empire"refers only to that part of the monarchy excluding Hungary and Bosnia-Herzegovina. István Deák, *Beyond Nationalism: A Social and Political History of the Habsburg Officer Corps*

1848-1918 (New York: Oxford, 1990), 11. The population of the Habsburg monarchy consisted of eleven officially recognized *Volksstämme* (nationalities), twelve ethnic subgroups, and sixteen religions. However, no official language existed in the Austrian half of the dual monarchy. Any real sense of "Austrianness" was upheld primarily by the bureaucracy, army officers, some of the nobility, and many Jews; these were the only groups whose self-identification relied heavily on multiple levels and loyalties. Michael John, "'We Do Not Even Possess Our Selves': On Identity and Ethnicity in Austria, 1880–1937," *Austrian History Yearbook* 30 (1999): 19–20, 44.

18. John Boyer points out that many Jews considered the aristocratic classes that ruled Austria-Hungary far too balanced to condone violent antisemitism. See *Culture and Political Crisis in Vienna: Christian Socialism in Power, 1897–1918* (Chicago: University of Chicago Press, 1995), 76. Rozenblit notes that in contrast to Jews in the German army, Jews in the Habsburg army felt especially comfortable, since they were allowed to serve as reserve officers and even, in a small number of cases, as career officers. Moreover, the army refused to investigate charges against Jews shirking their responsibility; however, this did not lead to greater integration but rather strengthened their self-identification as Jews. See Rozenblit, *Reconstructing*, 82, 93–94.
19. Some scholars have questioned whether life in Austria-Hungary can really be called a "Golden Age" of security for Jews. Siegfried Mattl suggests that political representation had become increasingly divided along ethnonational lines. See Malachi Hacohen, "Kosmopoliten in einer ethnonationalen Zeit? Juden und Österreicher in der Ersten Republik," in . . . *der Rest ist Österreich. Das Werden der Ersten Republik*, vol. 1, ed. Helmut Konrad and Wolfgang Maderthaner (Vienna: Carl Gerold's Sohn Verlag, 2008), 284. Nevertheless, what matters most here is how secure Jews considered their place in Austria-Hungary to be, and the effects of that emotional state, regardless of how safe it really was.
20. Joseph Bloch, *Der nationale Zwist und die Juden in Österreich* (Vienna: Gottlieb, 1886), 41.
21. Joseph Bloch, "Nichts gelernt und nichts vergessen," *Österreichische Wochenschrift*, June 22, 1917, 390. On Bloch's civic Austrian nationalism and belief in a supraethnic Austrian nationhood, see Ian Reifowitz, *Imagining an Austrian Nation: Joseph Samuel Bloch and the Search for a Supraethnic Austrian Identity, 1846–1918* (New York: Columbia University Press, 2003). As evidence that the unconditional loyalty of Austrian Jews to the state did not go unnoticed, many cite Franz Theodor Csokor's 1936 play about the dissolution of the Habsburg monarchy titled *3. November 1918*, which features army officers who declare their various national loyalties—Hungary, Poland, etc.—as they throw earth into a grave; the Jewish army doctor is the only one to declare his loyalty as "Austrian."
22. Here, this book diverges from Michael Brenner's definition of Jewish culture in his study of Jews in Weimar Germany, which he describes as "All literary, artistic,

and scholarly expressions ... that consciously advanced a collective identity among German Jews, which differed from that of their non-Jewish surroundings ... It follows that German-Jewish culture must not be misunderstood to mean any literary, scholarly, or artistic production created by German speaking-Jews." *The Renaissance of Jewish Culture in Weimar Germany* (New Haven: Yale University Press, 1998), 5.

23. For examples of how such processes functioned among Viennese Jews at the turn of the century, see Klaus Hödl, "The Blurring of Distinction: Performance and Jewish Identities in Late Nineteenth-Century Vienna," *European Journal of Jewish Studies* (November 2009): 249. I agree with Hödl that definitions of the "Jewish" cannot be fixed, and that stressing performance allows for instantaneous articulations that more accurately describe the processes of their formation. Nevertheless, I claim that the *idea* of fixed binary categories defining the Jewish and the non-Jewish is apparent in a wide range of contexts, and as such needs to be taken seriously as a crucial component of how Austrians defined themselves and others.

24. Otto Weininger was one of the first to explicitly detail the abstract, analytical terms of Jewish difference. In his study *Geschlecht und Charakter* (1903; *Sex and Character*), he describes the "Jewish" as a negative *Gattung* (category) related to the "feminine" that can take any shape precisely because of its lack of qualities. He also stressed that these catgories stemmed from, but were not equal to, actual Jews and non-Jews: ". . . one should not confuse *Judentum* (Jewishness) with Jews." See *Geschlecht und Charakter* (München: Matthes und Seitz, 1997), 407. Weininger's thoughts on this issue are unfortunately accompanied by—and in that sense, are inseparable from—vitriolic, hate-filled rhetoric against Jews and women. But the fact that this book resonated with such a broad spectrum of Austrians, including Jews, indicates the necessity of looking beyond its rhetoric to its underlying assumptions. For discussion of Weininger and others' ideas about Jewishness and gender, see Nancy A. Harrowitz, *Antisemitism, Misogyny and the Logic of Cultural Difference* (Lincoln: University of Nebraska Press, 1995); and Nancy A. Harrowitz and Barbara Hymans, eds. *Jews and Gender, Responses to Otto Weininger* (Philadelphia: Temple University Press, 1995). On reading Weininger in the intellectual climate of his time, see David S. Luft, *Eros and Inwardness in Vienna: Weininger, Musil, Doderer* (Chicago: University of Chicago Press), 2003.

25. Judith Butler briefly hints at such a framework: "The 'Jew' is no more defined by Israel than by antisemitism. The 'Jew' exceeds both determinations, and is to be found, substantively, as a historically and culturally changing identity that takes no single form and has no single telos." See "The Charge of Anti-Semitism: the Risks of Public Critique" in *Prophets Outcast: A Century of Dissident Jewish Writing about Zionism and Israel*, ed. Adam Schatz (New York: Nation Books, 2004), 367. On the benefits of a broader, more inclusive approach to Jewish Studies, see Steven Beller, "Knowing Your Elephant: Why Jewish Studies is not

the same as Judaistik, and why that is a good thing," in *Jüdische Studien: Reflexionen zu Theorie und Praxis eines wissenschaftlichen Feldes: Schriften des Centrums für jüdische Studien* 4, ed. Klaus Hödl (Innsbruck: Studienverlag, 2003).

26. I explore Jewish difference as a category of critical analysis in the modern era further in "Beyond Antisemitism: A Critical Approach to German Jewish Cultural History," *Nexus: Essays in German Jewish Studies* 1 (2011). My understanding of the uses of gendered analysis in historical study is indebted to Joan W. Scott's article, "Gender: A Useful Category of Historical Analysis," *American Historical Review* 91, no. 5 (1986). On the use of Jewish difference as a category of analysis for texts from earlier eras, see Lisa Lampert, *Gender and Jewish Difference from Paul to Shakespeare* (Philadelphia: University of Pennsylvania Press, 2004).
27. Here, I draw from Judith Halberstam's insightful work on the concept of "female masculinity" and the utility of considering the "masculine" as a concept separate from the male body. See *Female Masculinity* (Durham: Duke University Press, 1998).
28. Georg Stefan Troller describes the separation of the "Jew" from the "Jewish" as follows: "Whoever didn't participate in the 'masquerade' of Austrian folklore counted as a Jew, and if he didn't happen to be one, he would be characterized by such 'tasteful' labels like 'tinged, polluted, infected with Jewishness.'" Troller, *Das fidele Grab*, 11. Others idealized the "Jewish" essence more positively as typified by an "authentic" *Ostjude*, who stemmed from humble origins in a Galician shtetl, spoke Yiddish, and who was, ideally, uninterested in material pusuits and steeped in age-old, wise Jewish religious practice.
29. Butler's stress on the performative underscores her contention that "gender" is a always a "doing" rather than a static state of being. Judith Butler, *Gender Trouble: Feminism and the Subversion of Identity* (New York: Routledge, 1999), 33, 45. Butler also refers to the "transferability of the attributes" of gender, which means that men can perform femininity and women can perform masculinity. *Undoing Gender* (New York: Routledge, 2004), 213. The same holds true for Jewish difference. In emphasizing this simple binary system of Jewish difference, I do not wish to exclude the range of possible identifications beyond the simple categories of "Jewish" and "not-Jewish" that arise from it. Like gender, this binary system only represents the basis for a range of possible identifications along a continuum. A person, place, or thing be coded as neither, both, or some form of hybrid. My point is that, even though the world is far more complex than the "Jewish"/"not-Jewish" binary appears to offer, we cannot ignore that the culture of this period reflects the fact that people often acted as if this simple binary existed.
30. Scott Spector suggests that evincing the German/Jewish dialectical structure requires both a sceptical attitude toward these traditional categories, as well as a "sensitivity to the conditions under which they were produced and painstaking care in following how these conditions were actually lived." See "Forget assimilation: Introducing subjectivity to German-Jewish history," *Jewish History* 20, nos. 3–4 (2006): 361.

31. Rozenblit, *Reconstructing*, 7–8.
32. Klaus Hödl, *Wiener Juden—jüdische Wiener: Identität, Gedächtnis und Performanz im 19. Jahrhundert* (Innsbruck: Studienverlag, 2006), 50–63. Hödl maps Jewish culture in Vienna along similar lines, although he cautions that binaries like "center/periphery" and "Jewish/not-Jewish" risk excluding other processes of cultural exchange.
33. For Jews in the dual monarchy, "Austrian" was never a concept of national identity along the same lines as other forms of national self-identification. Jews imagined Habsburg Austria along the lines of a "civic" nation to which they could remain loyal. See Rozenblit, "Sustaining Austrian 'National' Identity," 180. Rozenblit also claims that a lack of Austrian "national identity" was a factor in facilitating Jewish "ethnic identity." See Rozenblit, *Reconstructing*, 177 n. 34; and Rozenblit, "Jewish Ethnicity," 134–53. For many Austrians, "Austrianness" had less to do with patriotism and national self-identification than it did with forming collective self-identifications along other lines, such as geography, religion, or even occupation. As William Bowman points out, "National activists and politicians may have wanted to put the nation and nationality first in policy and quotidian developments; it is far from clear that 'Austrians' always did or do so." See his review essay of *Essay über Österreich: Grundfragen von Identität und Geschichte, 1918–2000*, by Dieter A. Binder and Ernst Bruckmüller, *From Vienna to Chicago and Back: Essays on Intellectual History and Political Thought in Europe and America*, by Gerald Stourzh, and *Der österreichische Mensch: Kulturgeschichte der Eigenart Österreichs*, by William M. Johnston, *Journal of Modern History* 83, no. 1 (March 2011): 227. Moreover, Jews who immigrated to Vienna before the First World War from Galicia, Bohemia, Moravia, and Hungary stemmed from a broad range of backgrounds even within those groupings, and often maintained these distinctions after they migrated to the city. See Marsha L. Rozenblit, "Jewish Immigrants in Vienna before the First World War, *Aschkenas—Zeitschrift für Geschichte und Kultur der Juden* 17, no. 1 (2007): 45. For a useful and original argument about "national indifference"rather than national distinctions as a category of historical analysis, see Tara Zahra, *Kidnapped Souls: National Indifference and the Battle for Children in the Bohemian Lands 1900–1948* (Ithaca, NY: Cornell University Press, 2008).
34. See also Leora Auslander's article outlining the issues involved in considering what was implicitly "Jewish" about modern European culture, "The Boundaries of Jewishness or When Is a Cultural Practice Jewish?" *Journal of Modern Jewish Studies* 8, no. 1 (2009).
35. Michael P. Steinberg, *Judaism Musical and Unmusical* (Chicago: University of Chicago Press, 2007), 18. Darcy Buerkle outlines this problem clearly in her work on Norbert Elias and his preoccupation with manners, according to which an engagement with Jewishness appears not explicitly but rather as an "elaborately circumscribed absence." See "Caught in the Act. Norbert Elias, Emotion and the Ancient Law," *Journal of Modern Jewish Studies* 8, no. 1 (2009).

36. While other states like Czechoslovakia gained territory, Austria became a republic comprised of the lands that remained after the formation of other successor states. Austrians' general lack of enthusiasm for the formation of a new country has been well-documented. Many thought annexation to Germany represented the best solution, and others longed for a return of the former monarchy. But after World War I, the French were particularly adamant that Austria not be allowed to fortify the German Reich by joining Germany and rejected Austrian requests for regaining land that it lost to other territories during the peace negotiations.
37. Eric Hobsbawm, *Interesting Times: A Twentieth-Century Life* (New York: Pantheon, 2002), 8.
38. Stefan Zweig, *The World of Yesterday: An Autobiography* (New York: Viking, 2008), 215.
39. Austrians intensely debated the name for their new nation; Gerald Strouzh suggests this in itself to be a symptom of a broader identity crisis. Gerald Stourzh, *Vom Reich zur Republik: Studium zum Österreichbewußtsein im 20. Jahrhundert* (Vienna: Wiener Journal Schriftenverlag, 1990), 76. See also Gerald Stourzh, "Erschütterung und Konsolidierung des Österreichbewußtseins vom Zusammenbruch der Monarchie zur zweiten Republik," in *Was Heißt Österreich? Inhalt uns Umfang des Österreichbegriffs vom 10. Jahrhundert bis heute*, ed. Richard G. Plaschka, Gerald Stourzh, and Jan Niederkorn (Vienna: Archiv für österreichische Geschichte, 1995).
40. John W. Boyer, "The End of an Old Regime: Visions of Political Reform in Late Imperial Austria," in *Journal of Modern History* 58, no. 1 (1986): 161 and Boyer, *Culture and Political Crisis*, 369.
41. Modris Eksteins, *Rites of Spring: the Great War and the birth of the Modern Age* (New York: Mariner, 1989), 255.
42. Edward Timms, *Karl Kraus: Apocalyptic Satirist: Culture and Catastrophe in Habsburg Vienna* (New Haven: Yale University Press, 1989), 30–31.
43. Marsha L. Rozenblit, "The Dilemma of Identity: The Impact of the First World War on Habsburg Jewry," *Austrian Studies 5: The Habsburg Legacy. National Identity in Historical Perspective* (1994): 151.
44. Their numbers fluctuated throughout the war, reaching its highest point in 1915 with 77,090, most of whom would eventually return to their original residences, usually Galicia or the Bukovina. Beatrix Hoffmann-Holter, *'Abreisendmachung:' Jüdische Kriegsflüchtlinge in Wien 1914 bis 1923* (Vienna: Böhlau, 1995), 97, 283. See also David Rechter, "Galicia in Vienna: Jewish Refugees in the First World War," *Austrian History Yearbook* 28 (1997).
45. Minna Lachs recounts her shame at having been born in Poland, and remembers that catcalls of "*Judensau*" (Jew pig) increased when refugees arrived in Vienna, although she points out that these prejudices were by no means limited to those years. Minna Lachs, *Warum schaust du zurück: Erinnerungen 1907–1941* (Vienna: Europaverlag, 1986), 48.

46. An antisemitic rally held on September 25, 1919, in front of city hall attracted five thousand members; eight speakers complained that Galician Jewish refugees caused Aryans to starve. A rally on October 5 drew a crowd of fifteen thousand. In 1920, one rally erupted into an assault on passersby who "looked Jewish." Pauley, *From Prejudice to Persecution*, 81.
47. On negative attitudes toward Eastern European Jews held by other Jews in Central Europe see Steven E. Aschheim, *Brothers and Strangers: The East European Jew in German and German Jewish Consciousness 1800–1923* (Madison: University of Wisconsin Press, 1983).
48. On the relationship between the turbulent politics and cultural achievements at this time in Germany, see Eric Weitz, *Weimar Germany: Promise and Tragedy* (Princeton: Princeton University Press, 2007), 2–3.
49. Melech Rawitsch, *Das Geschichtenbuch meines Lebens: Auswahl*, trans. Armin Eidherr (Salzburg: Otto Müller, 1996), 171.
50. Helmut Gruber, *Red Vienna: Experiment in Working-Class Culture, 1919–1934* (New York: Oxford University Press, 1991), 28, 196 n. 80. Olaf Blaschke argues that latent antisemitism was fundamental to Catholic culture in Germany, even if it was not high on their agenda of issues, and even if Catholic leaders made efforts to distance themselves politically from overt antisemites. *Katholizismus und Antisemitismus im deutschen Kaiserreich* (Göttingen: Vandenhoeck & Ruprecht, 1999).
51. See Anton Staudinger, "Katholischer Antisemitismus in der ersten Republik" in *Eine zerstörte Kultur: Jüdisches Leben und Antisemitismus in Wien seit dem 19. Jahrhundert*, 2nd ed., ed. Gerhard Botz, Ivar Oxaal, and Michael Pollak (Vienna: Czernin, 2002); and Gruber, *Red Vienna*, 28. John Boyer notes that the close connection between early Christian Social leaders and Catholicism had as much to do with its perception as a source of social and cultural stability as it did with privileging its religious norms. *Culture and Political Crisis*, 460.
52. Of course, there were many Catholics in Weimar Germany, too, but they were outnumbered by Protestants. Many of them considered Germany to be a "Protestant creation" in which they held little power. See Weitz, *Weimar Germany*, 89. Michael P. Steinberg helpfully identifies two intersecting spectra of culture in Austria between 1890 and 1938: a political one proceeding from the critical, avant-garde, or revolutionary to the conservative, and then a cultural/religious spectrum, according to which Jewishness is least integrated into mainstream society, Catholicity is the most integrated, and Protestantness falls somewhere in the middle. *Austria as Theater and Ideology: The Meaning of the Salzburg Festival* (Ithaca, NY: Cornell University Press, 1990), 172.
53. David Josef Bach, "Politik der Schuljungen," *Arbeiter-Zeitung*, January 3, 1905.
54. Beverley Driver Eddy, *Felix Salten: Man of Many Faces* (Riverside, CA: Ariadne, 2010), 23. This early immersion in Catholicism did not preclude his support for Jews and Zionism, which would grow in later years. However, Judaism

never became a significant part of Salten's Jewish self-identification. See Hilary Hope Herzog, *"Vienna is Different:" Jewish Writers in Austria from the fin de Siècle to the Present* (New York: Berghahn, 2011), 114–21; similarly, Joseph Roth turned to Catholicism even though his self-identification as a Jew developed steadily over his lifetime. Karl Kraus claimed he was motivated to leave the Catholic church in 1923 (he had joined in 1911) "primarily by antisemitism," alluding to his critique of the Salzburg Festival. Edward Timms, *Karl Kraus, Apocalyptic Satirist: The Post-War Crisis and the Rise of the Swastika* (New Haven: Yale University Press, 2005), 283.

55. Unlike other religious officials, Catholic priests were still paid by the state and allowed to hold public office after the end of World War I. See Gruber, *Red Vienna*, 27.

56. Elias Canetti, *Crowds and Power*, trans. Carol Stewart (New York: Farrar, 1984), 154–55, 179. Canetti states that a main defining characteristic of Catholic culture is its *lack* of a crowd: "The image of this multitude moving year after year through the desert has become the crowd symbol of the Jews. It has remained to this day as distinct and comprehensible as it was then. . . . In this state of density they received their law." On the other hand, "Catholicism owes the calm which, after its spaciousness, is for many its strongest attraction, to its great age and its aversion to anything violently crowd-like. Its suspicion of the crowd is long-standing." Long ago, he claims, the Church decided the "open crowd" was its main enemy.

57. Jewish apostates increased from 349 in 1891 to 1401 in 1919. In 1923, a total of 1158 Jews converted, among them 649 men and 509 women. Though the overall numbers of Jewish apostates in Vienna dipped after 1923, the number of female converts remained steady at around 45 percent until 1930, when it rose to 52 percent. *Beiträge zur Statistik der Stadt Wien*, vol. 14 (Vienna: Gerlach & Wiedling, 1923), 1, 5; *Beiträge zur Statistik der Stadt Wien*, vol. 5 (Vienna: Gerlach & Wiedling, 1924), 6; *Statistische Mitteilung der Stadt Wien*, vol. 10–12 (Vienna: Gemeinde Wien, 1926); *Mitteilungen aus Statistik und Verwaltung der Stadt Wien*, vols. 1–12 (Vienna: Magistratsabteilung für Statistik, 1929); *Mitteilungen aus Statistik und Verwaltung der Stadt Wien*, vols. 1–12 (Vienna: Magistratsabteilung für Statistik, 1930).

58. According to Boyer, the increased mortality rates and decreasing birth rates after the First World War represented not only a "biological catastrophe" but also "exploded the very political culture within which all Austrian political parties operated." *Culture and Political Crisis*, 369. And as Maureen Healy notes, the growing centrality of the state during World War I in everyday matters such as "work, food, leisure and mourning" soon led to more concern among the general population about civic membership. See "Becoming Austrian: Women, the State, and Citizenship in World War I," *Central European History* 35, no. 1 (2002), 2.

59. Weitz, *Weimar Germany*, 2–3. Indeed, Jews's highly visible activity in Weimar Berlin is one reason why interwar Jewish experiences in Vienna have been overlooked.
60. Titles were officially abolished on April 3, 1919, although the government could not prohibit their use in private social situations. See William H. Johnston, *The Austrian Mind: An Intellectual and Social History, 1848–1938* (Berkeley: University of California Press, 1972), 39.
61. Joseph Wechsberg, *The Vienna I knew: Memories of a European Childhood* (New York: Doubleday, 1979), 76.
62. Boyer notes that the war was a traumatic and disruptive event, even for those who remained at home and faced fewer and more subtle instances of violence. *Culture and Political Crisis*, 419. Maureen Healy notes in particular the association of Galician refugees with disease, and the language in which it was described, that served to distance the resident population from the refugees in official doctors' reports. See *Vienna and the Fall of the Habsburg Empire: Total War and Everyday Life in World War I* (Cambridge: Cambridge University Press, 2004), 7–8.
63. For example, Jews in Czechoslovakia could register their nationality as Jewish, and many chose to do so; Jews in Austria did not have this option. Rozenblit, "Sustaining Austrian 'National' Identity," 186. Rozenblit also argues that "The dissolution of the Habsburg Monarchy and the creation of German-Austria called into question all the fundamental assumptions on which the identity of the majority of Vienna's Jews rested . . . the ordinary Jews of Vienna faced the most complicated identity crisis of all the former Habsburg Jews." Rozenblit, *Reconstructing*, 155–56. For a comparative view of Jews in the dissolved states of the dual monarchy, see Dahlmann and Hilbrenner, *Zwischen großen Erwartungen und bösem Erwachen*.
64. David Rechter emphasizes Jewish religious and ideological continuities, noting that despite the "seismic upheaval in Jewish society" wrought by the collapse, "pre-war Jewish ideologies survived almost intact the wholesale transformation of their external environment . . . [they] remained firmly grounded in their pre-war assumptions and frameworks." See *The Jews of Vienna and the First World War* (London: Littman Library, 2001), 187–88.
65. N.H. Tur-Sinai, "Viennese Jewry," in *The Jews of Austria: Essays on their Life, History and Desctruction*, ed. Josef Fraenkel (London: Vallentine Mitchell, 1967), 317. Indeed, emigration was an option chosen by a number of Austria's Jews. Between 1923 and 1934, the number of Jews in Austria dropped from 221,003 to 191,481, and in Vienna from 201,513 to 176,034. Michael John attributes this decrease to both emigration and low birth rates. See "We Do Not Even Possess Our Selves," 59.
66. Pauley, *From Prejudice to Persecution*, 230.

67. Marie Langer, Jaime del Palacio, and Enrique Guinsberg, *From Vienna to Managua: Journey of a Psychoanalyst* (London: Free Association Books, 1989), 33, 39–40. Langer made her home in Latin America after 1936.
68. Elias Canetti, *The Tongue Set Free: Remembrance of a European Childhood*, trans. Joachim Neugroschel (New York: Seabury Press, 1979), 170.
69. See Eleonore Lappin, "Jüdische Lebenserinnerungen. Rekonstruktionen von jüdischer Kindheit und Jugend im Wien der Zwischenkriegzeit," in Stern and Eichinger, *Wien und die jüdische Erfahrung*, 25. Of course, just as there was no one definition of "Austrian," neither was there one of "Viennese." For some, it was a close connection with bourgeois culture. For others, it was longing for life in the Habsburg monarchy. For example, Monroe E. Price, who was born in Vienna in August, 1938 and left with his family for the United States at the age of seven months, recalls his impression of his family's continued identification with Vienna: "One version of being Viennese was that you shouldn't wear your work on your sleeve. You shouldn't be preoccupied by money or achievement. You should think about the life of the Crown Prince and emulate it to some extent. When I was a child, I was told about a much-celebrated relative, my father's Uncle Emil, a paragon of sorts, a well-known *fiaker* (horse-drawn carriage) driver, with his top hat and formal coat, much like successors in Central Park, in business with his horse and carriage. His task, highly appreciated, was to bring beauty and pleasure into people's existence. The Vienna of the *fiaker* driver should be the model for life. It was the operetta, not the opera, that should be the goal of existence." See *Objects of Remembrance: A Memoir of American Opportunities and Viennese Dreams* (New York: Central European University Press, 2009), 13.
70. Peter G. J. Pulzer claims that despite the common elements between liberalism and socialism, Jews were driven to socialism in both Germany and Austria because they felt slighted by the bourgeoisie, did not feel equal in the political system, and because careers in conservative politics were impossible. See *The Rise of Political Anti-Semitism*, 253.
71. Gruber, *Red Vienna*, 6 and 213n14. See also Anson Rabinbach, ed., *The Austrian Socialist Experiment: Social Democracy and Austromarxism, 1918–1934* (Boulder, CO: Westview, 1985). Janek Wasserman aptly points out that during the interwar period, the term "Red Vienna" was deprecatory, polemical, and used most frequently by conservatives who opposed the city's government; it was only rarely, if ever, used by socialists and moderates. "Black Vienna, Red Vienna: the Struggle for Intellectual and Political Hegemony in Interwar Vienna, 1918–1938" (Ph.D. diss., Washington University, 2010), 3.
72. Pauley, *From Prejudice to Persecution*, 78. Of the major theorists of Austro-Marxism, only Karl Renner was not of Jewish descent. See Beller, *Vienna and the Jews*, 17. On the divergence between Renner and Otto Bauer on the topics of Jews and nationalism, see Ian Reifowitz, "Otto Bauer and Karl Renner on Nationalism, Ethnicity and Jews," *Journal of Jewish Identities* 2, no. 2 (July, 2009). As many

scholars have pointed out, Jews had no choice after the war to vote for any other party, given the demise of the Liberal Party and the antisemitic platforms of both the Christian Socials and German Nationalists. However, that fact alone cannot explain the presence of Jews as driving forces and committed supporters of Socialist programs. Social Democratic leaders with Jewish backgrounds include Friedrich Austerlitz, editor of the *Arbeiter-Zeitung*, Wilhelm Ellenbogen, Friedrich Adler, Max Adler, Hugo Breitner, Julius Tandler, and top intellectuals such as Heinrich Braun, Friedrich Stampfer, Rudolf Hilferding, and Gustav Eckstein who made their careers with the German labor movement. Those who remained in Austria included Oskar Pollak, Julius Braunthal, Thérèse Schlesinger, Helene Bauer, Sigmund Kaff, Benno Karpeles, and Julius Deutsch. Robert S. Wistrich characterizes socialism as an escape for most Jewish leaders from their backgrounds. "They found in the labour movement not only a new political home but an escape from the ghetto, from their Jewish background and social marginality." See *Socialism and the Jews: The Dilemmas of Assimilation in Germany and Austria-Hungary* (East Brunswick, NJ: Associated UP, 1982), 333.

73. For example, Robert Stricker's *Jüdischnationale Partei* (Jewish National Party) campaigned in parliamentary and community elections; the party had also called for a Jewish Nationalrat (parliament) of its own when it became apparent in 1918 that Jews would not gain recognition as a national group within the monarchy. After the war, when their demand became obsolete, Stricker's party sought a Jewish national parliament composed of other Jewish parties from German-Austria. Some Jews considered this demand nothing less than a "Jewish revolution." See Dieter Hecht, "Die Jüdischnationale Partei in Österreich 1918–1938," *Chilufim: Zeitschrift für jüdische Kulturgeschichte* 7 (2009); and David Rechter, *The Jews of Vienna*, esp. 195–200. For a comparative view of the efforts of Jews in Weimar Germany to rejuvenate Jewish culture, see Brenner, *The Renaissance of Jewish Culture in Weimar Germany* and Sharon Gillerman, *Germans into Jews: Remaking the Jewish Social Body in the Weimar Republic* (Stanford: Stanford University Press, 2009).

74. In 1925 Hakoah became the first Austrian champion in the professional league and won the national championship in hockey; its soccer team became popular in the United States. Jewish youth groups included Hashomer Hazair, Blau-Weiß, and Maccabi Hazair. Lappin, "Jüdische Lebenserinnerungen," 31–32. One of the explicit goals of Hakoah was to refute antisemitism by countering images of Jews as weak and dishonorable through a show of physical strength, discipline, and power. See John Bunzl, "Hakoah Vienna: Reflections on a Legend," in *Emancipation through Muscles: Jews and Sports in Europe*, ed. Michael Brenner and Gideon Reuveni (Lincoln: University of Nebraska Press, 2006), 113. See also John Bunzl, *Hoppauf Hakoah. Jüdischer Sport in Österreich: Von den Anfängen bis in die Gegenwart* (Vienna: Janus, 1987); and Susanne Helene Betz, Monika Löscher, and Pia Schölnberger, eds. *". . . m . . . ehr als ein Sportsverein": 100 Jahre Hakoah Wien 1909–2009* (Vienna: Studienverlag, 2009). Michael Brenner suggests that

Hakoah made a deep impression on Jews even if they had no other connection to Judaism or Jewish communal life. See "Introduction: Why Jews and Sports," in Brenner and Reuveni, *Emancipation through Muscles*, 6.

75. Relatively few autobiographies written by interwar Austrian Jews mention their involvement in or enthusiasm for Jewish politics, the Jewish community, or Zionist organizations. Lappin, "Jüdische Lebenserinnerungen," 30. For an exception, see the diaries of Galician-born Emanuel Fiscus, which describe his euphoric hopes for the Jewish national party. *Tagebücher von Emanuel Fiscus (1916–1921)*, ed. Evelyn Adunka (Innsbruck: Studienverlag, 2008).

76. "Austria" (also called Amateure) was one of many other Cityclubs, a nickname used for bourgeois clubs based in the coffeehouses of Vienna's first district, as opposed to the more proletarian clubs like Admira and Rapid, which were based in the suburbs. Writer Friedrich Torberg claims that Hakoah attracted Zionists, "Austria" drew assimilated Jews, and the sport club Rapid, which maintained a proud proletarian self-identification throughout the First Republic, was more or less off limits to Jews. Nevertheless, Jewish textile company director Rudolf Mütz headed the successful Admira team from the proletarian district of Floridsdorf. Jews also supported and served as officials of smaller teams from other working-class districts where few Jews lived, like Simmering. Finally, Jewish publisher Leo Schidrowitz remained a leader and representative of Rapid up until February 1938. In a 1923 newspaper article, Schidrowitz made derogatory comments about the members of Amateure, whom he described as "rich Jewish businesspeople." Significantly, Schidrowitz was also head of the Gloriette-Verlag from 1920–1924, which published erotic and sex-based literature, as well as five novels by Hugo Bettauer, including *Die Stadt ohne Juden* (see Chapter 2). Schidrowitz's visibility in public life is clear from Heimito von Doderer's 1956 novel *Die Dämonen*, in which the author portrays him satirically as "Direktor Szindrowits," the head of a publisher named "Pornberger & Graff" who speaks terrible German. See Jakob Rosenberg and Georg Spitaler, "Grün-weiß unterm Hakenkreuz. Der Sportklub Rapid im Nationalsozialismus (1938–1945)" and Georg Spitaler, "Rudolf Mütz—der vergessene Präsident," in *Wo die Wuchtel fliegt: Legendäre Orte des Wiener Fußballs*, ed. Peter Eppel, Bernhard Hachleitner, Werner Michael Schwarz, and Georg Spitaler, (Vienna: Löcker, 2008), 21–24 and 66. See also Matthias Marschik and Georg Spitaler, "Leo Schidrowitz: Propagandist des Wiener Fußballs," *Sportzeiten* 2 (2008): 10. Many thanks to Georg Spitaler for this information. See also Michael John, "Ein 'kultureller Code'? Antisemitismus im österreichischen Sport der ersten Republik," in *Emanzipation durch Muskelkraft, Juden und Sport in Europa*, ed. Michael Brenner and Gideon Reuveni (Göttingen: 2006).

77. In *Watermarks*, Yaron Zilberman's 2004 documentary about Hakoah's women's swim team, Ann Marie Pisker implies that her father disapproved of her membership. Friedrich Torberg, an extremely enthusiastic member of the team, also

suggests that his parents were not happy about his desire to join the group. According to them, "A well-brought up young man from a good home should play tennis at the WAC [Vienna Athletic Sports Club], not soccer for Hakoah." See Friedrich Torberg, "Warum ich stolz darauf bin," in Arthur Baar, *50 Jahr Hakoah, 1909–1959* (Tel-Aviv: Verlagskomittee Hakoah, 1959), 278.

78. Georg Stefan Troller claims Jews "soaked up" many of the general prejudices of the city against modernism: "provincial was better than urban, Germans were better than Frenchmen (or even Italians, those 'wops'), vague feelings better than lucid intellect. In the end, the 'Germanic Aryans' were nobler than all the others, and especially nobler than we were. We accepted this in principle and were determined to work our way up to the Aryans!" *Das fidele Grab*, 57.

79. Friedrich Torberg, *Die Tante Jolesch, oder der Untergang des Abendlandes in Anekdoten* (Munich: Langen-Müller, 1977), 213. For a detailed account of this phenomenon see Steven Beller, *Vienna and the Jews*. See also Sander L. Gilman, *Jewish Self-Hatred: Anti-Semitism and the Hidden Language of the Jews* (Baltimore: Johns Hopkins University Press, 1985). Ritchie Robertson refers to these exaggerated efforts as "hyperacculturation." See *The 'Jewish Question' in German Literature* 1759–1939 (New York: Oxford University Press, 1999), 345–379.

80. Marjorie Perloff, *The Vienna Paradox: A Memoir* (New York: New Directions, 2003), xiv, 2, 31, 39.

81. F. R. Bienenfeld, *The Religion of the Non-Religious Jews: Lecture delivered to the Sociological Society of Vienna, November 10, 1937*, trans. (London: Museum Press, 1944), 83.

82. See Joan W. Scott, "The Evidence of Experience," *Critical Inquiry* 17, no. 4 (Summer 1991), 777.

83. For an extensive discussion of the historiography of this issue see Spector, "Forget assimilation," 359. See also David Sorkin's foundational study *The Transformation of German Jewry, 1780–1840* (New York: Oxford University Press, 1987); David Sorkin, "Emancipation and Assimilation: Two Concepts and their Application to German-Jewish History," *Leo Baeck Institute Year-Book* 35 (1990); and David Sorkin, "The Impact of Emancipation on German Jewry: A Reconsideration," in *Assimilation and Community: The Jews in Nineteenth-Century Europe*, ed. Jonathan Frankel and Steven J. Zipperstein (Cambridge: Cambridge University Press, 1992).

84. Shulamit Volkov refers to these two linked reponses as "assimilation" and "dissimilation." See "The Dynamics of Dissimilation: Ostjuden and German Jews," in *The Jewish Response to German Culture from the Enlightenment to the Second World War*, ed. Jehuda Reinharz and Walter Schatzberg (Hanover, NH: University Press of New England, 1985).

85. There were thirty-five total newspapers catering to the Jewish community at any given time in Vienna between 1918 and 1938. They included the Zionist daily *Wiener Morgenzeitung*, which appeared from 1919 to 1927, the weekly *Jüdische Presse* published by Agudas Yisroel, the *Misrachi Jüdisches Wochenblatt*, and

many others. *Dr. Blochs Österreichische Wochenschrift* remained an important news source for the Jewish community until 1920; the weekly *Die Neue Welt*, edited by Zionist leader Robert Stricker, was published from September 23, 1927, until the *Anschluss*. See Dieter Hecht, "Die Stimme und Wahrheit der jüdischen Welt," in Stern and Eichinger, *Wien und die jüdische Erfahrung*, 101. See also Jonas Kreppel, *Juden und Judentum von Heute: Ein Handbuch* (Vienna: Amalthea, 1925), 715–16.

86. The need for materials in Yiddish was not as urgent in German-speaking cities due to the similarities of the two languages. See Rozenblit, *Assimilation and Identity*, 151 and Meir Hainisch, "Galician Jews in Vienna," in *The Jews of Austria*, ed. Josef Fraenkel (London: Vallentine Mitchell, 1967), 362, 364.

87. Berlin's thriving Yiddish culture during the Weimar era has been the subject of recent study. See *Studies in Yiddish* 8: *Yiddish in Weimar Berlin: At the Crossroads of Diaspora Politics and Culture*, ed. Gennady Estraikh and Mikhail Krutikov (Oxford: Legenda, 2010). On Eastern European Jews in Berlin after World War I, see Verena Dohrn and Gertrud Pickhan, eds., *Transit und Transformation. Osteuropäisch-jüdische Migranten in Berlin 1918–1939* (Göttingen: Wallstein, 2010).

88. Just after World War I, Hebrew and Yiddish writers and intellectuals, some of whom wrote in two or three languages, formed an extraordinary group in Vienna. These writers, most of whom were from Galicia, included Abraham Moshe Fuchs, Melech Ravitsch, Mendel Neugroschel, Melech Chmelnitzki, Shmuel Yakov Imber, Moshe Silburg, and Ber Horowitz. Uriel Birnbaum, best known for his German-language works, was also a member of this circle. See Gabriele Kohlbauer-Fritz, "Das Bild Wiens in der jiddischen Literatur," and Thomas Soxberger, "Zwischen Partei- und Selbstverlag: Die jiddische Literatur und Publizistik in Wien," in *Zwischenwelt* 8: *Jiddische Kultur und Literatur aus Österreich*, ed. Armin Eidherr und Karl Müller (Klagenfurt: Drava, 2003); and Pinsker, *Literary Passports*.

89. In a discussion of Fritz Grünbaum and Karl Farkas, two of the most well-known Austrian Jewish cabaret artists, Peter Jelavich argues that the genre's "distance from elite theatre was directly correlated with its ability to address Jewish themes." See "How 'Jewish' was Theatre in Imperial Berlin?" in *Jews and the Making of Modern German Theatre*, ed. Jeanette R. Malkin and Freddie Rokem (Iowa City: University of Iowa Press, 2010), 49–50. See also Marline Otte, *Jewish Identities in German Popular Entertainment* (New York: Cambridge University Press, 2006).

90. Oskar A.H. Schmitz, *Der österreichische Mensch: Zum Anschauungsunterricht für Europäer, insbesondere für Reichsdeutsche* (Vienna-Leipzig: Wiener literarische Anstalt, 1924), 16. For a discussion of Schmitz's work, see William H. Johnston, *Der österreichische Mensch: Kulturgeschichte der Eigenart Österreichs* (Vienna: Böhlau, 2010), 190–92.

91. Carl Paumgartten, *Repablick: Eine galgenfröhliche Wiener Legende aus der Zeit der gelben Pest und des roten Todes* (Graz: Stocker, 1924). Paumgartten (Karl/Carl Huffnagl, pseud.), the author of several antisemitic publications during the 1920s, also contributed to the satirical magazine *Die Muskete* and condemned Schnitzler as a Jewish playwright during the controversy over *Reigen* in 1921. See also Johann Sonnleitner, "Völkische Literatur und Antisemitismus in der Zwischenkriegszeit," in *Judentum und Antisemitismus. Studien zur Literatur und Germanistik in Österreich*, ed. Anne Betten und Konstanze Fliedl (Berlin: Erich Schmidt Verlag, 2003), 90–92; and Friedrich Achberger, *Fluchtpunkt 1938: Essays zur österreichischen Literatur zwischen 1918 und 1938*, (Vienna:Verlag für Gesellschaftskritik, 1994), 127–28.
92. Albert Lichtblau, "Antisemitismus 1900–1938," in Stern and Eichinger, *Wien und die jüdische Erfahrung*, 43.
93. Michael John, "Aggressiver Antisemitismus im österreichischen Sportgeschehen der Zwischenkriegszeit: Manifestationen und Reaktionen anhand ausgewählter Beispiele," *zeitgeschichte* 3 (1999): 206. Lotte Hümbelin recalls her dismissive reactions to the boys who drove through the Leopoldstadt on trucks yelling antisemitic slurs in the 1920s. *Mein eigener Kopf: Ein Frauenleben in Wien, Moskau, Prag, Paris und Zürich* (Zurich: Edition 8, 1999), 80–81.
94. Kadison described the experience as follows: "Escorted by a convoy of police, the whole troupe, still in costume and makeup with bundles under our arms, the men in full beard and long black coats, were led through the streets of Baden. Jeering crowds followed us, whistling and hooting. Some threw stones." Luba Kadison, "Vilna Troupe," unpublished lecture, 15–16, Joseph Buloff Jewish Theater Archive, Harvard University, Buloff Papers, Collection 3, BQA4959, Folder: LK/Vilna Troupe.
95. An article in the *Neue Freie Presse* describes the site of the lecture, which took place at the Vienna Konzerthaus, as a scene of pandemonium that included bloody attacks on both women and men; Hirschfeld was forced to retreat to a smaller room behind the podium. Many were wounded in an attack the article described as "extremely un-Viennese." "Stormszenen im Konzerthaussaale," *Neue Freie Presse*, February 5, 1923, 7. The right-wing *Reichspost* blamed Hirschfeld, whom they referred to as a "wandering preacher of immorality." See "Eine Hirschfeld-Versammlung gesprengt," *Reichspost*, February 5, 1923, 4.
96. According to Holtzmann (born Henriette Nussbaum), both her father and Stricker were arrested for defending themselves with their walking sticks. Lappin, "Jüdische Lebenserinnerungen," 30.
97. Muriel Gardiner, *Code Name "Mary:" Memoirs of an American Woman in the Austrian Underground* (New Haven: Yale University Press, 1983), 43–44.
98. Two photographs in the archive of the Austrian National Library document signs that read, JUDEN EINTRITT VERBOTEN on the main entrance to the university. Austrian National Library (ÖNB), Bildarchiv, Inventarnummer H 747

B and H 748 B. The university remained a center of antisemitism even during the more general lull in violent attacks after 1923. Jews could not gain appointments as full professors at the university; some students remained convinced that some professors failed them solely because they were Jews. Pauley, *From Prejudice to Persecution*, 121, 260. George E. Berkley notes that the university, unlike other institutions, was immune from police intervention, which may have contributed to its concentration there. See *Vienna and its Jews: The Tragedy of Success, 1880s–1980s* (Cambridge, MA: Abt Books/Madison Books, 1988), 149–61, 168–69.

99. In her seminal study, Shulamit Volkov identifies antisemitism's function in modernity as an important cultural code for articulating other political and social tensions in modern German society. "Antisemitism as a Cultural Code: Reflections on the History and Historiography of Antisemitism in Imperial Germany," *Leo Baeck Institute Year-Book* 23 (1978): 39.

100. Friedrich Heer, "Die beiden Republiken," in *Wien. Spektrum einer Stadt*, ed. Hilde Spiel (Vienna: Jugend und Volk, 1971), 350.

101. Ritchie Robertson notes that the contrast between city and country is a recurrent theme in Austrian literature between the wars. See "Austrian Prose Fiction 1918–1945," in *A History of Austrian Literature*, ed. Katrin Kohl and Ritchie Robertson (Rochester, NY: Camden House, 2006), 54.

102. Karl Schönherr, *Bühnenwerke II: Briefe, Dokumentation*, ed. Franz Hadamowsky (Vienna: Kremayr & Scheriau, 1974), 629. On the other hand, Gustav Mahler, Sigmund Freud, Peter Altenberg, and Arthur Schnitzler maintained that they often needed to be outside the city in places like the Salzkammergut or Semmering in order to complete their work. Tag Gronberg, *Vienna: City of Modernity* (Bern: Peter Lang, 2007), 32–33. Hermann Broch, whose degree of Jewish self-identification and its impact on his work remains a subject of debate, engaged the province/city divide in his novel *Die Verzauberung*, a *Bergroman* (mountain novel) that he began writing in 1935. It was first published in 1954 under the title *Der Versucher* three years after his death in 1951. Edward Timms notes that Broch's *Die Schlafwandler* of 1931 suggests that he did not feel entirely at home in Vienna. See "Musil's Vienna and Kafka's Prague," in *Unreal City: Urban Experience in Modern European Literature and Art*, ed. Edward Timms and David Kelley (Manchester: Manchester University Press, 1985), 259.

103. John, "We Do Not Even Possess Our Selves," 29.

104. According to British diplomat Malcolm Bullock, Austrian citizens needed passports to enter different provinces immediately after the end of the war. *Austria 1918–1938: A Study in Failure* (London: Macmillan, 1939), 21.

105. As Christian Koller notes, Vienna was home to the overwhelming majority of the Social Democratic party membership; between 1919 and 1929, the number of

members in Vienna doubled, while all the provinces except Burgenland showed a significant decline. See "'. . . der Wiener Judenstaat, von dem wir uns unter allen Umständen trennen wollen.' Die Vorarlberger Anschlussbewegung an die Schweiz," in Konrad and Maderthaner, . . . *der rest ist Österreich*, 92.

106. In the elections of 1919, the Social Democrats gained control of the Viennese municipality. They governed the nation in a coalition with the Christian Socials until 1920, when the Christian Socials gained control of the national government.
107. Lichtblau, "Antisemitismus 1900–1930," 43.
108. The Christian Social leadership, which had viewed Vienna positively before 1918, now shifted to a platform of clear aversion for this "verjudet" (jewified) city. Lichtblau, "Das fragile Korsett," 33.
109. Friedrich Heer, *Der Glaube des Adolf Hitler: Anatomie einer politischen Religiosität* (Munich: Bechtle, 1968), 77. Lueger served as mayor of Vienna from 1897 to 1910.
110. "Christian Socials approved of and defended Christian religious identities, but did not emphasize 'Catholicism' as an independent political variable deserving decisive and exclusive prominence on its own." Boyer, *Culture and Political Crisis*, 164, 167.
111. Vienna's separation from Lower Austria allowed it to collect its own taxes for Red Vienna's social programs, which fostered even more tension between the city and the provinces. Christian Social and German National parties launched antisemitic campaigns against Vienna's councilman in charge of financial affairs Hugo Breitner. See Wolfgang Fritz, *Der Kopf des Asiaten Breitner: Politik und Ökonomie im roten Wien* (Vienna: Löcker, 2000). For a discussion of often overlooked political tensions in Vienna during the interwar period, see Wasserman, "Black Vienna, Red Vienna." Wasserman rightly emphasizes the importance of the hostile intellectual and political backdrop to the reforms of the Social Democrats.
112. In her excellent study of Jewish performer and strongman Siegmund Breitbart in Vienna, Sharon Gillerman illustrates how performances in both courtroom and theater opened up the possibilities for reconfiguring and recasting a host of supposedly "fixed" Jewish stereotypes. "Samson in Vienna: The Theatrics of Jewish Masculinity," *Jewish Social Studies* 9, no. 2 (2003).
113. Judith Beniston, "Drama in Austria, 1918–45," 21.

CHAPTER 1

1. In 1925, Bruno Wolf, an editor at the *Neues Wiener Journal*, formally accused Oskar Pöffel (also spelled Pöffl), editor of the newspaper's financial section, of threatening to write derogatory articles about firms unless they purchased advertising. As a result, the newspaper's publisher, Jakob Lippowitz, fired Pöffel. Newspaper reports at the time speculate that Lippowitz's absence from the murder trial indicates that he had likely colluded in such activities, a point that Pöffel's defense

lawyers Walter Riehl and Hans Gürtler seized upon in order to convince the jury of their client's innocence. See "Ein Märtyrer des Journalismus: Der tragische Tod Bruno Wolfs," *Neue Freie Presse*, June 20, 1928, 1–5; "Freigesprochen! Wegen angeblicher Sinnesverwirrung," *Das Kleine Blatt*, January 20, 1929, 1–4; Hans Gürtler, *Der Freispruch Pöffel* (Vienna: Verlag Moritz Perles, 1929), 107–36.

2. "Wie Pöffel den Mord verübt hat," *Das Kleine Blatt*, January 19, 1929, 5.
3. The court carried out a reenactment of the events of the murder on the morning of January 19 in the Hietzing courtroom, where the witnesses recalled their former roles. Later that morning, the entire company boarded a tram and headed back to court, where those involved in the reconstruction of the libel trial all reassumed their roles as witnesses in the murder trial.
4. In his closing statement, defense lawyer Walter Riehl, who was the leader of the Nazi Party in Vienna between 1919 and 1922, used highly charged, Jewish-coded language to denigrate unions and journalists to his client's benefit. He argued that both Wolf and Pöffel had been victims of a "surge of the union mentality in the postwar period," according to which all journalists banded together to pursue the class struggle. He described Pöffel as an impoverished, downtrodden man punished by the journalism "machine" for merely being a man from the "good old days." Riehl also capitalized on the fact that the jury members stemmed from the Burgenland to tell them that "men from the provinces had no reason to allow the Viennese to teach them the rules of justice." Wiener Stadt- und Landesarchiv (WStLA), Landesgericht für Strafsachen, A 11: II Vr 2652/28 (Oskar Pöffel). See also Gürtler, *Der Freispruch Pöffel*, 129–36 and *Das Kleine Blatt*, January 20, 1929. By this time, Riehl had already achieved notoriety for the acquittal of Otto Rothstock in 1925 for the murder of writer Hugo Bettauer based on a similar vilification of the Jewish media at his trial (covered in detail in this chapter) as well as for the 1927 acquittal of the murderers of an invalid and a child in Schattendorf (Burgenland) during a clash of paramilitary groups on the right and left. The Schattendorf acquittals set off the so-called July revolt of 1927 in Vienna, which led to the burning of the Justizpalast (Palace of Justice) and the deaths of almost one hundred people. For more on Riehl, his Nazi leadership, and the antisemitic ideology he acted upon throughout his life, see Rudolf Brandstötter, "Dr. Walter Riehl und die Geschichte der Nationalsozialistischen Bewegung in Österreich" (Ph.D. diss., University of Vienna, 1969.) Peter Haslinger suggests that the Burgenland was the only province in Austria (except for the city-province of Vienna) that had never existed as its own self-contained entity. For this reason, its insecurities after World War I not only led to particularly intense disorientation and apathy, but also opened up wide spaces for competition in regional self-identification and fractured discourse over what constituted "Burgenländerness." See "Building a Regional Identity: The Burgenland 1921–1938," *Austrian History Yearbook* 32 (2001).
5. Heinrich Eduard Jacob, "Pöffls Freispruch," *Fazit: Erzähler einer Generation*, ed. Herbert Reinoss, (Munich: F.A. Herbig, 1972), 228. The murder of the

forty-four-year-old, well-established journalist Bruno Wolf and the news of Oskar Pöffel's acquittal featured in the headlines of many newspapers in Vienna and several in Berlin, including the *Berliner Tageblatt* and the *Vossische Zeitung*. See *Neues Wiener Journal*, "Der Mord an Bruno Wolf," June 20, 1928, 4. However, the murder and subsequent trial did not receive much international attention. When foreign newspapers did report briefly on it, they (unlike their German-language counterparts) tended to frame the murder as an antisemitic act. Beyond merely displaying evidence of "antisemitic atittudes," the complicated configuration of Jewish and non-Jewish lawyers, defendants, victims, and witnesses involved in this trial and their statements to the court reveals the significant role of Jewish difference as an ordering system that lawyers for both sides of the case could draw upon to serve their needs. At the trial Pöffel admitted that his mother was Jewish and that his father had likely converted to Judaism. But Pöffel also staunchly maintained that nobody knew about his Jewish background, and so, as a Protestant, he faced persecution by his Jewish colleagues. Moreover, Jewish lawyer Richard Pressburger briefly served as defense lawyer for Oskar Pöffel in this murder trial; by that time, he had already served as defense lawyer for Philipp Halsmann at his first trial one month earlier. On the third day of Pöffel's trial, however, he claimed to be ill with a cold and bowed out. At that point, antisemitic lawyer Walter Riehl took over Pöffel's case. In his attempts to downplay the murder as an antisemitic act, Riehl portrayed Pöffel's father as a loyal Austrian involved in an unfortunate mixed marriage that undoubtedly affected his son's state of mind. On the other hand, Eduard Frischauer, the Jewish lawyer for Wolf's widow, did his best to call into question Pöffel's Jewish roots in an attempt to stress the role of antisemitism in the deed. "Oskar Pöffel" WStLA, Landesgericht für Strafsachen, A 11: II Vr 2652/28 (Oskar Pöffel). "Ein überraschender Zwischenfall im Mordprozess Pöffel," *Neue Freie Presse*, January 17, 1929, 8–9; "Die Ermordung des Redakteurs Wolf im Gerichtssaale: Dr. Pressburger legt die Verteidigung nieder," *Neue Freie Presse*, January 18, 1929, 12–13.

6. As Daniel Vyleta notes, criminal accusations against Jews often hinged on claims that they willfully lied and sabotaged the justice system; moreover, they frequently implicated not only the accused, but also Jewish lawyers, journalists, editors, psychologists, and others. See "Jewish Crimes and Misdemeanours: In Search of Jewish Criminality (Germany and Austria, 1890–1914)," *European History Quarterly* 35, no. 2 (2005).
7. Schlick was descended from Prussian aristocrats, and Bettauer converted from Judaism to Protestantism in 1890 at the age of eighteen. Bettauer's conversion surely did not make him any less Jewish in the eyes of his Nazi-affiliated murderer and other outspoken racial antisemites. But simply labeling his killer's act as a racially-motivated crime obscures the powerful symbolic codings of Jewish difference that helped him gain the jury's sympathy.

8. On medieval and modern accounts of Jewish ritual murder accusations, see Hillel Kieval, "Representation and Knowledge in Medieval and Modern Accounts of Jewish Ritual Murder, " *Jewish Social Studies* 1, no. 1(1994): 2.
9. Julie Stone Peters, "Legal Performance Good and Bad," *Law, Culture, and the Humanities* 4, no. 2 (2008): 182. See also Martha Merrill Umphrey, "Histories of the Live: Trials as Speech and Performance" (lecture, Association for the Study of Law, Culture and the Humanities, Brown University, Providence, RI, March 19, 2010).
10. "This repetition is at once a reenactment and reexperiencing of a set of meanings already socially established; and it is the mundane and ritualized form of their legitimization . . . indeed, the performance is effected with the strategic aim of maintaining gender within its binary frame—an aim that cannot be attributed to a subject, but, rather, must be understood to found and consolidate the subject." Judith Butler, *Gender Trouble: Feminism and the Subversion of Identity* (New York: Routledge, 1999), 45.
11. Philippe Halsman, *Jump Book* (New York: Simon and Schuster, 1959), 7–8. In later interviews, he concedes that Freud and Adler actually did influence his work.
12. Halsmann holds the record for the most photographs on the covers of *Life* magazine: 101. Though he later changed the spelling of his name to Philippe Halsman, in this chapter, I will use the spelling of his name at the time of the trial, Philipp Halsmann. For an insightful, detailed account of the trials drawn from a variety of sources, see Martin Pollack, *Anklage Vatermord: Der Fall Philipp Halsmann* (Vienna: Zsolnay, 2002).
13. Tiroler Landesarchiv (TLA), File St 3972/28 6 Vr 1380/28, Innsbrucker Landesgericht. Halsmann was studying engineering in Dresden and on an extended holiday with his family at the time of the murder.
14. Letter from Albert Einstein to President Wilhelm Miklas dated February 20, 1930. Österreichische Staatsarchiv (ÖStA), Bundespräsident (BP), File Z 36.305/30, IX Zahl 1710. The "Liga für Menschenrechte" (League of Human Rights) in Paris sent a telegram on March 10, 1930, to Miklas asking for him to pardon Halsmann since he had been the "victim of the xenophobia and antisemitism of the Tyrolean jury." ÖStA, BP, File Z 36.305/30, VIII Zahl 2015. Phillipp himself expressed to his friend Ruth Römer how pleased he was that Jakob Wassermann had come to his defense. Philipp Halsmann, *Briefe aus der Haft an eine Freundin*, ed. Karl Blanck (Stuttgart: J. Engelhorns Nachf., 1930), 54.
15. ÖStA, BP, File Z 36.305/30, V Zahl 4893.
16. Bruce Downes, "Philippe Halsman," *Popular Photography* 2 (February 1946): 20–59, 158–62; 160. Halsman left for New York in November, 1940, two days before Paris fell to the Nazis.
17. Zuckerkandl, whose sister Sophie was the sister in law of French prime minister Georges Clemenceau, plays up her role in interventing with well-placed French officials

like Paul Painlevé to achieve clemency for Halsmann in her memoirs. See Bertha Zuckerkandl, *Österreich Intim: Erinnerungen 1892–1942*, ed. Reinhard Federmann (Frankfurt: Ullstein, 1970), 180. However, letters and other documents indicate that Philipp's twenty-year-old sister Liouba was actually most instrumental behind the scenes in gaining his release. She traveled to Vienna, Dresden, Berlin, Munich, Paris, Basel, and Zurich in order to garner support for her brother. Nicole Emanuel is currently writing a book about her grandmother Liouba's involvement in mobilizing support for Philipp. I am deeply grateful to Nicole Emanuel for so generously sharing her research and family photographs with me.

18. TLA, File St 3972/28 6 Vr 1380/28, Innsbrucker Landesgericht.
19. Sigmund Freud, "Das Fakultätsgutachten im Prozess Halsmann," *Neue Freie Presse*, December 14, 1930, 13.
20. Karl Marbe, *Der Strafprozess gegen Philipp Halsmann, aktenmäßige Darstellung und kriminalpsychologische Würdigung* (Leipzig: C.L. Hirschfeld, 1932), 14.
21. Barnet Hartston, *Sensationalizing the Jewish Question: Anti-Semitic Trials and the Press in the Early German Empire* (Leiden: Brill, 2005), 131–32. Here, the work of Sander Gilman has been instrumental in uncovering links between criminality and negative stereotypes about Jewish sexual perversity, madness, and physiognomy as manifested through their dark complexions, large noses, abnormal feet, secret language, and strong sex drive. See especially Sander L. Gilman, *Jewish Self-Hatred: Anti-Semitism and the Hidden Language of the Jews* (Baltimore: Johns Hopkins University Press, 1986); *The Jew's Body* (New York: New York University Press, 1991); and *The Case of Sigmund Freud: Medicine and Identity at the Fin de Siècle* (Baltimore: Johns Hopkins University Press, 1993).
22. From 1926 to 1929, the only major violent public event that resulted in death was the demonstration surrounding the the storming and subsequent burning of the *Justizpalast* in 1927. See Bruce F. Pauley, *From Prejudice to Persecution: A History of Austrian Anti-Semitism* (Chapel Hill: University of North Carolina Press, 1992), 116. Nevertheless, as this book makes clear, isolated incidents of violence against Jews—along with the acquittal of their persecutors—continued throughout this period.
23. On the development of what he terms chimerical antisemitism, see Gavin I. Langmuir, *Toward a Definition of Antisemitism* (Berkeley: University of California Press, 1996), 336–45.
24. For more on this topic, see Andreas Maislinger and Günther Pallaver, "Antisemitismus ohne Juden: Das Beispiel Tirol," in *Voll Leben und voll Tod ist diese Erde: Bilder aus der Geschichte der jüdischen Österreicher (1190 bis 1945)*, ed. Wolfgang Plat (Vienna: Herold Verlag, 1988).
25. Jews were expelled from Tyrol in the seventeenth century, and in 1776 only 37 Jews resided there. By the 1920s, the Jewish population peaked at 225, including southern Tyrol. The only large store in the city of Innsbruck, Bauer and Schwarz, was Jewish-owned. There were also a few Jewish doctors and lawyers, a bank

director, and two or three in high positions in the railway. See E.S. Rimalt, "The Jews of Tyrol," in *The Jews of Austria*, ed. Josef Fraenkel (London: Valentine Mitchell, 1967), 380–381; and Pauley, *From Prejudice to Persecution*, 17. Protestants in the Zillertal were driven out of their homes between 1832 and 1837, and Tyrol had been one of the main supporters of the 1855 Concordat, a conservative document aiming to balance religion and society that strengthened Catholicism in Austria. Tyroleans continued to fight against Liberals in the national government in Vienna in the 1860s and 1870s. See William D. Bowman, "Regional History and the Austrian Nation," *Journal of Modern History*, 67, no. 4 (1995): 880–82.

26. Tyroleans demonstrated against annexation and against the division between North and South Tyrol. Andreas Hofer (1767–1810) was a Tyrolean innkeeper who led an uprising against the French and Bavarians in 1809, and who had been immortalized as a national hero around 1900 in the service of Catholic-conservative ideology. From 1920 until 1936, the "Andreas Hofer Association" sponsored a "Landestrauertag"—a day of mourning for the state—on October 10, the day the annexation of South Tyrol to Italy was made official. Newspaper articles complaining about the annexation appeared frequently until 1933, after which they began to drop off. See Rolf Steininger, "1918/1919: Die Teilung Tirols: Wie das Südtirolproblem enststand," in . . . *der Rest ist Österreich: Das Werden der Ersten Republik*, vol. 1, ed. Helmut Konrad and Wolfgang Maderthaner (Vienna: Carl Gerold's Sohn Verlag, 2008), 117; Niko Hofinger, "'Unser Lösung ist: Tirol den Tirolern!': Antisemitism in Tirol 1918–1938," *zeitgeschichte* 21, no. 3–4 (1994): 83; and Laurence Cole, *Andreas Hofer: The Social and Cultural Construction of a National Myth in Tirol, 1809–1904* (Florence: European University Institute, 1994), 5–8. On Hofer see also n. 59 and Chapter 2.

27. Angered over the loss of South Tyrol to Italy in 1920, 98.5 percent of the citizens in North Tyrol voted to join postwar Germany in April 1921. See Josef Riedmann, "Geschichte Tirols" in *Geschichte der österreichischen Bundesländer*, ed. Johann Rainer, 2nd ed. (Vienna: Geschichte und Politik, 1988).

28. Rainer Amstädter, *Der Alpinismus: Kultur—Organisation—Politik* (Vienna: WUV-Universitätsverlag, 1996), 218.

29. Bowman, "Regional History," 882.

30. For example, Jewish author Felix Salten (born Siegmund Salzmann), one of the fin-de-siècle "Young Vienna" circle of writers, published his 1923 novel *Bambi: eine Lebensgeschichte aus dem Walde* with Ullstein in Berlin after a stay in the Austrian Alps. The book was made into a Disney film in 1942. Salten also published *Fünfzehn Hasen: Schicksale in Wald und Feld* (1929) with Zsolnay in Vienna. These two books were among a spate of Salten's animal-centered literature aimed at adults and youth alike, including *Bambi's Children*, the sequel, which Salten published in English while in exile in Switzerland in 1939. Karl Kraus wrote "Jüdelnde

Hasen," ("Jüdeln" was a way to refer derogatorily to speaking with an accent of dialect associated with Jews. This title best translates as "Rabbits talking like Jews") an essay mocking the "Jewish" speech of Salten's rabbits, as well as their fear of enemies in the forest, in *Die Fackel* 820–26 (1929): 45–46. See Wendelin Schmidt-Dengler, *Ohne Nostalgie: Zur österreichischen Literatur der Zwischenkriegszeit* (Vienna: Bohlau, 2002), 158; Harold B. Segel, *The Vienna Coffeeehouse Wits* 1890–1938 (West Lafayette, IN: Purdue University Press, 1993), 104, 165–70; and Beverley Driver Eddy, *Felix Salten: Man of Many Faces* (Riverside, CA: Ariadne, 2010).

31. Amstädter, *Der Alpinismus*, 150–51. Alison Frank notes that crosses placed at the summit of Austrian mountains in the nineteenth and twentieth centuries marked not only their proximity to God, but also staked them out as "Christian" spaces. "The Pleasant and the Useful: Pilgrimage and Tourism in Habsburg Mariazell," *Austrian History Yearbook* 40 (2009): 158.
32. Photojournalist Alice Schalek and her family, for example, were avid mountain climbers, and Schalek was a member of the "Austria" branch of the Deutscher und österreichischer Alpenverein (DÖAV). In 1921 she published an article decrying the group's establishment of an *Arierparagraph* for their former hiking club. Alice Schalek, "Der Arierparagraph der Sektion Austria," *Neue Freie Presse*, February 22, 1921, 6. Walter Riehl, the antisemitic lawyer linked to several cases in this chapter, was a member of "Austria's" leadership during the year that the group implemented the *Arierparagraph*—a process they referred to as a "völkische Reinigung" (ethnic purification) of the group. See *Nachrichten der Sektion "Austria" des Deutschen und Österreichischen Alpenvereins*, no. 3(May 1921). Some Alpine clubs implemented these paragraphs even when they had no Jewish members, a move that, at least according to one newspaper, was intended as a dig at the Social Democrats. *Steyrer Tagblatt*, January 8, 1922, 5.
33. Martin H. Ross, *Marrano* (Boston: Branden, 1976), 17. The memoirs of a number of Jews indicate that they strongly identified with and felt connected to the physical beauty of Austria's landscape. For more details on the enthusiasm of many Austrian Jews for the mountains, see the exhibition catalogue *"Hast du meine Alpen gesehen?" Eine jüdische Beziehungsgeschichte*, ed. Hanno Loewy and Gerhard Milchram (Vienna: Bücher Verlag Hohenems-Wien, 2009), esp. 14.
34. Varon notes, "Yes, a Jew certainly could feel at home in Vienna. But the countryside was another matter: the Austrian peasant, the Styrian mountaineer, the yodelling Tyrolean were hopelessly prejudiced . . . Hotel owners, restaurateurs, chambermaids, waiters, porters, busboys and bellboys were all confirmed anti-Semites. The more money they made from Jewish tourists, domestic and foreign, the more anti-Semitic they seemed to become." *Professions of a Lucky Jew* (London: Cornwall, 1992), 30–31. See also Jacqueline Vansant, *Reclaiming Heimat: Trauma and Mourning in Memoirs by Jewish Austrian Reémigés* (Detroit: Wayne State University Press, 2001), 106–110.

35. Perloff notes, "In the photographs taken on summer vacations in the Salzkammergut or the Tyrol, we children—and here even my mother (but not Great-grandmother Rosenthal)—are dressed in dirndls or lederhosen." *The Vienna Paradox: A Memoir* (New York: New Directions, 2003), 39. Leo Spitzer, who was born in La Paz, Bolivia, to Austrian Jewish refugees, includes photographs of his parents and other refugees in traditional Tyrolean dress and holding "Dirndl Balls," pointing out that attempting to reproduce their Austrianness this way was also an act of defiance, since Jews had been barred from wearing "national costume" when the Nazis came to power. Leo Spitzer, "Back Through the Future: Nostalgic Memory and Critical Memory in a Refuge from Nazism," in *Acts of Memory: Cultural Recall in the Present*, ed. Mieke Bal, Jonathan Crewe, and Leo Spitzer (Hanover: University Press of New England, 1999), 88–89.
36. According to the first Donauland newsletter, the group was established to provide a gathering place for those affected by the recent "wave of hatred" among other branches of the DÖAV. In response, the leaders of "Austria" encouraged other members of the DÖAV to formally protest the acceptance of this "Jewish" group. *Nachrichten der Sektion "Donauland" des Deutschen und Österreichischen Alpenvereins*, no. 1, August 1, 1921.
37. Amstädter, *Der Alpinismus*, 310. On the conflicts among the hiking groups regarding the *Schutzhütte* in the Zillertal, see also Pollack, *Anklage Vatermord*, 85. By this time, ninety-six of Austria's one hundred Alpine clubs had instituted *Arierparagraphen*. At a meeting of the Österreichischer Touristenklub (Austrian Tourists' Club, ÖTK), Walter Riehl spoke in favor of the *Arierparagraph*, proclaiming, "It's infuriating when, for example, one sees blonde German girls on the Rax [a popular mountain for hikers] being led by a *Schieberjude* (Jewish black-marketeer)," "Annahme des Arierparagraphen im Österreichischen Touristenklub," *Neue Freie Presse*, April 30, 1921, 7. After applause, the measure was approved by 3056 to 784 votes. During the discussion, one member noted that the huts of the ÖTK had been built with "Jewish money." In advance of the meeting, the *Reichspost* reported: "Just like the group 'Austria' of the German and Austrian Alpine clubs, the central leadership of the ÖTK is attempting to block the unwanted growth of racially foreign, non-Aryan elements" and urged Aryan members to participate in the group's vote to hinder the continued *Verjudung* of Austria's largest Alpine club. See "Der Arierparagraph im Österrreichischen Touristenklub," *Der Reichspost*, April 12, 1921, 5.
38. Josef Wahl claimed that neither of the Halsmanns carried snow goggles or ice picks; another witness noted that Philipp spoke "very poor German." TLA, File St 3972/28 6 Vr 1380/28, Innsbrucker Landesgericht, 32.
39. The phrase he used was "gänzlich unalpin ausgerüstet" (outfitted in an extremely un-Alpine way). Moreover, they did not strike him as a father-son pair, and he believed they were Italian and could not understand what they said. Testimony of

Wilhelm Geilenkirchen, TLA, File St 3972/28 6 Vr 1380/28, Innsbrucker Landesgericht, 104.

40. Karl Meixner notes, "The shoes of both Halsmanns were actually nailed together in a very strange way, which none of those involved had ever seen before, even though foreigners from all over the world come to climb the mountains of the Tyrol." "Lehren des Halsmannprozesses (Mit 28 Abbildungen)," in *Beiträge zur gerichtlichen Medizin*, vol 10, ed. Albin Haberda (Leipzig and Vienna: Franz Deuticke Verlag, 1930), 57.
41. Robert A. Kann, *A History of the Habsburg Empire, 1526–1918* (Berkeley: University of California Press, 1974), 186.
42. See Robert Musil, "*Anschluss* with Germany," in *Robert Musil: Precision and Soul: Essays and Addresses*, eds. and trans. Burton Pike and David Luft (Chicago: University of Chicago Press, 1990), 96.
43. The first passion play took place in 1634 in Oberammergau, Bavaria. The town's residents took a vow that if God would spare them from the bubonic plague, they would have thousands of participants perform in plays in the first five months of each ten-year period. The play featured dramatic text, choral music, and tableaux vivants representing Christianity's supersession of Judaism and the crucifixion. See Robert Michael, *A History of Catholic Antisemitism: The Dark Side of the Church* (New York: Palgrave McMillan, 2008), 105. Perforances of passion plays and other religious folk plays featured as important parts of the cultural history of several Tyrolean towns in the vicinity of Innsbruck, including Wattens, Amras, Axams, Jenbach, and many others. See Adalbert Sikora, "Zur Geschichte der Volksschauspiele in Tirol," *Zeitschrift des Ferdinandeums für Tirol und Vorarlberg*, no. 50 (1906).
44. On the social function of blood libel trials in the communities in which they took place, see Kieval, "Representation and Knowledge," 55–56.
45. Three blood libel accusations took place in the Tyrol, including that of Ursula of Lienz (1442), Anderl of Rinn (1462), and Simon of Trent (1475). Accusations against Jews also occurred throughout Lower Austria, Styria, and Carinthia. See Norman Roth, ed. *Medieval Jewish Civilization* (New York: Routledge, 2001), 300. Major blood libel trials also occurred in Tisza-Eszlár (Austria-Hungary), Skurcz bei Danzig, Lutscha (Austria-Hungary), Breslau, Corfu (Greece), and Xanten (Germany) between 1880 and 1895.
46. See Langmuir, *Toward a Definition of Antisemitism*, especially chapter 9; and David Biale, *Blood and Belief: The Circulation of a Symbol between Jews and Christians* (Berkeley: University of California Press, 2007), 111–12.
47. Walser Smith also points out that the first ritual murder accusations in the twelfth century, which claimed that Jews killed boys and nailed them to crosses, later morphed into accusations of Jews having murdered children for their blood and for host desecration. Thirteenth-century historian Matthew Paris's account of the

twelfth-century death of William of Norwich claimed that in carrying out their ritual reenactment, Jews assigned themselves expanded roles, including that of Pontius Pilate and other Romans; they forced Christ to die an even more gruesome and torturous death. "Anti-semitic violence as reenactment: An essay in cultural history," 338. Ritual murder trials have long served as the basis not only for passion plays, but also for poems and dramas. For a list of early popular works based upon ritual murder accusations, see Alan Dundes, ed., *The Blood Libel Legend: A Casebook in Anti-Semitic Folklore*. (Madison: University of Wisconsin Press, 1991), 363 n. 42. On the power of folklore to influence historical events and the adaptation of accusations of blood libel to new circumstances over the centuries, see Georg R. Schroubek, "Zur Tradierung und Diffusion einer europäischen Aberglaubensvorstellung," in *Die Legende vom Ritualmord. Zur Geschichte der Blutbeschuldigung gegen Juden*, ed. Rainer Erb (Berlin: Metropol, 1993). Here, I also draw upon Walser Smith's illuminating account of the ritual murder accusation and ensuing violence in Konitz, Germany in 1900, in which he underscores the importance of the process according to which long-standing anti-semitic attitudes are transformed into acts, and how, in such cases, stories are made to conform to pre-existing religious and political patterns. See *The Butcher's Tale: Murder and Anti-Semitism in a German Town* (New York: W.W. Norton, 2002), 22. Walser Smith also notes that art historian Aby Warburg was one of the first cultural historians to seriously pursue how blood libel accusations could become lodged in the "social memory" of communities over time and then instrumentalized in the service of modern political needs. Warburg, who collected material on the Konitz case in particular, was interested in how they functioned to shape the "social memory" of a community. See also Charlotte Schoell-Glass, *Aby Warburg and Anti-Semitism: Political Perspectives on Images and Culture*. Detroit, MI (Wayne State University Press, 2008), 60.

48. Walser Smith distinguishes between two types of reenactment that were deeply embedded in German cultural history: ritual murder charges that sparked outbursts of violence against Jews, and those that were ritually bound, in which Jews were threatened and and denigrated but not killed. He links passion plays and other forms of theatrical reenactments to the latter form. "Anti-Semitic violence as reenactment: An essay in cultural history," *Rethinking History* 11, no. 3 (2007): 339–40.
49. Kieval, "Representation and Knowledge," 52–72. On the debates about ritual murder accusations in the parliament of Austria-Hungary at the end of the nineteenth century, see Albert Lichtblau, "Die Debatten über die Ritualmordbeschuldigungen im österreichischen Abgeordnetenhaus am Ende des 19. Jahrhunderts," in Erb, *Die Legende vom Ritualmord*.
50. Robert S. Wistrich, *Socialism and the Jews: The Dilemmas of Assimilation in Germany and Austria-Hungary* (East Brunswick, NJ: Associated University Press,

1982), 187–88. On the reasons behind the nineteenth-century resurgence of blood libel accusations see Hartston, *Sensationalizing the Jewish Question*, 129.

51. David Biale notes that antisemitic publications like *Der Stürmer* evoked ritual murder symbols explicitly in the interwar period. Biale, *Blood and Belief*, 130. However, ritual murder did not only spark the imaginations of Nazis. On the tropes of ritual murder in dramas and novels by authors such as Thomas Mann, Arnold Zweig, and Franz Kafka, see Arnold J. Band, "Refractions of the Blood Libel in Modern Literature," in *Studies in Modern Jewish Literature* (Philadelphia: Jewish Publication Society, 2003), 317–38; and Sander L. Gilman, *Franz Kafka: The Jewish Patient* (New York: Routledge, 1995), esp. 121–51.
52. Rimalt, "The Jews of Tyrol," 376. Of the three ritual murder accusations against Jews that took place in the Tyrol, the legend of Anderl of Rinn was the most popular. Hofinger, "Tirol den Tirolern!," 83–84.
53. According to the legend, in 1462, Jewish salesmen passing through the area on their way to the fair in Bolzano supposedly tortured, slaughtered, and hung a three-year old boy named Andreas Oxner; miracles were said to have taken place on his grave. In 1620–21, a Jesuit play based on the events was first performed; there were also regular liturgical processions to the site of his supposed murder, the *Judenstein*. The local parish church featured a painting of the events of the murder. Richard Utz attests to the "strong ceremonial and memorial ties between conservative Tyrolean identity and the story." See "Remembering Ritual Murder: The Anti-Semitic Blood Accusation Narrative in Medieval and Contemporary Cultural Memory," in *Genre and Ritual: The Cultural Heritage of Medieval Rituals*, ed. Eyolf Østrem, Mette Birkedal Bruun, Nils Holger Petersen, and Jens Fleischer (Copenhagen: Museum Tusculanum Press, 2005), 155–57. Leander Petzoldt's research attests to the depth to which the veneration of Anderl was firmly implanted in the local culture. "Religion between Sentiment and Protest: the Suspension of the Cult of 'Andreas[Anderl] von Rinn in the Tyrol," *International Folklore Review* 10: (1995), 24; Georg R. Schroubek, "Andreas von Rinn: Der Kult eines 'heiligen Ritualmordopfers' im historischen Wandel," *Österreichische Zeitschrift für Volkskunde*, 49 no. 4 (1995); and Schroubek, "Judenfeindliche Kulte und regionale Identität. Religiöse Verehrung von Ritualmordopfern und die Folgen," in *Denn das Sterben des Menschen hört nie auf. Askpekte jüdischen Lebens in Vergangenheit und Gegenwart*, ed. Ulrich Wagner (Würzburg: Schöningh, 1997), 157–68.
54. For more details on the cult surrounding Anderl von Rinn and its continued—and contested—importance to the construction of self-identification in Tyrol throughout the twentieth century, see Petzoldt, "Religion between Sentiment and Protest," 21–34.
55. Ernst Ruzicka, *Max Halsmanns Ermordung: Der Schlüssel der Wahrheit* (Vienna: Krystall-Verlag, 1930).

56. See the account of the events Philipp Halsmann gave at the first trial in December, 1928. TLA, File St 3972/28 6 Vr 1380/28, Innsbrucker Landesgericht, 21.
57. Marbe, *Der Strafprozess gegen Philipp Halsmann*, 41. Philipp and others later pointed out, to no avail, that it would make little sense for a guilty murderer to point to the bloodiest spot as his standing place. See Carl Brockhausen, "Geleitwort," in *Der Fall Halsmann: Schriften der österreichischen Liga für Menschenrechte*, vol. 3 (Vienna: Verlag Gilhofer & Anschburg, 1931), 2. For more on the "pathologized, lying Jew" as well as Jews and sexualized, criminalized acitivity, see Sander L. Gilman, *The Case of Sigmund Freud. Medicine and Identity at the Fin de Siècle* (Baltimore: Johns Hopkins University Press, 1993).
58. As the prosecutor in Innsbruck indicated in his September 26, 1929, report to the federal ministry of justice in Vienna, the jury found Halsmann guilty largely based on statements by court experts, who ruled out that Halsmann could have died accidentally based on the bloody stone and bloodstains found at the top of the cliff; they also concluded that Halsmann's contention that he was only fifteen to twenty steps away from his father when he fell ruled out the possibility that a third party could have murdered Halsmann. ÖStA, Bundesministerium für Justiz (BfJ), File 33901/1931, VI Karton 3402, Folder 34414/1931, GZ 36.504-4/29, VZ 36.388/29, NZ 36.628 /29. Philipp's appeal of the first guilty verdict claimed that the jury had been mistaken in deeming the death as the result of murder, and not an accident. By the time of the retrial, however, it was clear to Philipp and the defense that Max Halsmann's extensive wounds could not have resulted from an accident.
59. In 1935, the Jewish community of Innsbruck appealed to the Tyrolean Landestag to censor the antisemitic portrayal of Jews in a performance in Rinn of a new version of what one government official called the "well-known Judenstein legend." They asked the authorities to strike phrases such as: "Godless Jews," "a pious, kosher, Christian child," "the Jews killed a child there," "we need the child's blood for our Osterbrot (matzoh)," and a scene in which the Jews "sharpen their knives" while the child wails. The official attests to the justifiable complaints of the Jewish community about the negative language and characterizations of Jews, but also emphasizes how dismayed the townspeople are about the possible ban on or censorship of the play. One local leader suggested that defending the play from the Jews' attempts at censorship led to a positive outcome: it greatly unified the (non-Jewish) townspeople. The drama was immensely popular and played to sold-out audiences from Innsbruck, Hall, and the Zillertal. Although some performances were apparently censored according to a ruling of the Landestag, a memo in the files of the Union of Austrian Jews suggests that later performances reverted to the original antisemitic language. See the memo of the Präsidium des Amtes der Landesregierung von Tirol, November 1935; letter to the Bezirkshauptmannschaft in Rinn from the Gendarmeriepostenkommando Rinn, November 8, 1935; letter from Heinrich Schuler,

Prämonstratenser-Chorherrenstift Wilten, November 11, 1935; *Tiroler Anzeiger*, April 9, 1936, TLA, Amt der Landesregierung für Tirol, Präsidium, Geschäftszahl XII 61-1549. See also the memo of the December 13, 1935 visit of rabbi E. S. Rimalt to Oskar Hirschfeld, Records of the Union österreicher Juden, Wien, Fond 714, manuscript RG-11.001M.29, Reel 103, archive of the United States Holocaust Memorial Museum.

60. As Sander L. Gilman reminds us, the imagine of the Eastern European Jew as a sexually deviant murderer was an important part of how the public visualized the figure of Jack the Ripper, murderer of prostitutes in London's East End, at the end of the nineteenth century. A high proportion of the 130 men questioned in the case of Jack the Ripper were Jews. Sander L. Gilman, *The Jew's Body* (New York: Routledge, 1991), 113, 119.
61. When it became clear that Philipp and his family in fact became poorer as a result of Max's death, the prosecution was forced to drop the absurd assertion that Philipp stood to profit from his father's death. Another witness, however, highlighted the fact that that Max Halsmann had haggled over the price of the tour.
62. TLA, File St 3972/28 6 Vr 1380/28, Innsbrucker Landesgericht, 11.
63. Alfred Kastil, "Denkschrift," in *Der Fall Halsmann, Schriften der Österreichischen Liga für Menschenrechte III* (Vienna: Gilhofer & Ranschburg, 1931), 23. Jews were considered to be rational, clever, modern and acting on their own volition; if they occupied powerful social positions, they sabotaged crime investigations and trials, and victims of their schemes were portrayed as innocent and helpless. See Vyleta, *Crime, News, and Jews*, 316. See also Gilman, *The Jews' Body*, 128–49.
64. Meixner, "Lehren des Halsmannprozesses," 84–85. Meixner was not the only medical expert commissioned by the court with prejudices against Halsmann. In his own published account, Dr. Eduard Gamper described his character as "impenetrable" and "nervous" and claimed that the positive statements made by his character witnesses during the second trial made sense if one recognized these as the result of his efforts to hide his true "hidden"—and much more negative—character: "Behind the austere seriousness of his outward demeanor lies hidden a peculiar conflicting nature and inner insecurity." Dr. Eduard Gamper, "Der Gutachten der medizinischen Fakultät Innsbruck in der Strafsache gegen Philipp Halsmann," *Beiträge zur gerichtlichen Medizin*, band 10, ed. Prof. Dr. Albin Haberda (Leipzig and Vienna: Franz Deuticke, 1930), 127. That Jews were two-faced and possessed a keen ability to hide their true nature had long been a common antisemitic accusation. For more on antisemitism in Innsbruck during the interwar period, see Pauley, *From Prejudice to Persecution*, 99.
65. As Philipp's defense frequently pointed out, this contention made little sense in light of the fact that Max Halsmann's death had a negative effect on the family's financial situation. However, one witness who knew Philipp as a student in Dresden claimed that, during a visit in 1924, his father had made "inappropriate comments" and referred to Philipp as "Nasletnik" which, he admitted, meant

"successor." Oskar Grünberg, TLA, File St 3972/28 6 Vr 1380/28, Innsbrucker Landesgericht, 106.

66. "It's possible that my father said at that time that I wanted to succeed him. That was a favorite joke of his. He often tended to present me as his heir." Philipp Halsmann, TLA, File St 3972/28 6 Vr 1380/28, Innsbrucker Landesgericht, 16.
67. "Regarding defense lawyer Pessler's question about whether he said to the witness Gaus that when he comes across a Jew, he should keep left, and when he comes across a Christian he should keep right, the witness explained: That is untrue, I did not say that. On the contrary—I told the witnesses from the Zillertal that nobody should mention Jews, otherwise the whole thing would immediately be labeled a *Judenhetzerei* (attack against Jews)." The court then explains that "keeping left" in this sense (*linkshalten*) is slang expression meaning "to lie." TLA, File St 3972/28 6 Vr 1380/28, Innsbrucker Landesgericht, 52.
68. Later, under pressure from Halsmann's defense, Wimmer retracted his statement: He told his congregation it was not for him to say whether Halsmann had actually murdered his father. This episode is related by Artur Glaser in the same report. ÖStA, BfJ, File 33901/1931, VI Karton 3402, Folder 34414/1931, GZ 36.388-4/29, VZ 36.327/29, NZ 36.504 /29.
69. Richard Pressburger includes a copy of this poster with a letter to the federal ministry of justice in Vienna in which he complains again about the antisemitic atmosphere in Innsbruck that is negatively influencing the trial. Report of October 11, 1929, ÖStA, BfJ, File 33901/1931, VI Karton 3402, Folder 34414/1931, GZ 6.721-4/29, VZ 36.661/29, NZ 36.937/09. Pressburger also wrote that he had been attacked on his way from the courtroom back to his hotel, which is the reason he decided not to continue to act as defense lawyer for Halsmann. "From the first day of this trial it was my impression that I was in the land of the enemy." Letter from Richard Pressburger to the federal ministry of justice in Vienna of October 10, 1929. Pressburger also ends his letter with the assurance that he is not only an experienced defense attorney, but also an "old Austrian, who views the Tyrol as a part of his beloved fatherland" and in this capacity asks that the ministry reverse this error of justice. Letter from Pressburger to federal ministry of justice, September 24, 1929. Just how overdetermined the Jewishness of Halsmann's lawyer was is apparent from the fact that, for the second trial, Halsmann chose the non-Jewish, Tyrolean lawyer Pessler as his leading defense attorney, although that did not stop unfounded rumors that he, too, was actually a Jew.
70. Halsmann's lawyers visited the federal ministry of justice on September 25, 1929 to claim there was new evidence that Max Halsmann had been robbed, and to complain that local antisemitism was negatively influencing the trial. ÖStA, BfJ, File 33901/1931, VI Karton 3402, Folder 34414/1931, GZ 36.388-4/29, VZ 36.327/29, NZ 36.504 /29.
71. In the same file, an undated report on the "Prozess Halsmann," notes that Dr. Glaser [Artur], the editor of the *Neues Wiener Tagblatt*, had visited the federal

ministry of justice and had confirmed that a jury member named Diemetz had claimed "Ja, die Juden werden wir schon hineintunken." (We'll surely bring down the Jews.) A report of the Innsbruck police confirms witness statements that Diemetz accompanied this statement with a "thumbs up" gesture. Report of the Städtische Polizei Kriminaldienst, October 1, 1929. ÖStA, BfJ, File 33901/1931, VI Karton 3402, Folder 34414/1931, GZ 36.388-4/29, VZ 36.327/29, NZ 36.504 /29.

72. On psychoanalysis as a "Jewish science," see Sander L. Gilman, *The Case of Sigmund Freud.*
73. On antisemitic associations of Jews with the "circulation" of both blood and money, see Biale, *Blood and Belief*, 7–8.
74. For the prosecution's reasoning for Halsmann's indictment on November 29, 1928, see ÖStA, BfJ, File 33901/1931, VI Karton 3402, Folder 34414/1931, GZ 38.381-4/28, VZ 37.676/28, NZ 35.452 /29.
75. In the indictment, the prosecutor noted only that Eder claimed the grass looked as though a "heavy body" had been pulled through it. For Eder's complete statement to the court, see TLA, File St 3972/28 6 Vr 1380/28, Innsbrucker Landesgericht, 54–56. References to Jews as pigs and Jewish publications as "piglike" were common; the term "Saujud" (Jew pig) was a slur that Philipp's (non-Jewish) lawyer Franz Pessler often heard uttered in the courtroom. Pessler, "Ein Bild des Prozesses," in *Der Fall Halsmann*, 42, 44.
76. On the association of the murder of Simon of Trent with the *Judensau*, see Avner Falk, *A Psychoanalytic History of the Jews* (Cranbury, NJ: Associated University Press, 1996), 498–500. On the motif of the Judensau, see Isaiah Shachar, *The Judensau: A Medieval Anti-Jewish Motif and Its History* (London: Warburg Institute, 1974).
77. Eder, TLA, File St 3972/28 6 Vr 1380/28, Innsbrucker Landesgericht, 55.
78. Moreover, as an innkeeper, Eder occupied a special position. As Ian F.D. Morrow's guidebook suggests, the tradition of viewing innkeepers as community leaders and their legendary roles in Tyrolean folklore was a popular marketing tool for tourism. "As in war so as in peace, the innkeepers of Tyrol have not seldom proved themselves the leaders of the small communities to which their inns serve as a meeting-place. In the village councils the innkeepers frequently exercise an influence second only to that of the village priest, and they are often to be found wielding the by no means insignificant authority with which the *Bürgermeister* [mayor] is invested." The guidebook also mentions that Andreas Hofer and at least one other of his "warriors" had been innkeepers. See *The Austrian Tyrol: The Land in the Mountains* (London: Faber and Faber, 1931), 304–5.
79. Letter from Philipp Halsmann to the federal ministry of justice, June 15, 1931, ÖStA, BfJ, File 33901/1931, VI Karton 3402, Folder 34414/1931, GZ 34.417–4
80. Meixner was born in Vienna in 1879 and completed his *Habilitation* in 1912 at Vienna's Institute of Forensic Medicine. He came to Innsbruck only in 1927. In

Vienna, he had been an honorary member of the radical Burschenschaft "Olympia," a group popular with antisemitic leaders that had included an *Arierparagraph* in its bylaws as early as 1889. See Niko Hofinger, "'. . . man spricht nicht gerne von dem Prozeß, es sind noch zu viele Fremde da': Die Halsmann-Affäre 1928–1930," in *Politische Skandale und Affären in Österreich: von Mayerling bis Waldheim*, ed. Michael Gehler and Hubert Sickinger (Thaur: Kulturverlag, 1995), 195, n.3; and *Deutsche Zeitschrift für gerichtliche Medizin* 44 (1955): 341–42.

81. TLA, File St 3972/28 6 Vr 1380/28, Innsbrucker Landesgericht, 153.
82. ÖStA, BP, File Z 36.305/30.
83. Nicole Emanuel, "Philippe Halsman, a personal story," *In Touch, Newsletter of the Friends of the Jewish Museum Hohenems* 9, no. 1 (January 2008): 8–11. According to Emanuel (Philipp's grand-niece), Liouba was on vacation in Paris at the time and did not learn of her father's death until ten days after the murder, when she travelled immediately to Innsbruck and found her mother, Ita, wandering the streets in shock. See also Pollack, *Anklage Vatermord*, 64.
84. Pessler, *Der Fall Halsmann*, 76.
85. Until that point, Max Halsmann's head was still preserved at the University of Innsbruck medical school; only upon the insistence of the Austrian minister of science and research did the university contact the Jewish community about arranging for its interment with the rest of Max Halsmann's body in 1991. See the letter from Erhard Busek to Rainer Sprung, University of Innsbruck, dated March 7, 1991; copy available in the TLA, File St 3972/28 6 Vr 1380/28, Innsbrucker Landesgericht. Only upon the intervention of journalists and various other university and state officials was the head returned to his grave. Ironically, it was immediately dug up again due to questions regarding the legitimacy of the original request for its interment; Max's head was returned to the grave for the last time at a ceremony on November 12, 1991. See Hofinger, "'. . . man spricht nicht gerne," 220–21.
86. Ross, *Marrano*, 21.
87. *Arbeiter-Zeitung*, September 15, 1929.
88. *Der Morgen*, December 2, 1929.
89. The telegram of September 21, 1929 sent to the minister of justice and to the president was signed by editors and reporters of over thirty national and international newspapers from Vienna, Berlin, Munich, Dresden, Paris, Madrid, Riga, New York, and Chicago. ÖStA, BfJ, File 33901/1931, VI Karton 3402, Folder 34414/1931, GZ 36.324-4/29, VZ 35.452/29, NZ 36.327 /29. The BfJ relates Baldauf's statement in an undated report. ÖStA, BfJ, File 33901/1931, VI Karton 3402, Folder 34414/1931, GZ 36.388-4/29, VZ 36.327/29, NZ 36.504 /29.
90. Report of the Innsbruck Staatsanwaltschaft (public prosecutor) on the visit of Franz Baldauf, editor of the *Tiroler Anzeiger*, on September 25, 1929. ÖStA, BfJ.
91. Report of the Innsbruck Oberstaatsanwaltschaft (senior public prosecutor), December 28, 1928 to the BmJ, ÖStA, BfJ, File 33901/1931, VI Karton 3402, Folder 34414/1931, GZ 36.324-4/29, VZ 35.452/29, NZ 36.327 /29.

92. Report of the Innsbruck Oberstaatsanwaltschaft (senior public prosecutor), December 28, 1928 to the BmJ, ÖStA, BfJ, File 33901/1931, VI Karton 3402, Folder 34414/1931, GZ 36.388-4/29, VZ 36.327/29, NZ 36.504 /29.
93. Report of the Innsbruck public prosecutor to the Innsbruck senior public prosecutor, December 18, 1928.
94. Only the ultra–right-wing newspapers reminded readers in vain that the occasion of a Jew killing another Jew is an event to be celebrated, not condemned: *Kikeriki*, September 22, 1929, and *Der eiserne Besen*, September 27 and October 25, 1929. In his report of October 3, 1929, the prosecutor admits that the *Der eiserne Besen* has published negative articles about Halsmann and Pressburger, but insists it is an "unknown" and "fully irrelevant" newspaper from Salzburg, the influence of which cannot be compared to the "big Viennese daily papers." ÖstA, BfJ, File 33901/1931, VI Karton 3402, Folder 34414/1931, GZ 36.661/29
95. TLA, File St 3972/28 6 Vr 1380/28, Innsbrucker Landesgericht, 87.
96. "Das Momentbild des nach rückwärts geneigten Vaters war wie auf einer photographischen Platte fixiert. Mit fixiert meine ich nicht deutlich sondern bewegungslos und fix . . . Ich habe den Absturz selbst nicht gesehen." TLA, File St 3972/28 6 Vr 1380/28, Innsbrucker Landesgericht, 21
97. Marsha Rozenblit notes that Jews in Vienna converted at a higher rate than anyone else in the dual monarchy, and that Protestantism may have been a more comfortable choice than "ornate, ritualistic Catholicism." See Marsha L. Rozenblit, *The Jews of Vienna, 1867–1914: Assimilation and Identity* (Albany: State University of New York Press, 1983), 128, 136. On Jewish conversion in the interwar period, see the Introduction.
98. See John W. Boyer, *Political Radicalism in Late Imperial Vienna. Origins of the Christian Social Movement 1848–1897* (Chicago: University of Chicago Press, 1981), 88.
99. Bettauer died sixteen days later, on March 26, 1925, of serious injuries caused by the shooting. Before he died, Balder Olden, the brother of Bettauer's partner Rudolf, claimed that Bettauer was apparently eager to get back to work and resolved to continue holding *Sprechstunden* (consultation hours) despite the shooting. Bettauer also apparently retained his wry sense of humor after the shooting. "In the hospital he complained to the doctor, 'You want to keep me from my work' and promised that 'During future consultations I'll keep a revolver on the table.'" Balder Olden, *Die Literarische Welt*, March 23, 1928, 3.
100. He launched the publication in 1924 together with Rudolf Olden. The first week's circulation of 60,000 increased to 200,000 within five weeks; that number was greater than the circulation of most of Vienna's daily political papers. See Beth Noveck, "Hugo Bettauer and the Political Culture of the First Republic," *Contemporary Austrian Studies* 3 (1995), 141.
101. Noveck, "Hugo Bettauer," 148.
102. Noveck, "Hugo Bettauer," 140. For a discussion of both the book and the film, see Chapter 2.

103. Despite their innovations in health care and marriage counseling, the Social Democratic municipal government was notoriously timid on matters of birth control and abortion. See Helmut Gruber, *Red Vienna: Experiment in Working Class Culture 1919–1934* (New York: Oxford University Press, 1991), 179.
104. *Er und Sie: Wochenschrift für Lebenskultur und Erotik*, Nr. 1, February, 14, 1924, and Nr. 2, February 31, 1924.
105. The fact that the number of ads rose from 14 to 123 in only one month speaks to their popularity. Both men and women placed ads, and those who wrote them frequently referred to themselves as "Jew" or "Aryan," or indicated one or the other as a preferred partner.
106. Bruce Pauley characterizes Seipel's antisemitism as restrained compared to that of other politicians, but at times ambiguous and tinged with racial overtones. See *From Prejudice to Persecution*, 163.
107. "Stenographischer Bericht über die Sitzung des Gemeinderates," March 21, 1924, Archiv der Universität Wien, 1058. In 1921, Anton Orel had published a political tract that denounced the Austrian constitution and its principle of popular sovereignty as having created a "miserable Jews' republic" in which Catholics were subjected to a "Jewish overlord." See *Das Verfassungsmachwerk der 'Republik Österreich' von der Warte der immerwährenden Philosophie aus und im Lichte von der Idee, Natur und Geschichte Österreichs geprüft und verworfen*, (Vienna: Vogelsang, 1921), 30. Orel had already participated in one of the biggest antisemitic rallies in the early postwar years, the International Congress of the *Antisemitenbund* held from March 11–13, 1921. In a speech there he called Jews the "incarnation of the anti-Christ" who were destroying Christian-German culture; he also warned against world domination by Jews. Pauley, *From Prejudice to Persecution*, 82.
108. *Der Volkssturm*, March 30, 1924, 1. Cited in Murray G. Hall, "Hugo Bettauer," in *Elektrische Schatten: Beiträge zur österreichischen Stummfilmgeschichte*, ed. Francesco Bono, Paolo Caneppele, and Günter Kren (Vienna: Filmarchiv, 1999), 150–51. Hall points out that this trial placed Bettauer in the middle of the tense political situation between Red Vienna and the Christian Social national government.
109. WStLa, 2.3.4.A11–VrLGI (1920–1938 auch LG II) | 1851–1950, 1953–1958 1776/24 (Hugo Bettauer and Rudolf Olden); Noveck, "Hugo Bettauer," 147.
110. *Bettauers Wochenschrift* 9 (1925).
111. Noveck, "Hugo Bettauer," 102, 141.
112. The performances took place in Vienna's Volkstheater beginning on February 1, 1921, under the direction of Alfred Bernau. Antisemitic disturbances on February 8 and 16 also led to a deepening of tensions between the Christian Social federal government and the Social Democrat leadership of Vienna, as the federal minister for the interior and education Egon Glanz overrode the decisions of local authorities and banned future performances. Alfred Pfoser, "Der Wiener '*Reigen*-Skandal,' Sexualangst als politisches Syndrom der Ersten Republik," in *Neuere Studien zur Arbeitergeschichte*, vol. 3, ed. Helmut Konrad and Wolfgang

Maderthaner (Vienna: Europaverlag, 1984), 676–89. In his article about the "scandal" for the *Reichspost*, Karl Paumgartten (see Introduction) castigates Social Democrats as the protectors of the "Jews" Schnitzler and Bernau. "Hinter den Kulissen der 'Reigen'-Schützer," February 14, 1921, 1–2. The *Neue Freie Presse* reported that men and women in the audience were mishandled and that the theater suffered damages. "Gewaltsame Verhinderung der heutigen 'Reigen' Aufführung," *Neue Freie Presse*, February 17, 1921, 1.

113. Daniel Vyleta points out that before 1914, right-wing newspapers in Central Europe often connected criminal acts to Jews even when there was no Jewish suspect or defendant, while other newspapers used antisemitic idioms only occasionally—though always consciously. Vyleta, *Crime, Jews, and News*, 115, 223. The widespread antisemitism in Vienna's newspapers during this trial suggests that at least some newspapers intensified their use of antisemitic rhetoric during the interwar period.
114. Even when they opposed the Christian Social stance against pornography, Social Democrats waffled on issues of public morality. Murray Hall also suggests that the press, not Rothstock, worked hardest to play up antisemitism as a reason for the killing, and that Riehl pushed Rothstock in this direction as well. See Murray G. Hall, *Der Fall Bettauer* (Vienna: Löcker,1978), 205 n. 8.
115. Noveck, "Hugo Bettauer," 149–50.
116. "Ein Revolverattentat," *Reichspost*, March 11, 1925, 1.
117. Rode, whose name was Johann Walter Rosenzweig until he converted to Catholicism in 1899, was the son of Czernowitz merchant and politician Leon Rosenzweig, who published the anonymous book "Wir Juden: Betrachtungen und Vorschläge" (1883) and advocated for full Jewish assimilation. See *Walther Rode: Leben und Werk*, ed. Gerd Baumgartner (Vienna: Löcker, 2007).
118. WStLA MA 8; 2.3.4.A11—Vr LG I, 1851–1956, Vr 1748/25 Rothstock; Noveck, "Hugo Bettauer," 149–50.
119. WStLA MA 8; 2.3.4.A11—Vr LG I, 1851–1956, Vr 1748/25, Hauptverhandlung. Rudolf Olden, co-publisher of *Bettauers Wochenschrift*, claimed the deck was stacked against Bettauer since the judge refused to question Rothstock's statements. Instead, the judge read to the court a dozen evaluations against his writings, allowed the police to testify that prostitutes regularly read Bettauer's novels, and let Rothstock's lawyer Riehl "sing an aria to the young hero who had done a knightly deed protecting Austrians, who had been so deeply poisoned by Jews that they didn't deserve him. So for the whole day the trial was about Bettauer, Jews, and the 'immoral' media. Just not about Rothstock." "Oesterreichische Köpfe," *Die Weltbühne* 21:2 (1925): 591–94. As noted above, Riehl's talent for turning murder trials into rants against the corrupt, Jewish media would prove useful to his defense of Oskar Pöffel in 1928.
120. Police memo dated March 11, 1925, WStLA, MA 8; 2.3.4.A11—Vr LG I, 1851–1956, Vr 1748/25.

121. WStLA MA 8; 2.3.4.A11—Vr LG I, 1851–1956, Vr 1748/25 Rothstock.
122. WStLA MA 8; 2.3.4.A11—Vr LG I, 1851–1956, Vr 1748/25 Rothstock.
123. Polizeidirektion Wien, March 11, 1925. WStLA MA 8; 2.3.4.A11—Vr LG I, 1851–1956, Vr 1748/25. The Jewish community of Vienna holds no record of Eisler having either been born or registered as Jewish. (He is apparently not related to the Austrian Jewish philosopher of the same name born in 1873, who was father of the composer Hanns Eisler.) There are a number of other Rudolf Eislers registered in the community during that time, but none born in 1872.
124. "Dass ich bei Eisler blieb, ist darauf zurückzuführen, weil ich froh war, überhaupt einen Posten gefunden zu haben. Ich war übrigens auch bei einem Juden, den ich sehr geschätzt habe. Doch Eisler war ein Sohn der Lüge und des Satans, und ich musste doch dort bleiben." WStLA MA 8; 2.3.4.A11—Vr LG I, 1851–1956, Vr 1748/25, Hauptverhandlung, 9.
125. "Prozess Rothstock," *Bettauers Wochenschrift* 40 (1925), 1.
126. See also Murray Hall, "Hugo Bettauer," in *Elektrische Schatten. Beiträge zur österreichischen Stummfilmgeschichte*, ed. Francesco Bono, Paolo Caneppele, and Günter Kren (Vienna: Filmarchiv, 1999), 168.
127. In a letter from September 7, 1976 to the German Parliament, Rothstock continued his "crusade" against pornography from his home in Germany. See Hall, *Der Fall Bettauer*, 182, 184. And in a September 6, 1976, letter to Murray Hall, who first extensively researched this case decades ago, Otto Rothstock admitted that he had lied in his testimony; the letter also suggests that his antisemitic motives were real, yet also trumped up for the purposes of the trial. "Despite my youth, as I shot B. face to face on March 10, 1925, I knew I wasn't eliminating the main culprit in the demoralization of young Germans. Back then, like today, I wasn't an outspoken antisemite, I was only rebelling against the fact that a Jew wanted to eroticize the youth and started a business to do it. I also explained at the time of my arrest that I carried out the act out of love for my contemporaries, as it was intended to serve as a warning shot for our leaders. Nobody knew of my intention, and I bought the pistol myself in a gun shop. There was no conspiracy; my statement to that effect was a bluff." See also Hall, *Der Fall Bettauer*, 182, 184. Rothstock also made this statement in a remarkable interview for the Austrian television program *teleobjektiv* in 1977, in which he reveals himself as a racist and antisemite. He expresses his longing for the higher moral standards of the past and decries the current mixing of races; he even goes so far as to praise Jews for "their tendency not to engage in race-mixing." When asked whether he had truly been *Sinnesverwirrt* at the time of the murder, he chuckles and states that, in contrast to what he had claimed in court, he had never been confused, nobody else had put him up to the task, and he "had always known what he was doing." He claimed his motive was to send an *Alarmschuss* (alarm shot) to the government. I am grateful to Murray Hall for making this interview available to me.

128. WStLA, MA 8; 2.3.4.A11—Vr LG I, 1851–1956, Vr 1748/25 Rothstock
129. "Es wird sich doch ein Rothstock finden" became a popular phrase used to threaten professors at the University in Vienna between 1934 and 1938. For example, it was used specifically to threaten Jewish-born law professor and drafter of the Austrian constitution Hans Kelsen in 1930; he emigrated soon thereafter. See Renate Lotz-Rimbach, "Mord verjährt nicht: Psychogramm eines politischen Mordes," in *Stationen: dem Philosophen und Physiker Moritz Schlick zum 125. Geburtstag*, ed. Friedrich Stadler and Hans Jürgen Wendel (Vienna: Springer-Verlag 2009), 83.
130. "So Hund, du verfluchter, jetzt hast du es." WStLA, 5.
131. For more details, see Peter Malina, "Tatort: Philosophenstiege. Zur Ermordung von Moritz Schlick am 22. Juni 1936," in *Bewußtsein, Sprache und die Kunst: Metamorphosen der Wahrheit*, ed. Michael Benedikt and Rudolf Burger (Vienna: Verlag der österreichischen Staatsdruckerei, 1988). Schlick had served as adviser for his doctoral dissertation, *Die Bedeutung der Logik im Empirismus und Positivismus* (The Meaning of Logic in Empiricism and Positivism); soon after receiving his degree in 1931, Nelböck began harassing him.
132. He also had a personal relationship with the scientist and played with him in a chamber music ensemble after meeting him in Germany. Michael Siegert, "Mit dem Browning philosophiert: Der Mord an Moritz Schlick am 22. Juni 1936," *FORUM* 28, no. 331/332 (July/August 1981), 26.
133. Hans-Joachim Dahms, "The Emigration of the Vienna Circle," in *Vertreibung der Vernunft: The Cultural Exodus from Austria*, ed. Friedrich Stadler and Peter Weibel (Vienna: Springer, 1995), 58, 61.
134. I was unable to read, or to find anyone else who could decipher, the handwritten minutes from a committee meeting of February 7, 1914. Archiv der Universität Wien, Moritz Schlick, PHS 34.24. For Friedrich Stadler's interpretation of these minutes, see "The Vienna Circle and the University of Vienna," in Stadler and Weibel, eds., *Vertreibung der Vernunft*, 48. The committee asked Emil Reich, who taught practical philosophy, and Richard von Wettstein, a botanist. Stadler implies they did not want Schlick in any case and had been searching for an excuse not to appoint him—but did not find it. Schlick was ultimately appointed despite opposition.
135. Lotz-Rimbach outlines the career of Leo Gabriel and his ties to the leadership of the Vaterländischen Front. It is through representing Gabriel at the Volksheim Brigittenau that Nelböck switched from positivism to antipositivism. Renate Lotz-Rimbach, "Zur Biografie Leo Gabriels: Revision und Ergänzung der Selbstdarstellung eines Philosophen und Rektors der Universität Wien," *zeitgeschichte* 6, no. 31 (2004).
136. Lotz-Rimbach, "Mord verjährt nicht," 91.
137. He was in part successful, and they held some lectures in 1934-35. These files make it clear that Gabriel encouraged Nelböck to apply for a position as lecturer even though he knew it had already been filled by Zilsel. When Nelböck was

rejected for the position, Gabriel told him it was Schlick's fault; Nelböck then threatened to murder him again. ÖVHA, Bestand Ottakring, Protokolle 1934, cited in Lotz-Rimbach, "Mord verjährt nicht," 92–93.

138. WStLA, MA 8, 2.3.4.A11—Vr LG I, 1851–1956, 20 Vr 5867/36, Nelböck.
139. Siegert, "Mit dem Browning philosophiert," 19–20, 25.
140. WStLA, MA 8, 2.3.4.A11—Vr LG I, 1851–1956, 20 Vr 5867/36, Nelböck, 5–6.
141. According to his appeal, he had "played down" the real ideological reasons for killing Schlick in an attempt to avoid damaging the reputation of the Nazi party.
142. Senior public prosecutor to the provincial court in Wels, May 12, 1941. WstLA, MA 8, 2.3.4.A11—Vr LG I, 1851–1956, 20 Vr 5867/36, Nelböck. In 1950, Nelböck asked to view his files in order to appeal his sentence and to see the testimony of witnesses for "personal reasons"; he was informed that the files had been sent to the German federal ministry of justice in Berlin, where they were most likely destroyed in an air attack. WstLA, MA 8, 2.3.4.A11—Vr LG I, 1851–1956, 20 Vr 5867/36, Nelböck.
143. Stadler, "The Vienna Circle," 51.
144. "This is something we can really understand. The Jew, after all, is a born antimetaphysicist: in philosophy he loves logicism, mathematicism, formalism, and positivism, in other words, all the characteristics that Schlick embodied to the highest degree. We would like to point out, however, that we Christians live in a Christian-German state, and that it is up to us to determine which philosophy is good and appropriate." Prof. Dr. Austriacus [Johannes Sauter, pseud.], "Der Fall des Wiener Professors Schlick—eine Mahnung zur Gewissenserforschung," *Schönere Zukunft* 11, no. 41, July 12, 1936, 1079–1080. Sauter was a member of the circle around the Austro-fascist philosopher and political economist Othmar Spann. See Wolfgang Maderthaner and Lisa Silverman, "'Wiener Kreise': Jewishness, Politics and Culture in Interwar Vienna," in *Interwar Vienna: Culture between Tradition and Modernity*, ed. Deborah Holmes and Lisa Silverman (Rochester, NY: Camden House, 2009), 59–62.
145. Hilde Spiel, *Die hellen und die finsteren Zeiten: Erinnerungen 1911–1946* (Munich: List, 1989), 135. More than thirty years later, at least one Austrian journalist was still under the impression that antisemitism had been part of his murderer's motive. See Hellmut Andics, *Der Staat, den keiner wollte* (Vienna: Herder, 1968), 344. The catalogue for the Vienna Jewish Museum's 2004 exhibition *Wien, Stadt der Juden* (Vienna, City of Jews) includes Schlick's murder as an example of an act of antisemitism and includes Schlick in its index. See Joachim Riedl, "Füreinander, ineinander, gegeneinander. Wien und die letzte Blüte des Wiener Judentums" in *Wien, Stadt der Juden*, ed. Joachim Riedl (Vienna: Zsolnay, 2004), 13, 396. Other authors also include Schlick in their lists of Viennese Jews. See, for example, Barbara Toth, "Gegeneinander, füreinander, ineinander: Juden in Wien in der Zwischenkriegszeit," in *Wie wir gelebt haben: Wiener Juden*

erinnern sich an ihr 20. Jahrhundert, ed. Tanja Eckstein and Julia Kaldori (Vienna: Mandelbaum, 2008), 12–14, 13.

146. Manfred Geier, *Der Wiener Kreis* (Reinbek bei Hamburg: Rowohlt, 1998), 90.
147. Vyleta notes that in 1907, the *Deutsche Volksblatt* reported a case of prostitution and paedophilia that was considered a "Jewish crime," even though no Jews were involved. Vyleta, "Jewish Crimes and Misdemeanours," 317.
148. Walser Smith, "Anti-semitic violence," 339.

CHAPTER 2

1. Obituary of Ludwig Zwieback, *Neue Freie Presse*, January 23, 1906, 28. When Ludwig died, he divided his fortune among daughters Ella, Gisela, and Malwine. Ella was born in 1878 in Vienna and died in 1970 in the United States. She married Alexander Zirner on January 8, 1899; they lived together in an apartment next to the Hotel Bristol at Kärntnerring 1 in Vienna. Alexander Zirner founded and served as honorary president of the Verband der Wiener Damenmodenfirmen (Association of Viennese Women's Fashion Companies), vice president of the Verband für österreichischen Modeexport (Association for Austrian Fashion Exports), and president of Ludwig Zwieback & Co. until his death on December 7, 1924, after which Ella took over from her husband and ran the company. She was sometimes referred to as Ella Zirner-Zwieback and Ella Zwieback Zirner. Giles MacDonogh, *1938: Hitler's Gamble* (New York: Basic Books, 2009), 257–61; obituaries of Alexander Zirner, *Neue Freie Presse*, December 10, 1924, 15; Laura Wärndorfer, unpublished autobiography, 40–29. I am deeply grateful to August Zirner for sharing his mother's autobiography with me.
2. According to Ludwig Zirner's wife, Laura Wärndorfer, her husband had studied cello, piano, and composition with Franz Schmidt in Vienna, but did not realize that Schmidt was his father until after he had emigrated to the United States. However, she claimed that most of Viennese society had been aware of his paternity. See Laura Wärndorfer's unpublished autobiography, 40–49; Carmen Ottner, "Quellen zu Leben und Werk der letzten Lebensjahre Franz Schmidts," in *Studien zu Franz Schmidt*, Band 15*: Musik in Wien 1938–1945, Symposion 2004*, ed. Carmen Ottner (Vienna: Franz-Schmidt-Gesellschaft, 2006), 108–09; and *Studien zu Franz Schmidt, Band 5: Quellen II zu Franz Schmidt: Briefe, Autographen, Aufzeichnungen in Privatbesitz, Erinnerungen*, ed. Carmen Ottner (Vienna: Ludwig Doblinger, 1987), 106.
3. Ella commissioned Adalbert Franz Seligmann to paint an eight-panel frieze titled "Franz Schmidt's 2nd Symphony" for the music salon in her apartment. The frieze was Aryanized when she and her son Ludwig fled the country. See the 2006 report on the city's restitution of the artwork, 191–94, http://www.wienmuseum.at/fileadmin/user_upload/PDFs/Restitutionsbericht_2006.pdf.

4. Ella had two other children with Alexander Zirner: Katharina Renée von Erös, who died of tuberculosis in England in 1948, and Hans Erich Zirner, who fled to Paris in 1938 and died in Monte Carlo in 1960. See MacDonogh, *Hitler's Gamble*, 257–61. According to Laura Wärndorfer, her mother-in-law Ella redecorated the store and pressured Ludwig to join the family business; after the war, Ella wanted to return to Vienna to reclaim the family business, but they remained in the United States upon Ludwig's wishes. They received restitution for the business in 1958. At that time, Ella was living with the artist Wilhelm Victor Krausz in New York. See Wärndorfer, unpublished autobiography, 40–49.
5. According to Gerhard Botz, the resurrection and rebirth of the German Reich were common themes in Nazi musical compositions in Austria after the *Anschluss*. Schmidt was not a member of the Nazi Party, but he had not been forced to take this commission. See Gerhard Botz, "'Deutsche Auferstehung': Die Verführung des greisen Tonsetzers Franz Schmidt," in *Studien zu Franz Schmidt*, Band 15, 47.
6. Bettauer published the novel in 1922. The version used in this chapter is *The City without Jews*, trans. Salomea Neumark Brainin (New York: Bloch, 1997), hereafter cited in the text as *CwJ*.
7. Hilde Spiel, "Jewish Women in Austrian Culture," in *The Jews of Austria: Essays on their Life, History and Destruction*, ed. Josef Fraenkel (London: Vallentine Mitchell, 1967), 108.
8. See Murray G. Hall, "'Hinaus mit den Juden!' Von Graffiti und der Zeitung bis zur Leinwand," in *Wien und die jüdische Erfahrung 1900–1938*, ed. Frank Stern and Barbara Eichinger (Vienna: Böhlau, 2009), 62.
9. Recognizable public figures in the novel include a composer's wife who has an affair with a writer (likely Alma Mahler-Werfel) and Zionist representative Minkus Wassertrilling (likely Robert Stricker). A journalist named Karpeles may refer to German Jewish journalist Gustav Karpeles. The novel also mentions a proprietor of a banking house in Vienna named Herr Strauss, which may refer to the bank *Herz & Strauss* on the Schottenring. Peter Höyng claims that the character Herbert Villoner refers to Arthur Schnitzler. See Peter Höyng, "A Dream of a White Vienna after World War I: Hugo Bettauer's *The City without Jews* and *The Blue Stain*" in *At Home and Abroad: Historicizing Twentieth-Century Whiteness in Literature and Performance*, ed. La Vinia Delois Jennings (Knoxville: University of Tennessee Press, 2009), 44. The composer Wallner may be Gustav Mahler, and the playwright Walter Haberer may refer to Franz Werfel. The two Pan-Germans Wondratschek and Jiratschek, who both speak with "strong Bohemian accents," may refer to well-known antisemitic legislators descended from Czech immigrants Josef Jerzabek (member of the Christian Social city council and leader of the Federation of Antisemites) and Anton Pumera, who had served as Lueger's treasurer in the city council. Michael John, "'We Do Not Even Possess Our Selves': On Identity and Ethnicity in Austria, 1880–1937," *Austrian History Yearbook* 30 (1999): 38.

10. The first issue of *Er und Sie: Wochenschrift für Lebenskultur und Erotik*, published on February 14, 1924, included an article titled "The Erotic Revolution" chiding the hypocrisy of those who force women to work as hard as men, yet who do not permit them the sexual freedom to which they themselves are entitled.
11. Here the film addresses fears surrounding the ability of the Jewish "New Woman" to "pass" or, at the very least, to successfully cross the boundaries between German and Jewish. For a discussion of this issue, see Kerry Wallach, "Observable Type: Jewish Women and the Jewish Press in Weimar Germany" (Ph.D. diss., University of Pennsylvania, 2011), 7.
12. One cannot infer from the typecasting of Werbezirk, however, that Jewish women were always exclusively assigned to playing such characters. Elisabeth Bergner (born Elisabeth Ettel in Drohobycz, Galicia), a popular Jewish actress, appeared in a wide variety of roles on stage and screen in Vienna, Berlin, and Munich during the interwar period. Her ability to "pass" for non-Jewish in a way that Werbezirk could not was linked to her aura of mystery. On stage she appeared in *Miss Julie* by August Strindberg, and in 1926, Max Reinhardt directed her in the title role of G.B. Shaw's *Saint Joan* at the Deutsches Volkstheater. Mela Hartwig suggested that Bergner play the lead in a stage adaptation of her novel *Das Weib ist ein Nichts*, but the play was never realized. Letter from Mela Hartwig to Zsolnay Verlag, October 3, 1931, APZ. In 1930–1931, Bergner's future husband Paul Czinner directed her in the film *Ariane* (based on the popular novel *Ariane, jeune fille russe* by French writer Claude Anet); the film's protagonist is a Russian-born university student studying math in Berlin. Zsolnay published the German translation of the novel, and published it again with Bergner on the cover when the film was released. (The Nazis confiscated the book and would not allow it to be sold as long as Bergner was featured on the cover. Many thanks to Murray Hall for this information.) Significantly, in her one "Jewish" role, Bergner appeared as a man: She played the thirteen-year-old boy Moritz Scharf in Arnold Zweig's 1918 play *Die Sendung Semaels: Jüdische Tragödie in fünf Aufzügen*, originally published in 1914 as *Ritualmord in Ungarn: Jüdische Tragödie in fünf Aufzügen* based on a ritual murder case of 1882 in the Hungarian town of Tisza-Eszlár. Bergner's androgynous appearance and ability to play both the "fragile child-woman" as well as the "femme fatale" contributed greatly to her popularity. Elfi Pracht-Jörns, "Elisabeth Bergner," in *Jewish Women: A Comprehensive Historical Encyclopedia*, March 1, 2009, Jewish Women's Archive, http://jwa.org/encyclopedia/article/bergner-elisabeth. Kerry Wallach explores the marketing of Mascha Kaléko as a "new woman" whose image remains open to a wide range of intepretations, including boyish, feminine, fashionable, and even unruly. See "Mascha Kaléko Advertises the New Jewish Woman," in *"Not an Essence but a Positioning": German-Jewish Women Writers (1900–1938)*, ed. Andrea Hammel and Godela Weiss-Sussex (Munich: Meidenbauer, 2009), 217. Vienna-born Fritzi Massary (Friederika Massaryk), who converted to Protestantism around the turn of the

century, became known as "die Massary" in Berlin due to the popularity of her extensive cabaret, revue, and operetta performances; like Bergner, her wide repertoire of characters did not include Jewish women. Marline Otte, *Jewish Identities in German Popular Entertainment* (New York: Cambridge University Press, 2006), 239. This was also true for Galician-born actor Salka Viertel (born Salomea Sara Steuermann), who joined the Neue Wiener Bühne in 1908, where she met her future husband, Viennese Jewish screenwriter and film director Berthold Viertel. They founded an Expressionist theater company together in 1923 and moved to the United States in 1928, where they pursued successful careers in the entertainment industry. Salka Viertel, *The Kindness of Strangers* (New York: Holt, Rinehart and Winston, 1969).

13. Coincidentally, the plot of Baum's first novel, *Der Eingang zur Bühne*, first published as a serial in the *Vossische Zeitung* in April 1920, revolves around an affair at the Vienna Conservatory—although it involves a music teacher and two female students who are in love with him. Baum's first-hand knowledge of the atmosphere at the Conservatory is clear from her writing. Nicole Nottelmann, *Die Karrieren der Vicki Baum: Eine Biographie* (Cologne: Kiepenheuer & Witsch, 2007), 68–70.
14. According to Nadia Valman, the popularity of British literature in which the Jewish woman is depicted as a "blank" indicates that the figure of the Jewess functions as the ultimate empty and unreadable category upon which all the fears of the era regarding sexuality, nationality, race and religion may be projected. See *The Jewess in Nineteenth-Century British Literary Culture* (Cambridge: Cambridge University Press, 2007), 1–3.
15. For a more information on *Er und Sie*, see Chapter 1.
16. The Gloriette-Verlag published five of Bettauer's novels between 1922 and 1924: *Die Stadt ohne Juden* (1922), *Das blaue Mal: der Roman eines Ausgestoßenen* (1922), *Der Frauenmörder* (1922), *Der Herr auf der Galgenleiter. Ein Tag aus dem Leben eines Normalmenschen* (1922), and *Die freudlose Gasse. Ein Wiener Roman aus unseren Tagen* (1924). The sixth, *Der Kampf um Wien: Ein Roman vom Tage* was serialized in *Der Tag* in 1922/23, published by the Verlag Der Tag in 1923, and reprinted in a shorter version by the R. Löwitt Verlag under the title *Ralph und Hilde. Roman eines Wiener Mädels* in 1926. The Gloriette-Verlag, characterized by Murray Hall as one of the many short-lived new publishers in the early years of the First Republic, was founded in 1920 and was run until 1923 by Leo Schidrowitz, who had a reputation as a publisher of "erotic literature"; for example, his book of erotic folk songs *Das schamlose Volkslied* appeared with Gloriette in 1921. The fact that the press also published Else Feldmann and Anna Nussbaum's edited volume of letters, essays, and drawings by Viennese children, *Das Reisebuch des Wiener Kindes: Eine Sammlung von Briefen, Aufsätzen und Zeichnungen der Wiener Schulkinder im Ausland* in 1921 indicates that its range extended somewhat more

broadly. Hall describes Schidrowitz, who also served as an editor and critic for the Viennese newspapers *Wiener Mittags-Zeitung* and *Der Merker*, founded the magazines *Die Ernte*, *Der Maßstab*, and *Der Aufbau*, led the literature section of the Zinnen Verlag and founded his own Leo Schidrowitz Verlag in 1924, was one of the most involved and connected men in the publishing world of interwar Austria. See *Österreichische Verlagsgeschichte 1918–1938*, vol. 2, entries for the Leo Schidrowitz Verlag and Gloriette-Verlag, http://www.verlagsgeschichte.murrayhall.com. On Schidrowitz's activities in Vienna's sports' teams, see Chapter 1.

17. *Die Börse*, July 13, 1922, 16.
18. Bruce Pauley refers to the novel as the "most powerful attack made on anti-Semitism during the First Austrian Republic." See *From Prejudice to Persecution: A History of Austrian Anti-Semitism* (Chapel Hill: University of North Carolina Press, 1992), 103. Scott Spector describes both book and film as attempts to "conjure the utopian fantasy of Jewish absence in order to refute anti-Semitism." See "Modernism without Jews: A Counter-Historical Argument," *Modernism/Modernity* 13, no. 4 (2006): 618.
19. As Michael André Bernstein has pointed out, the gravity of the catastrophe of the Holocaust has rendered ethical literary analysis in the post-Holocaust age a considerable challenge. See Michael André Bernstein, "Victims-in-Waiting: Backshadowing and the Representation of European Jewry," *New Literary History* 29, no. 4 (Autumn, 1998): 625.
20. Florian Krobb, for example, maintains that the "conciliatory resolution of the novel contains a plea for better understanding and co-existence" between Jews and non-Jews and that Bettauer intended the novel to serve as a reminder to "behave unobtrusively and not to offend any rules of Gentile society." Florian Krobb, "'Vienna Goes to Pot without Jews:' Hugo Bettauer's *Die Stadt ohne Juden* (*The City without Jews*)," *Jewish Quarterly* 41, no. 2 (1994): 20.
21. The names of Leo Strakosch and his alias, Frenchman Henry Dufresne, likely refer but do not exactly correspond to the names of real people. The Strakosch family was a well-known, ennobled Viennese Jewish family originally from Bohemia; Dufresne was the name of a prominent Jewish family from Berlin; Jacob Ephraim changed his name to Dufresne, and his son Jean became a well-known chess master. I found no evidence of a "Leopold Strakosch" or "Henry Dufresne" active in Vienna in the 1920s. The multimillionaire Sir Henry Strakosch (1871–1943) was born in Austria and was chairman of the Union Corporation (South African Goldmines) in the 1920s; Siegfried Strakosch published the book *Selbstmord eines Volkes* with the Rikola Verlag in 1922; he and his wife Wally presided over a salon attended by authors like Felix Salten. Leopold Dufresne was a French painter who achieved some success in Paris at that time. On the Strakosch family see Marie Therese Arnborn, *Friedmann, Gutmann, Lieben, Mandl, Strakosch: Fünf Familien Porträts aus Wien vor 1938* (Vienna: Böhlau, 2002).

22. "Thirty enormous trains" transported Jews from Vienna (*CwJ*, 57). These attempts were unsuccessful. See Anton Staudinger, "Katholischer Antisemitismus in der Ersten Republik," in *Eine zerstörte Kultur: Jüdisches Leben und Antisemitismus in Wien seit dem 19. Jahrhundert*, ed. Gerhard Botz, Ivar Oxaal, Michael Pollak, and Nina Scholz (Vienna: Czernin, 2002). The 1919 attempt occurred at the behest of a Social Democrat, but in 1920, the Christian Socials instigated the deportation attempt. See Margarete Gradner, "Staatsbürger und Ausländer: Zum Umgang Österreichs mit den jüdischen Flüchtlingen nach 1918," in *Asylland wider Willen: Flüchtlinge in Österreich im europäischen Kontext seit 1914*, ed. Gernot Heiss and Oliver Rathkolb (Vienna: Ludwig-Boltzmann-Institut für Geschichte und Gesellschaft, 1995): 25.
23. Kallop almost certainly refers to Ignaz Mandl, Lueger's colleague, whom some considered the "real" driving force behind the mayor's political successes before Lueger ultimately dropped him. As Joseph Bloch, who knew Lueger personally, wrote, "His best buddy was a Dr. Ig. Mandl, who directed him into communal life and showed him the way in politics." See Joseph S. Bloch, *Errinerungen aus meinem Leben* (Vienna: R. Löwit Verlag, 1922), 240. On Mandl's role in broadening Lueger's world view, see John W. Boyer, *Political Radicalism in Late Imperial Vienna: Origins of the Christian Social Movement 1848–1897*, (Chicago: University of Chicago Press, 1981), 191–99.
24. From November 21–23, 1918, a total of seventy-three Jews were killed and hundreds more injured in the largest of a number of violent pogroms that broke out in 1918 in the context of the conflict between Poland and Ukraine for the control over Galicia. Marsha L. Rozenblit, *Reconstructing a National Identity: The Jews of Habsburg Austria during World War I* (New York: Oxford University Press, 2001), 137.
25. Joseph Scheicher, *Aus dem Jahre 1920: Ein Traum vom Landtags- und Reichratsabgeordneten Dr. Joseph Scheicher* . . . (St. Pölten: Verlag von Johann Gregora's Buchhandlung, 1900). Scheicher served as a Christian Social representative in the national parliament from 1894 to 1918. He edited the Catholic periodical *St. Pöltner Boten*, was close to Karl Lueger, and gave virulently antisemitic speeches in the *Landtag*. See Richard S. Geehr, *Karl Lueger: Mayor of fin-de-siècle Vienna* (Detroit: Wayne State University Press, 1990), 354 n. 20. Scheicher was instrumental in organizing support for a unified group of clerical, nationalist, and antisemitic protestors against Liberalism in 1887. According to John Boyer, his career was one of the most "colorful and provocative in modern Austrian ecclesiastiscal history." See Boyer, *Political Radicalism*, 140. According to Friedrich Heer, Scheicher came up with the idea to change the name of the Anti-Liberal League formed under Lueger to the Party of United Christians. *Der Glaube des Adolf Hitler: Anatomie einer politischen Religiosität* (Munich: Bechtle, 1968), 77.
26. As Sander L. Gilman has pointed out, the Jews' foot became a central image in German and Austrian antisemitic representations of Jews in the late nineteenth-century.

Jews' "flat" and otherwise deformed feet became a hallmark of Jewish difference and separated them from others. Freud also dealt with the Jews' foot—and the supposed limping gait caused by it, as well as its links to criminality—in the course of his degeneracy theory. See the chapter "The Degenerate Foot and the Search for Oedipus" in Sander L. Gilman, *The Case of Sigmund Freud: Medicine and Identity at the Fin de Siècle* (Baltimore: Johns Hopkins University Press, 1993), 113–68, esp. 118.

27. Heer notes how similar these details were to Hitler's actual plans, as well as the irony of Scheicher's claim that his animosity toward Jews was not "personal" and his absurd statement that he "would be the first to jump in the water if he saw a drowning Jew." See *Der Glaube des Adolf Hitler*, 108–13.
28. Hans Tietze recognized its equally satirical treatment of both Aryans and Jews. *Die Juden Wiens: Geschichte, Wissenschaft, Kultur* (Leipzig, Vienna: E.P. Tal & Co. Verlag, 1935), 279.
29. Kraus converted to Catholicism in 1911 but left the church in 1923. Robert S. Wistrich maintains that Kraus, in his use of antisemitic stereotypes, "seriously underestimated the power of antisemitism and reinforced rather than weakened it." See Robert S. Wistrich, review of Paul Reitter, *The anti-Journalist: Karl Kraus and Jewish Self-Fashioning in Fin-de-Siècle Europe*, *American Historical Review* 114, no. 5 (2009).
30. See Paul Reitter, *The anti-Journalist: Karl Kraus and Jewish Self-Fashioning in Fin-de-Siècle Europe* (Chicago: University of Chicago Press, 2008).
31. Judith Butler, *Gender Trouble: Feminism and the Subversion of Identity* (London: Routledge, 1999), 144–47, 177.
32. Journalist Anton Kuh complained in 1923 about the "*Verdorfung*" (provincialization) of Vienna, exemplified in particular through its Catholic festivities and parades. "That Vienna is by the mountains . . . can be felt more and more each day since the end of the war. Since then the law of "unter sich" (among ourselves) rules is becoming clearer." Anton Kuh, "Wien am Gebirge," *Die Stunde* 1, no. 101, July 4, 1923, 3.
33. Here Bettauer mocks the cult surrounding Andreas Hofer (1767–1810), a Tyrolean innkeeper who led an uprising against the French and Bavarians in 1809 and who was immortalized as a national hero around 1900 in the service of Catholic-conservative ideology. On Hofer, see also Chapter 1.
34. Hanns Haas, "Der Traum von Dazugehören—Juden auf Sommerfrische," in *Der Geschmack der Vergänglichkeit: Jüdische Sommerfrische in Salzburg*, ed. Robert Kriechbaumer (Vienna: Böhlau, 2002). The popularity of Jews' spending summers in the provinces began long before the interwar period and was not restricted to Austria. There is evidence, however, suggesting that the nature of the antisemitism Jews experienced in Austrian *Sommerfrische* in particular intensified between the wars. See Frank Bajohr, *"Unser Hotel ist Judenfrei": Bäder-Antisemitismus im 19. und 20. Jahrhundert* (Frankfurt: Fischer Taschenbuch, 2003).

35. In Austria, as in Germany, Jewish men were more likely than Jewish women to intermarry for a variety of reasons. However, in Austria, interfaith marriage was not allowed unless one of the partners either converted to their partner's religion or declared themselves *konfessionslos* (without religion). Nevertheless, Jewish women were still frequently part of interfaith couples. Of the 155 Jews who married non-Jewish partners in 1910, 64 (forty percent) were women. Marsha L. Rozenblit, *The Jews of Vienna: Assimilation and Identity 1867–1914* (Albany: State University of New York Press, 1983), 128. According to Austrian government statistics, from 1914–1918, Jewish women accounted for 30 percent of the brides of interfaith marriages involving one Jewish partner. After the war ended and the Austrian requirement for one partner to convert or claim to be *konfessionslos* before marrying a partner of a different faith was lifted, the total number of interfaith marriages in Vienna rose. And in both 1919 and 1920, the percentage of Jewish women in interfaith marriages involving one Jewish partner increased again to 40 percent. In 1922, Jewish women accounted for 38 percent of interfaith marriages in which Jews were involved. The majority of Jewish men and women in all cases married *konfessionslos* partners. *Beiträge zur Statistik der Republik Österreich, Statistik des Bundesstaates Österreichs*, vol 8., *Die Bewegung der Bevölkerung in den Jahren 1914 bis 1921*, ed. Bundesamt für Statistik (Vienna: Druck und Verlag der österreichischen Staatsdruckerei, 1923), 9, 113; *Beiträge zur Statistik der Stadt Wien*, ed. Bundesamt für Statistik (Vienna: Gerlach & Wiedling) 14 (1923), 8. On Jewish intermarriage in Vienna before World War I, as well as detailed caveats about the possible underreporting of these statistics, see Rozenblit, *The Jews of Vienna*, 128–140; on Jewish intermarriage in Germany see Steven M. Lowenstein, "Intermarriage and Conversion," *Modern Judaism* 25, no. 1 (2005); and Kerstin Meiring, *Die christlich-jüdische Mischehe in Deutschland 1840-1933* (Hamburg: Dölling & Gallitz, 1998).
36. Here, I draw extensively upon Franka Marquardt's introduction of the concept of the "narrated" Jew and the importance of distinguishing its presence in texts, as opposed to the visualized "image" of the Jew typically discussed in literature. See *Erzählte Juden: Untersuchungen zu Thomas Manns Joseph und seine Brüder und Robert Musils Mann ohne Eigenschaften* (Münster: Lit Verlag, 2003), 279. In *The City without Jews*, the one minor instance of such a "narrated" Jewish woman evoked before the expulsion is a passing reference to the Jewish wife of the archbishop's brother (*CwJ*, 44).
37. In Arthur Schnitzler's novel dealing explicitly with Jewish issues, *Der Weg ins Freie* (*Road to the Open*, 1908), its aristocratic protagonist Georg von Wergenthin has Jewish friends, attends Jewish salons, and has a Catholic mistress, not a Jewish one, "against every expectation" (according to Schnitzler's friend the Danish critic Georg Brandes). In answering a question from Brandes about why he did not make Wergenthin's mistress a Jewish woman, Schnitzler wrote in a letter of April 7, 1908, "I could not. The figure of Anna appeared to me from the very start

as incontrovertibly Catholic." Nevertheless, most reviewers at the time still "read" her as Jewish. See Abigail Gilman, *Viennese Jewish Modernism. Freud, Hofmannsthal, Beer-Hofmann and Schnitzler* (University Park: Penn State University Press, 2009, 114–15).

38. On the feminized male Jew, see Sander L. Gilman, *Freud, Race, and Gender* (Princeton: Princeton University Press, 1993).
39. Otto Weininger published his theories on the constructed categories of "Jew" and "woman" at the turn of the century. His *Geschlecht und Charakter* (1903; *Sex and Character*) is the first widely-disseminated text that explicitly describes the "Jewish" as a negative *Gattung* (category) related to the "feminine" that can take any shape precisely because of its lack of qualities. The absence of any inner reality, according to Weininger, is what determines the presence of the Jew. "Man sieht, wie schwierig es ist, das Judentum zu definieren . . . **'Jüdisch'** ist also eine **Kategorie** und psychologisch nicht weiter zurückzuführen uns zu bestimmen" (One sees how difficult it is to define Judaism . . . **"Jewish"** is thus a **category** and we cannot take its psychological determination any further). (Emphasis is Weininger's.) *Geschlecht und Charakter* (Munich: Matthes & Seitz, 1997), 591, note to p. 436. See also Nancy Harrowitz, *Antisemitism, Misogyny, and the Logic of Cultural Difference* (Lincoln: University of Nebraska Press, 1995).
40. The Hungarian Jewish brothers Ludwig, Samuel, and Emanuel Zwieback established the department store Ludwig Zwieback & Bruder Co. in 1877. In 1895, the Hungarian-born Jewish architect Friedrich Schön designed a new store for them located at Kärntnerstrasse 11/15, at the corner of Weihburggasse, very close to St. Stephen's Cathedral in the center of the city. On the occasion of Schön's eightieth birthday, the *Neue Freie Presse* referred to the "Haus Zwieback" in the Kärntnerstrasse as "one of his most beautiful works in this area." *Neue Freie Presse*, August 28, 1937, 7. See Fredric Bedoire, *The Jewish Contribution to Modern Architecture 1830–1930* (Jersey City, NJ: Ktav, 2004), 327.
41. The property was Aryanized in 1938. In 1951, Ella was awarded restitution of the Kärntnerstrasse building, which she then sold in 1957. Catharina Christ, *Jüdische k. und k. Hoflieferanten in der Textilbranche mit Niederlassung in Wien in der Zeit von 1870 bis 1938* (Diplomarbeit, University of Vienna, 2000).
42. The absence of Jewish women characters from the book is especially curious given that Bettauer's other novels that do not deal directly with Jewish topics, such as *Die freudlose Gasse* (1924; translated as *Viennese Love* in1929) actually *do* contain several Jewish women characters who are not portrayed as negatively as they are in other popular novels. For example, one of the most popular books in Vienna in 1920 was Rudolf Hans Bartsch's *Seine Jüdin oder Jakob Böhmes Schusterkugel* (Vienna: L Staackmann, 1920) in which a former army officer marries a "beautiful Jewess" who attempts to lure him into a new, possibly shady business career, instead of becoming a trusty shoemaker. According to Georg Stefan Troller, the book, which sold 25,000 copies in its first year, typified the fundamental, and

easily understandable, differences between stereotypes about "Jewish greed" and "noble alpine humanity" that a post–World War I public without social and political orientation craved. Georg Stefan Troller, *Das fidele Grab an der Donau: Mein Wien 1918–1938* (Düsseldorf: Artemis & Winkler, 2004), 61.

43. In Paris, the general public was well aware that Jews were actively involved in the construction of new department stores. In Berlin, Wertheim, Tiezt, and Adolf Jandorf's Kaufhaus des Westens (KaDeWe) were Jewish-owned. In Vienna, the non-Jewish company Philip Haas created the first department store in Vienna on the Stephansplatz in 1855; the Jewish textile company Rothberger and Kramer soon followed suit by building one across from it in 1880. See Bedoire, *The Jewish Contribution*, 190–201, 250, 326.
44. Paul Lerner, "Consuming Pathologies: Kleptomania, Magazinitis, and the Problem of Female Consumption in Wilhelmine and Weimar Germany," *WerkstattGeschichte* 42 (2006): 47. See also "Consuming Powers: The 'Jewish Department Store' in German Politics and Culture," in *The Economy in Jewish History: New Perspectives on the Interrelationship between Ethnicity and Economic Life*(New York: Berghahn, 2011).
45. "This representation is confirmed in the development of Austrian department stores; Jews really dominate here as opposed to the large chain stores (*Filialunternehmungen*), especially the specialty grocery stores, where non-Jewish firms are decisive (Meinl)." Friedrich Tannenbaum, *Das Warenhaus in Österreich: Auszug aus der Dissertation zur Erlangung des Doktorats der Staatswissenschaften an der rechts—und staatswissenschaftlichen Fakultät der Wiener Universität* (1932), Vienna: University of Vienna, 30.
46. Belinda Davis, "Food Scarcity and the Empowerment of the Female Consumer in World War I Berlin," *The Sex of Things: Gender and Consumption in Historical Perspective*, ed. Victoria de Grazia and Ellen Furlough (Berkeley: University of California Press, 1996), 289. In Vienna, Maureen Healy points out that the Imperial Organization of Austrian Housewives likewise assumed that consumers were women. Healy, "Becoming Austrian: Women, the State, and Citizenship in World War I," *Central European History* 35, no. 1 (2002):12.
47. "Vienne Oblige. Eine Eintragung im Handbuch der Wiener Gesellschaft," cited in the exhibition catalogue *Wien: Stadt der Juden—Die Welt der Tante Jolesch*, ed. Joachim Riedl (Vienna: Zsolnay, 2004), 34–35. She is also praised in Ludwig Hirschfeld's *Was nicht im Baedeker steht: Wien und Budapest* of 1927: "Zwieback, however, is no mere outfitter; it is a fashionable outfitters with a pronouncedly personal tone, a tone supplied by Frau Ella Zirner-Zwieback, the head of the house, a striking Vienna personality, at the same time a perfect lady of society and a good business-woman, full of ambition and good taste, and a wonderful pianist to boot. The 'lines and colors' noticeable on a great number of Vienna women are of Frau Zirner's composition." *The Vienna That's Not in the Baedeker*, trans. T.W. Maccallum (Munich: R. Piper & Co. Verlag, 1929), 188.

48. Darcy Buerkle, "Gendered Spectatorship, Jewish Women, and Psychological Advertising in Weimar Germany," *Women's History Review* 15, no. 4 (2006): 631.
49. Karin Maria Schmidlechner, "Sozialökonomische Position und kulturelle Lage der Frauen," in . . . *d* . . . D*er Rest ist Österreich: Das Werden der Ersten Republik*, Band 2, ed. Wolfgang Maderthaner and Helmut Konrad (Vienna: Carl Gerold's Sohn, 2008), 99.
50. Healy, "Becoming Austrian," 5–6. Healy refers here to Gerald Stourzh's concept of *Gesinnung*. See also Gerald Stourzh, "Ethnic Attribution in Late Imperial Austria: Good Intentions, Evil Consequences," in *Austrian Studies 5: The Habsburg Legacy: National Identity in Historical Perspective* (1994).
51. At the turn of the century, L. Keimer described Austria as "perhaps the most backward in Europe on the woman question. Nearly every profession was closed to women." *The International Congress of Women of 1899: Women in Professions*, ed. the Countess of Aberdeen (London: T. Fisher Unwin, 1900), 45–46.
52. *Die Fackel* 59 (1900): 28.
53. Jewish women continue to bear the brunt of complaints about materialistic society, as typified in the stereotype of the "JAP" (Jewish American Princess) and jokes relating to the supposed materialism, frigidity, showiness, and superficiality of American Jewish women. See Riv-Ellen Prell, *Fighting to Become Americans: Jews, Gender, and the Anxiety of Assimilation* (Boston: Beacon, 1999). See also Evelyn Torton-Beck, "From 'Kike to Jap': How Misogyny, Anti-Semitism, and Racism Construct the Jewish American Princess," in *Race, Class, and Gender*, eds. Margaret Andersen and Patricia Hill Collins (Belmont, CA: Wadsworth, 1992), 91. Edward Timms points out that Kraus, who was able to publish *Die Fackel* because he received a private income from his wealthy father, was not anticapitalist, and repudiated the material needs that he himself had never faced. See Edward Timms, *Karl Kraus: Apocalyptic Satirist: The Post-War Crisis and the Rise of the Swastika* (New Haven: Yale University Press, 2005), 257.
54. Joseph Roth, *The Wandering Jews: A Classic Portrait of a Vanished People*, trans. Michael Hofmann (New York: W. W. Norton & Company, 2001 [1927]), 85. Hereafter cited in text as *WJ*.
55. Roth is often lauded for celebrating Eastern European Jewish life in his texts, but some provide a more critical analysis of Roth's attitude toward Eastern European Jews. For the privileging of East over West in his rhetoric, see Mark H. Gelber, "*Juden auf Wanderschaft* und die Rhetoriker der Ost-West Debatte im Werk Joseph Roths," in *Joseph Roth: Interpretation-Kritik-Rezeption*, ed. Michael Kessler and Fritz Hackert (Tübingen: Stauffenburg 1990).
56. Roth, *The Wandering Jews*, 84–85.
57. Later in the text, Roth mentions that few Jews live in Marseilles.
58. The first is in reference to the wives of Jewish scholars in the East, who are responsible for caring for the children and who "carry on a small trade with maize in summer and naptha in winter, as well as pickled cucumbers, beans, and baked

goods" (*WJ*, 27). Other mentions include the description of the Eastern "wonder rabbi"—"The enjoyment of his wife is a sacred duty to him and is a pleasure only because it is a duty. . . . All other women are banished from his immediate circle" (*WJ*, 33). During Yom Kippur, "All the women now weep in front of the silver candelabra" (*WJ*, 41). At a funeral "The women run through the streets, crying out their grief to every stranger. . . . The most shattering scenes take place at the cemetery. Women refuse to leave the graves; they have to be dragged away; they require taming as much as comforting" (*WJ*, 43–44). On Roth's portrayal of Eastern European Jewish women as pathologized stereotypes of the "beautiful Jewess" in his 1930 novel *Hiob*, see Ritchie Robertson, *The 'Jewish Question' in German Literature 1759–1939* (New York: Oxford University Press, 1999), 424–425.

59. Paula E. Hyman, *Gender and Assimilation in Modern Jewish History: The Roles and Representation of Women* (Seattle: University of Washington Press, 1995), 134–35.
60. Hugo Bettauer, "Das Warenhaus Stafa," *Bettauers Wochenschrift*, no. 8, 1925, 23. Ironically, the management of the store limited the number of Jews they employed. Ernst Epler recalls his father being turned away from a job as a salesman at Stafa with the following words: "Dear Comrade Epler, we already have enough Jews here, you must understand that it's not good for sales." Ernst Epler, "Du bist ein Jud . . .," in *Die Mazzesinsel*, ed. Ruth Beckermann (Vienna: Löcker, 1984), 80.
61. In contrast, most American silent films of the 1920s depict Jewish women as hardworking, strong, and nurturing and maintaining and fostering "Jewish family values." Sharon Pucker Rivo, "Projected Images: Portraits of Jewish Women in Early American Film," *Talking Back: Images of Jewish Women in American Popular Culture*, ed. Joyce Antler (Hanover: University Press of New England, 1998), 35.
62. However, the industry shrank due to lack of funding, high interest rates, and the impossibility of keeping even large film production companies afloat. Filmmakers born in Austria include Billy Wilder, Josef von Sternberg, and Otto Preminger; Jewish directors who made films in Vienna include Paul Czinner, Alexander Korda, and Michael Curtiz (all Hungarian born), Richard Oswald, and Robert Wiene. Already by the end of the First World War, around three hundred feature films had been produced in Austria. S.S. Prawer, *Between Two Worlds: The Jewish Presence in German and Austrian Film, 1910–1933* (New York: Berghahn, 1995), ix. See also Alys George, "Hollywood on the Danube? Vienna and Austrian Silent Film of the 1920s," in *Interwar Vienna: Culture between Tradition and Modernity*, ed. Deborah Holmes and Lisa Silverman (Rochester: Camden House, 2009).
63. Riemann, born in 1892 in Berlin, made over fifty films in forty years; he acted in his first film in 1916. In 1937 he was awarded the title *Staatsschauspieler* (state

actor) by the Nazis. Anna Milety (Anna Krbetz) was born in 1896 in Lower Austria and grew up in Budapest. She married Breslauer in 1925 and subsequently stopped acting. Armin Loacker, "Biografisches zu den Filmschaffenden sowie Haupt—und Nebendarstellern von Die Stadt ohne Juden," in *Die Stadt ohne Juden*, ed. Guntram Geser and Armin Loacker (Vienna: Filmarchiv Austria, 2000), 193, 201. One article about the film claimed viewers would immediately recognize her from roles as the sweet "Wiener Mädel," the "genre that fits her so well and in which she displays her innate charm." *Die Filmwelt* 15 (1924), 5.

64. One other Jewish actress, Laura Glücksmann, appears in a bit part in the film as a saleswoman. She was later killed in a Nazi death camp. Loacker, "Biografisches," 175, 209.
65. Suicide was becoming increasingly prevalent at this time among Jewish women, though this phenomenon was rarely spoken about. See the work of Darcy Buerkle on the effacement of Jewish women's suicide in Germany: "Historical Effacements. Facing Charlotte Salomon," in *Reading Charlotte Salomon*, ed. Michael P. Steinberg and Monica Bohn-Duchen (Ithaca, NY: Cornell University Press, 2006); and *Nothing Happened: Charlotte Salomon and an Archive of Suicide* (Ann Arbor: University of Michigan Press, 2012).
66. Gisela Werbezirk was born in 1875 in Pressburg. She fled to the United States after 1938, where she continued her career as an actress; she died in 1956. Werbezirk often played in comedic stage productions in the Rolandbühne in the Leopoldstadt, where she performed regularly between 1919 and 1925–1926 in roles written especially for her by Alfred Deutsch-German and Armin Friedmann. Typically, she played strong women who had to care for themselves and their children in the absence of their husbands. See Brigitte Dalinger, "Popular Jewish Drama in Vienna in the 1920s," in *Jewish Theatre: A Global View*, ed. Edna Nahshon (Leiden: Brill, 2009), 184. In her discussion of *Jargon* and Revue theater in Berlin, Marline Otte indicates that performances by Jewish actors on stage and the limits of their roles indicate that the tensions between Jews and non-Jews in popular entertainment intensified after World War I, when Jews' performances of their "ethnic" Jewish difference on stage to mixed audiences became increasingly less acceptable. Revue theaters providing popular entertainment, such as Berlin's Metropol, suggested that the degree of "acceptable difference" accepted by the upper echelons of German society eroded after the end of the war due to social instability, rising antisemitism, and the politicization of culture—elements that characterized culture in Vienna, too. See Otte, *Jewish Identities*, 201–58, esp. 278.
67. On the development of the Jewish mother as a stock character provoking both ridicule and blame in American popular culture, see Joyce Antler, *You never call! You never Write! A History of the Jewish Mother* (New York: Oxford University Press, 2007).
68. Both kinds of characters are prototypes for more modern figurations of the "Jewish mother" and "Jewish American Princess" in popular culture.

69. As Brigitte Dalinger notes, women likely did work in some roles beyond that of actress in the Yiddish troupes, albeit behind the scenes. Brigitte Dalinger, "Yiddish Theater in Vienna." *Jewish Women: A Comprehensive Historical Encyclopedia.* March 20, 2009. Jewish Women's Archive, http://jwa.org/encyclopedia/article/yiddish-theater-in-vienna.
70. "Das ist die ganze Frau Werbezirk, dieser unwahrscheinliche Fauxpas der Schöpfung, dieses Jargonwunder an Leib, Seele und Stimme!" Anton Kuh, "Bezirk der Werbezirk," in *Luftlinien, Feuilletons, Essays und Publizistik*, ed. Ruth Greuner (Vienna: Löcker, 1981), 449–51.
71. Friedrich Torberg, "Die Erben der Tante Jolesch: Anhang. Nachrufe: Gisela Werbezirk oder Frau Breier aus Gaya in Hollywood," in *Die Erben der Tante Jolesch* (Munich: Langen/Müller 2008), 638–40.
72. For the Othering of Jewish women in both Europe and America, see Paula Hyman, *Gender and Assimilation* and Tamar Garb, "Modernity, Identity, Textuality," in *The Jew in the Text: Modernity and the Construction of Identity*, ed. Linda Nochlin and Tamar Garb (London: Thames and Hudson: 1995). For more detailed discussions of the fin-de-siècle Viennese context of anxieties Jewish men projected onto women, see Alison Rose, *Jewish Women in Fin-de-Siècle Vienna* (Austin: University of Texas Press, 2008); and Michaela Raggam-Blesch, *Zwischen Ost und West. Identitätskonstruktionen jüdischer Frauen in Wien* (Innsbruck: Studienverlag, 2008).
73. Jenbach, born Ida Jakobovits, 1868, in Hungary, first trained as an actress and later became a dramaturge and screenwriter. She collaborated at least five times with Breslauer, and also worked on screenplays for other German films. She was deported to Minsk at the end of 1941, where she was probably murdered. Loacker, "Biografisches," 175. In Yiddish theater, Jewish women rarely served in any role other than actress, indicating that cabaret and film provided more of an opportunity for Jewish women in Vienna to advance in the entertainment industry.
74. These are likely the only two other Jewish actresses in the film. See Brigitte Dalinger and Silvia Stastny "'. . . und 68 weitere Darsteller' Verbindungen zwischen jüdischen Filmen und jüdischen Theater im Wien der 20er Jahre," in Geser and Loacker, *Die Stadt ohne Juden*. Salcia Weinberg, born Sarah Licht in Galicia in 1878, was active in Jewish theater between 1909 and 1930. She married actor Hermann Weinberg when she was fifteen, sang in the choir of the Lemberg Polish Opera, then entered Gimpel's Jewish theater and toured as part of a Jewish cabaret company with her husband through Hungary, Bulgaria, and Germany. She died in 1940. Laura Glücksmann, born in 1885 in Lemberg, was active in the Jewish theater in Vienna starting in 1914; in the 1920s also participated in the Freie Jüdische Volksbühne, and acted in Warsaw, Romania, Czechoslovakia, Belgium, Paris and London. Later, she starred in the classic American Yiddish film *Yidl mitn Fidl* in 1936. She died in a concentration camp. See Brigitte Dalinger,

Quellenedition zur Geschichte des jüdischen Theaters in Wien (Tübingen: Niemeyer, 2003), 157, 165.

75. Nathan Birnbaum [Mathias Acher, pseud.], "Eine ostjüdische Bühne in Wien: Ein kleiner Beitrag zum jüdischen Kulturproblem," *Ost und West* 2, no. 4 (1902): 235–40. Here, he refers to her as "Frau Weinberg."
76. American silent films of the 1920s often depict themes about intermarriage, but only one film depicts a Jewish woman intermarrying. Rivo, "Projected Images," 35.
77. See note 35. Especially interesting in this context is that fact that intermarriage was commonly undertaken as a means to social advancement among partners of different classes, but the interfaith couples in this film portray partners of the same class. See also Ivar Oxaal, "The Jews of Young Hitler's Vienna: Historical and Sociological Aspects," in *Jews, Antisemitism and Culture in Vienna*, ed. Ivar Oxaal, Michael Pollak, and Gerhard Botz (London: Routledge, 1987), 34. For more on Jewish interfaith marriage before World War I, see Rozenblit, *Assimilation and Identity*, 128–29.
78. In Berlin the film premiered in 1926. Guntram Geser, "Start in Sechs Wiener Kinos," in Geser and Lacker, *Die Stadt ohne Juden*, 95.
79. See *Das Kino-Journal*, vol. 731 (1924) and *Der Kinematograph*, vol. 912 (1924), 33.
80. Other mainstream films in Austria with explicitly Jewish themes, such as Otto Kreisler's film version of Grillparzer's play *Die Jüdin von Toledo* (1919), and *Theodor Herzl: Bannerträger des jüdischen Volkes* (1919) are retellings of historical stories. The film *Das alte Gesetz* (dir. E.A. Dupont), which was set in Vienna but premiered in Berlin in 1923, tells a story of assimilation, as does the Austrian film *Der Fluch*. Notably, both *Der Fluch* and *Die Stadt ohne Juden*, described by contemporaneous publications as two Viennese films that take place in the "Jewish milieu," were both banned in Linz in 1924. See *Wiener Kino: Das Blatt des Kinobesuchers*, third week of August, 1924.
81. Though he and his work are barely acknowledged today, the film's director H.K. Breslauer was one of the most important film directors in Austria after World War I. *Die Stadt ohne Juden* was his last film. Later, he joined the Nazi party. Loacker, "Biografisches," 67.
82. Bettauer never went on record with his detailed critique of the film. However, the September 25, 1924, issue of *Bettauers Wochenschrift* featured a "letter" to Bettauer from the film's director (likely satirical and written by Bettauer himself) in which Breslauer protests that the film's poor quality is not his fault.
83. The film also replaces Zionist representative Minkus Wassertrilling with a rabbi and includes scenes inside a synagogue that do not appear in the book. See Murray G. Hall, "Hugo Bettauer," in *Elektrische Schatten: Beiträge zur österreichischen Stummfilmgeschichte*, ed. Francesco Bono, Paolo Caneppele, and Günter Kren (Vienna: Filmarchiv, 1999), 154–55.
84. Using remains found in Amsterdam, the Filmarchiv Austria reconstructed 1,635 of the film's original 2,400 meters. See Geser and Loacker, *Die Stadt ohne Juden*, 14.

85. Dieter Hecht notes that there were more than fifty Jewish women who wrote for Jewish newspapers in the First Republic, and also that non-Jewish women occasionally wrote for these papers. Topics covered included family, culture, social, politics, economics, and women's emancipation. See "Die Stimme und Wahrheit der jüdischen Welt," in *Wien und die jüdische Erfahrung 1900–1938*, ed. Frank Stern and Barbara Eichinger (Vienna: Böhlau, 2009), 105.
86. The careers of women with a range of Jewish backgrounds in interwar Vienna spanned many fields, including social welfare, pedagogy, medicine, bookkeeping, civil service, politics, and business; some had already begun their careers before the interwar period, and there are far too many to list in their entirety here. Gertrud Bodenwieser began her own dance group from her studio and was an instrumental founder of *Ausdruckstanz*; in 1928 she was awarded a professorship in choreography at the Vienna State Academy of Music and Dramatic Arts. Cilli Pam opened a gymnastics studio and a massage studio at her apartment. E-mail from Frank Pam to author, April 27, 2010. Marietta Blau studied physics at the University of Vienna and became a pioneer in radioactivity research. Portrait photographers Trude Fleischmann and Dora Kallmus (Madame d'Ora) both ran their own successful photography studios. Marta Friedländer-Garelik was one of the first women in Vienna to study law. Käthe Leichter (Marianne Katharina Pick) became the leading Socialist feminist in "Red Vienna," along with Stella Klein-Löw and Therese Schlesinger Eckstein. Helene Deutsch became head of the Training Institute of the Vienna Psychoanalytic Society; other Jewish women leaders in the field of psychoanalysis included Melanie Klein, Margaret Mahler, and Anna Freud. Charlotte Bühler from Berlin studied psychology in Munich before marrying (non-Jewish) psychologist Karl Bühler in 1916. Helene Scheu-Riesz started the Sesam Verlag for children in 1923. Elise Richter was one of the first women in Vienna to earn a doctorate and to hold an academic appointment at an Austrian university even before World War I. However, only in 1919 did women become officially eligible to complete the *Habilitation*—the postdoctoral degree necessary for a permanent job at universities. Women were allowed to become full-fledged lawyers and clerks after women were allowed to take the bar examinations in Austria and Germany in 1922. Information regarding the broad range of careers of many lesser-known Jewish women can be accessed via claims for restitution of their Aryanized property. See http://www.crt-ii.org/_awards (accessed November 14, 2010). For example, Lily Margarethe Bader, née Stern, was the owner and director of a girls' boarding school, the Pensionat Stern. Marianne Bardach and her brother owned a jewelry factory called Turiet & Bardach. Anna Bogart was owner and executive of a company named Damenmodenhaus Ignatz Weiss, which had been established by her father. Rosa Egré and her husband owned and operated a fur business that included a store. Rosa Salzmann managed a shoe store that was owned by her husband. On the achievements of Anitta Müller-Cohen, Eugenia Schwarzwald, and others at the turn of

the century through 1938, see Dieter Hecht, *Zwischen Feminismus und Zionismus: Die Biographie einer Wiener Jüdin, Anitta Müller-Cohen (1890–1962)* (Vienna: Böhlau, 2008); Rose, *Jewish Women*; and Raggam-Blesch, *Zwischen Ost und West.*

87. Harriet Pass Freidenreich, *Female, Jewish, Educated: The Lives of Central European University Women* (Bloomington: Indiana University Press, 2002), 68.
88. The elimination of the restrictive conditions for licenses and censorship in the Austria-Hungary accounted for the flourishing of publishing in general. See Murray G. Hall, "Publishers and Institutions in Austria, 1918–45," in *A History of Austrian Literature 1918–2000*, ed. Katrin Kohl and Ritchie Robertson (Rochester, NY: Camden House, 2006), 75–77.
89. Jewish university women, despite being excluded from typical male networks, often chose Jewish men as their mentors, and relied upon the help of male colleagues and professors. Freidenreich, *Female, Jewish, Educated*, 66.
90. One of the most successful—yet understudied—Jewish woman writers in interwar Vienna, novelist Gina Kaus (Regina Wiener), faced similar discrimination in Vienna; she even spoke about the different expectations for male and female writers. She wrote about themes including the New Woman and gender roles, including a favorable review of Vicki Baum's novel *Helene*. She became Ella Zwieback's sister-in-law in 1913 when she married Alexander Zirner's brother Josef; he was killed in battle two years later. Her first drama, *Diebe im Haus* appeared in 1917. Her first novella, *Der Aufstieg* appeared in 1921 and her first novel, *Die Verliebten* appeared with Ullstein in 1928. She fled Austria in 1938 and became a screenwriter in Hollywood. For a biographical study of the life and works of Gina Kaus, as well as her position in the interwar Austrian and German contexts, see Hildegard Atzinger, *Gina Kaus: Schriftstellerin und Öffentlichkeit: Zur Stellung einer Schriftstellerin in der literarischen Öffentlichkeit der Zwischenkriegszeit in Österreich und Deutschland* (Frankfurt am Main: Peter Lang, 2008).
91. According to Georg Stefan Troller, the few women who frequented the literary circles in these cafés usually served as a combination of artist and muse for men; these also included successful writer Gina Kaus, actress Lina Loos, wife of the architect Adolf Loos, writer Emma von Alesch (neé Rudolph), also known as "Ea," who became the mistress of Hermann Broch, and Bibiana Amon, who was "discovered" by Peter Altenberg. Troller, *Das fidele Grab*, 30–31. Vicki Baum was not only a prolific writer, but also a shrewd businesswoman who was keenly aware of audiences' tastes, and knew just how much to critique women's role in society in her works without being so radical as to alienate readers. She was aware of the gender discrimination she faced, but referred to it flippantly—and humorously—in her autobiography, as well as in private letters. In one letter to Donald B. Elder, her editor at the New York publisher Doubleday, she jokes that she is surprised he still speaks to her, given the social gap between them, noting her hopes that he was not "the gentleman who made derogatory remarks about my posterior while I cleaned

his bathtub" when she worked as a chambermaid at the Berlin Hotel Adlon years ago. Letter from Vicki Baum to Don Elder, dated "July I don't know which 1942," State University of New York at Albany, Vicki Baum Papers.

92. Vicki Baum, *It Was All Quite Different* (New York: Funk & Wagnalls, 1964), 164, 173.
93. Ibid., 229, 263. *Menschen im Hotel* first appeared as a serial in the *Berliner Illustrirte Zeitung*. It was performed as a play directed by Max Reinhardt in Berlin in 1929–1930, and in Vienna directed by Rudolf Beer in 1930, of which he was the director from 1924 to 1932. It was performed on Broadway as *Grand Hotel* in 1931. The 1932 film starring Greta Garbo, John Barrymore, and Joan Crawford won the Academy Award for Best Picture. See also Nottelmann, *Die Karrieren der Vicki Baum*, 148.
94. Freidenreich, *Female, Jewish, Educated*, 16. Lynne Frame points to the "apparent Jewishness of the character of Helene" in her analysis of Baum's book. See "Gretchen, Girl, Garçonne? Weimar Science and Popular Culture in Search of the Ideal New Woman," in *Women in the Metropolis: Gender and Modernity in Weimar Culture*, ed. Katharina von Ankum (Berkeley: University of California Press, 1997).
95. Lynda King, *Best-Sellers by Design: Vicki Baum and the House of Ullstein* (Detroit: Wayne State University Press, 1988), 94. Baum notes that she wrote the narrative with the help of physicians and scientists. Baum, *It was all Quite Different*, 259. For an informative discussion on Baum's reification of common Jewish and gender stereotypes in this novel, see Katie Sutton, *The Masculine Woman in Weimar Germany* (New York: Berghahn, 2011), 155–57.
96. The contradictory messages of *Stud. chem. Helene Willfüer* may have accounted for its enormous popularity at the time of its publication. While Helene asserts her independence by pursuing her career and getting an abortion, in the end she upholds conservative values by marrying her true love, her former professor. Nottelmann, *Die Karrieren der Vicki Baum*, 128–30.
97. King, *Best-Sellers by Design*, 72–75, 87.
98. Atina Grossmann, "The New Woman and the Rationalization of Sexuality in Weimar Germany," in *Powers of Desire: The Politics of Sexuality*, ed. Ann Snitow, Christine Stansel, and Sharon Thompson (New York: Monthly Review Press, 1983), 167.
99. In her research on Jewish women and the Jewish press in Weimar Germany, Kerry Wallach suggests that the "Jewish" values of the New Woman often remained subtly hidden below the surface. She notes that Jewish women participating in Weimar culture at times presented themselves as "unique and discernibly Jewish" even if their outer appearance and modes of self-presentation did not appear on the surface to differ from those of other women. See "Observable Type," 2, 5.
100. The papers of Mela Hartwig's sister Greta (Hartwig) Manschiger, who emigrated to the United States with her husband Kurt Manschinger, at SUNY-Albany contain a trove of information about the family's life, including the

death of their brother Kurt in 1924 and about their parents, who were divorced. After 1938, Mela and Greta supported their mother financially, although she joined Mela and her husband in England. Soon before her death, according to her wishes, Mela had her mother transferred to a Jewish convalescent home. Letters from Theodor Hartwig, who lived with his third wife, Berta Hartwigova (Skribany), in Brno to Greta reveal a somewhat strained relationship between Mela and her father. Letters Mela wrote to her sister refer to her continued efforts to write after she and husband Robert Spira emigrated to the United Kingdom; one dated November 4, 1965, mentions a novel abandoned after only two chapters. However, in a letter dated April 17, 1954, Robert Spira describes to his in-laws that Mela has turned to painting. He proudly describes a painting she has done of Tauplitz, a small mountain village in Austria where Mela and he owned a second home that was Aryanized. SUNY-Albany, Papers of Greta Hartwig Manschinger and Kurt (Ashley Vernon) Manschinger (MP).

101. "Theodor Hartwig, der Altmeister der sozialistischen Freidenkerbewegung gestorben," Typescript, MP, undated. Mela's mother did not convert, and Mela herself was unfamiliar with Jewish rituals. Upon her mother's death in 1956 in London, Mela wrote to Greta in a letter dated May 21 that others had made the arrangements with the synagogue for the funeral. "The 20–30 minute Jewish service, which is so foreign to me, was very bleak." MP.

102. Roles she played included Elektra, Hedda Gabler, Lulu, and the Jewess of Toledo. Max Hilscher, "Die künstlerische Doppelnatur von Mela Spira (Mela Hartwig)," undated, MP. Once she moved back to Austria, she was part of an artistic circle including poet Hans Leifhelm, dramatist and later politician Ernst Fischer, and painter Alfred Wickenburg. A collection of her poetry, *Spiegelungen*, appeared in 1953 thanks to the interventions of her brother-in-law. Letter from Mela to Greta, September 13, 1952. MP.

103. Letter from Mela Hartwig to the Zsolnay Verlag, June 13, 1928, APZV.

104. See Bettina Fraisl, *Körper und Text: (De-) Konstruktionen von Weiblichkeit und Leiblichkeit bei Mela Hartwig* (Vienna: Passagen, 2002), 140.

105. Letter from Mela Hartwig to the Zsolnay Verlag, May 14, 1927, APZV.

106. Because the censorship regulations of the Habsburg monarchy had made it difficult for authors to publish freely, pre–World War I Austrian authors often turned to Berlin and Leipzig-based publishers to disseminate their books to the broadest possible markets. Austrian publishing companies usually specialized narrowly; it was not until 1899 with the establishment of the Wiener Verlag that the first publishing house devoted strictly to literature was founded in Vienna. Hall, "Publishers and Institutions in Austria," 75–77. Oskar Friedmann, brother of Egon Friedell, founded the Wiener Verlag in 1899, but only after Fritz Freund took over did it begin to draw well-known authors such as Hugo von Hofmannsthal, Arthur Schnitzler, and Robert Musil.

107. Other Jewish men who founded successful publishing houses in Vienna included Ernst Peter Rosenthal (E.P. Tal & Co. Verlag), Friedrich (Fritz) Ungar, Ludwig Goldscheider and Bela Horowitz (Phaidon Verlag), and the Suschitzky brothers (Anzengruber Verlag). Fritz Ungar broke off and began the Saturn Verlag in 1926, which he ran until it was Aryanized in 1938. He first became interested in publishing works with explicitly Jewish topics in 1935 due to the worsening political situation for Jews in Germany; these included two edited volumes by Fritz Kobler, *Juden und Judentum in deutschen Briefen aus zwei Jahrhunderten* and *Jüdische Briefe aus Ost und West*. Interview with Frederick Ungar by Rose Stein, New York City, April 28, 1981, 4. SUNY-Albany, Papers of Frederick Ungar.
108. As Arthur Schnitzler, who frequented his mother's salon, noted in a diary entry of November 25, 1923, "One of her sons wanted to found a publishing company as a side project, not with a view to profits." Arthur Schnitzler, *Tagebücher 1909–1926* (Vienna: Verlag der österreichischen Akademie der Wissenschaften, 1981–2000), vol 9.
109. Murray G. Hall and Herbert Ohrlinger, *Der Paul Zsolnay Verlag 1924–1999. Dokumente und Zeugnisse* (Vienna: Zsolnay, 1999), 16, 61–62. Costa's father, Karl Costa, was a librettist, editor, and theatre director. Costa's mother, Rosa Goldstern, was Jewish; in August 1941, Costa and his family were deported to Minsk. See also Murray G. Hall, *Der Paul Zsolnay Verlag: Von der Gründung bis zur Rückkehr aus dem Exil* (Tübingen: Niemeyer, 1994), 186.
110. These included translations into German of both French writer Colette and American author Fannie Hurst. Hall, *Der Paul Zsolnay Verlag: Von der Gründung*, 175.
111. Gertrude Grunwaldt sent Hartwig and Zsolnay an adaptation of the novel for the stage, which she filed for copyright in 1931 in the United States. Letter from Gertrude Grunwaldt to the Paul Zsolnay Verlag, December 26, 1931. According to Grunwaldt, the directors of Vienna's Theater in der Josefstadt and Apollo Theater wanted to stage the play, and she had also been in contact with interested theaters on Broadway in New York, as well as playwright and producer Anne Nichols. Letter from Gertrude Grunwaldt to Paul Zsolnay Verlag, September 19, 1931, APZV.
112. Robert Neumann intervened twice on behalf of Lili Grün. After his initial recommendation of her manuscript *Herz über Bord* to the publisher, he attempted to secure funding for her when she fell ill two years later. Letter from Felix Costa to Lili Grün, November 30, 1935, and letter from the Paul Zsolnay Verlag to Lili Grün from October 16, 1933, APZV. Neumann also helped Hilde Spiel sign her contract with Zsolnay. See Hall, *Der Zsolnay Verlag: von der Gründung*, 186–87.
113. Felix Costa to Hilde Spiel, January 4, 1935, APZV.
114. Even when Zsolnay did not publish Jewish women writers, he provided them with translation work, an important source of income and creative achievement,

though admittedly one that also kept the translator "invisible." Eric Hobsbawm, whose mother published a novel and also worked as a translator in Vienna, claims that she "clearly took great and legitimate pride in the professionalism and literary quality of her translations" *Interesting Times. A Twentieth-Century Life* (New York: Pantheon, 2003), 39. Berta Zuckerkandl, who wrote newspaper articles, translated French and English novels into German, and acted as a kind of literary agent by procuring manuscripts for Zsolnay from foreign authors, played several important roles in Vienna's cultural sphere. Dozens of letters between Zuckerkandl and the Zsolnay Verlag from the interwar years attest to their close working relationship. In one, Berta Zuckerkandl informs Zsolnay they should expect to receive a new play by Alfred Savoir in which she is trying to interest Max Reinhardt in producing. Letter from Zuckerkandl to Zsolnay, November 26, 1928, APZV. Letters from various women to Zsolnay inquire about the possibilities of translating German authors into Yiddish and Polish. See letters from Lena Israel-Gedin of Berlin, December 22, 1930, and Pauline Sandauer of Lvov of December 16, 1930, APZV.

115. On other German writers covering similar topics at that time, such as Irmgard Keun, see Mila Ganeva, *Women in Weimar Fashion: Discourses and Displays in German Culture, 1918–1933* (Rochester, NY: Camden House, 2008).

116. "Ich glaube, ich würde aufhören zu leben, wenn ich dich verliere, nicht sterben, nein, aufhören zu leben, begreifst du das? Ich lebe ja nicht mich, ich lebe—ich glaube, ich lebe dich." Hartwig, *Das Weib ist ein Nichts* (Vienna: Droschl, 2002), 36. The title of the novel is taken from a line attributed to Friedrich Hebbel, "Ein Weib ist ein Nichts; nur durch den Mann kann sie etwas werden." The marketing materials for the original publication describe it as follows in English and German: "It is the woman's fate to become absorbed in the man, in a great and life-enhancing or in a tragic sense. Bibiana, who belongs in turn to an adventurer, a powerful financier, and a revolutionary, experiences the tragedy of womanhood, in that she always becomes the passive creation of her lover." [Es ist des Weibes' Schicksal, in hohem und lebensteigerndem oder im tragischem Sinne im Manne aufzugehen. Bibiana, die nacheinander einem Abenteurer, einem Geldgewaltigen und einem Revolutionär angehört, erlebt die Tragik der Weibeshörigkeit, indem sie stets zum willenlosen Geschöpf des Geliebten wird.] APZV.

117. Sigrid Schmid-Bortenschlager points out that the revolver is a thinly disguised phallic symbol, as well as a symbol of power over life and death. "Der zerbrochene Spiegel: Weibliche Kritik der Psychoanalyse in Mela Hartwigs Novellen," *Modern Austrian Literature: Special Issue on Austrian Women Writers*, 12, no. 3/4 (1979): 80, 82.

118. Mela Hartwig, *Ekstasen* (Berlin: Ullstein, 1992), 54.

119. Schmid-Bortenschlager, "Der zerbrochene Spiegel," 89.

120. "Sie wissen, sehr verehrte gnädige Frau, daß das Weltbild des deutschen Lesepublikums und besonders der deutschen Frau heute ein anderes ist als die Lebensanschauung, die aus Ihrem Werke spricht." Letter from the Paul Zsolnay Verlag to Mela Hartwig, March 16, 1933, APZV. Faced with an extreme financial crisis due to the stigma of being a "Jewish" publisher, Zsolnay was forced to hire authors more acceptable to the new public tastes. A 1934 letter from a journal published in Danzig under the direction of the Nazi Senator für Gesundheitswesen und Bevölkerungspolitik (representative for public health and population policy) and signed "mit deutschem Gruss!" cites its interest in "questions about German life and German culture and questions about the German eastern borderlands and how to see [them] in hereditary terms, which is more popular today than ever" and asks if Zsolnay would be interested in issuing their publication. Costa declined his request. Letter from the "Verlag Wacht im Osten" (Danzig) dated March 23, 1934, and letter from C/B (perhaps Costa) dated March 26, 1934 to Dr. Jürgen M-S. APZV.
121. "Es handelt sich—darüber sind auch sie schon wohl klar—um ein absolut publikumsunwirksames und abseitiges Werk, das in der heutigen Zeit einem heutigen Publikum vorzulegen einen sicheren Misserfolg bedeuten würde." Letter from Zsolnay to Hartwig, April 24, 1931, APZV. "Wenn wir eine Frauenbeilage mit einem Romanteil hätten, so würde ich Ihren Roman . . . sofort erwerben. Da wir aber nur einen Roman bringen können und nicht, wie die meisten Parteizeitungen, zwei, ist es mir auf absehbare Zeit unmöglich, Ihren interessanten Roman zu erwerben." Letter from David Joseph Bach, *Arbeiter-Zeitung* to Mela Hartwig, July 13, 1932, APZV. Other Jewish women writers like Veza Canetti and Else Feldmann faced similar limitations and ambivalent support. *Arbeiter-Zeitung* editor Otto Koenig forbade Veza Canetti from publishing under her own name, claiming that articles written by a Jewish woman would reflect badly on the newspaper. In her letters to Koenig, Else Feldmann expresses her deep appreciation to both Koenig and Josef Luitpold Stern, head of the Socialist Writers' Association, though she also complains that he let her stories to pile up without payment and began letters to her with "Dear gentleman." Letter from Else Feldmann to Otto Koenig dated June 12, 1925 Wienbibliothek, Tagblatt-Archiv, Papers of Else Feldmann, 1026/44-1.
122. However, *Das Weib ist ein Nichts* was translated into Italian in 1931. In 1930, Metro-Goldwyn-Mayer expressed interest in turning the book either into a film starring Greta Garbo or a play along the lines of the already successful Broadway hit *Grand Hotel*. Admittedly, however, Gertrude Grunwaldt, who worked for MGM in New York, noted that Hartwig's book would have to be rewritten with a "happy end" to fit the tastes of the American public. Plans for the film were never realized; MGM went on to produce the film *Grand Hotel* in 1932 based on Baum's novel and stage production. Nevertheless, in 1931, Grunwaldt adapted Hartwig's novel into a play, *The Woman Won—A Play in 4 Acts*. Letters from

Gertrude Grunwaldt to Mela Hartwig dated January 30, 1930, and August 1, 1931, and letter from Gertrude Grunwaldt to the Paul Zsolnay Verlag dated October 5, 1933. APZV.

123. Letter from Mela Hartwig to Zsolnay, June 12, 1934, APZV.
124. See Murray G. Hall, "Publishing in the Thirties in Vienna: The Paul Zsolnay Verlag," in *Austria in the Thirties: Culture and Politics*, ed. Kenneth Segar and John Warren (Riverside, CA: Ariadne, 1991).
125. See Hall, *Der Paul Zsolnay Verlag: Von der Gründung*, 353.
126. In 1935, he wrote a letter to Eugenie Schwarzwald on her behalf. Letter from Felix Costa to Eugenie Schwarzwald, February 8, 1935, APZV. His letters show that Costa made every effort to procure a forum in which Grün could publish, in order for her to gain a source of income. After Costa succeeded in having the newspaper *Der Wiener Tag* publish her novel *Loni in der Kleinstadt*, and he also obtained small grants for her from the PEN club and the Concordia organizations. See file on Lili Grün, APZV. For the most recent work on Schwarzwald and her role in the Austrian public sphere during the interwar period, see Deborah Holmes, "Die neue Pädagogik und die Intellektuellen: Der Beitrag Eugenie Schwarzwalds zur Reformpädagogik in Österreich" in Konrad and Maderthaner, *. . . der Rest ist Österreich*, vol. 2.
127. Letters from Schriftleitung von Velhagen & Klasings Monatsheften to Zsolnay Verlag dated June 20, 1928 and July 14, 1928, APZV.
128. On the difficulty Jewish women writers faced in overcoming what Tamar Garb has called "the dead weight of phantasmic projections that circulated around the category Jewess," see "Modernity, Identity, Textuality," 27.
129. In 1910, possibly due to connections through Prels, Baum became the first woman to publish a story in *Ost und West*, a Berlin magazine aimed at rendering Eastern European Jewish culture palatable to middle-class German Jewish readers. See David A. Brenner, "Neglected 'Women's' Texts and Contexts: Vicki Baum's Jewish Ghetto Stories," *Women in German Yearbook* 13 (1997): 102. "Raffael Gutmann" was also serialized in three issues of the *Leipziger Illustrierte Zeitung* in 1922. October 12, 307–8; October 19, 353–54; November 2, 403–5.
130. Letter from Mela Hartwig to the Paul Zsolnay Verlag, June 24, 1934, APZV.
131. The same was true for Jewish women who competed in beauty contests. In 1929, Lisl Goldarbeiter won both Miss Austria and Miss Universe, and came in second place in the Miss Europe competitions, but rarely acknowledged her Jewish background. As Kerry Wallach points out, the Jewish press championed her to promote the Jewish people in general, but the fact that Jewish Central European beauty queens did not look "visibly Jewish" was often the key to their success. "'Recognition for the Beautiful Jewess': Beauty Queens Crowned by Modern Jewish Print Media," in *Globalizing Beauty: Aesthetics in the Twentieth Century*, ed. Hartmut Berghoff and Thomas Kühne (Washington, D.C.: German Historical Institute, forthcoming).

132. A list of Aryanized Jewish properties compiled by the Gestapo in 1938 includes their homes in Gösting and Tauplitz. Dokumentationsarchiv des österreichischen Widerstandes, File 19.400/170. Mela and her husband both struggled with financial difficulties while in England despite the fact that Mela achieved some success as a painter in the 1950s and early 1960s.
133. While in England, Hartwig worked as a teacher and a translator of English poems into German. However, her difficulties in publishing may have inspired her turn to painting in the 1950s. Her endeavors as a painter proved successful; several London galleries exhibited and/or sold her work. In 2011–2012, the Austrian Cultural Forum in London presented an exhibition of her artwork.

CHAPTER 3

1. Georg Simmel, "The Metropolis and Mental Life," cited in *Georg Simmel*, ed. David Frisby and Mike Featherstone (London: Routledge, 2002), ix.
2. Interview with Helen Blank (Bilber), born 1917 in Vienna, Leo Baeck Institute (LBI), Austrian Heritage Collection (AHC), Number 1928. Blank came to the United States with her younger sister and mother in 1939.
3. Marsha L. Rozenblit notes that this trend began when an increasing number of Jewish business employees chose Neubau (VII) as their home. They rarely chose to live in Ottakring (XVI) and Hernals (XVII) or in the other working-class districts of the city; however, a growing number of poor Jewish artisans lived outside the Gürtel. When they did, they tended to live in those two working-class districts. *The Jews of Vienna, 1867–1914: Assimilation and Identity* (Albany: SUNY Press, 1983), 91. According to census data from 1923 and 1934, these trends continued throughout the interwar period. See *Beiträge zur Statistik der Republik Österreich, Statistik des Bundesstaates Österreichs*, vol. 12, "Vorläufige Ergebnisse der Volkszählung vom 7. März 1923," ed. Bundesamt für Statistik (Vienna: Druck und Verlag der österreichischen Staatsdruckerei, 1923); and *Die Ergebnisse der österreichischen Volkszählung vom 22. März 1934*, vol. 3: Wien, ed. Bundesamt für Statistik (Vienna: Druck und Verlag der österreichischen Staatsdruckerei, 1935), 2–3. However, the reliability of these statistics, in particular those of 1923, has been called into question; they should be treated only as estimates. See Gudrun Exner, Josef Kytir, and Alexander Pinwinkler, eds. *Bevölkerungswissenschaft in Österreich in der Zwischenkriegszeit (1918–1938): Personen, Institutionen, Diskurse* (Vienna: Böhlau, 2004), 170–72; 292–95.
4. Jews typically preferred to live in the *Villenviertel* (villa districts) like Währing (XVIII) and Döbling (XIX). The Bundeserziehungsanstalt für Mädchen (previously known as the k.u.k. Officierstöchter-Erziehungs-Institut) was located in Hernals (XVII) when Helen Blank attended. It relocated to Landstrasse (III) in 1934.

5. Helen Blank notes that when she expressed anxiety to her non-Jewish classmates about their brothers' activities, they answered with "hollow replies" of "Don't worry—we'll protect you."
6. Historians claim that Viennese Jews far exceeded their proportional representation both in education for girls and in Social Democratic voting and leadership patterns. On the predominance of Viennese Jews in the *Gymnasium*, see Rozenblit, *Assimilation and Identity*, 99–125; on Jewish girls in the Viennese *Gymnasium* see Harriet Pass Freidenreich, *Female, Jewish, Educated: The Lives of Central European University Women* (Bloomington: Indiana University Press, 2002), 1–20; on Jews and Socialism see Robert S. Wistrich, *Socialism and the Jews: The Dilemmas of Assimilation in Germany and Austria-Hungary* (East Brunswick, NJ: Associated University Press, 1982). For a discussion about whether and when a general cultural practice can be usefully described as "Jewish," see Leora Auslander, "The Boundaries of Jewishness or When Is a Cultural Practice Jewish?" *Modern Jewish Studies* 8, no. 1 (2009).
7. In 1910, for example, Jews made up only 3 percent of the population in proletarian Ottakring, but 11 percent in the more middle-class Neubau (VII). In contrast, Jews made up 34 percent of the population in the Leopoldstadt, 20 percent in the first district inside the Ring, and 21 percent in the district of Alsergrund (IX). Ivar Oxaal, "The Jews of Young Hitler's Vienna: Historical and Sociological Aspects," in *Jews, Antisemitism, and Culture in Vienna*, ed. Ivar Oxaal, Michael Pollak, and Gerhard Botz (London: Routledge, 1987), 30. Rozenblit points out that between 1870 and 1910, "Jews in Vienna adjusted their choice of neighborhood to conform to their changing occupations and social status." She notes that the proportion of Jews making up the population of Alsergrund doubled from 10 percent to 20 percent, and tripled from 4 percent to 12 percent in Mariahilf and Neubau. *Assimilation and Identity*, 88–89.
8. Kevin Lynch with Alvin K. Lukashok, "Some Childhood Memories of the City" [1956], reprinted in *City Sense and City Design. Writings and Projects of Kevin Lynch*, ed. Tridib Banerjee and Michael Southworth (Cambridge: MIT Press, 1996), 161.
9. For more on the relationship between the overlapping of personal and spatial boundaries and their importance for children's development of their self-understandings, see David Sibley, "Families and Domestic Routines: Constructing the Boundaries of Childhood," in *Geographies of Cultural Transformation*, ed. Steve Pile and Nigel Thrift (London: Routledge, 1995). On the impact of urban life and social thought on Jewish self-identification, see Joachim Schlör, *Das Ich der Stadt: Debatten über Judentum und Urbanität, 1822–1938* (Göttingen: Vandenhoeck & Ruprecht, 2005).
10. Helen Blank, LBI, AHC, 3. Gitta Deutsch also reflects on the details of the streets near her home in her memoir *Böcklinstrassenelegie: Erinnerungen* (*The Red Thread*) (Vienna: Picus, 1993).

11. According to Kevin Lynch, the "legibility" of a cityscape refers to the ease with which a person can recognize its parts and organize them into a coherent pattern. A legible city, he suggests, offers security and both deepens and intensifies human experience. See *The Image of the City* (Boston: MIT Press, 1960), 5.
12. Robert S. Wistrich notes that associating the "Red Fear" with the "Jewish Question" began as part of Mayor Karl Lueger's propaganda when he took office in 1897. Robert S. Wistrich, "Social Democracy, Antisemitism, and the Jews," in Oxaal et al., *Jews, Antisemitism, and Culture*, 116. According to Josef Hindels, both teachers and students, with few exceptions, expressed antisemitism by decrying "Red Vienna." "For them anti-Semitism was accepted, but they had only hate and scorn for the plans to build up Red Vienna. The students, with few exceptions, came from bourgeois homes, and were full of prejudices against 'the Reds' and 'the Jews.'" See his undated autobiography, 5, cited in Eleonore Lappin, "Jüdische Lebenserinnerungen: Rekonstruktionen von jüdischer Kindheit und Jugend im Wien der Zwischenkriegzeit," in *Wien und die jüdische Erfahrung 1900–1938*, ed. Frank Stern and Barbara Eichinger (Vienna: Böhlau, 2009), 36.
13. Rozenblit, *Assimilation and Identity*, 17. In 1869, Jews represented 6.4 percent of the total population of Vienna. The percentage rose to 8.6 percent in 1910 percent and to 9.4 percent in 1934. However, between 1923 and 1934, the number of Jews in Vienna actually fell from 201,513 to 176,034. *Die Ergebnisse der österreichischen Volkszählung vom 22. März 1934*, vol. 1: "Bundesstaat," ed. Bundesamt für Statistik (Vienna: Druck und Verlag der österreichischen Staatsdruckerei, 1935), 50. Michael John attributes the decrease in numbers to both emigration and low birth rates. "'We Do Not Even Possess Our Selves': On Identity and Ethnicity in Austria, 1880–1937," *Austrian History Yearbook* 30 (1999): 59.
14. Rozenblit points out that the Jewish population grew rapidly after 1850 and the government's lifting of residence restrictions that had kept most Jews from living in Vienna. Unlike non-Jewish immigrants, Jews came from different areas of Austria-Hungary, and for different reasons, tended to move as families, and were not unfamiliar with city life. When they came to the city, they tended to reside near other Jews, regardless of class—a trait that set them apart from the non-Jewish Viennese. Rozenblit, *Assimilation and Identity*, 16–19.
15. David Vogel's (also spelled Fogel) Hebrew novel was published as *Haye nisu'im* (Jerusalem: Mitspeh, 1929–30). The version used in this chapter is *Married Life*, trans. Dalya Bilu (New Milford, CT: Toby Press, 2007), hereafter cited in the text as *ML*; Abraham Moshe Fuchs's Yiddish novel was originally published as *unter der brik un andere derzejlungen* (Warsaw: Kultur-lige, 1924). The version used in this chapter is *Unter der Brücke*, trans. Armin Eidherr (Salzburg: Otto Müller Verlag, 1997), hereafter cited in the text as *UdB*; Veza Canetti's stories were first published in the *Arbeiter-Zeitung* between 1932–1933. Elias Canetti published them after Veza's death as *Die gelbe Strasse: Roman* (Munich: Hanser, 1990). The

version used in this chapter is *Yellow Street*, trans. Ian Mitchell (London: Halban, 1990), hereafter cited in the text as *YS*.

16. An *eruv*, for example, is a physical expression of a symbolic private domain area in which observant Jews may complete a range of activities on the Sabbath that can typically only be done at home. But the *eruv* can also take on unintended meanings that address the nature of community formation. Moreover, given Jews' history of living behind ghettos, walls, and fences set up to delineate the community, the *eruv* by definition echoes this process regardless of the intent of its builders. See Charlotte Elisheva Fonrobert, "The Political Symbolism of the Eruv," *Jewish Social Studies* 11, no. 3 (2005): 10.
17. For an excellent overview of this type of examination, see Charlotte Elisheva Fonrobert and Vered Shemtov, "Introduction: Jewish Conceptions and Practices of Space," *Jewish Social Studies* 11, no. 3 (2005). See also *Jewish Topographies: Visions of Space, Traditions of Place*, ed. Anna Lipphardt, Julia Brauch, and Alexandra Nocke (Aldershot: Ashgate, 2008); and *Makom: Orte und Räume im Judentum—Real—Abstrak—Imaginär*, ed. Michal Kümper, Barbara Rösch, Ulrike Schneider, and Helen Thein (Hildesheim: Georg Olms Verlag, 2007). Scott Spector's innovative use of "territory"—in reference to both physical and metaphorical space—is a useful analytical frame for understanding the complexities of the political, social, and cultural context for German-Jewish writers in Prague during the fin-de-siècle. In some instances, those writers' challenges to conceptions of nation, language, and the degree to which they self-identified with both echo those of writers in Hebrew and Yiddish in Vienna. See *Prague Territories: National Conflict and Cultural Innovation in Franz Kafka's Fin de Siècle* (Berkeley: University of California Press, 2000).
18. Henri Lefebvre, *The Production of Space*, trans. Donald Nicholson-Smith (Malden, MA: Blackwell Publishers, 1984), 44–45.
19. The roots of its use lie in Heidegger's foregrounding of the dialectical, constitutive relationship between people and their physical environment in his notion of *Dasein* (being-in-the-world). The term suggests that the world around us cannot exist independently of the people who inhabit it. It is only through our consciousness, actions, and interactions that the physical landscape is brought into being.
20. Setha M. Low and other scholars of the built environment refer to this site of social engagement as "place"; however, since most in Jewish studies speak of Jewish "space" rather than Jewish "place," I will continue to use the term "space" to refer to this reconceptualized area. See *On the Plaza: The Politics of Public Space and Culture* (Austin: University of Texas Press, 2000), 127–53. I am grateful to Arijit Sen for introducing me to the use of these terms in the context of the built environment.
21. Robert Rotenberg, *Landscape and Power in Vienna* (Baltimore: Johns Hopkins University Press, 1995), 5.

22. The earliest documented evidence of Jews in Austria stems from 799 and 906, but it was not until 1244 that they received official permission to live in Vienna. The area where they lived, the *Judenviertel*, was delimited by walls and accessible only through gates, but because Jews with privileges could live outside its bounds, it was not a ghetto per se. In 1420, Archduke Albrecht V, under the pretense of host-desecration, ordered Jews banished from Austria except for 210 wealthy Jews who were imprisoned, plundered, and then burned in 1421 in an event called the "Wiener Geserah." The area was renamed "Neuer Platz" in 1423, and since 1437 called "Judenplatz." A plaque in Latin "celebrating" the burning of the "Hebrew dogs" in 1421 still remains today on the *Haus zum großen Jordan*, across the way from the Rachel Whiteread's 2000 memorial to Austrian Jews murdered in the Holocaust. Today the area remains a Jewish space with a contested history in Vienna. On the complicated history of Vienna's Judenplatz as a memorial space, see Monika Sommer, "Der Wiener Judenplatz als Museum ohne Mauern: Eine Kritik," *transversal: Zeitschrift des Zentrums jüdische Studien* 3, no. 1 (2002).
23. Due to financial burdens during the Thirty Year's War, Emperor Ferdinand III decreed in 1624 that Jews should inhabit an area of the *Unteren Werd* (lower marsh); they were free to engage in trade and commerce in other parts of the city, but restricted in where they lived. Though never completely walled in physically, the fact that Jews were required to live there rendered it a *quasi*-ghetto.
24. By 1580, a number of Jewish families had returned to Vienna, and by the early seventeenth century Jews formed a new community in the inner city around the inner city's Kienmarkt, where most Jewish businesses were located. In 1669, a mandate issued in the name of Leopold I expelled all Jews from Austria; the decree was carried out in 1670. Leopold, the Habsburg emperor who expelled the Jews, made sure to dedicate the church to a namesake: the canonized Bamburg duke, Leopold III. Several nineteenth-century sources allege that at its dedication, he laid a foundation stone with the following inscription on the back in Latin: "After driving out the unfaithful Jews, his most serene highness Emperor Leopold of Austria toppled the synagogue that stood here, cleaned this den of iniquity, and in 1670 turned it into a house of God dedicated according to Catholic ritual to St. Leopold, margrave and patron of Austria." See, for example, Leopold Matthias Wechsel, *Die Leopoldstadt bey Wien: Quellen und Quellschriftstellern, in Verbindung mit einer Skizze der Landesgeschichte, historisch dargestellt* (Vienna: Anton Strauss, 1824), 296–97. Only three years after the expulsion decree, Jews returned, with even fewer rights. They were forbidden to practice their religion in public, and Leopold did not issue general residence permits to them; with the exception of a few wealthy court Jews, most remained unable to choose their place of residence or own their property. Nathan von Arnstein was allowed to rent a residence on the Hoher Markt in 1796, although he also owned a small chateau in what is now the fifteenth district. By 1772, Vienna was home to 594 Jews who had to pay high special taxes. See R. Po-chia Hsia, "The Jews and

the Emperors," in *State and Society in Early Modern Austria*, ed. Charles W. Ingrao (West Lafayette, IN: Purdue University Press, 1994), 78; John P. Spielman, *The City and the Crown: Vienna and the Imperial Court, 1600–1740* (West Lafayette, IN: Purdue University Press, 1993), 130–32; Michaela Feurstein and Gerhard Milchram, *Jewish Vienna* (Vienna: Mandelbaum, 2004), 38–39, 45–48; Oxaal, "The Jews of Young Hitler's Vienna," 15–24; Felix Czeike, *Wien wie es war: Ein Nachschlagewerk für Freunde des alten und neuen Wien* (Vienna: Fritz Molden, 1965), esp. 269–70; Erika Weinzierl and Otto D. Kulka, eds., *Vertreibung und Neubeginn: Israelische Bürger österreichischer Herkunft* (Vienna: Böhlau, 1992), 20–21.

25. In 1782, Joseph II's *Toleranzpatent* eased numerous restrictions for Jews, including some of the restrictions on residence and professions, after which, some Jews started retail businesses in the city center; Vienna's central synagogue was built there in 1826. However, it was not until 1860, when restrictions on purchasing real estate were finally lifted, that Jews began to play a crucial role in shaping the city's cultural landscape outside the Leopoldstadt.
26. Dell Upton, "Seen, Unseen, and Scene," in *Understanding Ordinary Landscapes*, ed. Paul Erling Groth and Todd W. Bressi (New Haven: Yale University Press, 1997), 175.
27. See in particular Eve Blau's chapter "The Historical City. Patterns of Growth in Urban Life," in *The Architecture of Red Vienna 1919–1934* (Cambridge: MIT University Press, 1999), 48–87.
28. Carl E. Schorske, *Fin-de-Siècle Vienna: Culture and Politics* (New York: Vintage: 1980), 24–114.
29. However, Schorske does mention that the *Postsparkasse* (Postal Savings Bank) built in 1906 by Otto Wagner, with its emphasis on small accounts for the "little man," represented the antisemitic response of the Christian Social Party to the "Rothschild" Jewish banking houses. Attempts to include in the building a bust of their hero, the bank's founder Georg Coch, were allegedly thwarted by "influential Jewish opposition." Schorske, *Fin-de-Siècle Vienna*, 90.
30. Fredric Bedoire, *The Jewish Contribution to Modern Architecture 1830–1930* (Jersey City, NJ: Ktav, 2004), 312–13. On the significance of Jews' participation in developing both private and public buildings on the Ringstrasse, see Elana Shapira, "Jüdisches Mäzenatentum zwischen Assimilation und Identitätsstiftung in Wien, 1800–1930," in *Jüdische Friedhöfe. Kultstätte, Erinnerungsort, Denkmal*, ed. Claudia Theune and Tina Walzer (Vienna: Böhlau, 2010), 174–75.
31. Once restrictions were lifted, Jewish bankers, supported by a few non-Jewish aristocrats, were also at the forefront of funding building projects on this area of prime real estate; some of them developed entire blocks. Jewish banking families such as Epstein and Ephrussi built palaces on or just off the Ringstrasse; some constructed *Mietspaläste* "rental palaces." See Bedoire, *The Jewish Contribution to Modern Architecture*, 216, 303, 308, 318. For informative details about the life of

the Ephrussi family in Vienna, see Edmund de Waal, *The Hare with Amber Eyes: A Hidden Inheritance* (London: Vintage, 2010), 111–284.

32. Bedoire, *The Jewish Contribution to Modern Architecture*, 318. On Viennese Jews who turned away from the Historicist style and supported the avant-garde movement, see Elana Shapira, "Jewish Patronage and the Avant-Garde in Vienna," in *Jewish Collectors and their Contribution to Modern Culture,* ed. Annette Weber. Heidelberg: Universitätsverlag, 2011.
33. Botstein notes that most Viennese Jews tended to concentrate in areas with close and easy access to the cultural events on the Ringstrasse. See Leon Botstein, "Sozialgeschichte und die Politik des Ästhetischen: Juden und Musik in Wien 1870–1938," in Leon Botstein and Werner Hanak, eds., *Quasi una fantasia: Juden und die Musikstadt Wien*, exhibition catalogue (Hofheim: Wolke Verlag, 2003), 47.
34. Franz Friedrich Masaidek, *Wien und die Wiener aus der Spottvogelperspektive: Wien's Sehens-, Merk- und Nichtswürdigkeiten* (Vienna: Waldheim, 1873), 21, 30.
35. "Intense rivalry gripped the Viennese citizens and the rich Jewish bankers thanks to emancipation, finally! Having received the right to be human, to be able to own one's own house and home, they were proud to build grand houses for themselves and rental houses, too. They had first-rate artists construct their grandiose buildings on the Ringstrasse in order to say: Here we are, we're here to stay, it's beautiful here, we want to build our palaces here! Rothschild, Todesco and Springer, Wiener and Schey, Königswarter and Epstein and all the others became landlords on Vienna's Ringstrasse, those men who were not able to own land or property before 1848." Cited in Elana Shapira, *"Assimilating with Style": Jewish Assimilation and Modern Architecture and Design: The Case of the "Outfitters" Adolf Loos and Leopold Goldman and the Making of the Goldman & Salatsch Building*, (Ph.D. diss., University of Applied Arts, Vienna, 2004), 26. Uhl's mother came from a prominent Jewish family in Silesia and converted to Catholicism when she was married. Monica Strauss, *Cruel Banquet, The Life and Loves of Frida Strindberg*, (New York: Harcourt, 2000), 3.
36. Wer uns're Wienerstadt/Hübsch lang nicht g'sehen hat/Der find't kein Haus mehr fast;/Denn wo man nur hinschaut steht A Palast!/Der Ring ist ein Juwel/Dort wohnt ganz Israel/In zehn Jahren baun's bequem/Sich dorten ein neues Jerusalem. Elana Shapira notes that these lyrics were written by Jewish journalist Josef Weyl around 1869. See "Jüdisches Mäzenatentum," 175 and n.18. The original *An der schönen blauen Donau* premiered in 1867.
37. He names specifically the "millionaires" David von Gutmann, Ludwig von Gutmann, Albert Freiherr von Rothschild, Nathaniel Baron Rothschld, and Carl Wittgenstein. Joseph Scheicher, *Aus dem Jahre 1920: Ein Traum vom Landtags- und Reichratsabgeordneten Dr. Joseph Scheicher* . . . (St. Pölten: Verlag von Johann Gregora's Buchhandlung, 1900), 82. In his memoirs, Scheicher exhibits the

common antisemitic trope that "Jews are everywhere" when he notes, "The eternal Jew travels the world and leeches money and property from all peoples. There is almost no town or market, or even a village, in which trade is not a Jewish monopoly or has good prospects to become one. There, too, the inhabitants are poor." *Erlebnisse und Erinnerungen: Aus der Jugendzeit* (Vienna: Carl Fromme, 1907–1912), 7. For more on Joseph Scheicher, see Chapter 3.

38. Oxaal, "The Jews of Young Hitler's Vienna," 30. Wealthy Jews rarely chose to live in Wieden. Rozenblit, *Assimilation and Identity*, 78.

39. Philipp and Wilhelm Suschitzky had difficulties obtaining permission to open their bookstore selling mainly socialist literature in the proletarian district of Favoriten (X). Wilhelm's son Wolfgang Suschitzky states that the "Brüder Suschitzky" bookstore also functioned as a library and well-known meeting place for intellectuals and authors from the brothers' publishing company, the Anzengruber Verlag. The family lived nearby. Julia Winckler, "Gespräch mit Wolfgang Suschitzky, Fotograf und Kameramann," *Exilforschung: Ein Internationales Jahrbuch*, ed. Claus-Dieter Krohn, et al., 21 (2003), 256–57. As Rozenblit notes, although Favoriten was a popular home for Czechs in Vienna, few Czech Jews—or any Jews at all—chose to live in that district. Rozenblit, *Assimilation and Identity*, 96. In 1934, Jews comprised only 2.3 percent of that district's population and represented only 2 percent of the city's total Jewish population. *Statistik des Bundesstaates Österreichs*, vol. 2: Bundesstaat, ed. Bundesamt für Statistik (Vienna: Druck und Verlag der österreichischen Staatsdruckerei, 1935), 2–3. Between 1920 and 1933, the Suschitzkys were obliged to appear in court at least seven times to respond to charges for supposed violations of the city's ordinance against selling pornography. They were found guilty only once, in 1933, for selling erotic literature. Annette Lechner, *Die Wiener Verlagsbuchhandlung Anzengruber-Verlag, Brüder Suschitzky (1901–1938) im Spiegel der Zeit*, (M.A. Diplomarbeit, University of Vienna, 1994), 147. Originally, the Suschitzky brothers wanted to build their store on the Himbergerstrasse between Keplerplatz and Landgutgasse. In their application to the Ministry of the Interior, they argued that such a store was necessary in a district with such a large population and so many schools. See Allgemeines Verwaltungsarchiv, Zl. 23.018 a.a.O. as cited in Lechner, *Die Wiener Verlagsbuchhandlung*, 13.

40. Rozenblit, *Assimilation and Identity*, 74–76. As evidence of the complex reality of the residential situation underlying the coding of Jewish space is Ivar Oxaal's point that many Jews in the inner city and Leopoldstadt lived in apartment buildings with Christians, in contrast to the residential patterns of Jews in late nineteenth-century Prague. Oxaal, "The Jews of young Hitler's Vienna," 25. Michael John notes a striking difference in the segregation patterns of the Jews and Czechs, the two largest minorities in Vienna. Compared to the Jewish population, the middle-class immigrant Czech population soon reached a level of geographical integration that their Jewish counterparts did not. John, "'We Do Not

Even Possess Our Selves,'" 31. Of course, this does not preclude the fact that Jews lived in other districts, or that other parts of the city could be coded as Jewish. For example, the Jewish population in the districts of Fünfhaus and Sechshaus also grew in the mid-nineteenth century. See Julius Müller, "Die Bewohnerinnen der jüdsichen Gemeinde 'Sechshausen' und ihre mährischen 'Heimatstadt," in *Das Dreieck meiner Kindheit: Eine jüdische Vorstadtgemeinde in Wien*, eds. Michael Kofler, Judith Pühringer, and Georg Traska (Vienna, Mandelbaum: 2008), 73.

41. Rozenblit, *Assimilation and Identity*, 85.
42. Benno Weiser Varon, *Professions of a Lucky Jew* (London: Cornwall, 1992), 21–22.
43. For a history of the theater, see Richard S. Geehr, *Adam Müller-Guttenbrunn and the Aryan Theater of Vienna: 1898–1903: The Approach of Cultural Fascism* (Göppingen: Kümmerle, 1973).
44. The Burgtheater on the Ringstrasse was not finished until 1870, by which time other theaters had emerged focussing on operetta and targeting middle-class audiences who were moving to the districts surrounding the inner city. W. E. Yates, *Theatre in Vienna: A Critical History, 1776–1995* (Cambridge: Cambridge University Press, 1996), 159.
45. "The Viennese theater was, to a great extent, a Jewish affair. Though many actors were Gentiles, the stars and prominent playwrights and directors were predominantly Jews." Varon, *Professions of a Lucky Jew*, 29. For more on Jews' attendance of musical and theater performances in Vienna, see Leon Botstein, *Judentum und Modernität: Essays zur Rolle der Juden in der deutschen und österreichischen Kultur, 1848 bis 1938* (Vienna: Böhlau, 1991). See also the exhibition catalogue *Quasi una fantasia: Juden und die Musikstadt Wien*, ed. Leon Botstein and Werner Hanak (Hofheim: Wolke Verlag, 2003).
46. Although the city's oldest commercial theater, established in 1780, was located in the Leopoldstadt, it never served as a rival to the court theaters. Yates, *Theatre in Vienna*, 18.
47. Adam Müller-Guttenbrunn was a Pan-German theater critic and writer who first gained notoriety with his antisemitic pamphlet *Wien war ein Theaterstadt* (Vienna: Graeser, 1885). He was director-designate of the Raimundtheater since its inception in 1893 near the border of Vienna's 6th district, close to the Gürtel. He became director of the Kaiserjubiläums-Stadttheater, which he helped establish in 1898; with 1,855 seats, it was one of Vienna's largest commercial theaters. Ironically, Müller-Guttenbrunn claims to have tried to convince the Board members not to completely exclude Jews from membership in this antisemitic theater; he feared that doing so would lead to disfavor among Jewish newspaper critics. Adam Müller-Guttenbrunn [Roderich Meinhart, pseud.], *Erinnerungen eines Theaterdirektors* (Leipzig: L. Staackmann Verlag, 1924), 15–16. The theater produced plays with antisemitic content, and only occasionally broke the rule about not hiring Jewish actors or including Jewish playwrights on the program. The

brief history of the original theater was filled with missteps, blunders, and financial mismanagement. For more details see Yates, *Theatre in Vienna*, 168–77. See also "Aryan Theater," in *A Historical Encyclopedia of Prejudice and Antisemitism*, vol. 1, ed. Richard S. Levy (Santa Barbara, CA: ABC-CLIO, 2005), 40–41. Today, the building is home to Vienna's Volksoper, a popular venue for music and theater performances. It features two large plaques in its lobby honoring both Adam Müller-Guttenbrunn and the mayor who helped enable the buildings' construction, Karl Lueger, with no mention of their original antisemitic intentions.

48. Müller-Guttenbrunn, *Erinnerungen*, 10. In the decades before the First World War, the districts of both Währing (XVIII) and Döbling (XIX) began to attract more Jews. See Rozenblit, *Assimilation and Identity*, 91.
49. Friedrich Schütz was a Jewish editor at the *Neue Freie Presse*.
50. During the interwar period, Müller-Guttenbrunn continued to receive accolades as he developed his antisemitic outlook. Upon being named *Ehrendoktor* (Honorary doctor) in 1922, none other than Walter Riehl, head of the Nazi Party in Vienna, who would later serve as the defense lawyer for both Hugo Bettauer's murderer Otto Rothstock and Bruno Wolf's murderer Oskar Pöffel (see Chapter 1), wrote the following congratulatory note: "We will never forget that it was you who has been especially good to our party. We consistently recommend your novels, which count among the best German literature of all time, to our followers." Letter from Walter Riehl to Adam Müller-Guttenbrunn, November 2, 1922, WB, HS, WRP, IN 35.370.
51. Dr. Ignaz Schwarz, *Das Wiener Ghetto: Seine Häuser und Seine Bewohner* (Vienna: Wilhelm Braumüller, 1909).
52. Part I: Of the 69 houses of the *Judenviertel* at the time of its destruction in 1421, 50 were privately owned by Jews. In addition to listing the owners of each building, to whom it was sold and the cost, the study also describes the rooms in each house. The afterword to the reprint of Schwarz's study by Andreas Weigl indicates that part of this map is incorrect. Part II of the study covers what would later become the Leopoldstadt, the "The Jewish City in the Lower Werd" (*Die Judenstadt im Unteren Werd* 1625–1670).
53. Schwarz explicitly states that the study was meant to serve as a counterpart to G. Wolf's, *Die Juden in der Leopoldstadt im 17. Jahrhundert in Wien* (Vienna: Verlag Herzfeld and Bauer, 1864), commissioned by the city. Though Schwarz does not mention it, Ludwig August Frankl's *Zur Geschichte der Juden in Wien* (Vienna: Druck und Verlag von J.P. Sollinger's Witwe, 1853) lists the addresses and owners of Jewish properties in the Judenstadt before their expulsion in 1669, but does not map them. Significantly, Frankl also documents the preservation of the oldest Jewish cemetery in Vienna (1582) in the suburb of Rossau in the Seegasse, which continued to exist even after the 1669–1670 expulsions since the Fränkel brothers paid the city 4000 Gulden to secure the cemetery. *Zur Geschichte*, 6–7, 18. Between 1912 and 1917, Bernard Wachstein documented the cemetery

in a scholarly study of its tombstone inscriptions. *Die Inschriften des alten Judenfriedhofes in Wien* (Vienna: Wilhelm Braumüller, 1912–1917) included a plan and description of each stone, as well as a number of biographies of the people who were buried there. This study of Jews literally "embedded" in the city provides an important counterpart to the community's documentation of the areas where Jews lived in the past.

54. See the afterward to the reprint of Schwarz's study by Andreas Weigl, 320.
55. One of these, by Leopold Wechsel, emphasizes how many Christian residents had lived in the *Unteren Werd* before the expulsion of the Jews in order to "prove" the district's nature as a Christian area. Wechsel, *Die Leopoldstadt bey Wien*, 262.
56. Wolfgang Maderthaner and Lutz Musner point out that a solid ring of densely constructed working-class suburbs surround the districts within the Gürtel and the city center; those districts with villa estates (XIII, XVIII, XIX) alone were designed for upper- and upper-middle class residents. See *Unruly Masses: The Other Side of Fin-de-Siècle Vienna* (New York: Berghahn, 2008), 34.
57. Schorske, *Fin-de- Siècle Vienna*, 32–33.
58. Maderthaner and Musner, *Unruly Masses*, 34. The authors claim that these buildings are an integral part of the city's fractured political history, since the construction of large tenements in the working-class districts beyond the Gürtel with facades that mimic the grandiose buildings of the Ringstrasse actually served to conceal the miserable living conditions within, and obscured residents' awareness of the economic reality of their situation.
59. Stephen Templ and Tina Walzer's *Unser Wien:"Ariesierung" auf österreichisch* (Berlin: Aufbau, 2001) fulfills a similar function to Schwarz's 1909 report. Using records of Aryanizations and forced sales, they create a figurative map of many of the major areas where Jews in Vienna lived and worked before 1938. To be sure, however, many Jews did not necessarily own property and lived in a variety of other spaces and districts throughout the city. For example, Rabbi Joseph Bloch lived in Floridsdorf, which, according to the 1934 census, featured a Jewish population of only 1857, representing 1.7 percent of the district's population. Of all Vienna's districts, only Simmering had a smaller Jewish population, although even that district featured its own synagogue. Of the numerous former Austrian Jews interviewed in the Leo Baeck Institute's Austrian Heritage Collection, at least a few came from districts in Vienna with low Jewish populations, like Ottakring and Rudolfsheim. Recently published local histories about Viennese Jews who lived in districts where few other Jews resided all seek, to some extent, to (rightly) challenge the essentializing notion that *all* Viennese Jews lived in heavily Jewish-populated areas of the city. See Kofler, et al., *Das Dreieck meiner Kindheit*; and Herbert Exenberger, *Gleich dem kleinen Häuflein der Makkabäer: Die jüdische Gemeinde in Simmering: 1848–1945* (Vienna: Mandelbaum, 2009) about Jews in Simmering (XI).
60. "Die Vorstadt führt!" *Illustriertes Sportblatt* 41 (1927), 7.

61. Renate Banik-Schweitzer, "Vienna. Development of the City," in *Architecture in Vienna*, ed. August Sarnitz (Vienna: Springer, 1998), 18.
62. Vienna and Lower Austria officially became separate states on December 29, 1921, although in practice they had functioned separately in some ways as early as December 1920.
63. Sándor Békési, "Shrinking City? Stadtbilder und Stadtentwicklung im Wien der Zwischenkriegszeit," in the exhibition catalogue *Kampf um die Stadt*, ed. Wolfgang Kos (Vienna: 2009), 99, 102.
64. On the basis of research on autobiographies stemming from the first quarter of the twentieth century, Eleonore Lappin claims that many Jews reconfigured their self-identifications as politically Austrian, culturally Viennese, and ethnically Jewish. See Lappin, "Jüdische Erinnerungen," 25. For more on the phenomenon of *Alt-Wien*, see the exhibition catalogue *Alt Wien. Die Stadt, die niemals war*, ed. Wolfgang Kos and Christian Rapp (Vienna: Czernin, 2004).
65. Varon, *Professions of a Lucky Jew*, 31.
66. Anton Kuh, "Wien am Gebirge," *Die Stunde*, July 4, 1923, 3. Kuh is best known for his scathing public polemic against Karl Kraus delivered before an audience at the Vienna Konzerthaus on October 25, 1925, and later published as "Der Affe Zarathustras (Karl Kraus)." See Harold B. Segel, ed. and trans., *The Vienna Coffeehouse Wits, 1890–1938* (West Lafayette, IN: Purdue University Press, 1993), 296–98.
67. David Matless notes a similar preoccupation in England between 1918 and 1939, when there emerged a "particular landscaped version of English citizenship" that accompanied the increase in scale and scope of open-air leisure. David Matless, "The Art of Right Living: Landscape and Citizenship, 1918–39," in *Mapping the Subject. Geographies of Cultural Transformation*, ed. Steven Pile and Nigel Thrift (London: Routledge, 1995), 93.
68. Anton Kuh, "Theaterfest in Wien: Ein Premierenbericht," *Prager Tagblatt*, October 1, 1924, 3.
69. Leo Perutz, "Skizzen aus Ukraine" in *Mainacht in Wien* (Vienna: Zsolnay, 1996), 153.
70. According to Manès Sperber, it was not only the longest street in the Leopoldstadt, but also the most visibly poor. Manès Sperber, "Die Demütigung," in *Die Mazzesinsel: Juden in der Wiener Leopoldstadt 1918–1938*, ed. Ruth Beckermann (Vienna: Löcker, 1984), 50.
71. This ambivalence about its function may explain why many of the now-celebrated Jewish writers, composers, and thinkers from the fin-de-siècle through the interwar period tended to—in the words of Georg Stefan Troller "ashamedly repress"—their ties to the Leopoldstadt in their works, despite the fact that many had spent their formative years there. Troller includes among them Arthur Schnitzler, Theodor Herzl, Sigmund Freud, Gustav Mahler, Arnold Schönberg, Peter Altenberg, Felix Salten, and Alfred Polgar. Georg Stefan Troller, *Das fidele*

Grab an der Donau: Mein Wien 1918–1938 (Düsseldorf: Artemis & Winkler, 2004), 16.

72. Leon Askin, cited in Werner Hanak and Mechtild Widrich, eds., *Wien II: Leopoldstadt: Die andere Heimatkunde* (Vienna: Brandstätter, 1999), 9.
73. Peter Herz, "Entzauberte Praterstraße," in Beckermann, *Die Mazzesinsel*, 82–85.
74. Rozenblit notes that registered members of the Jewish community tended to live on more major streets such as the Taborstrasse, Rembrandtstrasse, Untere Augartenstrasse, Stefaniestrasse, Praterstrasse, and Obere Donaustrasse. The wealthier among them lived to the east of the Taborstrasse, while poorer Jews tended to live in side streets and back alleys to its west. In 1910, Jews made up 33.9 percent of the total population of the Leopoldstadt. Rozenblit, *Assimilation and Identity*, 78, 84. In 1934, 50, 922 of Vienna's 176, 034 Jews (29 percent) lived there. *Die Ergebnisse der österreichischen Volkszählung vom 22. März 1934*, vol. 3: Wien, ed. Bundesamt für Statistik (Vienna: Druck und Verlag der österreichischen Staatsdruckerei, 1935), 2–3. It retained its character as the "core Jewish district" despite the fact that Jews of all origins and social classes lived there; the highest concentration of Galician Jews remained in Brigittenau, which was part of the Leopoldstadt until 1900. Oxaal, "The Jews of Young Hitler's Vienna," 29. That the Deutschösterreichische Schutzverein Antisemitenbund (German-Austrian Antisemitic Defense League) chose to stage an armed demonstration in the Leopoldstadt in 1919 also visibly and violently signalled its continued role as the symbolic Jewish district. Some Jews from Vienna, such Stella Klein-Löw and Ernst Epler, refer to it as the "Judenbezirk" in their memoirs. Beckermann, *Mazzesinsel*, 74.
75. Herz also names the smaller Roland-Bühne as a place of lively interest, especially the Budapester Orpheum in the Taborstrasse. Peter Herz, "Entzauberte Praterstraße," in Beckermann, *Mazzesinsel*, 82–83.
76. Eva Brueck, LBI, 4–5.
77. Beckermann, *Mazzesinsel*, 75.
78. Lotte Hümbelin, *Mein eigener Kopf: Ein Frauenleben in Wien, Moskau, Prag, Paris und Zürich* (Zürich: Edition 8, 1999), 27, 46.
79. Stella Klein-Löw, *Erinnerungen* (Vienna: Jugend und Volk, 1980), 188–89.
80. Sonia Wachstein, "Hagenberggasse 49: Memories of a Viennese Jewish Childhood" (1997), LBI, Sonia Wachstein Papers, 8–9.
81. Wachstein, "Hagenberggasse," 16.
82. She notes that under the heading 'Böcklinstrasse," her father wrote in the margins his initials, "OED" and "No. 26 = 1919–1939," the number of their house and the years they lived there. The book itself appears to be something of an act of defiance, in that it contains an extensive section on the history of the Jews in the Leopoldstadt, a sympathetic account of their expulsion and expropriation in the seventeenth century, as well as the history of the building of its synagogues. See Karl Artner, Otto Guth, Emil Nekovar, Hans Schedling, Paul Sekora, Otto Selig, Leopold Steiner, and Dr. Michael Tennenhaus, *Die Leopoldstadt: Ein Heimatbuch*

published by the Teachers' Association of the Second District, Heimatkunde division, (Vienna: Selbstverlag der Lehrer-Arbeitergemeinschaft, 1937). Max Eisler, a Jewish professor of art history at the University of Vienna, alludes to this role in his foreword, in which he writes that the history of the district is tied not only to the city, or to Austria, but also with that of Europe.

83. As a refugee from Eastern Europe growing up in the Leopoldstadt, he said he felt he suffered less antisemitism than those Jews in other areas of the city. Varon, *Professions of a Lucky Jew*, 21–22.
84. Joseph Roth, *The Wandering Jews: A Classic Portrait of a Vanished People*, trans. Michael Hofmann (New York: W. W. Norton & Company, 2001), 55. Of note is that some writers emphasize further distinctions even within the bounds of the Leopoldstadt: in the same book, Joseph Roth idealizes the Prater an "antisemitism-free" zone, while Felix Salten treats its Wurstelprater as a utopian space separate from the rest of the city. See a discussion of Salten's 1911 essay "Wurstelprater" in Hilary Hope Herzog, *"Vienna Is Different:" Jewish Writers in Austria from the fin de Siècle to the Present* (New York: Berghahn, 2011), 48–49; on both Roth and Salten, 135.
85. Michel de Certeau, *The Practice of Everyday Life* (Berkeley: University of California Press, 1984), 169.
86. Daniel Vyleta points out that liberal publications were more likely to emphasize the Leopoldstadt as a site with a high crime rate than right-wing, antisemitic publications. For true antisemites, Jews were ubiquitous. See Daniel Vyleta, *Crime, Jews and News: Vienna 1895–1914* (New York: Berghahn, 2007), 161, 261.
87. Eric Zakim points out that this scene is only the first of many in which the text refers to Gurdweill being poked, pierced, or otherwise invaded. Later, he will even become the indistinct object of his own thoughts, such as "The pointless thought pierced him," and even minor incidents take on more authorial perspective than Gurdweill's own. As Zakim suggests, "The further inside we go into Gurdweill's mind, the more the external world of objects affects and influences the very thoughts and feelings that we expect to be private and inviolable; immanent authority does not exist separate from the materiality of the exterior world." "Between Fragment and Authority in David Fogel's (Re)Presentation of Subjectivity," *Prooftexts* 13, no. 1 (1993): 106, 110.
88. By having the woman convert to Judaism, Vogel maintains the "standard" narrative of the Jewish man-Christian woman interfaith relationship, also reverses its terms by his remaining Jewish.
89. Editor's introduction to Michel de Certeau, "Walking in the City," in *The Cultural Studies Reader*, ed. Simon During (London: Routledge, 1993), 151.
90. Michel de Certeau, *The Practice of Everyday Life* (Berkeley: University of California Press, 1984), 36–37.
91. *Leutnant Gustl*, one of the first novellas to employ the stream of consciousness technique, appeared in serialized form in the *Neue Freie Presse* in 1900 and in

book form in 1901. For another example of a fin de siècle text in which walking the streets of Vienna helps the protagonist develop a sense of his own self-identification, see Felix Salten, "Die Wiener Strasse," in *Das Österreichische Antlitz: Essays* (Berlin: S. Fischer, 1910), 11–22.

92. Vogel took pains to learn and read novels in German and in translation. His attachment to Hebrew was neither sentimental nor nationalist, and his diary gives no indication why he continued to write in Hebrew while in Vienna. Robert Alter suggests that for Vogel, Yiddish may have "lacked the aura of literary prestige . . . and was no doubt too much associated with the world of pious earlocks and dirty caftans and musty prayer rooms that he wanted to put behind him." Vogel did, however, switch to Yiddish in 1942. Robert Alter, "Fogel and the Forging of a Hebrew Self," *Prooftexts* 13, no. 1 (1993), 4–5.
93. David Vogel, *Das Ende der Tage: Tagebücher und autobiographische Aufzeichnungen 1912–1922 und 1941–42*, trans. Ruth Achlama (Munich: List, 1995), entry dated December 13, 1912.
94. Vogel, *Das Ende der Tage*, entries dated January 28, 1913, October 4, 1913, and June 30, 1914.
95. Gershon Shofman, another Hebrew modernist writer in Vienna at that time, also wrote stories based in and describing the city. See Shachar M. Pinsker, *Literary Passports: The Making of Modernist Hebrew Fiction in Europe* (Stanford: Stanford University Press, 2011), 93. One researcher recently discovered an unpublished manuscript for a second Hebrew novel by Vogel set in interwar Vienna. *Viennese Romance* is expected to be published in 2012. *Haaretz,* January 20, 2012.
96. Alter, "Fogel and the Forging of a Hebrew Self," 7. Gershon Shaked also notes that Vogel's texts contained new idioms he created, using words from German and Yiddish, deliberately not paying attention to "normative Hebrew." *The New Tradition: Essays on Modern Hebrew Literature* (Cinncinnati: Hebrew Union College Press, 2006), 312. See also Gershon Shaked, "David Vogel: A Hebrew Novelist in Vienna," in *Austrians and Jews in the Twentieth Century: From Franz Joseph to Waldheim*, ed. Robert S. Wistrich (New York: St. Martin's Press, 1992), 98. It should also be noted that some authors may not have written novels in Hebrew, but made use of the Hebrew (and Yiddish) language in their German texts. As Christina Pareigis points out, writer Klara Blum's use of Hebrew and Yiddish in her German texts serves as a literary strategy that opens up new perspectives on the relationship between these languages and German beyond simply standing in as representatives of the foreign or Other. "Glasperlenhebräisch. Das Fremd-Wort in den Schriften von Klara Blum und Getrud Kolmar," in *'Not an Essence but a Positioning:' German-Jewish Women Writers (1900–1938)*, ed. Andrea Hammel and Godela Weiss-Sussex (Munich: Meidenbauer, 2009, 154–58.
97. Thomas Soxberger, "Die Jüdisch-Nationalen und das Jiddische in Wien in den Jahren 1918–1919," *Chilufim: Zeitschrift für jüdische Kulturgeschichte* 7 (2009),

93–94. According to Soxberger, these modernist writers founded a Yiddish publishing company, *Der Kwall* [der kval], in 1919.

98. Rozenblit, *Assimilation and Identity*, 77.

99. Certeau, *The Practice of Everyday Life*, 128–29.

100. Maureen Healy argues that in Vienna, World War I became a "total war" in the sense that Viennese undertaking common daily activities not directly linked to it, such as shopping, child-rearing, and leisure activities, nonetheless reinterpreted them according to the conditions imposed by war. Fuch's text underscores an impression of this area of the Leopoldstadt as one section of the city where such everyday activities were "refracted through the lens of war" in an even more distorted way. See *Vienna and the Fall of the Habsburg Empire: Total War and Everyday Life in World War I* (Cambridge: Cambridge University Press, 2004), 3.

101. This required appearance, called the *Musterung*, figured in novels and films as an ultimate determinant of men's weakness or strength. It also contributed to the more widespread stereotype that men of draftable age not selected for service were necessarily weak, sick, or otherwise "unfit," which was not always the case. See Healy, *Vienna and the Fall*, 264–67.

102. See, for example, Franz Werfel's 1926 fragment "Pogrom," in *Franz Werfel: Erzählungen aus zwei Welten*, ed. Adolf D. Klarmann, vol. 2 (Frankfurt: Fischer, 1952), 336–75. On the ambivalences of literary depictions of the *Ostjude* in Austrian literature after 1918 see Helga Schreckenberger, "Literarische Reaktionen zur ostjüdischen Zuwanderung nach 1918," in *Österreich 1918 und die Folgen: Geschichte, Literatur, Theater und Film*, eds. Karl Müller and Hans Wagener (Böhlau: Vienna, 2009).

103. Beatrix Hoffmann-Holter, "'Ostjuden hinaus!' Jüdische Kriegsflüchtlinge in Wien 1914–1924," in *Die Stadt ohne Juden*, ed. Guntram Geser and Armin Loacker (Vienna: Filmarchiv Austria, 2000), 319.

104. On home-front violence among men in Vienna during World War I, see Healy, *Vienna and the Fall*, 264–65.

105. This story may represent a "literary inversion" of Yiddish writers' hopes for a lively Yiddish life in the new capital of the old Empire. See Karl Müller, "Aspekte jiddischer Prosa am Beispiel von Abraham Mosche Fuchs," in *Zwischenwelt: Jiddische Kultur und Literatur aus Österreich*, ed. Armin Eidherr and Karl Müller (Klagenfurt: Theodor Kramer Gesellschaft and Drava, 2003), 171.

106. Allison Schachter, "Bergelson and the Landscape of Yiddish Modernism," in *East European Jewish Affairs* 30:1 (2008), 11. Schachter explores David Bergelson's modernist short stories further in *Diasporic Modernisms: Hebrew and Yiddish Literatures in the Twentieth Century* (New York: Oxford University Press, 2011).

107. Franz Werfel gave a speech on November 30, 1930, in honor of Asch's fiftieth birthday, and even Max Reinhardt sent a telegram of birthday wishes to Asch through Zsolnay that year, noting that the success of the poet filled him with "pride and happiness" (ÖLA, Zsolnay). In addition, Jewish periodicals like

Menorah, Ost und West, Israelitisches Familienblatt and *Das Jüdische Echo* also published Yiddish literature in translation in the 1920s.

108. APZV.

109. Joseph Roth, "The Moscow Yiddish Theater," in *The Moscow Yiddish Theater: Art on Stage in the Time of Revolution*, ed. Benjamin Harshav (New Haven, CT: Yale University Press, 2008), 110–117, 113. In addition, An-sky himself was critical of Asch, at one point accusing him of being a "literary shnorrer" (beggar) who was "ready to pray to any god you want, so long as it's fashionable and they pay." Safran, *Wandering Soul*, 163. However, Asch's reception in Vienna was mainly enthusiastic. For an overview, see Evelyn Adunka, "Scholem Asch und Wien," in *Zwischenwelt: Jiddische Kultur und Literatur aus Österreich*, ed. Armin Eidherr and Karl Müller (Klagenfurt: Theodor Kramer Gesellschaft and Drava, 2003).

110. Isaac Bashevis Singer, "a.m. fuchs der derzeiler" in *a.m. fukss: di nacht und der tog*, ed. Melech Rawitsch (New York: der kwal, 1961), 5–8. Critic Joseph Leftwich, one of Fuchs' contemporaries, described him as "one of our best Yiddish story writers." "Thinking of Vienna," in *The Jews of Austria*: *Essays on their Life, History and Destruction*, ed Josef Fraenkel (London: Vallentine Mitchell 1967), 231. Thomas Soxberger characterizes him as the most important Yiddish prose author in Vienna. Other stories by Fuchs take place in the Leopoldstadt and likewise portray Jewish working-class characters, shocking themes (like sexual abuse) but never lose their bias for the underdog and critique of the elite Jews of Vienna. See Thomas Soxberger, ed. and trans., *Nackte Lieder: Jiddische Literatur aus Wien 1915–1938* (Vienna: Mandelbaum, 2008), 14–15.

111. Armin Eidherr, "Abraham Mosche Fuchs: Der Chronist des Wiener Vorstadtelends und des galizischen Landlebens," in *UdB*, 92–93. Fuchs also headed the "Literature and Art" section of *Di naje zajt*, a Yiddish periodical that was founded in 1924 in Vienna, though it lasted only three months. See also Gabriele Kohlbauer-Fritz, "Jiddische Subkultur in Wien," in *Ist jetzt hier der wahre Heimat? Östjüdische Einwanderung nach Wien*, ed. Peter Bettelheim and Michael Ley (Vienna: Picus, 1993), 99; Gabriele Kohlbauer-Fritz, ed. and trans., *In a Schtodt woss schtarbt/In einer Stadt, die stirbt. Jiddische Lyrik aus Wien* (Vienna: Picus, 1995).

112. On the history of Sephardic Jews in Vienna, see the exhibition catalogue *Die Türken in Wien: Geschichte einer jüdischen Gemeinde*, ed. Felicitas Heimann-Jelinek, Gabriela Kohlbauer-Fritz, and Gerhard Milchram (Vienna: Jewish Museum der Stadt Wien, 2010); and Ruth Burstyn, "Die Geschichte der türkisch-spaniolischen Juden im Habsburgerreich: Die Ursprünge der sephardischen/spanischen Einwanderung in Wien," in Bettelheim and Ley, *Ist jetzt hier die "wahre Heimat?*.

113. Hermann Taubner, Rachel Calderon's second husband and Veza Canetti's father, died in Belgrade on December 1, 1904, in unknown circumstances. In 1910, her mother married Menachem Alkaley, who, according to a number of sources,

physically abused both Veza and her mother. Angelika Schedel, "Vita Veza Canetti," *Text + Kritik, Zeitschrift für Literatur*, ed. Heinz Ludwig Arnold, X/02:156 (2002), 95–97; see also Anne D. Peiter, *Komik und Gewalt. Zur literarischen Verarbeitung der beiden Weltkriege und der Shoah* (Vienna: Böhlau, 2007), 210–269.

114. The titles of each of the stories in the order they appear in the novel are: "The Monster," "The Ogre," "The Canal," "The Tiger," and "The Fixer."

115. Koppstein also attempts to seduce Lina, the girl in Trafik, and when she does not respond to his advances, he has her fired; Graf tells Knut Tell about it, referring to Koppstein as a "leather swindler." Both sexual perversity and swindling were common antisemitic stereotypes. The *Adressbuch* (address book) for Vienna from 1930 lists over thirty separate entries for leather firms located on the Ferdinandstrasse. See *Adolph Lehmann's Allgemeiner Wohnungs-Anzeiger nebst Handels- und Gewerbe-Adreßbuch für die Bundeshauptstadt Wien* (Vienna: 1930), 336. On the potential "hidden" Jewishness of the other characters in *Yellow Street*, see Helmut Göbel, "Bemerkungen zum verdeckten Judentum in Veza Canettis *Die gelbe Straße*," in *"Ein Dichter braucht Ahnen." Elias Canetti und die europäische Tradition*, ed. Gerald Stieg and Jean-Marie Valentin (Bern: Peter Lang, 1997).

116. Veza Canetti wrote *Die Schildkröten* (*The Tortoises*) her first and only text to deal directly with Jewish issues, while in exile in England in 1939, but the book was not published until 1999. Mela Hartwig wrote *Das Wunder von Ulm*, her only novella to deal with Jewish themes, in 1934, though it was not published until 1936.

117. Veza Canetti, *Geduld bringt Rosen: Erzählungen* (Munich: Hanser, 1992), 54. In the original German, Canetti uses the word "jüdeln" to describe his speech; the word is term that means to speak with a Jewish accent or in Yiddish-tinged German. Lehmann's *Adressbuch* also includes a leather firm called Rosenzweig & Topf at Ferdinandstr. 30, located next door to her home, suggesting she may have based the character Topf from "Der Sieger" on a real person.

118. Helmut Göbel, afterword to Canetti, *Die gelbe Strasse*, 178. Julian Preece also suggests that she tailored both "The Victor" and "Patience Brings Roses" to fit the needs of both the *Arbeiter-Zeitung* and Wieland Herzfelde, the editor of an anthology in which the latter story was reprinted. See the introduction to *Veza Canetti: Viennese Short Stories*, ed., trans., and intr. Julian Preece (Riverside, CA: Ariadne, 2006), 5.

119. Elias Canetti, "Veza," foreword to Canetti, *Yellow Street*, ix.

120. Elias Canetti, *Yellow Street*, ix. She met future husband Elias Canetti in 1924 at one of Karl Kraus's lectures, which she regularly attended; the couple married in 1934, about a year after Elias moved into her apartment at Ferdinandstrasse 29. He published *Die gelbe Strasse* in 1990, twenty-seven years after her death.

121. Sadly, it would also become home to many more Jews immediately before deportation. According to records at the DÖW, at least 612 Jews gave the

Ferdinandstrasse as their last address before they were deported to their deaths; 28,691 of nearly 60,000 murdered Austrian Jews gave the Leopoldstadt as their last known address.

122. Helga Gibbs, *Leopoldstadt: Kleine Welt am großen Strom* (Vienna: Mohl, 1997), 130.
123. Julian Preece, *The Rediscovered Writings of Veza Canetti: Out of the Shadows of a Husband* (Rochester, NY: Camden House, 2007), 16.
124. Beckermann, *Mazzesinsel*, 74. Gitta Deutsch, who grew up in nearby Böcklinstrasse, mentions in her memoir both the Jewish grocer and the Roman Catholic Youth Organization, in whose processions she was pleased to take part as a Protestant. Gitta Deutsch, *The Red Thread* (Riverside: Ariadne, 1996), 5–6.
125. As Alexander Kosenina aptly points out, the character Vlk could be interpreted as displaying "Jewish"-coded qualities when he attempts to parse the meaning of a passage from the Book of Moses. "Veza Canetti – Fundstücke aus dem literarischen Nachlass," in Hammel and Weiss-Sussex, *Not an Essence but a Positioning*, 184.
126. Veza Canetti also told her brother-in-law that the fourth of the five tales in *Yellow Street* is the story of his (Jewish) cousin Mathilde Arditti. See Karen Lauer and Kristian Wachinger, eds. *"Dearest Georg." Love, Literature, and Power in Dark Times. The letters of Elias, Veza, and Georges Canetti 1933–1948*. Trans. David Dollenmayer. (New York: Other Press: 2009), 8. A few explicitly Jewish characters do appear in a few of her other stories, such as "Der Sieger," published in *Geduld bringt Rosen* (Munich: Carl Hanser, 1992).
127. Angelika Schedel, *Sozialismus und Psychoanalyse: Quellen von Veza Canettis literarischen Utopien* (Würzburg: Königshausen & Neumann, 2002), 38.
128. Stella Klein-Löw, who worked in the Ferdinandstrasse every day after school, described the Leopoldstadt negatively in her memoir. *Erinnerungen*, 189.
129. Elias Canetti, *The Torch in my Ear* (New York: Farrar, Straus and Giroux, 1982), 124. Canetti was correct: both men and women were apt to describe Veza as exotic. For example, Hilde Spiel, who knew both Canettis personally, compliments her "Spanish" beauty and describes her as "an exotic woman who radiated mystery." "Hilde Spiel über Veza Canetti," *Basta*, no. 7/8 (1990), "Lesezone" supplement, 6.
130. William Collins Donahue, *The End of Modernism. Canetti's Auto-da-Fé* (Chapel Hill: University of North Carolina Press, 2001), 2.
131. The reasons why she stopped writing remain unclear. Preece, *The Rediscovered Writings*, 16–18.

CHAPTER 4

1. Kadison suggests that he may have spoken the phrase in Yiddish: "Dos ist nicht ein shospiel. Dos ist ein Gottespiel!" Luba Kadison and Joseph Buloff, *On*

Stage, Off Stage: Memories of a Lifetime in the Yiddish Theater (Cambridge: Harvard University Library Press, 1992), 42–43; Joseph Buloff Jewish Theater Archive, Harvard University, Buloff Papers, Collection 3, BQA4959, Folder: LK/Lecture/Vilna Troupe, 8. Max Reinhardt apparently also attended performances of *Der Dybbuk* by Habima, a Hebrew-language theater troupe from Moscow, during their performance in Vienna in May-June 1926. Itzhak Norman, *Be-reshit Habimah* [The birth of Habima] (Jerusalem: ha-Sifriyah ha-Tsiyonit, 1966), 341. Reinhardt's involvement in the Yiddish theater began long before 1922; in 1908 he staged one of the first Yiddish dramas to be shown on the German stage in Berlin, Sholem Asch's early drama *Got fun nekome* (God of Vengeance); its setting in a Jewish-run bordello and inclusion of a Jewish prostitute caused controversy, particularly among Jewish groups. Brigitte Dalinger, *Quellenedition zur Geschichte des jüdischen Theaters in Wien*, Conditio Judaica 42 (Tübingen: Niemeyer, 2003), 134 n. 82.

2. Arnold Zweig's *Das ostjüdische Antlitz* (Berlin: Welt-Verlag, 1920) includes fifty drawings by Hermann Struck that typify common depictions of Eastern European Jews. Luba Kadison notes that Zweig and Struck encouraged the founding of the Federation of Yiddish Dramatic Actors (FADO), which later became the Vilna Troupe, and that they were the ones responsible for persuading the German military authorities in Vilna to allow them to perform in 1916. Kadison and Buloff, *On Stage*, 7. Other writers who idealized *Ostjuden* include Martin Buber, Else Lasker-Schüler, Joseph Roth, and Alfred Döblin. On the subject of *Ostjuden* in German and Austrian culture, see Michael Brenner, *The Renaissance of Jewish Culture in Weimar Germany* (New Haven: Yale University Press, 1996), 129–52; Steven Aschheim, *Brothers and Strangers: the East European Jew in German and German Jewish Consciousness* (Madison: University of Wisconsin Press, 1982); Jack Wertheimer, *Unwelcome Strangers: East European Jews in Imperial Germany* (New York: Oxford University Press, 1987); Armin A. Wallas, "Mythen der Übernationalität und revolutionäre Gegenmodelle: Österreich-Konzeptionen jüdischer Schriftsteller zwischen Monarchie und Exil," in *Österreich-Konzeptionen und jüdisches Selbstverständnis: Identitäts-Transfigurationen im 19. und 20. Jahrhundert*, ed. Hanni Mittelmann and Armin A. Wallas (Tübingen: Niemeyer, 2001). On the symbolism of using the term *Ostjude* see Leslie Morris, "Reading the Face of the Other: Arnold Zweig's and Hermann Struck's *Das ostjüdische Antlitz*," in *The Imperialist Imagination: German Colonialism and its Legacy*, ed. Sara Friedrichsmeyer, Sara Lennox, and Susanne Zantop (Ann Arbor: University of Michigan Press, 1998), 196.
3. As Michael Steinberg notes, "Salzburg was to reestablish the cultural roots of which the branches were Berlin, Vienna, Bayreuth, and Oberammergau. . . . Unlike larger cities, Salzburg as festival city signified a collectivity that would embrace both performers and audience into a communitarian solidarity." *Austria as Theater and Ideology: The Meaning of the Salzburg Festival* (Ithaca, NY: Cornell University Press, 1990), 3.

4. For a nuanced discussion of the theme of messianic redemption and its appeal to a range of Jewish writers and thinkers in Central Europe, see Ritchie Robertson, *The 'Jewish Question' in German Literature* 1759–1939 (New York: Oxford University Press, 1999), 390–399 and Michael Löwy, *Redemption and Utopia: Jewish Libertarian Thought in Central Europe*, trans. Hope Heaney (London: Athlone, 1992); on the general pervasiveness of messianism in the culture of the time, see Lisa Marie Anderson, *German Expressionism and the Messianism of a Generation* (Amsterdam: Rodopi, 2011).
5. Manès Sperber, *All our Yesterdays, vol. 1, God's Water Carriers*, trans. Joachim Neugroschel (New York: Holmes and Meier, 1987), 17–18.
6. Jews played a significant role in the flourishing cabaret culture and small alternative theaters. For an overview, see Christian Klösch, "'Wien, das fidele Grab an der Donau': Der Beitrag von Juden zu Kabarett und Kleinkunst im Wien der Zwischenkriegszeit," in the exhibition catalogue *Wien, Stadt der Juden. Die Welt der Tante Jolesch*, ed. Joachim Riedl (Vienna: Zsolnay, 2004). See also Alfred Pfoser, *Literatur und Austromarxismus* (Vienna: Löcker, 1980), 68.
7. Gershom Scholem, "Zum Verständnis des messianischen Idee im Judentum," *Eranos Jahrbuch* 28 (1959).
8. W.E. Yates, *Theatre in Vienna: A Critical History, 1776–1995* (Cambridge: Cambridge University Press, 1996), xv.
9. Bettina Riedmann, *"Ich bin Jude, Österreicher, Deutscher": Judentum in Arthur Schniztlers Tagebüchern und Briefen* (Tübingen: Niemeyer, 2002), 201.
10. Delphine Bechtel maintains that, for this reason, Yiddish theater was actually more firmly established in Vienna than in Berlin. See Delphine Bechtel, "Yiddish Theater and Its Impact on the German and Austrian Stage, " in *Jews and the Making of Modern German Theater*, ed. Jeanette R. Malkin and Freddie Rokem (Iowa City: University of Iowa Press, 2010).
11. Similar organizations were founded in Galicia, indicating that this drive to "reform" Jewish culture was not limited to Vienna. See *Jüdisches Theater*, June 1, 1921, as cited in Brigitte Dalinger, *Verloschene Sterne: Geschichte des jüdischen Theaters in Wien* (Vienna: Picus, 1998), 69. See also Brigitte Dalinger, "Yiddish Theater in Vienna, 1880–1938," in *Yiddish Theatre: New Approaches*, ed. Joel Berkowitz (Oxford: Littman Library, 2003).
12. Dalinger, *Verloschene Sterne*, 70. In addition to plays by S. An-sky, the troupe performed the works of Yiddish dramatists including Sholem Asch, David Pinski, Y.L. Peretz, and H. Leivick.
13. Melech Rawitsch, *Das Geschichtenbuch meines Lebens: Auswahl*, trans. Armin Eidherr (Salzburg: Otto Müller, 1996), 167.
14. Kadison and Buloff, *On Stage*, 43–44.
15. Oskar Kokoschka, *Mein Leben* (Munich: Bruckmann, 1971), 84. Musil wrote about the renaissance of Yiddish theater in "Wiener Theaterbericht," May 31, 1922 and "Die Wilnaer Truppe in Wien," December 8, 1922. Robert Musil,

Gesammelte Werke, vol. 2, ed. Adolf Frisé (Reinbek bei Hamburg: Rowohlt, 1978), 1613–1615. I am grateful to Murray Hall for these references.

16. Arthur Schnitzler, *Tagebücher* (Vienna: Verlag der österreichischen Akademie der Wissenschaften, 1993), May 2, 1921, 185. In another entry from December 19, 1922, he notes that he attended the performance of a play in Yiddish by the Vilna Troupe that was "just fair, as far as I understood it." See n. 22. The fact that Schnitzler made these remarks in his own diary suggests that not all German speakers could easily understand Yiddish. Performances of *Der Dybbuk* in German at the Rolandbühne in Vienna in 1925 were very well-received. Delphine Bechtel, "Yiddish Theater and its Impact"; see also Arnold Zweig, "Anskis 'Dybuk' deutsch," *Jüdische Rundschau*, January 29, 1926, 56. On the other hand, the Moscow-based Hebrew-language troupe Habima also found great success with performances of *Der Dybbuk* translated into Hebrew when they performed in Vienna in 1926; they were well-received again when they returned in 1928 and 1938. Hebrew-language performances resonated not only with Zionists, but also with wider audiences who didn't understand Hebrew but who may have found in it an even deeper connection to the drama's spiritual aims. Schnitzler, Reinhardt, and Helene and Hermann Thimig attended the 1926 opening of Richard Beer-Hofmann's *Jakobs Traum*; actor Alexander Moissi (who played the lead in *Jedermann* at the Salzburg Festival) greeted the troupe upon their arrival at the Carltheater. Dalinger, *Verloschene Sterne*, 150–152; Felix Salten, "Gastspiel Habima" Carl-Theater, *Neue Freie Presse*, May 30, 1926, reprinted in Dalinger, *Quellenedition*, 82–85.
17. Franz Kafka, letter to Felice Bauer, March 11, 1912, cited in Evelyn Torton-Beck, *Kafka and the Yiddish Theater: Its Impact on his Work* (Madison: University of Wisconsin Press, 1971), 15 n. 13.
18. Arnold Zweig, as cited in Joachim Hemmerle, "Jiddisches Theater im Spiegel deutschsprachiger Kritik von der Jahrhundertwende bis 1928: Eine Dokumentation," in *Beter und Rebellen: Aus 1000 Jahren Judentum in Polen*, ed. Michael Brocke (Frankfurt: Deutscher Koordinierungsrat der Gesellschaften für christlich-jüdische Zusammenarbeit, 1983), 290.
19. Sander L. Gilman, *Franz Kafka, The Jewish Patient* (New York: Routledge, 1995), 27. For a detailed discussion of Kafka and his circle of friends' complicated reception of Yiddish culture see Scott Spector, *Prague Territories: National Conflict and Cultural Innovation in Franz Kafka's Fin de Siècle*. Berkeley: University of California Press, 2000, 86–88.
20. Kadison and Buloff, *On Stage*, 43–44. Buloff noted, "We came to Vienna fleeing from Warsaw as if from a fire, because of the bad acoustics . . . Now we are housed in a worse theater, yet the problem here is not as grave, because here they don't understand our language anyhow. So, in a way, it is better that they can't hear us; besides, it doesn't seem to bother them."

21. Joseph Roth, *The Wandering Jews: A Classic Portrait of a Vanished People*, trans. Michael Hofmann (New York: W. W. Norton & Company, 2001), 48.
22. "Roland-bühne (Wilna Theater jüd.) 'Schwer zu sein a Jud' von Alejchem. Leidlich soweit ichs verstand." Arthur Schnitzler, *Tagebuch*, entry dated December 19, 1922.
23. Riedmann, *Ich bin Jude*, 168. The performances were advertised in the *Arbeiter-Zeitung* on October 6, 1922. An article two days later noted that the Vilna Troupe's guest performance would have to be postponed until October 17 due to technical difficulties.
24. Arthur Schnitzler, *Tagebuch*, entries dated September 14 and 15, 1909, and September 22, 1922.
25. Riedmann, *Ich bin Jude*, 201.
26. "My father didn't like to hear us singing Yiddish songs. He rejected Yiddish categorically as jargon and corrupt German . . . But then when the Vilna Troupe came from Lithuania to Vienna and brought the Jewish and non-Jewish Viennese critical public to storming applause, above all with Anski's strange and very unusual 'Dybuk,' later with Schalom Asch's 'Gott der Rache,' I triumphed over my father. He himself went with me to 'Dybuk' and he and Mama became loyal visitors in the subsequently established Yiddish theater in Vienna. I remember that Arthur Schnitzler, for example, never missed a première." Minna Lachs, *Warum schaust du zurück: Erinnnerungen 1907–1941* (Vienna: Europaverlag, 1986), 133–34.
27. Manès Sperber, *All das Vergangene*, vol. 2, *Die vergebliche Warnung* (Vienna: Europaverlag, 1975).
28. Although the Vilna Troupe performed *The Dybbuk* and other plays in Berlin, they did not develop as loyal an audience there as they did in Vienna. See Heidelore Riss, *Ansätze zu einer Geschichte des jüdischen Theaters in Berlin 1889–1936* (Frankfurt: Peter Lang, 2000), 243.
29. Hans-Peter Bayerdörfer makes a similar point about the attraction of non-Jews to Yiddish theater. "Jüdisches Theater der Zwischenkriegszeit—östliche Wurzeln, westliche Ziele? Umrisse einer Kontroverse," in *Theater der Region—Theater Europas: Kongress der Gesellschaft für Theaterwissenschaft*, ed. Andreas Kotte (Basel: Verlag Theaterkultur, 1995), 25. Joseph Roth writes that even the posters for those plays attracted attention and had a stronger effect than refined advertisements. He describes them as "made of cheap and loud yellow paper, without margins, stuck haphazardly on walls and not on the official poster boards, put up in nasty smelly corners." Joseph Roth, "The Moscow Yiddish Theater," in *The Moscow Yiddish Theater: Art on Stage in the Time of Revolution*, ed. Benjamin Harshav (New Haven: Yale University Press, 2008), 110–11.
30. Kadison and Buloff, *On Stage*, 43.
31. An-sky was not the only Yiddish writer who drew on Jewish mysticism to recreate an ethnic heritage to use as the basis of a people. For example, Der Nister (Pinkhas

Kahanovitch) and Y. L. Peretz also used Jewish mysticism for similar ends. See Neugroschel, *The Dybbuk*, 237.

32. An-sky witnessed the violence done to Jews during the Russian army's occupation of Galicia and other areas as part of his wartime experiences as an aid worker. He carried a draft of what would later become *Der Dybbuk* with him there already in 1913; he later reworked his wartime diaries and letters into a Yiddish memoir called *The Destruction of Galicia*. Safran, *Wandering Soul*, 3, 230–32. See also Shmuel Werses, "An-ski's 'Tsvishn tsvey veltn (Der Dibbuk)'/'Bein shney olamot'/'Hadybbuk'/'Between Two Worlds (The Dibbuk):' A Textual History" in *Studies in Yiddish Literature and Folklore* (Jerusalem: Hebrew University, 1986).
33. Nathaniel Deutsch, *The Jewish Dark Continent: Life and Death in the Russian Pale of Settlement* (Cambridge: Harvard University Press, 2011), 43.
34. For example, the play consists of different genres: Act I is a romance that ends in tragedy, Act II contains musical and dance elements, Act III is a ghost story, and Act IV contains a trial and exorcism. See Neugroschl, xiv. For more on the play as an expression of modernism, see Gabriella Safran and Steven J. Zipperstein, *The Worlds of S. An-sky: A Russian Jewish Intellectual at the Turn of the Century* (Stanford: Stanford University Press, 2006).
35. See Hans Tramer, "Der Expressionismus. Bemerkungen zum Anteil der Juden an einer Kunstepoche," *Bulletin des Leo Baeck Instituts* 2. no. 5 (1958): 33. See also Hanni Mittelmann, "Expressionismus und Judentum," in *Conditio Judaica: Judentum, Antisemitismus und deutschsprachige Literatur vom Ersten Weltkrieg bis 1933/1938*, ed. Hans Otto Horch and Horst Denkler (Tübingen: Niemeyer, 1993), 251 and Michael Stark, *Für und wider den Expressionismus: Die Entstehung der Intellektuellendebatte in der deutschen Literaturgeschichte* (Stuttgart: Metzler, 1982), 276.
36. Mittelmann, "Expressionismus und Judentum," 258–59. Gabriella Safran refers to An-sky as a "neo-Hasid" who drew selectively from its mystical legends but remained secular. *Wandering Soul: The Dybbuk's Creator, S. An-Sky* (Cambridge: Harvard University Press, 2010), 204.
37. "Nothing as redolent of study house folklore and Hasidic fantasy had ever been assembled on a Yiddish stage before. An-sky introduced a rich layering of literary and folkloristic motifs that give the play an authentic, 'mystical' feel even as it turns traditional narratives to secular, dramatic ends." David Roskies, ed., *The Dybbuk and Other Writings by S. Ansky* (New York: Schocken, 1992), xxvi.
38. Eugen Höflich, "Der Dybuk—Notizen anlässlich des Wiener Gastspieles der Wilnaer," *Komödie: Wochenrevue für Bühne und Film*, nos. 37/38, November 11, 1922, Leo Baeck Institute-New York, AR 2371 s43/2, Folder 1.
39. On An-sky's years in Paris, see Safran, *Wandering Soul*, 70-74. On his commitment to the survival of Jewish culture in the modern word and its connection to his writing of *The Dybbuk*, see Safran, *Wandering Soul*, 186–221 and Eugene Avrutin, ed., *Photographing the Jewish Nation: Pictures from S. An-sky's Ethnographic Expeditions*

(Hanover, NH: University Press of New England, 2009), 6–10. Nathaniel Deutsch's annotated translation of *The Jewish Ethnographic Program*, the extensive questionnaire An-sky used on his ethnographic expeditions, notes a number of instances in which questions relate to themes An-sky directly incorporated into *The Dybbuk*. See Deutsch, *The Jewish Dark Continent*, 195 n. 295 and 283–84 n. 599.

40. Letter from An-sky to Chaim Zhitlovsky, originally published in *Literarische Bleter* 11 (1924), reprinted in Neugroschel, *The Dybbuk*, 1. Moreover, Gabriella Safran points out that the earlier Russian version of this play from 1915 is full of much more ethnographic material, such as legends and folksongs, that was later edited out, revealing An-sky's "dedication to the ideals of cultural translatability" that he had earlier professed in essays advocating for translating "Jewishness" into Russian. "Theory and Practice of Secular Jewish Culture in Russian," in *Jewish Literatures and Cultures: Context and Intertext*, ed. Anita Norich and Yaron Z. Eliav (Providence, RI: Brown University Press, 2008), 200. Nathaniel Deutsch notes that the extraordinary lengths to which An-sky went during his ethnographic expeditions indicate that he attempted not merely to salvage Jewish culture, but rather to redeem it. *The Jewish Dark Continent*, 27.

41. *Wiener Morgenzeitung*, December 6, 1921. Other evidence exists that the mix of Jews and non-Jews in Viennese audiences did not go unnoticed: "Hier sitzen Juden im Kaftan und sind andachtsvolle Zuschauer ihres eigenen Wesens; junge Mädchen weinen und schluchzen in ihre Taschentücher; es sind aber auch Gojim mit jüdischen Köpfen da, und für diese schrieb ich diese Zeilen" (Here sit Jews in caftans, and are devoted spectators of their own nature; young women cry and sob in their handkerchiefs; there are also Goyim (non-Jews) with a Jewish sensibility there, and it is for them that I write these lines). *Sonn- und Morgenzeitung*, June 13, 1921, cited in Dalinger, *Verloschene Sterne*, 81. Minna Lachs also noted the mix of Jewish and non-Jewish Austrians at the Yiddish theater performances she attended in Vienna. See Lachs, *Warum schaust du zurück*, 133–34.

42. Felix Salten, "Gedenkrede" (for Herzl), *Neue Freie Presse*, June 23, 1929.

43. Robert Musil, rev. in the *Prager Presse* of April 21, 1922, reprinted in Robert Musil, *Gesammelte Werke in neun Bänden*, vol. 9 (Reinbek bei Hamburg: Rowohlt, 1981), 1570. In addition, Jewish writer Soma Morgenstern mentions that both Jewish and non-Jewish friends encouraged his friend, the non-Jewish composer Alban Berg, and him to attend the Vilna Troupe's performance of *Der Dybbuk* in 1926. Morgenstern described it as one of the most beautiful and unforgettable evenings at the theater in his life. Berg was impressed enough with the performance to attempt to acquire the German language rights and was "greatly disappointed" when he was not able to do so. Soma Morgenstern, "Zur Entstehung der Oper Lulu," in *Alban Berg und seine Idole. Erinnerungen und Briefe*, ed. Ingolf Schulte (Berlin: Aufbau, 1999), 130–33.

44. Helmut Gruber, *Red Vienna: Experiment in Working Class Culture 1919–1934* (New York: Oxford University Press, 1991), 27.

45. See William M. Johnston, *The Austrian Mind: An Intellectual and Social History 1848–1938* (Berkeley: University of California Press, 1972), 57.
46. Friedrich Torberg, "A Sentimental Preface" (1966), in *Tante Jolesch or the Decline of the West in Anecdotes*, ed. Sonat Birnecker Hart, trans. Maria Poglitsch Bauer (Riverside, CA: Ariadne, 2008).
47. Tim Bonyhady, *Good Living Street: Potrait of a Patron Family, Vienna 1900* (New York: Pantheon, 2011), 202.
48. See Marsha L. Rozenblit, *Reconstructing a National Identity: The Jews of Habsburg Austria during World War I* (New York: Oxford University Press, 2001).
49. On Käthe Braun-Prager, see Tatjana Popovic, ed., *Die Stadt der Ewigen und andere Novellen* (Klagenfurt: Alekto, 2000), 8–11.
50. Werfel, a German-language author born to a Jewish mother in Prague, was circumcized and also celebrated his bar mitzvah. Although he never converted, he expressed strong affinities to Catholicism in his works. His novel *Barbara oder die Frömmigkeit* of 1929 recounts the end of the monarchy through the lens of religion, although it remains unclear exactly which religion. See Armin A. Wallas "Seelenaufschlitzer und Gottsucher: Die Krisen jüdischer Identität im österreichischen Expressionismus," *Das jüdische Echo* 48 (1999): 39; and essays by Wolfgang Nehring, Konstanze Fliedl, and Jennifer E. Michaels in *Judentum in Leben und Werk von Franz Werfel*, ed. Hans Wagener and Wilhelm Hemecker (Berlin: De Gruyter, 2011.) Franz Werfel held the honorary speech for Yiddish writer Scholem Asch on the occasion of his fiftieth birthday on November 30, 1930 (APZV).
51. See Franz Werfel, "Erguß und Beichte" (1920), in *Franz Werfel, Zwischen oben und unten: Prosa—Tagebücher—Aphorismen—Literarische Nachträge*, ed. Adolf D. Klarmann (Munich: Langen Müller, 1975), 691.
52. Max Brod, "Franz Werfel's 'Christliche Sendung,'" *Der Jude* 1 (1916/1917), 721. Werfel's close friend Friedrich Torberg also maintained that Werfel's interest in Catholicism brought him closer to Judaism. See Adolf Klarmann, Notes of conversation with Friedrich Torberg, November 11, 1945, Werfel Collection, Van Pelt Library, University of Pennsylvania, as cited in Lionel B. Steiman, "Franz Werfel: The Formation of a non-Jewish Jew," in Wagener and Hemecker, *Judentum in Leben und Werk von Franz Werfel*, 1.
53. According to Edward Timms, in another letter to Maria von Thurn und Taxis, Rilke expounds in even more detail on what he terms the "Jewish mentality" that colors Werfel's work. For an excellent discussion of the relationship between Werfel, Rilke, and Karl Kraus, and the role the terms of Jewish difference played in their critiques of each others' lives and works, see Edward Timms, *Karl Kraus, Apocalyptic Satirist: The Post-War Crisis and the Rise of the Swastika* (New Haven: Yale University Press, 2005), 234–40. The letter to Hofmannsthal can be found in Rainer Maria Rilke, *Briefwechsel mit Hugo von Hofmannsthal*, ed. Rudolf

Hirsch and Ingeborg Schnack (Frankfurt, 1978), 77. The letter to Maria von Thurn und Taxis can be found in *Rainer Maria Rilke und Marie Thurn und Taxis—Briefwechsel*, ed. Ernst Zinn (Zurich: Niehans & Rokitansky, 1951), 1, 323–24. Both are cited in Timms, *Karl Kraus*, 237–38, 577, n. 42 and n. 43.

54. Helene Deutsch is known primarily for her two-volume *The Psychology of Women* (1944–1945) She led the Psychoanalytic Society's Training Institute until leaving Vienna for Boston in 1935. See Paul Roazen, *Helene Deutsch: A Psychoanalyst's Life* (New Brunswick, NJ: Transaction, 1992).
55. Brenner, *The Renaissance of Jewish Culture*, 152.
56. See, for example, Sonia Wachstein's memoir cited in Chapter 3. Moreover, Arthur Schnitzler's anticlericalism is apparent in his autobiography and in his play *Professor Bernhardi*. See Ritchie Robertson, *Occasions 9: Anticlericalism in Austrian Literature from Joseph II to Thomas Bernhard* (London: Austrian Cultural Forum, 2006), 26–27.
57. Yates, *Theatre in Vienna*, 15, 45.
58. The article claimed it was hoped that the next director would be "the long awaited Messiah, the healer, who will redeem this house form the heavy curse of the last decades." See Steinberg, *Austria as Theater and Ideology*, 52–53.
59. On the popularity of Jewish performer and strongman Siegmund Breitbart, for example, see Sharon Gillerman, "Samson in Vienna: The Theatrics of Jewish Masculinity," *Jewish Social Studies* 9, no. 2 (2003).
60. Adam Müller-Guttenbrunn, *Wien war eine Theaterstadt* (Vienna: Carl Gerold's Sohn, 1887), 42, 44, 65.
61. Adam Müller-Guttenbrunn [pseud. Roderich Meinhart], *Erinnerungen eines Theaterdirektors* (Leipzig: L. Staackmann, 1924), 15–16. On Müller-Guttenbrunn and the significance of the location of the theaters he established, see also Chapter 3.
62. Recent examinations include the less studied trend of the Catholic influence on the culture of the Burgtheater. See Robert Pyrah, *The Burgtheater and Austrian Identity: Theatre and Cultural Politics in Vienna, 1918–1938* (Oxford: Legenda, 2007), esp. 89–105.
63. Steinberg, *Austria as Theater and Ideology*, xix–xx.
64. In 1922, Reinhardt would transform the Kollegienkirche, a baroque church, into a temporary auditorium to stage *Das Salzburger große Welttheater*, which provoked a scathing article from Karl Kraus attacking the Festival as a fraud; according to Kraus, this event drove him to renounce Catholicism. See Karl Kraus, "Vom großen Welttheaterschwindel," *Die Fackel* 601–607 (1922): 4–7 and Timms, *Karl Kraus*, 282.
65. Josef Kaut, *Festspiele in Salzburg* (Salzburg: Residenz, 1965), 19.
66. Oskar Holl, "Dokumente zur Entstehung der Salzburger Festspiele: Unveröffentlichtes aus der Korrespondenz der Gründer," *Maske und Kothurn—Vierteljahrsschrift für Theaterwissenschaft* 13 (1967): 174–75.

67. Heinrich Damsich, *Der Merker*, Oktober 1917, as cited in Holl, "Dokumente," 171.
68. A letter from fellow founder Friedrich Gehmacher alludes to early fears that Reinhardt might turn Salzburg into a commercial affair. Letter from Friedrich Gemacher to Heinrich Damisch dated August 28, 1916, reprinted in Holl, "Dokumente," 158.
69. Steinberg, *Austria as Theater and Ideology*, 46–49.
70. Heinz Dopsch and Hans Spatzenegger, eds., *Geschichte Salzburgs: Stadt und Land*, vol. 2, pt. 2, *Neuzeit und Zeitgeschichte* (Salzburg: Universitätsverlag Anton Pustet, 1988), 833–871.
71. The quotes originally appeared in the *Salzburger Volksbote*, November, 27, 1918, and January 30, 1919, as cited in William D. Bowman, "Regional History and the Austrian Nation," *Journal of Modern History* 67, no. 4 (1995): 887, n. 44. Helga Embacher points out that already in 1918, the program of the Christian Social Party in Salzburg demanded the exclusion of "non-Germans" (meaning Jews) from public offices and the civil service. See "Lenin oder Jabotinsky? Jüdische Identitätssuche in Salzburg nach dem ersten Weltkrieg," in Deutsch-Jüdische Jugendliche im "Zeitalter der Jugend," ed. Yotam Hotam (Göttingen: Vandenhoeck & Ruprecht, 2009), 184.
72. Steinberg, *Austria as Theater and Ideology*, xix.
73. Paul Stefan, *Neue Züricher Zeitung*, August 27, 1920.
74. Hilde Albers-Frank, "Life in a Changing World," unpublished manuscript, August 22, 1978, LBI, AHC, 48.
75. Leon Botstein estimates that Jews made up at least one third of the audience of concerts and theater in interwar Austria. See Leon Botstein, "Musikkultur und die Juden: Wien als Beispiel," in *Judentum und Modernität: Essays zur Rolle der Juden in der deutschen und österreichischen Kultur 1848 bis 1938* (Vienna: Böhlau, 1991).
76. See Hanns Haas, "Der Traum vom Dazugehören—Juden auf Sommerfrische," in *Der Geschmack der Vergänglichkeit: Jüdische Sommerfrische in Salzburg*, ed. Robert Kriechbaumer (Vienna: Böhlau, 2002).
77. Wrote one journalist: "If my colleagues came to Salzburg and saw the Leopoldstadt-'Dirndls,' who often come to Salzburg from St. Gilgen, St. Wolfgang, and 'Ischeles,' then they'd lose their sense of humor." *Salzburger Volksblatt*, August 20, 1920, 3.
78. "Es gibt keinen Juden, der jetzt nicht in Salzburg ist, und seit Reinhardt da ist, sammelt sich das Volk wie schwarze Fliegen." Robert Kriechbaumer, "Statt eines Vorwortes—"Der Geschmack der Vergänglichkeit," in *Der Geschmack der Vergänglichkeit*, 12, n. 17.
79. In *The City without Jews*, Hugo Bettauer also notes mockingly that ". . . the appearance of anyone who might be suspected of being a Gentile would actually create a sensation in Ischl, Gmunden, Wolfgang, Gilgen, Strobl, Aussee, or on the

Attersee" as these were "places that had formerly disgusted the genuine Viennese" while Christians inhabited the "less expensive and less beautiful" resorts of Lower Austria, Styria, and some "out of the way" Tyrolean villages. Hugo Bettauer, *The City without Jews: A Novel of our Time*, trans. Salomea Neumark Brainin (New York: Bloch, 1997), 118–19. For an extensive discussion of *The City without Jews*, see Chapter 2.

80. Steinberg, *Austria as Theater and Ideology*, xxiv and 2. I am deeply indebted to the work of Michael Steinberg on Hofmannsthal and the Jewish roots of the Salzburg Festival, as well as on what he terms the "Catholic culture of the Austrian Jews," which represented a turn from a Jewish to a Catholic aesthetic that occurred out of a "desire to participate in public forms of meaning, to adapt their minds, intellectually and spiritually, to the dominant culture." Steinberg, *Austria as Theater*, esp. 164–70; here 170.
81. See Gottfried Reinhardt, *Der Liebhaber: Erinnerungen seines Sohnes Gottfried Reinhardt an Max Reinhardt* (Munich: Droemer Knaur, 1973), 373. Although Reinhardt was born in Baden (near Vienna), his father was born in Pressburg, and Max spent much of his childhood there and even had Hungarian citizenship. See Steinberg, 201 n. 5.
82. Helene Thimig-Reinhardt, *Wie Max Reinhardt lebte* (Percha am Starnberger See: Schulz, 1973), 99.
83. Letter from Max Reinhardt to Ferdinand Künzelmann, July 21, 1918 cited in Holl, "Dokumente," 175.
84. Heinrich Eduard Jacob, "Reinhardt, der Österreicher," *Musikblätter des Anbruch* 10, July 2, 1922.
85. Gottfried Reinhardt, *Der Liebhaber*, 107 and 205.
86. Thimig-Reinhard, *Wie Max Reinhardt lebte*, 101.
87. Gottfried Reinhardt, *Der Liebhaber*, 38.
88. Letter from Max Reinhardt to Ferdinand Künzelmann, July 21, 1918, cited in Holl, 175.
89. Thimig-Reinhardt, *Wie Max Reinhardt lebte*, 101.
90. Abigail Gillman, *Viennese Jewish Modernism: Freud, Hofmannsthal, Beer-Hofmann, and Schnitzler* (Pittsburgh: Penn State University Press, 2009).
91. Gillman, *Viennese Jewish Modernism*, 57–58. According to Gillman, the original manuscript called for casting Jewish characters of Eastern European origin—namely, a rabbi, his daughter, and a Yeshiva student, who Hofmannsthal switched to a more general "Alchimist" (alchemist) and student, and then ultimately retracted in its entirety for reasons that remain unclear.
92. Peter C. Pfeiffer, "Hugo von Hofmannsthal worries about his Jewish mixed ancestry," in *Yale Companion to Jewish Writing and Thought in German Culture, 1096–1996*, ed. Sander L. Gilman and Jack Zipes (New Haven: Yale University Press, 1997).

93. J.J., "Carl Bleibtreu und A. Baumberg," *Kikiriki-Anzeiger*, April 20, 1902, 3. It must be noted, however, that not only antisemites viewed him as a Jew. Stefan Zweig, for example, expressed how as a youth, he had become enamored of Hugo von Hofmannsthal's abilities as a poet since the first time he heard him give a public lecture, noting proudly that "For after all, his father, a banker, came from the same Jewish middle class as the rest of us; this genius had grown up in a house similar to our own, with similar furniture and similar manners. . . ." Hofmannsthal's status as a Jew able to overcome his "Jewishness" is part of what captivates Zweig. See Stefan Zweig, *The World of Yesterday: An Autobiography* (New York: Viking, 2008), 52.
94. Judith Beniston, "Drama in Austria, 1918–45," in *A History of Austrian Literature 1918–2000*, ed. Katrin Kohl and Ritchie Robertson (Rochester, NY: Camden House, 2006), 27.
95. Andrew Barker claims that Hofmannsthal contributed ". . . more than any of his contemporaries to the conscious literary demarcation of the Austrian from the German." Andrew Barker, "The Politics of Austrian Literature," in Kohl and Robertson, *A History of Austrian Literature*, 110.
96. Yates, *Theatre in Vienna*, 209–10.
97. Yates, *Theatre in Vienna*, 189.
98. Kaut, *Festspiele in Salzburg*, 22.
99. See Jacques Le Rider, "Hugo von Hofmannsthal and the Austrian Idea of Central Europe," *Austrian Studies 5: The Habsburg Legacy* (1994).
100. Yet, as Judith Beniston notes, Hofmannsthal attempted to make it more part of Austrian "folk tradition" than of religion, by referring to *Jedermann* as a *Märchen* (fairy tale) and hinting at comparisons to the Brothers Grimm. When staged on the steps of the cathedral, however, one could not help but see its religious appeal. For example, at the end of Hofmannsthal's text, Everyman is led off by a monk, while the staged version has him entering the cathedral. Judith Beniston, "Hofmannsthal and the Salzburg Festival," in *A Companion to the Works of Hugo von Hofmannsthal*, ed. Thomas A. Kovach (Rochester, NY: Camden House, 2002), 171–72.
101. Berta Zuckerkandl, "Gespräch über Österreich," Interview with Hugo von Hofmannsthal, 1920 in *Hugo von Hofmannsthal. Die Gestalt des Dichters im Spiegel der Freunde*, ed. Helmut A. Fiechtner (Vienna: Humboldt Verlag, 1949), 337–38.
102. Pfeiffer, "Hugo von Hofmannsthal," 213.
103. Hofmannsthal wrote the letter in reaction to Haas's inclusion of an entry on his life in Gustav Krojanker's anthology *Juden in der deutschen Literatur* (1922). Hugo von Hofmannsthal, letter to Willy Haas, June 4, 1922, in Hugo von Hofmannsthal and Willy Haas, *Ein Briefwechsel* (Berlin: Propyläen, 1968), 46–47.

104. "Wenn meine ganzen inneren Entwicklungen und Kämpfe nichts wären als Unruhen des ererbten Blutes, Aufstände der jüdischen Blutstropfen gegen die germanischen und romanischen, und Reactionen gegen diese Aufstände." See Jens Rieckmann, "Zwischen Bewußtsein und Verdrängung: Hofmannsthals jüdisches Erbe," *Deutsche Vierteljahrsschrift für Literaturwissenschaft und Geistesgeschichte* 67, no. 3 (1993): 466.
105. According to W.E. Yates, "Reinhardt produced more works by Hofmannsthal than by any other contemporary dramatist, and it was in his productions that Hofmannsthal's major works were introduced to Vienna." While he was grateful for Reinhardt's support, Hofmannsthal nevertheless remained bitter about the Burgtheater's neglect of his work. *Theatre in Vienna*, 189.
106. Albers-Frank, "Life in a Changing World," 48.
107. See Martin Stern, "Verschwiegener Antisemitismus: Bemerkungen zu einem widerrufenen Brief Hofmannsthals an Rudolf Pannwitz," *Hofmmansthal Jahrbuch* 12 (2004).
108. Pfeiffer, "Hugo von Hofmannsthal," 217–18.
109. Michael Steinberg also interprets Hofmannsthal's turn to a Catholic aesthetic as being directly linked to his desire to turn away from what he perceived as a Jewish—and therefore individualistic and least integrated—to a collective, national, and integrated one. Steinberg, *Austria as Theater and Ideology*, 170. Abigail Gillman brings to light the actual enactment of these concerns in *Der Schüler* (1901). See Gillman, *Viennese Jewish Modernism*, 57–58 and n. 91.
110. In a letter to Max Reinhardt of 1919 Hofmannsthal noted, "Here it seems even more necessary to me, that the group of artists (you, Strauss, Schalk, Roller, and I) remain fully and *tightly* in agreement; the Salzburg citizens of the committee must have the feeling that we guide them with secure hands, towards a certain direction that we have agreed upon. My draft program serves this purpose, among others. It seeks to solve the dilemma of opera versus great drama in that it includes both under the term festival." Hofmannsthal to Max Reinhardt, Rodaun, May 26, 1919, cited in Franz Hadamowsky, "Reinhardt und Salzburg" in *Katalog-Ausstellung Hugo von Hofmannsthal* (Salzburg: Amt der Salzburger Landesregierung, 1959), 31.
111. See Hans Liebstoeckl, "Von Sonntag auf Montag" *Ausgewählte Theaterfeuilletons*, (Vienna: Renaissance, 1925), xviii. Salzburger Festspiel, section 4. On antisemitism in Salzburg in general, including criticism of the Salzburg Festival in the press, see Günter Fellner, *Antisemitismus in Salzburg, 1918-1938* (Vienna: Geyer-Edition, 1979).
112. "Und nun zu Salzburg: Ich drahtete Ihnen und wiederhole nun die *dringende* Bitte: nehmen Sie die rein formale, keinerlei Betätigung erheischende Stelle an ... Reinhardt zum Präsidenten nehmen diese Spießbürger nie: sie hassen ihn, sie hassen ihn drei- und vierfach, als Juden, als Schloßherrn, als Künstler und einsamen Menschen, den sie nicht begreifen." Gottfried Reinhardt, *Der Liebhaber*, 205. Strauss accepted and served as President until 1923.

113. Camillo Castiglioni, son of the chief rabbi of Trieste, came to Vienna before World War I and became a leading figure known for his luxurious lifestyle, his speculation in international finance, and his support for the arts. He, Sigmund Bosel, and Richard Kola, two other wealthy Jewish speculators, went bankrupt in the interwar period. On the financial scandals, the social reaction, and the signficance of Jews in this period, see Peter Melichar, "Alter, neuer und verlorener Reichtum: Eine Skizze zu den großen Vermögen im Österreich der Zwischenkriegszeit," in *Armut und Reichtum in der Geschichte Österreichs*, ed. Ernst Bruckmüller (Vienna: Böhlau, 2010); Franz Mathis, "'. . . weil Herr Castiglioni in Österreich eben nicht verfolgt werden darf: Ein Justizskandal und seine mediale Rezeption," in *Politische Skandale und Affären in Österreich: von Mayerling bis Waldheim*, ed. Michael Gehler and Hubert Sickinger (Thaur, AT: Kulturverlag, 1995); George E. Berkley, *Vienna and Its Jews: The Tragedy of Success, 1880s–1980s* (Cambridge, MA: Abt Books/Madison Books, 1988), 149–61.
114. Edda Fuhrich-Leisler, "Max Reinhardt und Wien," in *Wien 1870–1930: Traum und Wirklichkeit*, (Salzburg: Residenz, 1984), 662.
115. Heinrich Pouthon, "Hofmannsthal-Jedermann-Salzburg," in Hadamowsky, "Reinhardt und Salzburg," 15.
116. According to Zifferer's wife, the first initiatives for the Salzburg Festival took place in the couple's salon in Paris, which was a center of French and Austrian cultural exchange. Wanda Zifferer, affidavit to Raoul Auernheimer, no date. DÖW 19214/2 (Papers of Raoul Auernheimer).
117. For example, the fact that Hofmannsthal asked Zifferer *not* to include Sophie (Szeps) Clemenceau, the wife of French prime minister Georges Clemenceau, despite her prominent position in Parisian society, indicates that the problem was likely her association with Clemenceau. See *Briefwechsel: Hugo von Hofmannsthal, Paul Zifferer*, ed. Hilde Burger (Vienna: Verlag der österrichischen Staatsdruckerei, 1983), 192.
118. "Die Freunde der Salzburger Festspiele, 1926," Salzburg Festival Archive.
119. Botstein, *Judentum und Modernität*, 142.
120. Leon Botstein, "Sozialgeschichte und die Politik des Ästhetischen: Juden und Musik in Wien 1870–1938," in Botstein and Hanak, *Quasi una fantasia*, 47.
121. *Salzburger Chronik*, May 28, 1918.
122. *Der eiserne Besen*, August 15, 1924. In 1924 they also campaigned against Reinhardt's *Das Mirakel* (the Miracle) being performed in the church.
123. "'Jedermann' in Salzburg," *Der Merkur*, Heft 17, September 1, 1920.
124. "Die Salzburger Festspiele: Vorbereitungen," *Wiener Allgemeine Zeitung*, August 14, 1920, 5.
125. "Der Fremdenteufel in Salzburg," *Linzer Tages-Post*, August 23, 1921, 5–6.
126. Judith Beniston, *Welttheater: Hofmannsthal, Richard von Kralik, and the Revival of Catholic Drama in Austria 1890–1934* (London: Maney, 1998), 108.

127. *Der Kunstgarten*, vol. 2, p.117–18 as cited in Judith Beniston, "Cultural Politics in the First Republic: Hans Brecka and the 'Kunststelle für christliche Volksbildung'" in *Catholicism and Austrian Culture*, ed. Judith Beniston and Ritchie Robertson, (Edinburgh: Edinburgh University Press, 1999), 108.
128. Joseph August Lux, *München-Augsburger Abendzeitung*, August 24, 1920.
129. Beniston, *Welttheater*, 209–11.
130. Joseph August Lux, "Die Festspielhaus-Architektur in Salzburg," *Salzburger Chronik*, October 9, 1921; and "Salzburger Festspielhaus im Spiegel der Kritik," *Reichspost*, June 6, 1926. See also "Die drei Salzburger Hanswurste," a satirical "Barockspiel" written by Lux that mocks the festival's prices and foreign tourists. Austrian National Library (ÖNB), Handschriftensammlung, Ser. n. 34.077. See also Mark Jarzombek, "Joseph August Lux: Werkbund Promoter, Historian of a Lost Modernity," *Journal of the Society of Architectural Historians* 63, no. 2 (2004): 205.
131. Kriechbaumer, "Statt eines Vorwortes," 14.
132. *Salzburger Chronik*, February 24, 1894.
133. Alfred Polgar, "Großes Theater in Salzburg! Stadt und Leute," *Prager Tagblatt*, August 17, 1922, 3.
134. Karl Kraus, *Die Fackel* 912–15 (1935): 34–62.
135. Hans Liebstoeckl, "Von Sonntag auf Montag," *Ausgewählte Theaterfeuilletons*, Verlag "Renaissance" Vienna 1925, XVIII. *Salzburger Festspiel*, sec 6. By populations from Bad Ischl and Bad Gastein, the writer clearly referred to popular Jewish *Sommerfrische* towns.
136. The population of the Salzburg Jewish community reached its high point with 285 in 1910; Jews were never more than 0.1 percent of the total population of Salzburg. Embacher, "Lenin oder Jabotinsky?," 182.
137. See the interview with Erwin Bonyhadi, in *Geduldet, Geschmäht und Vertrieben: Salzburger Juden erzählen*, ed. Daniela Ellmauer, Helga Embacher, and Albert Lichtblau (Salzburg: Otto Müller, 1998), esp. 114, 118–25.
138. Helga Embacher, "Exil als neue Heimat," in *Ein ewiges Dennoch: 125 Jahre Juden in Salzburg*, ed. Marko M. Feingold (Vienna: Böhlau, 1993), 456.
139. Bonyhadi, *Geduldet, Geschmäht und Vertrieben*, 118.
140. "Das Salzburger Grosse Welttheater," *Prager Tagblatt*, August 19, 1922, 2. Nina Lieberman recalls attending the Salzburg Festival in 1932 with her father, the community's rabbi. See Nina J. Lieberman, *The Salzburg Connection. An Adolescence Remembered* (New York: Vantage Press, 2004), 134.

Conclusion

1. Ironically, as Ruth Gruber shows, Jews' literal absence after 1945 is now palpable in the form of philosemitic events and memorabilia, forming a new Jewish "presence" that disturbs, questions, and reveals much about lingering European prejudices and stereotypes about Jews. Ruth Ellen Gruber, *Virtually Jewish: Reinventing Jewish Culture in Europe* (Berkeley: University of California Press, 2002).

2. There was some increase, however, in promoting explicitly Jewish themes and culture among some Jews in Austria after the situation worsened for Jews in Germany after 1933. See Chapter 2.
3. Janek Wasserman rightly notes that historians' overemphasis on 1938 as the turning point of the demise of the First Republic tends to obscure the importance of the events of 1934 for all Austrians. Here, too, Jews' options for political loyalty changed radically when the new regime outlawed the Social Democratic party, and ultimately, the civil war signaled the drastic worsening of conditions for Jews. Antisemites now decried the Jewish origins of the Social Democratic leaders more frequently, and Jews who remained loyal to the Social Democrats faced harassment. Many Jews began to separate from the Social Democrats, and some even shifted their support in favor of the new regime; these included Jewish intellectuals like Karl Kraus, Felix Salten, Franz Werfel, and Freud. See Malachi Hacohen, "Kosmopoliten in einer ethnonationalen Zeit? Juden und Österreicher in der Ersten Republik," in *. . . der Rest ist Österreich: Das Werden der Ersten Republik*, vol. I, ed. Helmut Konrad and Wolfgang Maderthaner (Vienna: Carl Gerold's Sohn, 2008); Harriet Pass Freidenreich, *Jewish Politics in Vienna, 1918–1938* (Bloomington: Indiana University Press, 1991), 195–203. However, despite new censorship laws, Viennese cabaret performances continued to articulate Jewish concerns during the years of the *Ständestaat*. Hans-Peter Bayerdörfer, "Jewish Cabaret Artists before 1933," in *Jews and the Making of Modern German Theatre*, ed. Jeanette Malkin and Freddie Rokem (Iowa City: University of Iowa Press, 2010), 147.
4. For more details on Jewish responses to the *Ständestaat*, see Sylvia Maderegger, *Die Juden im österreichischen Ständestaat 1934–1938* (Vienna: Geyer, 1973); and Freidenreich, *Jewish Politics in Vienna*, 180–203. On antisemitism after 1934, see Bruce F. Pauley, "Political Antisemitism in Interwar Vienna," in *Jews, Antisemitism, and Culture in Vienna*, ed. Ivar Oxaal, Michael Pollak, and Gerhard Botz, 168–71 (London: Routledge, 1987).
5. Andres Müry, "Das Fest der Antimoderne," in *Kleine Salzburger Festspielgeschichte*, ed. Andres Müry (Salzburg: Pustet, 2002), 36. See also "Verzeichnis der in der Ostmark eingezogenen bzw. beschlagnahmten Vermögenswerte," July 22, 1938, listing the confiscation of Schloss Leopoldskron in Salzburg. Dokumentationsarchiv des österreichischen Widerstandes, Vienna, File 19.400/170; Johannes Hofinger, *Die Akte Leopoldskron: Max Reinhardt—Das Schloss—Arisierung & Restitution* (Salzburg: Verlag Anton Pustet, 2005). On the fate of Reinhardt's private library in the Schloss Leopoldskron during the Nazi period, see Murray G. Hall, "Entgangene Trophäen I: Die Privatbibliothek von Max Reinhardt," in *". . . a . . . llerlei für die Nationalbibliothek zu ergattern . . .": Eine österreichische Institution in der NS-Zeit*, ed. Murray G. Hall and Christina Köstner (Vienna: Böhlau, 2006).
6. On this phenomenon during the interwar period in particular, see Steven Beller, *Was nicht im Baedeker steht: Juden und andere Österreicher im Wien der Zwischenkriegszeit* (Vienna: Picus, 2008).

7. Arthur Schnitzler, *Jugend in Wien: Eine Autobiographie* (Vienna: Molden, 1968), 322. As Bettina Riedmann makes clear, only after the First World War did Schnitzler become aware of his growing positive attitude toward being Jewish. *"Ich bin Jude, Österreicher, Deutscher": Judentum in Arthur Schniztlers Tagebüchern und Briefen* (Tübingen: Niemeyer, 2002), 405–6. In J.L. Benvenisti's 1923 interview with Schnitzler (published in 1924), Schnitzler describes his inclination to self-analysis as "Jewish." J.L. Benvenisti, "Arthur Schnitzler Foretells Jewish Renaissance," *The American Hebrew*, February 29, 1924, 460, 474.
8. Eric Hobsbawm, *Interesting Times: A Twentieth-Century Life* (New York: Pantheon, 2002), 21.
9. Georg Stefan Troller, *Das fidele Grab an der Donau: Mein Wien 1918–1938* (Düsseldorf: Artemis & Winkler, 2004), 57.
10. Musil's wife Martha Marcovaldi (née Heinemann) was Jewish.
11. See Stefan Jonsson, *Subject without Nation: Robert Musil and the History of Modern Identity* (Durham: Duke University Press, 2000), 2.
12. Robert Musil, "Ruminations of a Slow-witted mind" (1933), in *Robert Musil: Precision and Soul: Essays and Addresses*, ed. and trans. Burton Pike and David Luft (Chicago: University of Chicago Press, 1990), 229. Musil's intention for the essay to be published in *Die neue Rundschau* was not realized due to its critical political stance. Originally published in Robert Musil, *Gesammelte Werke*, vol. 8/9, ed. Adolf Frisé (Reinbek bei Hamburg: Rowohlt, 1978), 217–18. By 1933, Musil could no longer have had any illusions about what the Nazis' rise to power in Germany meant for cultural politics. On May 10, 1933, the Nazis burned books by Jews and political opponents, among them those of his mentor Alfred Kerr; at that point, the Jewish founding members of the first Musil Society went into exile. Karl Corino, "Der Fall Robert Musil," in *Vertriebene Vernunft*, vol. 2, *Emigration und Exil österreichischer Wissenschaft 1930–1940*, ed. Friedrich Stadler (Münster: LIT, 2004), 538.
13. "I count up us men of intellect . . . and I find approximately three times as many 'Aryans' as 'non-Aryans.' I pick out those who have been unquestionably overestimated as well as underestimated and find among them members of both camps. As a control, I look at what is merely the writing industry: there I find in the theater a preponderance of Jewish authors, but in the novel I find a lucrative, unconsciously sanctimonious, incredibly pernicious cerebral industry that is almost exclusively in the hands of Aryans." Musil, "Ruminations," 229. I am grateful to Florence Vatan for this reference.
14. Letter from Sigmund Freud to Oskar Pfister dated October 9, 1918, in *Sigmund Freud and Oskar Pfister, Briefe 1909–1939*, ed. Ernst L. Freud and Heinrich Meng (1963) as cited in Peter Gay, *A Godless Jew: Freud, Atheism and the Making of Psychoanalysis* (New Haven: Yale University Press, 1987), 37, 603. Sander Gilman claims that Freud's creation of psychoanalysis implicitly engaged Jewishness despite its lack of nonreligious, ethnic, or political characteristics, since psychoanalysis is itself a science in which "many of the claims against the Jew (such as the

special, sexualized nature of the Jew) are sanitized and made into universal claims for human nature." In other words, psychoanalysis represents an attempt to form a universal explanation for a stereotype blamed specifically on Jews. Sander L. Gilman, "Freud's Jewish Identity," review of Peter Gay, *A Godless Jew* and *Freud: A Life for our Time*, in Edward Timms and Ritchie Robertson, eds., *Vienna 1900: From Altenberg to Wittgenstein* (Edinburgh: Edinburgh University Press, 1990); 175. See also John M. Cuddihy, *The Ordeal of Civility* (New York: Basic, 1974). Freud described himself as a Jew who is neither German nor Austrian. *Sigmund Freud, Brautbriefe: Briefe an Martha Bernays aus den Jahren 1882–1886*, ed. Ernst L. Freud (Frankfurt: Fischer, 1988), 137.

15. For more on this phenomenon, see Steven Beller, "Is There a Jewish Aspect to Modern Austrian Identity?" in *Österreich-Konzeptionen und jüdisches Selbstverständnis: Identitäts-Transfigurationen um 19. und 20. Jahrhundert*, ed. Hanni Mittelmann and Armin Wallas (Tübingen: Max Niemeyer, 2001), esp. 45. Ernst Gombrich vehemently disagreed with attempts to address Jewish difference in the cases of assimilated Jewish Austrian art patrons who lived at the turn of the century. Ernst Gombrich, *The Visual Arts in Vienna circa 1900 & Reflections on the Jewish Catastrophe* (London: Austrian Cultural Institute, 1997).
16. Bruce Lincoln, *Method & Theory in the Study of Religion*, vol. 8 (1996): 225–27.
17. Joan W. Scott, "The Evidence of Experience," *Critical Inquiry*, 17, no. 4 (Summer 1991): 777.
18. Leora Auslander, "The Boundaries of Jewishness or When Is a Cultural Practice Jewish?" *Modern Jewish Studies* 8, no. 1 (2009). To name another example, in discussing Karl Popper's uncomfortable ambivalences about Jews, Malachi Hacohen sees no contradiction in accepting Popper's rejection of any label of "Jew" while recognizing that the context of his life and work as a marginal Jew is necessary in order to understand both the basis for the intensity of his views on cosmopolitanism, as well as the limits of Austrian society, which ultimately ensured their failure. *Karl Popper—the Formative Years, 1902–1945: Politics and Philosophy in Interwar Vienna*, (Cambridge: Cambridge University Press, 2000), 308–09.
19. As Michael Steinberg notes, studying and writing about music remains difficult due to music's "incongruity with words as well as other signifying practices." Michael P. Steinberg, *Judaism Musical and Unmusical* (Chicago: University of Chicago Press, 2007), 9.
20. In the German context, see Lily E. Hirsch, *A Jewish Orchestra in Nazi Germany: Musical Politics and the Berlin Jewish Culture League* (Ann Arbor: University of Michigan Press, 2010); *Jewish Musical Modernism, Old and New*, ed. Philip V. Bohlman (Chicago: University of Chicago Press, 2008); Klára Móricz, *Jewish Identities: Nationalism, Racism, and Utopianism in Twentieth-Century Music* (Berkeley: University of California Press, 2008). On Jews' relationship to music in Russia, see James Loeffler, *The Most Musical Nation: Jews and Culture in the Late Russian Empire* (New Haven: Yale University Press, 2010).

21. *Der Tonwille: Pamphlets in Witness of the Immutable Laws of Music*, ed. William Drabkin, trans. Ian Bent et al., vol. 1 (Oxford: Oxford University Press, 2004). Nicholas Cook notes that Schenker can be aligned with other composers who were often falsely accused of being Jewish due to their status as conspicuous representatives of the liberal tradition. See *The Schenker Project: Culture, Race, and Music Theory in Fin-de-Siècle Vienna* (New York: Oxford University Press, 2007), 54.
22. Ian Bent, "'That bright new light': Schenker, Universal Edition, and the origins of the Erläuterung series, 1901–1910," *Journal of the American Musicological Society* 58 (2005): 97–98, 114.
23. Leon Botstein, "Gedanken zu Heinrich Schenkers jüdischer Identität," in *Rebell und Visionär: Heinrich Schenker in Wien*, ed. Evelyn Fink (Vienna: Lafite, 2003); Cook, *The Schenker Project*, 213.
24. Cook, *The Schenker Project*, 13.
25. Móricz, *Jewish Identities*, 206. Additionally, Karen Painter's work underscores the important role the politicization of music and discourse surrounding antisemitism played in shaping Germanness and Austrianness between 1900–1945. See *Symphonic Aspirations: German Music and Politics, 1900–1945* (Cambridge, MA: Harvard University Press, 2007).
26. For more on Schoenberg's struggle to convince others of the Germanness of his music, see Hacohen, *Karl Popper*, 102.
27. Hacohen, *Karl Popper*, 6, 25, 53.
28. Mises wrote his dissertation on the development of economic relations in Galicia. See *Die Entwicklung des gutsherrlich-bäuerlichen Verhältnisses in Galizien bis zu seiner Auflösung (1772–1848)* (Vienna: Deuticke, 1903); see also *Gesellschaft österreichischer Volkswirte Jahrbuch 1920: Die politischen Beziehungen Wiens zu den Ländern im Lichte der Volkswirtschaft* (Vienna: Fromme, 1920).
29. See Hans Kelsen, ed., *Die Verfassungsgesetze der Republik Deutschösterreich*, vols. 1–3 (Vienna: Deuticke, 1919). According to William M. Johnston, Kelsen first became interested in philosophy after reading Otto Weininger. See *The Austrian Mind: An Intellectual and Social History 1848–1938* (Berkeley: University of California Press, 1972), 95. For a detailed survey of Kelsen's life in Vienna and beyond, see the exhibition catalogue edited by Maria Ettl and Gerhard Murauer, *Hans Kelsen und die Bundesverfassung: Geschichte einer Josefstädter Karriere* (Vienna: Bezirksmuseum Josefstadt, 2010).

BIBLIOGRAPHY

Primary Sources

ARCHIVES

Archiv der Israelitischen Kultusgemeinde Wien
Archiv der Paul Zsolnay Verlag (APZ)
Archiv der Universität Wien, Vienna (AUW)
Archivaliensammlung der Medizinischen Universität Wien, Vienna
Archive of the United States Holocaust Memorial Museum
Dokumentationsarchiv des österreichischen Widerstandes, Vienna (DÖW)
Houghton Library, Harvard University, Cambridge, MA
  bMS Ger 91, "My Life in Germany before and after January 30, 1933"
Joseph Buloff Jewish Theater Archive, Harvard University, Cambridge, MA
Leo Baeck Institute, New York (LBI)
  Austrian Heritage Collection (AHC)
    Albers-Frank, Hilde
    Blank, Helen
  Papers of Sonia Wachstein
Österreichische Nationalbibliothek, Vienna (ÖNB)
  Bildarchiv
  Handschriftensammlung
  Österreichisches Literaturarchiv, Vienna (ÖLA)
Österreichisches Staatsarchiv, Vienna (ÖStA)
  Bundesministerium für Justiz (BfJ)
    File 33901/1931, VI Karton 3402, Folder 34414/1931
  Bundespräsident (BP)
    File Z 36.305/30

Österreichisches Theatermuseum, Vienna
Salzburg Festival Archive, Salzburg
State University of New York at Albany, M. E. Grenander Department of Special Collections & Archives, German and Jewish Intellectual Émigré Collection, Albany, NY
  Papers of Vicki Baum
  Papers of Greta Hartwig Manschinger and Kurt (Ashley Vernon) Manschinger (MP)
  Papers of Friedrich Ungar
Tiroler Landesarchiv, Innsbruck (TLA)
  Amt der Landesregierung für Tirol, Präsidium, Geschäftszahl XII 61–1549.
  St 3972/28 6 Vr 1380/28, Innsbrucker Landesgericht
Wienbibliothek, Vienna (WB)
  Handschriftensammlung (HS)
    Papers of Mela Hartwig (MHP)
    Papers of Hilde Spiel
    Papers of Walter Riehl
  Tagblatt-Archiv
    Papers of Else Feldmann
Wiener Stadt- und Landesarchiv, Vienna (WStLA)
  MA 8, 2.3.4.A11—Vr LG I, 1851–1956, 20 Vr 5867/36 (Johannes Nelböck)
  MA 8, Landesgericht für Strafsachen A11: II Vr 2652/28 (Oskar Pöffel)
  MA 8, 2.3.4.A11—Vr LG I, 1851–1956, Vr 1748/25 (Otto Rothstock)
  2.3.4.A11 -VrGI (1920–1938 auch LG II)|1851–1950, 1953–1958, 1776/24 (Hugo Bettauer and Rudolf Olden)

NEWSPAPERS AND PERIODICALS

The American Hebrew, New York, 1924
Arbeiter-Zeitung, Vienna, 1905, 1929
Bettauers Wochenschrift, Vienna, 1925
Dr. Blochs Österreichische Wochenschrift, Vienna, 1920
Die Börse, Vienna, 1922
Der eiserne Besen, Vienna, 1924, 1929
Er und Sie: Wochenschrift für Lebenskultur und Erotik, Vienna, 1924
Die Fackel, Vienna, 1900, 1922, 1929, 1935
Die Filmwelt, Vienna, 1924
Illustriertes Sportblatt, Vienna, 1927
Der Jude, Berlin, 1916/1917
Jüdische Rundschau, Berlin, 1926
Kikeriki, Vienna, 1929
Der Kinematograph, Berlin, 1924
Das Kino-Journal, Vienna, 1924
Das kleine Blatt, Vienna, 1929

Komödie: Wochenrevue für Bühne und Film, Vienna, 1922
Leipziger Illustrirte Zeitung, Leipzig, 1922
Linzer Tages-Post, Linz, 1921
Literarische Bleter, Warsaw, 1924
Die Literarische Welt, Berlin, 1928
Der Merker, Vienna, 1917
Der Morgen, Vienna, 1929
München-Augsburger Abendzeitung, Munich, 1920
Musikblätter des Anbruch, Vienna, 1922
Nachrichten der Sektion "Austria" des Deutschen und Österreichischen Alpenvereins, Vienna, 1921.
Nachrichten der Sektion "Donauland" des Deutschen und Österreichischen Alpenvereins, Vienna, 1921.
Neue Freie Presse, Vienna, 1906, 1921, 1923, 1924, 1926, 1928–1930, 1937
Neues Wiener Journal, Vienna, 1925, 1928
Neue Züricher Zeitung, Zurich, 1920
Ost und West, Berlin, 1902
Österreichische Wochenschrift, Vienna, 1917
Prager Presse, Prague, 1922
Prager Tagblatt, Prague, 1922, 1924
Reichspost, Vienna, 1921, 1923, 1925–1926
Salzburger Chronik, Salzburg, 1894, 1918, 1921
Salzburger Volksblatt, Salzburg, 1920
Salzburger Volksbote, Salzburg, 1918–1919
Schönere Zukunft, Vienna, 1936
Steyrer Tagblatt, Steyr, 1922
Die Stunde, Vienna, 1923.
Tiroler Anzeiger, Innsbruck, 1928
Die Weltbühne, Berlin, 1925
Wiener Allgemeine Zeitung, Vienna, 1920
Wiener Kino: Das Blatt des Kinobesuchers, Vienna, 1924.
Wiener Morgenzeitung, Vienna, 1921

PUBLISHED INTERVIEWS

Winckler, Julia. "Gespräch mit Wolfgang Suschitzky, Fotograf und Kameramann." *Exilforschung: Ein Internationales Jahrbuch*. Edited by Claus-Dieter Krohn, et al. 21 (2003): 254–279.

PUBLISHED MEMOIRS

Baum, Vicki. *It Was All Quite Different*. New York: Funk & Wagnalls, 1964.

Bloch, Joseph S. *Errinerungen aus meinem Leben*. Vienna: R. Löwit, 1922.

Canetti, Elias. *The Tongue Set Free: Remembrance of a European Childhood*. Translated by Joachim Neugroschel. New York: Seabury Press, 1979 [1977].

———. *The Torch in My Ear*. Translated by Joachim Neugroschel. New York: Farrar, Straus, and Giroux, 1982 [1980].

Deutsch, Gitta. *The Red Thread*. Riverside, CA: Ariadne, 1996. Originally appeared as *Böcklinstrassenelegie: Erinnerungen*. Vienna: Picus, 1993.

Gardiner, Muriel. *Code Name "Mary": Memoirs of an American Woman in the Austrian Underground*. New Haven, CT: Yale University Press, 1983.

Hobsbawm, Eric. *Interesting Times: A Twentieth-Century Life*. New York: Pantheon, 2002.

Hümbelin, Lotte. *Mein eigener Kopf: Ein Frauenleben in Wien, Moskau, Prag, Paris und Zürich*. Zurich: Edition 8, 1999.

Kadison, Luba, and Joseph Buloff. *On Stage, Off Stage: Memories of a Lifetime in the Yiddish Theater*. Cambridge: Harvard University Library, 1992.

Klein-Löw, Stella. *Erinnerungen*. Vienna: Jugend und Volk, 1980.

Kokoschka, Oskar. *Mein Leben*. Munich: Bruckmann, 1971.

Lachs, Minna. *Warum schaust du zurück: Erinnerungen 1907–1941*. Vienna: Europaverlag, 1986.

Langer, Marie, with Jaime del Palacio and Enrique Guinsberg. *From Vienna to Managua: Journey of a Psychoanalyst*. Translated by Margaret Hooks. London: Free Association, 1989.

Lieberman, J. Nina. *The Salzburg Connection. An Adolescence Remembered*. New York: Vantage Press, 2004.

Müller-Guttenbrunn, Adam [pseud. Roderich Meinhart]. *Erinnerungen eines Theaterdirektors*. Leipzig: L. Staackmann, 1924.

Perloff, Marjorie. *The Vienna Paradox: A Memoir*. New York: New Directions, 2003.

Price, Monroe E. *Objects of Remembrance: A Memoir of American Opportunities and Viennese Dreams*. New York: Central European University Press, 2009.

Rawitsch, Melech. *Das Geschichtenbuch meines Lebens: Auswahl*. Translated by Armin Eidherr. Salzburg: Otto Müller, 1996.

Reinhardt, Gottfried. *Der Liebhaber. Erinnerungen seines Sohnes Gottfried Reinhardt an Max Reinhardt*. Munich: Droemer Knaur, 1973.

Scheicher, Joseph. *Erlebnisse und Erinnerungen: Aus der Jugendzeit*. Vienna: Carl Fromme, 1907–1912.

Schnitzler, Arthur. *Jugend in Wien: Eine Autobiographie*. Vienna: Molden, 1968.

Sperber, Manès. *All das Vergangene*, vol. 2, *Die vergebliche Warnung*. Vienna: Europaverlag, 1975.

———. *All Our Yesterdays*, vol. 1, *God's Water Carriers*. Translated by Joachim Neugroschel. New York: Holmes and Meier, 1987.

Spiel, Hilde. *Die hellen und die finsteren Zeiten: Erinnerungen 1911–1946*. Munich: List, 1989.

Thimig-Reinhardt, Helene. *Wie Max Reinhardt lebte.* Percha am Starnberger See: Schulz, 1973.

Troller, Georg Stefan. *Das fidele Grab an der Donau: Mein Wien 1918–1938.* Düsseldorf: Artemis & Winkler, 2004.

Varon, Benno Weiser. *Professions of a Lucky Jew.* London: Cornwall, 1992.

Viertel, Salka. *The Kindness of Strangers.* New York: Holt, Rinehart and Winston, 1969.

Wechsberg, Joseph. *The Vienna I Knew: Memories of a European Childhood.* New York: Doubleday, 1979.

Zuckerkandl, Bertha. *Osterreich Intim: Erinnerungen 1892–1942.* Edited by Reinhard Federmann. Frankfurt: Ullstein, 1970.

Zweig, Stefan. *The World of Yesterday: An Autobiography.* New York: Viking, 2008.

UNPUBLISHED MEMOIRS

Wärendorfer, Laura. Unpublished autobiography. Typescript.

PUBLISHED DIARIES

Fiscus, Emanuel. *Tagebücher (1916–1921).* Edited by Evelyn Adunka. Innsbruck: Studienverlag: 2008.

Schnitzler, Arthur. *Tagebücher 1909–1926.* Vienna: Verlag der österreichische Akademie der Wissenschaften, 1981–2000.

Vogel, David. *Das Ende der Tage: Tagebücher und autobiographische Aufzeichnungen 1912–1922 und 1941–42.* Translated by Ruth Achlama. Munich: List, 1995.

Werfel, Franz. *Erzählungen aus zwei Welten.* Edited by Adolf D. Klarmann. Vol. 2. Frankfurt: Fischer, 1952.

———. *Zwischen oben und unten: Prosa—Tagebücher—Aphorismen—Literarische Nachträge.* Edited by Adolf D. Klarmann. Munich: Langen Müller, 1975.

PUBLISHED LETTERS

Canetti, Elias. *"Dearest Georg." Love, Literature, and Power in Dark Times. The letters of Elias, Veza, and Georges Canetti 1933–1948.* Edited by Karen Lauer and Kristian Wachinger. Translated by David Dollenmayer. New York: Other Press, 2009.

Freud, Sigmund. *Sigmund Freud, Brautbriefe: Briefe an Martha Bernays aus den Jahren 1882–1886.* Edited by Ernst L. Freud. Frankfurt: Fischer, 1988.

Halsmann, Philipp. *Briefe aus der Haft an eine Freundin.* Edited by Karl Blanck. Stuttgart: J. Engelhorns Nachf., 1930.

Hofmannsthal, Hugo von. *Ein Briefwechsel: Hugo von Hofmannsthal und Willy Haas.* Berlin: Propyläen, 1968.

———. *Briefwechsel: Hugo von Hofmannsthal and Paul Zifferer* Edited by Hilde Burger. Vienna: Verlag der österrichischen Staatsdruckerei, 1983.

Rilke, Rainer Maria. *Briefwechsel mit Hugo von Hofmannsthal*. Edited by Rudolf Hirsch and Ingeborg Schnack. Frankfurt: Insel, 1978.

———. *Rainer Maria Rilke und Marie von Thurn und Taxis: Briefwechsel*. 2 vols. Edited by Ernst Zinn. Zurich: Niehans & Rokitansky, 1951.

Schönherr, Karl. *Bühnenwerke II: Briefe, Dokumentation*. Edited by Franz Hadamowsky. Vienna: Kremayr & Scheriau, 1974.

PUBLISHED STATISTICS

Beiträge zur Statistik der Republik Österreich, Statistik des Bundesstaates Österreichs. Vol. 8: "Die Bewegung der Bevölkerung in den Jahren 1914 bis 1921." Edited by Bundesamt für Statistik. Vienna: Druck und Verlag der österreichischen Staatsdruckerei, 1923.

Beiträge zur Statistik der Republik Österreich, Statistik des Bundesstaates Österreichs. Vol. 12: "Vorläufige Ergebnisse der Volkszählung vom 7. März 1923." Edited by Bundesamt für Statistik. Vienna: Druck und Verlag der österreichischen Staatsdruckerei, 1923.

Beiträge zur Statistik der Stadt Wien. Vol. 14. Vienna: Gerlach & Wiedling, 1923.

Beiträge zur Statistik der Stadt Wien. Vol. 5. Vienna: Gerlach & Wiedling, 1924.

Die Ergebnisse der österreichischen Volkszählung vom 22. März 1934. Vol. 1: "Bundesstaat." Edited by Bundesamt für Statistik. Vienna: Druck und Verlag der österreichischen Staatsdruckerei, 1935.

Die Ergebnisse der österreichischen Volkszählung vom 22. März 1934. Vol. 3: "Wien." Edited by Bundesamt für Statistik. Vienna: Druck und Verlag der österreichischen Staatsdruckerei, 1935.

Mitteilungen aus Statistik und Verwaltung der Stadt Wien. Vols. 1–12. Vienna: Magistratsabteilung für Statistik, 1929.

Mitteilungen aus Statistik und Verwaltung der Stadt Wien. Vols. 1–12. Vienna: Magistratsabteilung für Statistik, 1930.

Statistische Mitteilung der Stadt Wien. Vols. 10–12. Vienna: Gemeinde Wien, 1926.

Statistisches Handbuch für die Republik Österreich. Edited by Bundesamt für Statistik. Vienna: Verlag des Bundesamtes für Statistik, 1929.

OTHER PUBLISHED PRIMARY SOURCES

Ansky, S. *The Dybbuk and Other Writings*. Edited by David Roskies. New York: Schocken, 1992.

———. *The Dybbuk and the Yiddish Imagination*. Edited and translated by Joachim Neugroschl. Syracuse: Syracuse University Press, 2000.

Artner, Karl, Otto Guth, Emil Nekovar, Hans Schedling, Paul Sekora, Otto Selig, Leopold Steiner, and Dr. Michael Tennenhus. *Die Leopoldstadt: Ein Heimatbuch*. Vienna: Selbstverlag der Lehrer-Arbeitergemeinschaft, 1937.

Baumgartner, Gerd, ed. *Walther Rode: Leben und Werk*. Vienna: Löcker, 2007.

Benvenisti, J.L. "Arthur Schnitzler Foretells Jewish Renaissance: An Exclusive Interview with the Eminent Littérateur." *The American Hebrew*. February 29, 1924: 460, 474.

Bettauer, Hugo. *The City without Jews: A Novel of our Time*. Translated by Salomea Neumark Brainin. New York: Bloch, 1997 [1922].

Bienenfeld, Franz R. *The Religion of the Non-Religious Jews*. Lecture delivered to the Sociological Society of Vienna. November 10, 1937. London: Museum Press, 1944.

Bloch, Joseph. *Der nationale Zwist und die Juden in Österreich*. Vienna: Gottlieb, 1886.

Braun-Prager, Käthe. *Die Stadt der Ewigen und andere Novellen*. Edited and afterward by Tatjana Popovic. Klagenfurt: Alekto, 2000.

Bullock, Malcolm. *Austria 1918–1938. A Study in Failure*. London: Macmillan, 1939.

Canetti, Elias. *Crowds and Power*. Translated by Carol Stewart. New York: Farrar, 1984 [1960].

Canetti, Veza. *Die gelbe Strasse: Roman*. Munich: Hanser, 1990.

Der Fall Halsmann, Schriften der österreichischen Liga für Menschenrechte. Vol. 3. Vienna: Gilhofer & Anschburg, 1931.

Dalinger, Brigitte. *Quellenedition zur Geschichte des jüdischen Theaters in Wien*. Tübingen: Niemeyer, 2003.

Frankl, Ludwig August. *Zur Geschichte der Juden in Wien*. Vienna: Druck und Verlag von J.P. Sollinger's Witwe, 1853.

Fuchs, Abraham Moshe. *Unter der Brücke*. Translated by Armin Eidherr. Salzburg: Otto Müller Verlag, 1997 [1924].

Gamper, Eduard. "Der Gutachten der medizinischen Fakultät Innsbruck in der Strafsache gegen Philipp Halsmann." *Beiträge zur gerichtlichen Medizin Band X*. Edited by Prof. Dr. Albin Haberda. Leipzig and Vienna: Franz Deuticke, 1930.

Gombrich, Ernst. *The Visual Arts in Vienna circa 1900 & Reflections on the Jewish Catastrophe*. London: Austrian Cultural Institute, 1996.

Gürtler, Hans. *Der Freispruch Pöffel*. Vienna: Verlag Moritz Perles, 1929.

Halsman, Philippe. *Jump Book*. New York: Simon and Schuster, 1959.

Hartwig, Mela. *Bin ich ein überflüssiger Mensch?* Droschl: Graz, 2001[1929/1930].

———. *Das Weib ist ein Nichts*. Graz: Droschl, 2002 [1929].

———. *Ekstasen*. Berlin: Ullstein, 1992 [1928].

Hirschfeld, Ludwig. *Was nicht im Baedeker steht: Wien und Budapest*. Munich: Piper Verlag, 1927. Translated from the original as *The Vienna That's Not in the Baedeker* by T.W. Maccallum. Munich: R. Piper & Co. Verlag, 1929.

Holl, Oskar. "Dokumente zur Entstehung der Salzburger Festspiele: Unveröffentlichtes aus der Korrespondenz der Gründer." *Maske und Kothurn—Vierteljahrsschrift für Theaterwissenschaft* 13 (1967): 148–79.

Jacob, Heinrich Eduard. "Pöffls Freispruch." In *Fazit: Erzähler einer Generation*, edited by Herbert Reinoss, 228–32. Munich: F.A. Herbig, 1972.

Keimer, L. *The International Congress of Women of 1899: Women in Professions*. Edited by the Countess of Aberdeen. London: T. Fisher Unwin, 1900.

Kelsen, Hans, ed. *Die Verfassungsgesetze der Republik Deutschösterreich*. Vols. 1–3. Vienna: Deuticke, 1919.

Kreppel, Jonas. *Juden und Judentum von Heute: Ein Handbuch*. Vienna: Amalthea, 1925.

Kuh, Anton. "Bezirk der Werbezirk." In *Luftlinien, Feuilletons, Essays und Publizistik*, Edited by Ruth Greuner. Vienna: Kremayr und Scheria, 1981.

Adolph Lehmann's Allgemeiner Wohnungs-Anzeiger nebst Handels- und Gewerbe-Adreßbuch für die Bundeshauptstadt Wien. Vienna, 1930.

Liebstoeckl, Hans. "Von Sonntag auf Montag." In *Ausgewählte Theaterfeuilletons, XVIII. Salzburger Festspiel*. Vienna: Verlag Renaissance, 1925.

Marbe, Karl. *Der Strafprozess gegen Philipp Halsmann, aktenmäßige Darstellung und kriminalpsychologische Würdigung*. Leipzig: C.L. Hirschfeld, 1932.

Masaidek, Franz Friedrich. *Wien und die Wiener aus der Spottvogelperspektive: Wien's Sehens-, Merk- und Nichtswürdigkeiten*. Vienna: Waldheim, 1873.

Meixner, Karl. "Lehren des Halsmannprozesses: Mit 28 Abbildungen." *Beiträge zur gerichtlichen Medizin*, Band X. Edited by Albin Haberda. Leipzig and Vienna: Franz Deuticke, 1930.

Mises, Ludiwig von. *Die Entwicklung des gutsherrlich-bäuerlichen Verhältnisses in Galizien bis zu seiner Auflösung (1772–1848)*. Vienna: Deuticke, 1903.

———. *Gesellschaft österreichischer Volkswirte Jahrbuch 1920: Die politischen Beziehungen Wiens zu den Ländern im Lichte der Volkswirtschaft*. Vienna: Fromme, 1920.

Morgenstern, Soma. "Zur Entstehung der Oper Lulu." In *Alban Berg und seine Idole. Erinnerungen und Briefe*, edited by Ingolf Schulte, 129–40. Berlin: Aufbau, 1999.

Müller-Guttenbrunn, Adam. *Wien war eine Theaterstadt*. Vienna: Carl Gerold's Sohn, 1887.

Musil, Robert. "Anschluss with Germany." In *Robert Musil: Precision and Soul: Essays and Addresses*, edited and translated by Burton Pike and David Luft, 90–101. Chicago: University of Chicago Press, 1990.

———. *Gesammelte Werke*. Edited by Adolf Frisé. Reinbek bei Hamburg: Rowohlt, 1970; 1978; 1981.

Orel, Anton. *Das Verfassungsmachwerk der "Republik Österreich" von der Warte der immerwährenden Philosophie aus und im Lichte von der Idee, Natur und Geschichte Österreichs geprüft und verworfen*. Vienna: Vogelsang, 1921.

Paumgartten, Carl. *Repablick: Eine galgenfröhliche Wiener Legende aus der Zeit der gelben Pest und des roten Todes*. Graz: Stocker Verlag, 1924.

Perutz, Leo. "Skizzen aus Ukraine" (1918). In *Mainacht in Wien*, 149–53. Vienna: Zsolnay, 1996.

Ross, Martin H. *Marrano*. Boston: Branden, 1976.

Roth, Joseph. "The Moscow Yiddish Theater." In *The Moscow Yiddish Theater: Art on Stage in the Time of Revolution*, edited by Benjamin Harshav, 110–17. New Haven, CT: Yale University Press, 2008.

———. *The Wandering Jews: A Classic Portrait of a Vanished People*. Translated by Michael Hofmann. New York: W.W. Norton & Company, 2001.

Ruzicka, Ernst. *Max Halsmanns Ermordung: Der Schlüssel der Wahrheit.* Vienna: Krystall-Verlag, 1930.

Salten, Felix. *Das Österreichische Antlitz: Essays.* Berlin: S. Fischer, 1910.

Scheicher, Joseph. *Aus dem Jahre 1920: Ein Traum vom Landtags- und Reichsratsabgeordneten Dr. Joseph Scheicher.* St. Pölten: Verlag von Johann Gregora's Buchhandlung, 1900.

Schmidt, Franz. *Studien zu Franz Schmidt,* Band 5: *Quellen II zu Franz Schmidt: Briefe, Autographen, Aufzeichnungen in Privatbesitz, Erinnerungen.* Edited by Carmen Ottner. Vienna: Ludwig Doblinger, 1987.

Schmitz, Oskar A.H. *Der österreichische Mensch: Zum Anschauungsunterricht für Europäer, insbesondere für Reichsdeutsche.* Vienna-Leipzig: Wiener Literarische Anstalt, 1924.

Schönherr, Karl. *Bühnenwerke II: Briefe, Dokumentation.* Edited by Franz Hadamowsky. Vienna: Kremayr & Scheriau, 1974.

Schwarz, Dr. Ignaz. *Das Wiener Ghetto: Seine Häuser und seine Bewohner.* Vienna: Wilhelm Braumüller, 1909.

Sikora, Adalbert. "Zur Geschichte der Volksschauspiele in Tirol." *Zeitschrift des Ferdinandeums für Tirol und Vorarlberg* 50 (1906): 339–72.

Soxberger, Thomas, ed. and trans. *Nackte Lieder: Jiddische Literatur aus Wien 1915–1938.* Vienna: Mandelbaum, 2008.

Tannenbaum, Friedrich. *Das Warenhaus in Österreich. Auszug aus der Dissertation zur Erlangung des Doktorats der Staatswissenschaften an der rechts- und staatswissenschaftlichen Fakultät der Wiener Universität.* Vienna: University of Vienna, 1932.

Tietze, Hans. *Die Juden Wiens: Geschichte, Wissenschaft, Kultur.* Leipzig, Vienna: E.P. Tal & Co. Verlag, 1935.

Torberg, Friedrich. "A Sentimental Preface" (1966). In Hart, *Tante Jolesch or the Decline of the West in Anecdotes,* 186–93.

———. "Warum ich stolz darauf bin." In *50 Jahr Hakoah, 1909–1959,* edited by Arthur Baar, 278–83. Tel-Aviv: Verlagskomittee Hakoah, 1959.

———. *Die Erben der Tante Jolesch.* Munich: Langen/Müller 2008.

———. *Die Tante Jolesch, oder der Untergang des Abendlandes in Anekdoten.* Munich: Langen-Müller, 1977.

———. *Tante Jolesch or the Decline of the West in Anecdotes,* edited and afterward by Sonat Birnecker Hart. Translated by Maria Poglitsch Bauer. Riverside, CA: Ariadne, 2008.

Vogel, David, *Married Life.* Translated by Dalya Bilu. New Milford, CT: Toby Press, 2007[1929–30].

Wechsel, Leopold Matthias. *Die Leopoldstadt bey Wein: Quellen und Quellschriftstellern, in Verbindung mit einer Skizze der Landesgeschichte, historisch dargestellt.* Vienna: Anton Strauss, 1824.

Weininger, Otto. *Geschlecht und Charakter.* London: Senker and Warburg, 1997 [1903].

Werfel, Franz. *Erzählungen aus zwei Welten*. Vol. 2. Edited by Adolf D. Klarmann. Frankfurt: Fischer, 1952.

———. *Zwischen oben und unten: Prosa—Tagebücher—Aphorismen—Literarische Nachträge*. Edited by Adolf D. Klarmann. Munich: Langen Müller, 1975.

Zweig, Arnold. *Das ostjüdische Antlitz*. Berlin: Welt-Verlag, 1920.

Select Secondary Sources

Achberger, Friedrich. *Fluchtpunkt 1938. Essays zur österreichischen Literatur zwischen 1918 und 1938*. Vienna:Verlag für Gesellschaftskritik, 1994.

Adunka, Evelyn. "Schalom Asch und Wien." In Eidherr and Müller, *Zwischenwelt: Jiddische Kultur und Literatur aus Österreich*, 185–98.

Alter, Robert. "Fogel and the Forging of a Hebrew Self." *Prooftexts* 13, no. 1 (1993): 3–13.

Amstädter, Rainer. *Der Alpinismus. Kultur—Organisation—Politik*. Vienna: WUV-Universitätsverlag, 1996.

Anderson, Lisa Marie. *German Expressionism and the Messianism of a Generation*. Amsterdam: Rodopi, 2011.

Antler, Joyce, *You Never Call! You Never Write! A History of the Jewish Mother*. New York: Oxford University Press, 2007.

Arnborn, Marie Therese. *Friedmann, Gutmann, Lieben, Mandl, Strakosch: Fünf Familien Porträts aus Wien vor 1938*. Vienna: Böhlau, 2002.

Aschheim, Steven E. *Brothers and Strangers: The East European Jew in German and German Jewish Consciousness, 1800–1923*. Madison: University of Wisconsin Press, 1983.

Atzinger, Hildegard. *Gina Kaus: Schriftstellerin und Öffentlichkeit: Zur Stellung einer Schriftstellerin in der literarischen Öffentlichkeit der Zwischenkriegszeit in Österreich und Deutschland*. Frankfurt am Main: Peter Lang, 2008.

Auslander, Leora. "The Boundaries of Jewishness or When Is a Cultural Practice Jewish?" *Journal of Modern Jewish Studies* 8, no. 1 (2009): 47–64.

Avrutin, Eugene, ed. *Photographing the Jewish Nation: Pictures from S. An-sky's Ethnographic Expeditions*. Hanover, NH: University Press of New England, 2009.

Bajohr, Frank. *"Unser Hotel ist Judenfrei."Bäder-Antisemitismus im 19. und 20. Jahrhundert*. Frankfurt: Fischer Taschenbuch, 2003.

Band, Arnold J. "Refractions of the Blood Libel in Modern Literature." In *Studies in Modern Jewish Literature* (Philadelphia: Jewish Publication Society, 2003), 317–38.

Banik-Schweitzer, Renate. "Vienna: Development of the City." In *Architecture in Vienna*, edited by August Sarnitz, 8–22. Vienna: Springer, 1998.

Barkai, A. "The Austrian Social Democrats and the Jews." *Wiener Library Bulletin*, n.s., 18, Part 1 (1970): 31–40; n.s., 19, Part 2 (1970): 16–21.

Barker, Andrew. "The Politics of Austrian Literature." In Kohl and Robertson, *A History of Austrian Literature*, 107–25.

Bayerdörfer, Hans-Peter. "Jewish Cabaret Artists before 1933." In Malkin and Rokem, *Jews and the Making of Modern German Theatre*, 132–50.

———. "Jüdisches Theater der Zwischenkriegszeit—östliche Wurzeln, westliche Ziele? Umrisse einer Kontroverse." In *Theater der Region—Theater Europas. Kongress der Gesellschaft für Theaterwissenschaft*, edited by Andreas Kotte, 25–45. Basel: Verlag Theaterkultur, 1995.

Bechtel, Delphine. "Yiddish Theater and Its Impact on the German and Austrian Stage." In Malkin and Rokem, *Jews and the Making of Modern German Theatre*, 77–98.

Beckermann, Ruth, ed. *Die Mazzesinsel: Juden in der Wiener Leopoldstadt 1918–1938*. Vienna: Löcker, 1984.

Bedoire, Fredric. *The Jewish Contribution to Modern Architecture 1830–1930*. Jersey City, NJ: Ktav, 2004.

Beier, Nikolaj. *"Vor allem bin ich ich—": Judentum, Akkulturation und Antisemitismus in Arthur Schnitzlers Leben und Werk*. Göttingen: Wallstein, 2008.

Békési, Sándor. "Shrinking City? Stadtbilder und Stadtentwicklung im Wien der Zwischenkriegszeit." In Kos, *Kampf um die Stadt*, 98–107.

Beller, Steven. "Is There a Jewish Aspect to Modern Austrian Identity?" In Mittelmann and Wallas, *Österreich-Konzeptionen*, 43–52.

———. "Knowing your Elephant: Why Jewish Studies Is Not the same as Judaistik, and Why That Is a Good Thing." In *Jüdische Studien: Reflexionen zu Theorie und Praxis eines wissenschaftlichen Feldes. Schriften des Centrums für Jüdische Studien 4*, edited by Klaus Hoedl, 13–23. Innsbruck: Studienverlag, 2003.

———. "Patriotism and the National Identity of Habsburg Jewry, 1860–1914." *Leo Baeck Institute Year-Book* 41(1996): 215–38.

———, ed. *Rethinking Vienna 1900*. New York: Berghahn, 2001.

———. "Was *nicht* im Baedeker steht: Juden und andere Österreicher im Wien der Zwischenkriegszeit." In Stern and Eichinger, *Wien und die jüdische Erfahrung*, 1–16.

———. *Vienna and the Jews, 1867–1938: A Cultural History*. New York: Cambridge University Press, 1989.

Beniston, Judith. "Cultural Politics in the First Republic: Hans Brecka and the 'Kunststelle für christliche Volksbildung.'" In *Catholicism and Austrian Culture*, edited by Judith Beniston and Ritchie Robertson, 101–18. Edinburgh: Edinburgh University Press, 1999.

———. "Drama in Austria, 1918–45." In Kohl and Robertson, *A History of Austrian Literature*, 21–52.

———. "Hofmannsthal and the Salzburg Festival." In *A Companion to the Works of Hugo von Hofmannsthal*, edited by Thomas A. Kovach, 159–80. Rochester, NY: Camden House, 2002.

———. "Schnitzler in Red Vienna." In *Arthur Schnitzler: Zeitgenossenschaften/Contemporaneities*, edited by Ian Foster and Florian Krobb, 217–31. Bern: Peter Lang, 2002.

———. *Welttheater: Hofmannsthal, Richard von Kralik, and the Revival of Catholic Drama in Austria 1890–1934*. London: Maney, 1998.

Bent, Ian. "'That bright new light': Schenker, Universal Edition, and the Origins of the Erläuterung series, 1901–1910." *Journal of the American Musicological Society* 58 (2005): 69–138.

Berkley, George E. *Vienna and Its Jews: The Tragedy of Success, 1880s–1980s*. Cambridge, MA: Abt Books/Madison Books, 1988.

Bernstein, Michael André. "Victims-in-Waiting: Backshadowing and the Representation of European Jewry." *New Literary History* 29, no. 4 (Autumn 1998): 625–51.

Betz, Susanne Helene, Monika Löscher, and Pia Schölnberger. *". . . m . . . ehr als ein Sportsverein": 100 Jahre Hakoah Wien 1909–2009*. Vienna: Studienverlag, 2009.

Biale, David. *Blood and Belief: The Circulation of a Symbol between Jews and Christians*. Berkeley: University of California Press, 2007.

Blaschke, Olaf. *Katholizismus und Antisemitismus im deutschen Kaiserreich*. Göttingen: Vandenhoeck & Rupprecht, 1999.

Blau, Eve. *The Architecture of Red Vienna 1919–1934*. Cambridge: MIT University Press, 1999.

Botstein, Leon. "Gedanken zu Heinrich Schenkers jüdischer Identität." In *Rebell und Visionär: Heinrich Schenker in Wien*, edited by Evelyn Fink, 11–17. Vienna: Lafite, 2003.

———. *Judentum und Modernität: Essays zur Rolle der Juden in der deutschen und österreichischen Kultur, 1848 bis 1938*. Vienna: Böhlau, 1991.

———. "Musikkultur und die Juden: Wien als Beispiel." In *Judentum und Modernität*, 133–37.

———. "Sozialgeschichte und die Politik des Ästhetischen: Juden und Musik in Wien 1870–1938." In Botstein and Hanak, *Quasi una fantasia*, 43–64.

Botstein, Leon, and Werner Hanak, eds. *Quasi una fantasia: Juden und die Musikstadt Wien*. Hofheim: Wolke Verlag, 2003. Exhibition catalogue.

Botz, Gerhard. "'Deutsche Auferstehung.' Die Verführung des greisen Tonsetzers Franz Schmidt." In Ottner, *Studien zu Franz Schmidt*, 35–65.

Bowman, William D. "Regional History and the Austrian Nation." *Journal of Modern History* 67, no. 4 (1995): 873–97.

Boyer, John W. *Culture and Political Crisis in Vienna: Christian Socialism in Power, 1897–1918*. Chicago: University of Chicago Press, 1995.

———. "The End of an Old Regime: Visions of Political Reform in Late Imperial Austria." *Journal of Modern History* 58, no. 1 (1986): 159–93.

———. *Political Radicalism in Late Imperial Vienna: Origins of the Christian Social Movement, 1848–1897*. Chicago: University of Chicago Press, 1981.

Brandstötter, Rudolf. "Dr. Walter Riehl und die Geschichte der Nationalsozialistischen Bewegung in Österreich." Ph. D. diss., University of Vienna, 1969.

Brenner, David A. "Neglected 'Women's' Texts and Contexts: Vicki Baum's Jewish Ghetto Stories." *Women in German Yearbook* 13 (1997): 101–19.

Brenner, Michael, and Gideon Reuveni, eds. *Emancipation through Muscles: Jews and Sports in Europe*. Lincoln: University of Nebraska Press, 2006.

Brenner, Michael, and Derek Jonathan Penslar, eds. *In Search of Jewish Community: Jewish Identities in Germany and Austria, 1918–1933*. Bloomington: Indiana University Press, 1998.

Brenner, Michael. *The Renaissance of Jewish Culture in Weimar Germany*. New Haven, CT: Yale University Press, 1998.

Bruckmüller, Ernst. *The Austrian Nation: Cultural Consciousness and Socio-Political Processes*. Riverside, CA: Ariadne, 1996.

Bruegel, J.W. "The Antisemitism of the Austrian Socialists, A Reassessment." *Wiener Library Bulletin*, n.s., 24/25 (1972): 39–45.

Buerkle, Darcy. "Caught in the Act. Norbert Elias, Emotion and the Ancient Law." *Journal of Modern Jewish Studies* 8, no. 1 (2009): 83–102.

———. "Gendered Spectatorship, Jewish Women, and Psychological Advertising in Weimar Germany." *Women's History Review* 15, no. 4 (2006): 625–36.

———. "Historical Effacements: Facing Charlotte Salomon." In *Reading Charlotte Salomon*, edited by Michael P. Steinberg and Monica Bohm-Duchen, 73–87. Ithaca, NY: Cornell University Press, 2006.

Bunzl, John. "Arbeiterbewegung, 'Judenfrage' und Antisemitismus: am Beispiel des Wiener Bezirks Leopoldstadt." In *Bewegung und Klasse: Studien zur österreichischen Arbeitergeschichte*, edited by Gerhard Botz, Hans Hautmann, Helmut Konrad, and Josef Wiedenholzer, 743–63. Vienna: Europaverlag, 1979.

———. "Hakoah Vienna: Reflections on a Legend." In Brenner and Reuveni, *Emancipation through Muscles*, 106–18.

———. *Hoppauf Hakoah: Jüdischer Sport in Österreich: Von den Anfängen bis in die Gegenwart*. Vienna: Janus, 1987.

Butler, Judith. "The Charge of Anti-Semitism: The Risks of Public Critique." In *Prophets Outcast: A Century of Dissident Jewish Writing about Zionism and Israel*, edited by Adam Schatz, 357–70. New York: Nation Books, 2004.

———. *Gender Trouble: Feminism and the Subversion of Identity*. New York: Routledge, 1999.

———. *Undoing Gender*. New York: Routledge, 2004.

Certeau, Michel de. *The Practice of Everyday Life*. Berkeley: University of California Press, 1984.

Coen, Deborah R. *Vienna in the Age of Uncertainty: Science, Liberalism and Private Life*. Chicago: University of Chicago Press, 2007.

Cole, Laurence. *Andreas Hofer: The Social and Cultural Construction of a National Myth in Tirol, 1809–1904*. Florence: European University Institute, 1994.

Cook, Nicholas. *The Schenker Project: Culture, Race, and Music Theory in Fin-de-Siècle Vienna*. New York: Oxford University Press, 2007.

Corino, Karl. "Der Fall Robert Musil." In *Vertriebene Vernunft*, vol. 2, *Emigration und Exil österreichischer Wissenschaft 1930–1940*, edited by Friedrich Stadler, 538–45. Münster: LIT, 2004.

Czeike, Felix. *Wien wie es war: Ein Nachschlagewerk für Freunde des alten und neuen Wien*. Vienna: Fritz Molden, 1965.

Dahlmann, Dittmar, and Anke Hilbrenner, eds. *Zwischen großen Erwartungen und bösem Erwachen: Juden, Politik und Antisemitismus in Ost- und Südeuropa, 1918–1945*. Paderborn: Ferdinand Schöningh, 2010.

Dahms, Hans-Joachim. "The Emigration of the Vienna Circle." In *Vertreibung der Vernunft: The Cultural Exodus from Austria*, edited by Friedrich Stadler and Peter Weibel, 57–79. Vienna: Springer, 1995.

Dalinger, Brigitte. "Popular Jewish Drama in Vienna in the 1920s." In *Jewish Theatre: A Global View*, edited by Edna Nahshon, 175–96. Leiden: Brill, 2009.

———. "Yiddish Theater in Vienna, 1880–1938." In *Yiddish Theatre: New Approaches*, edited by Joel Berkowitz, 107–17. Oxford: Littman Library, 2003.

———. *Verloschene Sterne: Geschichte des jüdischen Theaters in Wien*. Vienna: Picus, 1998.

Dalinger, Brigitte, and Silvia Stastny. "'. . . und 68 weitere Darsteller': Verbindungen zwischen jüdischen Filmen und jüdischen Theater im Wien der 20er Jahre." In Geser and Loacker, *Die Stadt ohne Juden*, 213–39.

Dassanowsky, Robert. *Austrian Cinema: A History*. Jefferson, NC: McFarland, 2005.

Davis, Belinda. "Food Scarcity and the Empowerment of the Female Consumer in World War I Berlin." In *The Sex of Things: Gender and Consumption in Historical Perspective*, edited by Victoria de Grazia and Ellen Furlough, 287–310. Berkeley: University of California Press, 1996.

Deutsch, Nathaniel. *The Jewish Dark Continent: Life and Death in the Russian Pale of Settlement*. Cambridge: Harvard University Press, 2011.

Donahue, William Collins. *The End of Modernism: Canetti's Auto-da-Fé*. Chapel Hill: University of North Carolina Press, 2001.

Dopsch, Heinz, and Hans Spatzenegger, eds. *Geschichte Salzburgs: Stadt und Land*, vol. 2, pt. 2, *Neuzeit und Zeitgeschichte*. Salzburg: Universitatsverlag Anton Pustet, 1988.

Dundes, Alan, ed. *The Blood Libel Legend: A Casebook in Anti-Semitic Folklore*. Madison: University of Wisconsin Press, 1991.

Eksteins, Modris. *Rites of Spring: The Great War and the Birth of the Modern Age*. New York: Mariner, 1989.

Eddy, Beverley Driver. *Felix Salten: Man of Many Faces*. Riverside, CA: Ariadne, 2010.

Eidherr, Armin. "Abraham Mosche Fuchs: Der Chronist des Wiener Vorstadtelends und des galizischen Landlebens." In Fuchs, *Unter der Brücke*, 91–109.

Eidherr, Armin, and Karl Müller. *Zwischenwelt: Jiddische Kultur und Literatur aus Österreich*. Klagenfurt: Theodor Kramer Gesellschaft and Drava, 2003.

Ellmauer, Daniela, Helga Embacher, and Albert Lichtblau, eds. *Geduldet, Geschmäht und Vertrieben: Salzburger Juden erzählen*. Salzburg: Otto Müller, 1998.

Embacher, Helga. "Exil als neue Heimat." In *Ein ewiges Dennoch: 125 Jahre Juden in Salzburg*, edited by Marko M. Feingold, 435–59. Vienna: Böhlau, 1993.

———. "Lenin oder Jabotinsky? Jüdische Identitätssuche in Salzburg nach dem ersten Weltkrieg." In *Deutsch-Jüdische Jugendliche im "Zeitalter der Jugend,"* edited by Yotam Hotam, 181–92. Göttingen: Vandenhoeck & Ruprecht, 2009.

Epler, Ernst. "Du bist ein Jud . . ." In Beckermann, *Die Mazzesinsel*, 74–81.

Eppel, Peter, Bernhard Hachleitner, Werner Michael Schwarz, and Georg Spitaler, eds. *Wo die Wuchtel fliegt: Legendäre Orte des Wiener Fußballs*. Vienna: Löcker, 2008. Exhibition catalogue.

Erb, Rainer, ed. *Die Legende vom Ritualmord. Zur Geschichte der Blutbeschuldigung gegen Juden*. Berlin: Metropol, 1993.

Ettl, Maria, and Gerhard Murauer, eds. *Hans Kelsen und die Bundesverfassung: Geschichte einer Josefstädter Karriere*. Vienna: Bezirksmuseum Josefstadt, 2010. Exhibition catalogue.

Exenberger, Herbert. *Gleich dem kleinen Häuflein der Makkabäer: Die jüdische Gemeinde in Simmering, 1848–1945*. Vienna: Mandelbaum, 2009.

Exner, Gudrun, Josef Kytir, and Alexander Pinwinkler, eds. *Bevölkerungswissenschaft in Österreich in der Zwischenkriegszeit (1918–1938): Personen, Institutionen, Diskurse*. Vienna: Böhlau, 2004.

Fellner, Günter. *Antisemitismus in Salzburg, 1918–1938*. Vienna: Geyer-Edition, 1979.

Feurstein, Michaela, and Gerhard Milchram. *Jewish Vienna*. Vienna: Mandelbaum, 2004.

Fonrobert, Charlotte Elisheva. "The Political Symbolism of the Eruv." *Jewish Social Studies* 11, no. 3 (Spring/Summer 2005): 9–35.

Fonrobert, Charlotte Elisheva, and Vered Shemtov. "Introduction: Jewish Conceptions and Practices of Space." *Jewish Social Studies* 11, no. 3 (2005): 1–8.

Fraenkel, Josef, ed. *The Jews of Austria: Essays on their Life, History and Destruction*. London: Vallentine, Mitchell 1967.

Fraisl, Bettina. *Körper und Text: (De-) Konstruktionen von Weiblichkeit und Leiblichkeit bei Mela Hartwig*. Vienna: Passagen, 2002.

Frame, Lynne. "Gretchen, Girl, Garçonne? Weimar Science and Popular Culture in Search of the Ideal New Woman." In *Women in the Metropolis: Gender and Modernity in Weimar Culture*, edited by Katharina von Ankum, 12–40. Berkeley: University of California Press, 1997.

Frank, Alison. "The Pleasant and the Useful: Pilgrimage and Tourism in Habsburg Mariazell." *Austrian History Yearbook* 40 (2009): 157–82.

Freidenreich, Harriet Pass. *Female, Jewish, Educated: The Lives of Central European University Women*. Bloomington: Indiana University Press, 2002.

———. *Jewish Politics in Vienna, 1918–1938*. Bloomington: Indiana University Press, 1991.

Fritz, Wolfgang. *Der Kopf des Asiaten Breitner: Politik und Ökonomie im roten Wien*. Vienna, Löcker, 2000.

Fuhrich-Leisler, Edda. "Max Reinhardt und Wien." In *Wien 1870–1930: Traum und Wirklichkeit*. Salzburg: Residenz, 1984.

Ganeva, Mila. *Women in Weimar Fashion: Discourses and Displays in German Culture, 1918–1933*. Rochester, NY: Camden House, 2008.

Garb, Tamar. "Modernity, Identity, Textuality." In *The Jew in the Text: Modernity and the Construction of Identity*, edited by Linda Nochlin and Tamar Garb, 20–30. London: Thames and Hudson: 1995.

Gay, Peter. *A Godless Jew: Freud, Atheism and the Making of Psychoanalysis*. New Haven, CT: Yale University Press, 1987.

Geehr, Richard S. *Adam Müller-Guttenbrunn and the Aryan Theater of Vienna: 1898–1903: The Approach of Cultural Fascism*. Göppingen: Kümmerle, 1973.

———. *Karl Lueger: Mayor of Fin-de-Siècle Vienna*. Detroit, MI: Wayne State University Press, 1990.

Geier, Manfred. *Der Wiener Kreis*. Reinbek bei Hamburg: Rowohlt, 1998.

Gelber, Mark H. "*Juden auf Wanderschaft* und die Rhetoriker der Ost-West Debatte im Werk Joseph Roths." In *Joseph Roth: Interpretation-Kritik-Rezeption*, edited by Michael Kessler and Fritz Hackert, 127–35. Tübingen: Stauffenburg 1990.

George, Alys. "Hollywood on the Danube? Vienna and Austrian Silent Film of the 1920s." In Holmes and Silverman, *Interwar Vienna: Culture between Tradition and Modernity*, 143–60.

Geser, Guntram and Armin Loacker, eds. *Die Stadt ohne Juden*. Vienna: Filmarchiv Austria, 2000.

Gibbs, Helga. *Leopoldstadt: Kleine Welt am großen Strom*. Vienna: Mohl, 1997.

Gillerman, Sharon. "Samson in Vienna: The Theatrics of Jewish Masculinity." *Jewish Social Studies* 9, no. 2 (2003): 65–98.

Gillman, Abigail. *Viennese Jewish Modernism: Freud, Hofmannsthal, Beer-Hofmann and Schnitzler*. University Park: Penn State University Press, 2009.

Gilman, Sander L. *The Case of Sigmund Freud: Medicine and Identity at the Fin de Siècle*. Baltimore: Johns Hopkins University Press, 1993.

———. "Freud's Jewish Identity." Review of *A Godless Jew* and *Freud: A Life for our Time*, by Peter Gay. In *Vienna 1900: From Altenberg to Wittgenstein*, edited by Edward Timms and Ritchie Robertson, 174–77. Edinburgh: Edinburgh University Press, 1990.

———. *Franz Kafka, The Jewish Patient*. New York: Routledge, 1995.

———. *Freud, Race, and Gender*. Princeton: Princeton University Press, 1993.

———. *The Jews' Body*. New York: New York University Press, 1991.

———. *Jewish Self-Hatred: Anti-Semitism and the Hidden Language of the Jews*. Baltimore: Johns Hopkins University Press, 1985.

Göbel, Helmut. "Bemerkungen zum verdeckten Judentum in Veza Canettis *Die gelbe Straße*." In *"Ein Dichter braucht Ahnen." Elias Canetti und die europäische Tradition*, edited by Gerald Stieg and Jean-Marie Valentin, 283–95. Bern: Peter Lang, 1997.

Gradner, Margarete. "Staatsbürger und Ausländer: Zum Umgang Österreichs mit den jüdischen Flüchtlingen nach 1918." In *Asylland wider Willen: Flüchtlinge in Österreich im europäischen Kontext seit 1914*, edited by Gernot Heiss and Oliver Rathkolb, 60–86. Vienna: Ludwig-Boltzmann-Institut für Geschichte und Gesellschaft, 1995.

Gronberg, Tag. *Vienna: City of Modernity*. Bern: Peter Lang, 2007.

Grossmann, Atina. "The New Woman and the Rationalization of Sexuality in Weimar Germany." In *Powers of Desire: The Politics of Sexuality*, edited by Ann Snitow, Christine Stansel, and Sharon Thompson, 153–71. New York: Monthly Review Press, 1983.

Gruber, Helmut. *Red Vienna: Experiment in Working-Class Culture, 1919–1934*. New York: Oxford University Press, 1991.

Haas, Hanns. "Der Traum vom Dazugehören—Juden auf Sommerfrische." In Kriechbaumer, *Der Geschmack der Vergänglichkeit*, 41–58.

Hacohen, Malachi. "Dilemmas of Cosmopolitanism: Karl Popper, Jewish Identity and 'Central European Culture,'" *Journal of Modern History* 72 (March 1999): 105–49.

———. "Kosmopoliten in einer ethnonationalen Zeit? Juden und Österreicher in der ersten Republik." In Konrad und Maderthaner, . . . D*er Rest ist Österreich*, vol. 1, 281–316.

———. *Karl Popper: The Formative Years, 1902–1945*. Cambridge: Cambridge University Press, 2000.

Hadamowsky, Franz. "Reinhardt und Salzburg." In *Katalog-Ausstellung Hugo von Hofmannsthal*. Salzburg: Amt der Salzburger Landesregierung, 1959.

Hainisch, Meir. "Galician Jews in Vienna." In Fraenkel, *The Jews of Austria*, 361–73.

Hall, Murray G. "'Hinaus mit den Juden!' Von Graffiti und der Zeitung bis zur Leinwand." In Stern and Eichinger, *Wien und die jüdische Erfahrung*, 59–70.

———. "Publishing in the Thirties in Vienna: The Paul Zsolnay Verlag." In Segar and Warren, *Austria in the Thirties: Culture and Politics*, 204–18.

———. "Entgangene Trophäen I: Die Privatbibliothek von Max Reinhardt." In *"A . . . Allerlei für die Nationalbibliothek zu ergattern . . .": Eine österreichische Institution in der NS-Zeit*, edited by Murray G. Hall and Christina Köstner, 247–52. Vienna: Böhlau, 2006.

———. "Hugo Bettauer." In *Elektrische Schatten: Beiträge zur österreichischen Stummfilmgeschichte*, edited by Francesco Bono, Paolo Caneppele,. and Günter Kren, 149–68. Vienna: Filmarchiv, 1999.

———. "Publishers and Institutions in Austria, 1918–1945." In Kohl and Robertson, *A History of Austrian Literature*, 75–86.

———. *Der Fall Bettauer*. Vienna: Löcker, 1978.

———. *Der Paul Zsolnay Verlag: Von der Gründung bis zur Rückkehr aus dem Exil.* Tübingen: Niemeyer, 1994.

———. *Österreichische Verlagsgeschichte 1918–1938*, vol. 1. http://www.verlagsgeschichte.murrayhall.com.

Hall, Murray G., and Herbert Ohrlinger. *Der Paul Zsolnay Verlag 1924–1999. Dokumente und Zeugnisse*. Vienna: Zsolnay, 1999.

Hammel, Andrea and Godela Weiss-Sussex, eds. *"Not an Essence but a Positioning": German-Jewish Women Writers (1900–1938)*. Munich: Meidenbauer, 2009.

Hanak, Werner, and Mechtild Widrich, ed. *Wien II: Leopoldstadt, Die andere Heimatkunde*. Vienna: Brandstätter, 1999.

Harrowitz, Nancy A. *Antisemitism, Misogyny, and the Logic of Cultural Difference*. Lincoln: University of Nebraska Press, 1995.

Harrowitz, Nancy A., and Barbara Hymans, eds. *Jews and Gender, Responses to Otto Weininger*. Philadelphia: Temple University Press, 1995.

Harshav, Benjamin, ed. *The Moscow Yiddish Theater: Art on Stage in the Time of Revolution*. New Haven, CT: Yale University Press, 2008.

Hartston, Barnet. *Sensationalizing the Jewish Question: Anti-Semitic Trials and the Press in the Early German Empire*. Leiden: Brill, 2005.

Haslinger, Peter. "Building a Regional Identity: The Burgenland 1921–1938." *Austrian History Yearbook* 32 (2001): 105–23.

Healy, Maureen. "Becoming Austrian: Women, the State, and Citizenship in World War I." *Central European History* 35, no. 1 (2002): 1–35.

———. *Vienna and the Fall of the Habsburg Empire: Total War and Everyday Life in World War I*. Cambridge: Cambridge University Press, 2004.

Hecht, Dieter J. "Die Jüdischnationale Partei in Österreich 1918–1938." *Chilufim: Zeitschrift für jüdische Kulturgeschichte* 7 (2009): 109–36.

———. "Die Stimme und Wahrheit der Jüdischen Welt." In Stern and Eichinger, *Wien und die jüdische Erfahrung*, 99–114.

———. "Die Weltkongresse jüdischer Frauen in der Zwischenkriegszeit, Wien 1923, Hamburg 1929." In *Geschlecht, Religion und Engagement: Die jüdsiche Frauenbewegung im deutschsprachigen Raum*, edited by Edith Saurer and Margarete Grandner, 123–56. Vienna: Böhlau, 2005.

———. *Zwischen Feminismus und Zionismus: Die Biographie einer Wiener Jüdin, Anitta Müller-Cohen (1890–1962)*. Vienna: Böhlau, 2008.

Heer, Friedrich. "Die Beiden Republiken." In *Wien: Spektrum einer Stadt*, edited by Hilde Spiel, 342–61. Wien: Jugend und Volk, 1971.

———. *Der Glaube des Adolf Hitler: Anatomie einer politischen Religiosität*. Munich: Bechtle, 1968.

Hemmerle, Joachim. "Jiddisches Theater im Spiegel deutschsprachiger Kritik von der Jahrhundertwende bis 1928: Eine Dokumentation." In *Beter und Rebellen: Aus 1000 Jahren Judentum in Polen*, edited by Michael Brocke, 277–311. Frankfurt: Deutscher Koordinierungsrat der Gesellschaften für christlich-jüdische Zusammenarbeit, 1983.

Herzog, Hillary Hope. *"Vienna Is Different:" Jewish Writers in Austria from the Fin de Siècle to the Present*. New York: Berghahn, 2011.

Hödl, Klaus. "The Blurring of Distinction: Performance and Jewish Identities in Late Nineteenth-Century Vienna." *European Journal of Jewish Studies* (November 2009): 229–50.

———. *Wiener Juden—jüdische Wiener: Identität, Gedächtnis und Performanz im 19. Jahrhundert*. Innsbruck: Studienverlag, 2006.

Hoffmann-Holter, Beatrix. *"Abreisendmachung": Jüdische Kriegsflüchtlinge in Wien 1914 bis 1923*. Vienna: Böhlau, 1995.

———. "'Ostjuden hinaus!' Jüdische Kriegsflüchtlinge in Wien 1914–1924." In Geser and Loacker, *Die Stadt ohne Juden*, 301–41.

Hofinger, Johannes. *Die Akte Leopoldskron: Max Reinhardt—Das Schloss—Arisierung & Restitution*. Salzburg: Verlag Anton Pustet, 2005.

Hofinger, Niko. "'. . . Man spricht nicht gerne von dem Prozeß, es sind noch zu viele Fremde da': Die Halsmann-Affäre 1928–1930." In *Politische Skandale und Affären in Österreich: Von Mayerling bis Waldheim*, edited by Michael Gehler and Hubert Sickinger, 194–221. Thaur, AT: Kulturverlag, 1995.

———. "'Unser Lösung ist: Tirol den Tirolern!' Antisemitism in Tirol 1918–1938." *zeitgeschichte* 21, no. 3–4 (1994): 83–108.

Holmes, Deborah. "Die neue Pädagogik und die Intellektuellen: Der Beitrag Eugenie Schwarzwalds zur Reformpädagogik in Österreich." In Konrad and Maderthaner, *. . . der Rest ist Österreich*, vol. 2, 233–50.

Holmes, Deborah, and Lisa Silverman, eds. *Interwar Vienna: Culture between Tradition and Modernity*. Rochester, NY: Camden House, 2009.

Höyng, Peter. "A Dream of a White Vienna after World War I: Hugo Bettauer's The City without Jews and The Blue Stain." In *At Home and Abroad: Historicizing Twentieth-Century Whiteness in Literature and Performance*, edited by La Vinia Delois Jennings, 29–60. Knoxville: University of Tennessee Press, 2009.

Hsia, R. Po-chia. "The Jews and the Emperors." In *State and Society in Early Modern Austria*, edited by Charles W. Ingrao, 71–80. West Lafayette, IN: Purdue University Press, 1994.

Hyman, Paula E. *Gender and Assimilation in Modern Jewish History: The Roles and Representation of Women*. Seattle: University of Washington Press, 1995.

Janik, Allan, and Stephan Toulmin. *Wittgenstein's Vienna*. New York: Simon and Schuster, 1973.

Jelavich, Peter. "How 'Jewish' Was Theatre in Imperial Berlin?" In Malkin and Rokem, *Jews and the Making of Modern German Theatre*, 39–58.

John, Michael. "'We Do Not Even Possess Our Selves': On Identity and Ethnicity in Austria, 1880–1937." *Austrian History Yearbook* 30 (1999): 17–64.

———. "Aggressiver Antisemitismus im österreichischen Sportgeschehen der Zwischenkriegszeit: Manifestationen und Reaktionen anhand ausgewählter Beispiele." *zeitgeschichte* 25, no. 3 (1999): 203–23.

———. "Ein 'kultureller Code'? Antisemitismus im österreichischen Sport der ersten Republik." In Brenner and Reuveni, *Emanzipation durch Muskelkraft*, 121–42.

Johnston, William H. *The Austrian Mind: An Intellectual and Social History, 1848–1938*. Berkeley: University of California Press, 1972.

———. *Der österreichische Mensch: Kulturgeschichte der Eigenart Österreichs*. Vienna: Böhlau, 2010.

Jonsson, Stefan. *Subject without Nation: Robert Musil and the History of Modern Identity*. Durham, NC: Duke University Press, 2000.

Kadrnoska, Franz, ed. *Aufbruch und Untergang: Österreichische Kultur zwischen 1918 und 1938*. Vienna: Europaverlag, 1981.

Kann, Robert A. *A History of the Habsburg Empire, 1526–1918*. Berkeley: University of California Press, 1974.

Kaut, Josef. *Festspiele in Salzburg*. Salzburg: Residenz, 1965.

Kieval, Hillel. "Representation and Knowledge in Medieval and Modern Accounts of Jewish Ritual Murder." *Jewish Social Studies* 1, no. 1 (1994): 52–72.

King, Lynda. *Best-sellers by Design: Vicki Baum and the House of Ullstein*. Detroit, MI: Wayne State University Press, 1988.

Klösch, Christian. "'Wien, das fidele Grab an der Donau': Der Beitrag von Juden zu Kabarett und Kleinkunst im Wien der Zwischenkriegszeit." In Riedl, *Wien, Stadt der Juden*, 198–208.

Kofler, Michael, Judith Pühringer, and Georg Traska, eds. *Das Dreieck meiner Kindheit: Eine jüdische Vorstadtgemeinde in Wien*. Vienna: Mandelbaum, 2008.

Kohl, Katrin, and Ritchie Robertson, eds. *A History of Austrian Literature 1918–2000*. Rochester, NY: Camden House, 2006.

Kohlbauer-Fritz, Gabriele, ed. and trans. *In a Schtodt woss schtarbt/In einer Stadt, die stirbt. Jiddische Lyrik aus Wien*. Vienna: Picus, 1995.

Kohlbauer-Fritz, Gabriele. "Das Bild Wiens in der jiddischen Literatur." In Eidherr and Müller, *Zwischenwelt*, 154–66.

———. "Jiddische Subkultur in Wien." In *Ist jetzt hier der wahre Heimat? Östjüdische Einwanderung nach Wien*, edited by Peter Bettelheim and Michael Ley, 89–115. Vienna: Picus, 1993.

Koller, Christian. "'. . . Der Wiener Judenstaat, von dem wir uns unter allen Umständen trennen wollen': Die Vorarlberger Anschlussbewegung an die Schweiz," In Konrad and Maderthaner, *. . . der Rest ist Österreich*. Vol. 1, 83–102.

Konrad, Helmut, and Wolfgang Maderthaner, eds. . . . *d . . .* D*er Rest ist Österreich: Das Werden der ersten Republik*, vols. 1 and 2. Vienna: Carl Gerold's Sohn 2008.

Kos, Wolfgang, ed. *Kampf um die Stadt*. Vienna: Czernin, 2010. Exhibition catalogue.

Kosenina, Alexander. "Veza Canetti—Fundstücke aus dem literarischen Nachlass." In Hammel and Weiss-Sussex, *"Not an Essence, but a Positioning,"* 181–96.

Kriechbaumer, Robert, ed. *Der Geschmack der Vergänglichkeit: Jüdische Sommerfrische in Salzburg*. Vienna: Böhlau, 2002.

Krobb, Florian. "'Vienna goes to pot without Jews:' Hugo Bettauer's *Die Stadt ohne Juden (The City without Jews)*." *Jewish Quarterly* 41, no. 2 (1994): 17–20.

Langmuir, Gavin I. *Toward a Definition of Antisemitism*. Berkeley: University of California Press, 1996.

Lappin, Eleonore. "Jüdische Lebenserinnerungen: Rekonstruktionen von jüdischer Kindheit und Jugend im Wien der Zwischenkriegzeit." In Stern and Eichinger, *Wien und die jüdische Erfahrung*, 17–38.

Lechner, Annette. "Die Wiener Verlagsbuchhandlung Anzengruber-Verlag, Brüder Suschitzky (1901–1938) im Spiegel der Zeit." M.A. Diplomarbeit. University of Vienna, 1994.

Lefebvre, Henri. *The Production of Space*. Translated by Donald Nicholson-Smith. Malden, MA: Blackwell Publishers, 1984.

Le Rider, Jacques. "Hugo von Hofmannsthal and the Austrian Idea of Central Europe." *Austrian Studies 5: The Habsburg Legacy* (1994): 121–35.

Leftwich, Josef. "Thinking of Vienna." In Fraenkel, *The Jews of Austria*, 231–39.

Lerner, Paul. "Consuming Pathologies: Kleptomania, Magazinitis, and the Problem of Female Consumption in Wilhelmine and Weimar Germany." *WerkstattGeschichte* 42 (2006): 45–56.

———. "Consuming Powers: The 'Jewish Department Store' in German Politics and Culture." In Reuveni and Wobick-Segev, *The Economy in Jewish History*, 135–54.

Levy, Richard S., ed. *A Historical Encyclopedia of Prejudice and Antisemitism*. Santa Barbara, CA: ABC-CLIO, 2005.

Lichtblau, Albert. "Antisemitismus 1900–1938." In Stern and Eichinger, *Wien und die jüdische Erfahrung*, 39–58.

———. "Die Debatten über die Ritualmordbeschuldigungen im österreichischen Abgeordnetenhaus am Ende des 19. Jahrhunderts." In Erb, *Die Legende vom Ritualmord*, 267–292.

———. "Das fragile Korsett der Koexistenz: Zum Verhältnis von jüdischer und nichtjüdischer Bevölkerung in Österreich 1918 bis 1938." In Dahlmann and Hilbrenner, *Zwischen großen Erwartungen und bösem Erwachen*, 31–51.

———. "Partizipation und Isolation: Juden in Österreich in den 'langen' 1920er Jahren." *Archiv für Sozialgeschichte* 37 (1997): 231–53.

Lichtblau, Albert, and Michael John. "Jewries in Galicia and Bukovina, in Lemberg and Czernowitz: Two Divergent Examples of Jewish Communities in the Far East of the Austro-Hungarian Monarchy." In *Jewries at the Frontier: Accommodation, Identity, Conflict*, edited by Sander L. Gilman and Milton Shain, 29–66. Urbana: University of Illinois Press, 1999.

Lipphardt, Anna, Julia Brauch, and Alexandra Nocke, eds. *Jewish Topographies: Visions of Space, Traditions of Place*. Aldershot: Ashgate, 2008.

Loacker, Armin. "Biografisches zu den Filmschaffenden sowie Haupt- und Nebendarstellern von Die Stadt ohne Juden." In Geser and Loacker, *Die Stadt ohne Juden*, 167–211.

———. "Werkstätten der Seh(n)sucht: Produktionsgeschichte und Produktionsstrukturen des monumentalen Antikfilms in Österreich." In *Imaginierte Antike: Österreichische Monumental-Stummfilme, Historienbilder und Geschichtskonstruktion in Sodom und Gomorrha, Samson und Delila, Die Sklavenkönigen und Salammbô*, edited by Armin Loacker and Ines Steiner, 21–62. Vienna: Filmarchiv Austria, 2002.

Loewy, Hanno, and Gerhard Milchram, eds. *"Hast du meine Alpen gesehen?" Eine jüdische Beziehungsgeschichte*. Vienna: Bücher Verlag Hohenems-Wien, 2009. Exhibition Catalogue.

Lotz-Rimbach, Renate. "Mord verjährt nicht: Psychogramm eines politischen Mordes." In *Stationen: Dem Philosophen und Physiker Moritz Schlick zum 125. Geburtstag*, edited by Friedrich Stadler and Hans Jürgen Wendel, 81–104. Vienna: Springer-Verlag 2009.

———. "Zur Biografie Leo Gabriels: Revision und Ergänzung der Selbstdarstellung eines Philosophen und Rektors der Universität Wien." *zeitgeschichte* 6, no. 31 (2004): 270–91.

Low, Setha M. *On the Plaza: The Politics of Public Space and Culture*. Austin: University of Texas Press, 2000.

Löwy, Michael. *Redemption and Utopia: Jewish Libertarian Thought in Central Europe, A Study in Elective Affinity*. Translated by Hope Heaney. London: Athlone, 1992.

Luft, David S. *Eros and Inwardness in Vienna: Weininger, Musil, Doderer*. Chicago: University of Chicago Press, 2003.

Lützeler, Paul Michael. *Hermann Broch und die Moderne. Romane, Menschenrecht, Biografie*. Munich: Wilhelm Fink, 2011.

Lynch, Kevin. *The Image of the City*. Boston: MIT Press, 1960.

Lynch, Kevin, with Alvin K. Lukashok. "Some Childhood Memories of the City." In *City Sense and City Design. Writings and Projects of Kevin Lynch*, edited by Tridib Banerjee and Michael Southworth, 154–73. Cambridge: MIT Press, 1996.

MacDonogh, Giles. *1938: Hitler's Gamble*. New York: Basic Books, 2009.

Maderegger, Sylvia. *Die Juden im österreichischen Ständestaat 1934–1938*. Vienna: Geyer, 1973.

Maderthaner, Wolfgang, and Lisa Silverman. "'Wiener Kreise': Jewishness, Politics and Culture in Interwar Vienna." In Holmes and Silverman, *Interwar Vienna*, 59–80.

Maderthaner, Wolfgang, and Lutz Musner. *Unruly Masses: The Other Side of Fin-de-Siècle Vienna*. New York: Berghahn, 2008.

Maislinger, Andreas, and Günther Pallaver. "Antisemitismus ohne Juden: Das Beispiel Tirol." In *Voll Leben und voll Tod ist diese Erde: Bilder aus der Geschichte der jüdischen Österreicher (1190 bis 1945)*, edited by Wolfgang Plat, 171–87. Vienna: Herold Verlag, 1988.

Malina, Peter. "Tatort: Philosophenstiege: Zur Ermordung von Moritz Schlick am 22. Juni 1936." In *Bewußtsein, Sprache und die Kunst: Metamorphosen der Wahrheit,* edited by Michael Benedikt and Rudolf Burger, 231–53. Vienna: Verlag der österreichischen Staatsdruckerei, 1988.

Malkin, Jeanette, and Freddie Rokem. *Jews and the Making of Modern Jewish Theatre*. Iowa City: University of Iowa Press, 2010.

Marquardt, Franka. *Erzählte Juden: Untersuchungen zu Thomas Manns Joseph und seine Brüder und Robert Musils Mann ohne Eigenschaften*. Münster: LIT Verlag, 2003.

Marschik, Matthias, and Georg Spitaler. "Leo Schidrowitz: Propagandist des Wiener Fußballs." *Sportzeiten* 2 (2008): 7–30.

Mathis, Franz. "'. . . Weil Herr Castiglioni in Österreich eben nicht verfolgt werden darf:' Ein Justizskandal und seine mediale Rezeption." In *Politische Skandale und Affären in Österreich: Von Mayerling bis Waldheim*, edited by Michael Gehler and Hubert Sickinger, 185–93. Thaur, AT: Kulturverlag, 1995.

Matless, David. "The Art of Right Living: Landscape and Citizenship, 1918–39." In *Mapping the Subject: Geographies of Cultural Transformation*. Edited by Steven Pile and Nigel Thrift, 93–122. London: Routledge, 1995.

Melichar, Peter. "Alter, neuer und verlorener Reichtum: Eine Skizze zu den großen Vermögen im Österreich der Zwischenkriegszeit." In *Armut und Reichtum in der Geschichte Österreichs*, edited by Ernst Bruckmüller, 166–92. Vienna: Böhlau, 2010.

Michael, Robert. *A History of Catholic Antisemitism: The Dark Side of the Church*. New York: Palgrave McMillan, 2008.

Mittelmann, Hanni. "Expressionismus und Judentum." In *Conditio Judaica: Judentum, Antisemitismus und deutschsprachige Literatur vom ersten Weltkrieg bis 1933/1938*, edited by Hans Otto Horch and Horst Denkler, 251–59. Tübingen: Niemeyer, 1993.

Mittelmann, Hanni, and Armin A. Wallas, eds. *Österreich-Konzeptionen und jüdisches Selbstverständnis: Identitäts-Transfigurationen im 19. und 20. Jahrhundert*. Tübingen: Niemeyer, 2001.

Morris, Leslie. "Reading the Face of the Other: Arnold Zweig's and Hermann Struck's *Das ostjüdische Antlitz*." In *The Imperialist Imagination: German Colonialism and Its Legacy*, edited by Sara Friedrichsmeyer, Sara Lennox, and Susanne Zantop, 189–204. Ann Arbor: University of Michigan Press, 1998.

Müller, Julius. "Die Bewohnerinnen der jüdsichen Gemeinde 'Sechshausn' und ihre mährischen 'Heimatstadt.'" In *Das Dreieck meiner Kindheit: Eine jüdische Vorstadtgemeinde in Wien*, edited by Michael Kofler, Judith Pühringer, and Georg Traska, 59–88. Vienna, Mandelbaum: 2008.

Müller, Karl. "Aspekte jiddischer Prosa am Beispiel von Abraham Mosche Fuchs." In Eidherr and Müller, *Zwischenwelt*, 167–84.

Müller, Karl, and Hans Wagener. *Österreich 1918 und die Folgen: Geschichte, Literatur, Theater und Film*. Vienna: Böhlau, 2009.

Müry, Andres. "Das Fest der Antimoderne." In *Kleine Salzburger Festspielgeschichte*, edited by Andres Müry, 9–66. Salzburg: Pustet, 2002.

Neuhauser-Pfeiffer, Waltraud, and Karl Ramsmaier. *Vergessene Spuren: Die Geschichte der Juden in Steyr*. Grünbach, AT: Buchverlag Franz Steinmassl, 1998.

Nottelmann, Nicole. *Die Karrieren der Vicki Baum: Eine Biographie*. Cologne: Kiepenheuer & Witsch, 2007.

Noveck, Beth. "Hugo Bettauer and the Political Culture of the First Republic." *Contemporary Austrian Studies* 3 (1995): 138–69.

Østrem, Eyolf, Mette Birkedal Bruun, Nils Holger Petersen, and Jens Fleischer, eds. *Genre and Ritual: The Cultural Heritage of Medieval Rituals*. Copenhagen: Museum Tusculanum Press, 2005.

Otte, Marline. *Jewish Identities in German Popular Entertainment*. New York: Cambridge University Press, 2006.

Ottner, Carmen. "Quellen zu Leben und Werk der letzten Lebensjahre Franz Schmidts." In *Studien zu Franz Schmidt*, Band 15*: Musik in Wien 1938–1945, Symposion 2004*, edited by Carmen Ottner, 73–112. Vienna: Franz-Schmidt-Gesellschaft, 2006.

Oxaal, Ivar. "The Jews of Young Hitler's Vienna: Historical and Sociological Aspects," in Oxaal, et. al., *Jews, Antisemitism, and Culture in Vienna*, 11–38.

Oxaal, Ivar, Michael Pollak, and Gerhard Botz, eds. *Jews, Antisemitism, and Culture in Vienna*. London: Routledge, 1987.

Pareigis, Christina. "Glasperlenhebräisch. Das Fremd-Wort in den Schriften von Klara Blum und Getrud Kolmar." In Hammel and Weiss-Sussex, *"Not an Essence, but a Positioning,"* 151–64.

Painter, Karen, ed. *Mahler and his World*. Princeton: Princeton University Press, 2002.

———. *Symphonic Aspirations: German Music and Politics, 1900–1945*. Cambridge, MA: Harvard University Press, 2007.

Pauley, Bruce F. *From Prejudice to Persecution: A History of Austrian Anti-Semitism*. Chapel Hill: University of North Carolina Press, 1992.

Peters, Julie Stone. "Legal Performance Good and Bad." *Law, Culture and the Humanities* 4, no. 2 (2008):179–200.

Petzoldt, Leander. "Religion between Sentiment and Protest: The Suspension of the Cult of 'Andreas[Anderl] von Rinn in the Tyrol." *International Folklore Review* 10 (1995): 21–34.

Pfeiffer, Peter C. "Hugo von Hofmannsthal Worries about His Jewish Mixed Ancestry." In *Yale Companion to Jewish Writing and Thought in German Culture, 1096–1996*, edited by Sander L. Gilman and Jack Zipes, 212–18. New Haven, CT: Yale University Press, 1997.

Pfoser, Alfred. "Der Wiener 'Reigen-Skandal': Sexualangst als politisches Syndrom der ersten Republik." In *Neuere Studien zur Arbeitergeschichte*, vol. 3, edited by Helmut Konrad and Wolfgang Maderthaner, 663–719. Vienna: Europaverlag, 1984.

———. *Literatur und Austromarxismus*. Vienna: Löcker, 1980.

Pinsker, Shachar M. *Literary Passports: The Making of Modernist Hebrew Fiction in Europe*. Stanford: Stanford University Press, 2011.

Pollack, Martin. *Anklage Vatermord: Der Fall Philipp Halsmann*. Vienna: Zsolnay, 2002.

Prawer, S.S. *Between Two Worlds: The Jewish Presence in German and Austrian Film, 1910–1933*. New York: Berghahn, 1995.

Preece, Julian. *The Rediscovered Writings of Veza Canetti: Out of the Shadows of a Husband*. Rochester, NY: Camden House, 2007.

Prell, Riv-Ellen. *Fighting to Become Americans: Jews, Gender, and the Anxiety of Assimilation*. Boston: Beacon, 1999.

Pulzer, Peter G.J. *The Rise of Political Anti-Semitism in Germany and Austria*. London: Halban, 1988.

Pyrah, Robert. *The Burgtheater and Austrian Identity: Theater and Cultural Politics in Vienna, 1918–1938*. Oxford: Legenda, 2007.

Rabinbach, Anson, ed. *The Austrian Socialist Experiment: Social Democracy and Austromarxism, 1918–1934*. Boulder, CO: Westview, 1985.

Raggam-Blesch, Michaela. *Zwischen Ost und West: Identitätskonstruktionen jüdischer Frauen in Wien*. Innsbruck: Studienverlag, 2008.

Rechter, David. "Galicia in Vienna: Jewish Refugees in the First World War." *Austrian History Yearbook* 28 (1997): 113–30.

———. *The Jews of Vienna and the First World War*. London: Littman, 2001.

———. "Otto Bauer and Karl Renner on Nationalism, Ethnicity and Jews." *Journal of Jewish Identities* 2, no. 2 (July 2009): 1–19.

Reifowitz, Ian. *Imagining an Austrian Nation: Joseph Samuel Bloch and the Search for a Supraethnic Austrian Identity, 1846–1918*. New York: Columbia University Press, 2003.

Reitter, Paul. *The Anti-Journalist: Karl Kraus and Jewish Self-Fashioning in Fin-de-Siècle Europe*. Chicago: University of Chicago Press, 2008.

Reuveni, Gideon, and Sarah Wobick-Segev, eds. *The Economy in Jewish History: New Perspectives on the Interrelationship between Ethnicity and Economic Life*. New York: Berghahn, 2011.

Rieckmann, Jens. "Zwischen Bewußtsein und Verdrängung: Hofmannsthals jüdisches Erbe." *Deutsche Vierteljahrsschrift für Literaturwissenschaft und Geistesgeschichte* 67, no. 3 (1993): 466–83.

Riedl, Joachim, ed. *Wien, Stadt der Juden*. Vienna: Zsolnay, 2004. Exhibition Catalogue.

Riedmann, Bettina. "*Ich bin Jude, Österreicher, Deutscher.*" *Judentum in Arthur Schnitzlers Tagebüchern und Briefen*. Tübingen: Niemeyer, 2002.

———. "Arthur Schnitzler: Facetten einer jüdisch-österreichisch-deutschen Identität." In Stern and Eichinger, *Wien und die jüdische Erfahrung*, 370–84.

Riedmann, Josef. "Geschichte Tirols." In *Geschichte der österreichischen Bundesländer*, edited by Johann Rainer, 141–64. Vienna: Geschichte und Politik, 1988.

Rimalt, E.S. "The Jews of Tyrol." In Fraenkel, *The Jews of Austria*, 375–84.

Rismondo, Piero. "Schein und Sein." In *Wien. Spektrum einer Stadt*, edited by Hilde Spiel, 237–54. Vienna: Wiener, 1971.

Riss, Heidelore. *Ansätze zu einer Geschichte des jüdischen Theaters in Berlin 1889–1936.* Frankfurt: Peter Lang, 2000.

Rivo, Sharon Pucker. "Projected Images: Portraits of Jewish Women in Early American Film." In *Talking Back: Images of Jewish Women in American Popular Culture*, edited by Joyce Antler, 30–52. Hanover, NH: University Press of New England, 1998.

Roazen, Paul. *Helene Deutsch: A Psychoanalyst's Life.* New Brunswick, NJ: Transaction, 1992.

Robertson, Ritchie. *Occasions* 9: *Anticlericalism in Austrian Literature from Joseph II to Thomas Bernhard.* London: Austrian Cultural Forum, 2006.

———. "Austrian Prose Fiction 1918–1945." In Kohl and Robertson, *A History of Austrian Literature*, 53–74.

———. *The 'Jewish Question' in German Literature 1759–1939.* New York: Oxford University Press, 1999.

Rose, Alison. *Jewish Women in Fin-de-Siècle Vienna.* Austin: University of Texas Press, 2008.

Rosenberg, Jakob, and Georg Spitaler. "Grün-weiß unterm Hakenkreuz: Der Sportklub Rapid im Nationalsozialismus (1938–1945)." In Eppel, et. al., *Wo die Wuchtel fliegt*, 21–24.

Rotenberg, Robert. *Landscape and Power in Vienna.* Baltimore: Johns Hopkins University Press, 1995.

Roth, Norman, ed. *Medieval Jewish Civilization.* New York: Routledge, 2001.

Rozenblit, Marsha L. "Jewish Immigrants in Vienna before the First World War." *Aschkenas—Zeitschrift für Geschichte und Kultur der Juden* 17, no.1 (2007): 23–53.

———. "The Crisis of Identity in the Austrian Republic: Jewish Ethnicity in a New Nation-State." In Brenner and Penslar, *In Search of Jewish Community*, 134–53.

———. "The Dilemma of Identity: The Impact of the First World War on Habsburg Jewry." *Austrian Studies 5: The Habsburg Legacy: National Identity in Historical Perspective* (1994): 144–57.

———. *The Jews of Vienna, 1867–1914: Assimilation and Identity.* Albany: State University of New York Press, 1983.

———. *Reconstructing a National Identity: The Jews of Habsburg Austria during World War I.* New York: Oxford University Press, 2001.

———., "Sustaining Austrian 'National' Identity in Crisis: The Dilemma of the Jews in Habsburg Austria, 1914–1919." In *Constructing Nationalities in East Central Europe*, edited by Pieter M. Judson and Marsha L. Rozenblit, 178–91. New York: Berghahn, 2005.

Rubenstein, Richard L., and John K. Roth. *Approaches to Auschwitz: The Holocaust and Its Legacy.* Louisville, KY: Westminster John Knox Press, 2003.

Safran, Gabriella. "Theory and Practice of Secular Jewish Culture in Russian." In *Jewish Literatures and Cultures: Context and Intertext*, edited by Anita Norich and Yaron Z. Eliav, 177–200. Providence, RI: Brown University Press, 2008.

———. *Wandering Soul: The Dybbuk's Creator, S. An-sky*. Cambridge: Harvard University Press, 2010.

Safran, Gabriella, and Steven J. Zipperstein. *The Worlds of S. An-sky: A Russian Jewish Intellectual at the Turn of the Century*. Stanford: Stanford University Press, 2006.

Schachter, Allison. "Bergelson and the Landscape of Yiddish Modernism." *East European Jewish Affairs* 30, no. 1 (2008): 7–19.

———. *Diasporic Modernisms: Hebrew and Yiddish in the Twentieth Century*. New York: Oxford University Press, 2011.

Schedel, Angelika. "Vita Veza Canetti." In *Text + Kritik, Zeitschrift für Literatur*. Edited by Heinz Ludwig Arnold, X/02, Nr. 156 (October 2002): 95–104.

———. *Sozialismus und Psychoanalyse: Quellen von Veza Canettis literarischen Utopien*. Würzburg: Königshausen & Neumann, 2002.

Schlör, Joachim. *Das Ich der Stadt: Debatten über Judentum und Urbanität, 1822–1938*. Göttingen: Vandenhoeck & Ruprecht, 2005.

Schmid-Bortenschlager, Sigrid. "Der zerbrochene Spiegel: Weibliche Kritik der Psychoanalyse in Mela Hartwigs Novellen." *Modern Austrian Literature: Special Issue on Austrian Women Writers* 12, no. 3/4 (1979): 77–95.

Schmidlechner, Karin Maria. "Sozialökonomische Position und kulturelle Lage der Frauen." In Konrad and Maderthaner, . . . *der Rest ist Österreich*. vol. 2, 87–102.

Schmidt-Dengler, Wendelin. *Ohne Nostalgie: Zur österreichischen Literatur der Zwischenkriegszeit*. Vienna: Bohlau, 2002.

Schoell-Glass, Charlotte. *Aby Warburg and Anti-Semitism: Political Perspectives on Images and Culture*. Detroit, MI: Wayne State University Press, 2008.

Schorske, Carl. *Fin-de-Siècle Vienna: Politics and Culture*. New York: Vintage, 1981.

Schreckenberger, Helga. "Literarische Reaktionen zur ostjüdischen Zuwanderung nach 1918." In Müller and Wagener, *Österreich 1918 und die Folgen*, 71–88.

Schroubek, Georg R. "Andreas von Rinn: Der Kult eines 'heiligen Ritualmordopfers' im historischen Wandel." *Österreichische Zeitschrift für Volkskunde* 49, no. 4 (1995): 371–96.

———. "Zur Tradierung und Diffusion einer europäischen Aberglaubensvorstellung." In Erb, *Die Legende vom Ritualmord*, 17–24.

Schwarz, Robert. "Antisemitism and Socialism in Austria, 1918–1962." In Fraenkel, *The Jews of Austria*, 445–66.

Schwarz, Werner Michael. *Kino und Kinos in Wien: Eine Entwicklungsgeschichte bis 1934*. Vienna: Turia & Kant, 1992.

Scott, Joan W. "Gender: A Useful Category of Historical Analysis." *American Historical Review* 91, no. 5 (1986): 1053–75.

———. "The Evidence of Experience." *Critical Inquiry* 17, no. 4 (Summer 1991): 773–79.

Segar, Kenneth and John Warren, eds. *Austria in the Thirties: Culture and Politics*. Riverside, CA: Ariadne, 1991.

Segel, Harold B. *The Vienna Coffeeehouse Wits 1890–1938.* West Lafayette, IN: Purdue University Press, 1993.

Shaked, Gershon. "David Vogel: A Hebrew Novelist in Vienna." In Wistrich, *Austrians and Jews in the Twentieth Century*, 97–111.

———. *The New Tradition: Essays on Modern Hebrew Literature.* Cinncincnati: Hebrew Union College Press, 2006.

Shapira, Elana. *"Assimilating with Style": Jewish Assimilation and Modern Architecture and Design: The Case of the "Outfitters" Adolf Loos and Leopold Goldman and the Making of the Goldman & Salatsch Building.* Ph.D. diss. University of Applied Arts, Vienna, 2004.

———. "Jewish Patronage and the Avant-Garde in Vienna." In *Jewish Collectors and their Contribution to Modern Culture,* edited by Annette Weber, 219–235. Heidelberg: Universitätsverlag, 2011.

———. "Jüdisches Mäzenatentum zwischen Assimilation und Identitätsstiftung in Wien, 1800–1930." In *Jüdische Friedhöfe. Kultstätte, Erinnerungsort, Denkmal.* Edited by Claudia Theune and Tina Walzer, 171–86. Vienna: Böhlau, 2010.

Sibley, David. "Families and Domestic Routines: Constructing the Boundaries of Childhood." In *Geographies of Cultural Transformation*, edited by Steve Pile and Nigel Thrift, 123–42. London: Routledge, 1995.

Siegert, Michael. "Mit dem Browning philosophiert: Der Mord an Moritz Schlick am 22. Juni 1936," *FORUM* 28, no. 331/332 (July–August 1981): 18–26.

Silverman, Lisa. "Beyond Antisemitism: A Critical Approach to German Jewish Cultural History." *Nexus 1: The Duke Journal of German Jewish Studies* (2011): 27–45.

———. "Elias and Veza Canetti: German Writing, Sephardic Heritage." In *The Worlds of Elias Canetti: Centenary Essays*, edited by William Donahue and Julian Preece, 151–70. Newcastle, UK: Cambridge Scholars Publishing, 2007.

———. "Reconsidering the Margins: Jewishness as an Analytical Framework." *Journal of Modern Jewish Studies* 8, no. 1 (2009): 103–20.

———. "Zwischenzeit and *Zwischenort*: Veza Canetti, Else Feldmann, and Jewish Writing in Interwar Vienna." *Prooftexts: A Journal of Jewish Literary History* 26, nos. 1–2 (2006): 29–52.

Simon, Walter B. "The Jewish Vote in Austria." *Leo Baeck Institute Year-Book* 16 (1971): 97–121.

Singer, Isaac Bashevis. "a.m. fuchs der derzeiler." In *a.m. fukss: di nacht und der tog*, ed. Melech Rawitsch. New York: der Kwal, 1961, 5–8.

Sommer, Monika. "Der Wiener Judenplatz als Museum ohne Mauern: Eine Kritik." *transversal: Zeitschrift des Zentrums jüdische Studien* 3, no. 1 (2002): 69–89.

Sonnleitner, Johann. "Völkische Literatur und Antisemitismus in der Zwischenkriegszeit." In *Judentum und Antisemitisimus: Studien zur Literatur und Germanistik in Österreich*, edited by Anne Betten und Konstanze Fliedl, 84–92. Berlin: Erich Schmidt Verlag, 2003.

Sorkin, David. "Emancipation and Assimilation: Two Concepts and their Application to German-Jewish History." *Leo Baeck Institute Year-Book* 35 (1990): 17–33.

———. "The Impact of Emancipation on German Jewry: A Reconsideration." In *Assimilation and Community: The Jews in Nineteenth-Century Europe*, edited by Jonathan Frankel and Steven J. Zipperstein, 177–98. Cambridge: Cambridge University Press, 1992.

———. *The Transformation of German Jewry, 1780–1840.* New York: Oxford University Press, 1987.

Soxberger, Thomas, ed. and trans. *Nackte Lieder: Jiddische Literatur aus Wien 1915–1938.* Vienna: Mandelbaum, 2008.

Soxberger, Thomas. "Zwischen Partei- und Selbstverlag: Die jiddische Literatur und Publizistik in Wien." In Eidherr and Müller, *Zwischenwelt*, 250–63.

———."Die Jüdisch-Nationalen und das Jiddische in Wien in den Jahren 1918–1919." *Chilufim: Zeitschrift für jüdische Kulturgeschichte* 7 (2009): 83–107.

Spector, Scott. "Forget Assimilation: Introducing Subjectivity to German-Jewish history." *Jewish History* 20, no. 3–4 (2006): 349–61.

———. "Modernism without Jews: A Counter-Historical Argument." *Modernism/Modernity* 13, no. 4 (2006): 615–33.

———. *Prague Territories: National Conflict and Cultural Innovation in Franz Kafka's Fin de Siècle.* Berkeley: University of California Press, 2000.

Spiel, Hilde. "Jewish Women in Austrian Culture." In Fraenkel, *The Jews of Austria*, 97–110.

Spiel, Hilde, ed. *Wien: Spektrum einer Stadt.* Vienna: Jugend und Volk, 1971.

Spielman, John P. *The City and the Crown: Vienna and the Imperial Court, 1600–1740.* West Lafayette, IN: Purdue University Press, 1993.

Spitzer, Leo. "Back Through the Future: Nostalgic Memory and Critical Memory in a Refuge from Nazism." In *Acts of Memory: Cultural Recall in the Present*, edited by Mieke Bal, Jonathan Crewe, and Leo Spitzer, 87–104. Hanover, NH: University Press of New England, 1999.

Stadler, Friedrich. "The Vienna Circle and the University of Vienna." In *Vertreibung der Vernunft: The Cultural Exodus from Austria*, edited by Friedrich Stadler and Peter Weibel, 44–55. Vienna: Springer, 1995.

Stark, Michael. *Für und wider den Expressionismus: Die Entstehung der Intellektuellendebatte in der deutschen Literaturgeschichte.* Stuttgart: Metzler, 1982.

Staudinger, Anton. "Katholischer Antisemitismus in der ersten Republik." In *Eine Zerstörte Kultur: Jüdisches Leben und Antisemitismus in Wien seit dem 19. Jahrhundert*, 2nd ed. edited by Gerhard Botz, Ivar Oxaal, Michael Pollak, and Nina Scholz, 261–82. Vienna: Czernin, 2002.

Steiman, Lionel B. "Franz Werfel: The Formation of a non-Jewish Jew." In *Judentum in Leben und Werk von Franz Werfel*, edited by Hans Wagener and Wilhelm Hemecker, 1–18. Berlin: De Gruyter, 2011.

Steinberg, Michael P. *Austria as Theater and Ideology: The Meaning of the Salzburg Festival.* Ithaca, NY: Cornell University Press, 1990.

———. *Judaism Musical and Unmusical.* Chicago: University of Chicago Press, 2007.

Steininger, Rolf. "1918/1919: Die Teilung Tirols: Wie das Südtirolproblem enststand." In Konrad and Maderthaner, . . . *der Rest ist Österreich*, vol. 1, 103–18.

Stern, Frank, and Barbara Eichinger, eds. *Wien und die jüdische Erfahrung 1900–1938.* Vienna: Böhlau, 2009.

Stern, Martin. "Verschwiegener Antisemitismus: Bemerkungen zu einem widerrufenen Brief Hofmannsthals an Rudolf Pannwitz." *Hofmmansthal Jahrbuch* 12 (2004): 243–53.

Stourzh, Gerald. "Erschütterung und Konsolidierung des Österreichbewußtseins vom Zusammenbruch der Monarchie zur Zweiten Republik." In *Was heißt Österreich? Inhalt uns Umfang des Österreichbegriffs vom 10. Jahrhundert bis heute*, edited by Richard G. Plaschka, Gerald Stourzh, and Jan Niederkorn, 289–311. Vienna: Archiv für österreichische Geschichte, 1995.

———. "Ethnic Attribution in Late Imperial Austria: Good Intentions, Evil Consequences." *Austrian Studies 5. The Habsburg Legacy: National Identity in Historical Perspective* (1994), 67–83.

———. *Vom Reich zur Republik: Studium zum Österreichbewußtsein im 20. Jahrhundert.* Vienna: Wiener Journal Schriftenverlag, 1990.

Stratenwerth, Irene, and Hermann Simon, eds. *Pioniere in Celluloid: Juden in der frühen Filmwelt.* Berlin: Henschel, 2004.

Strauss, Monica. *Cruel Banquet, The Life and Loves of Frida Strindberg.* New York: Harcourt, 2000.

Sutton, Katie. *The Masculine Woman in Weimar Germany.* New York: Berghahn, 2011.

Templ, Stefan, and Tina Walzer. *Unser Wien "Ariesierung" auf österreichisch.* Berlin: Aufbau, 2001.

Timms, Edward. "Ambassador Herzl and the Blueprint for a Modern State." *Austrian Studies 8: Theodor Herzl and the Origins of Zionism* (1997): 12–26.

———. "Cultural Parameters between the Wars: A Reassessment of the Vienna Circles." In Holmes and Silverman, *Interwar Vienna*, 21–31.

———. *Karl Kraus: Apocalyptic Satirist. Culture and Catastrophe in Habsburg Vienna.* New Haven, CT: Yale University Press, 1989.

———. *Karl Kraus: Apocalyptic Satirist. The Post-War Crisis and the Rise of the Swastika.* New Haven, CT: Yale University Press, 2005.

———. "Musil's Vienna and Kafka's Prague: the Quest for a Spiritual City." In *Unreal City: Urban Experience in Modern European Literature and Art,* edited by Edward Timms and David Kelley, 247–263. Manchester: Manchester University Press, 1985.

———. "School for Socialism: Karl Seitz and the Culutral Politics of Vienna." *Austrian Studies 14: Culture and Politics in Red Vienna* (2006): 36–59.

Torton-Beck, Evelyn. "From 'Kike to Jap': How Misogyny, Anti-Semitism, and Racism Construct the Jewish American Princess." In *Race, Class, and Gender*, edited by Margaret Andersen and Patricia Hill Collins, 87–95. Belmont, CA: Wadsworth, 1992.

———. *Kafka and the Yiddish Theater: Its Impact on His Work*. Madison: University of Wisconsin Press, 1971.

Tramer, Hans. "Der Expressionismus: Bemerkungen zum Anteil der Juden an einer Kunstepoche." *Bulletin des Leo Baeck Instituts* 2, no. 5 (1958): 33.

Tur-Sinai, N.H. "Viennese Jewry." In Fraenkel, *The Jews of Austria*, 311–18.

Upton, Dell. "Seen, Unseen, and Scene." In *Understanding Ordinary Landscapes*, edited by Paul Erling Groth and Todd W. Bressi, 174–79. New Haven, CT: Yale University Press, 1997.

Utz, Richard. "Remembering Ritual Murder: The Anti-Semitic Blood Accusation Narrative in Medieval and Contemporary Cultural Memory." *Cultural Heritage of Medieval Rituals: Genre and Ritual, Transfiguration* 1–2: (2003): 145–62.

Valman, Nadia. *The Jewess in Nineteenth-Century British Literary Culture*. Cambridge: Cambridge University Press, 2007.

Vansant, Jacqueline. *Reclaiming Heimat: Trauma and Mourning in Memoirs by Jewish Austrian Reémigés*. Detroit, MI: Wayne State UP, 2001.

Volkov, Shulamit. "Antisemitism as a Cultural Code: Reflections on the History and Historiography of Antisemitism in Imperial Germany." *Leo Baeck Institute Year-Book* 23 (1978): 25–46.

———. "The Dynamics of Dissimilation: Ostjuden and German Jews." In *The Jewish Response to German Culture from the Enlightenment to the Second World War*, edited by Jehuda Reinharz and Walter Schatzberg, 195–211. Hanover, NH: University Press of New England, 1985.

Vyleta, Daniel M. *Crime, News, and Jews: Vienna 1895–1914*. New York: Berghahn, 2007.

———. "Jewish Crimes and Misdemeanours: In Search of Jewish Criminality (Germany and Austria, 1890–1914)." *European History Quarterly* 35, no. 2 (2005): 299–325.

de Waal, Edmund. *The Hare with the Amber Eyes: A Hidden Inheritance*. London: Vintage, 2010.

Wallach, Kerry. "Mascha Kaléko Advertises the New Jewish Woman." In Hammel and Weiss-Sussex, *"Not an Essence but a Positioning,"* 211–31.

———. "Observable Type: Jewish Women and the Jewish Press in Weimar Germany." Ph.D. diss. University of Pennsylvania, 2011.

———. "'Recognition for the Beautiful Jewess': Beauty Queens Crowned by Modern Jewish Print Media." In *Globalizing Beauty: Aesthetics in the Twentieth Century*, edited by Hartmut Berghoff and Thomas Kühne. Washington, D.C.: German Historical Institute (forthcoming).

Wallas, Armin A. "Mythen der Übernationalität und revolutionäre Gegenmodelle: Österreich-Konzeptionen jüdischer Schriftsteller zwischen Monarchie und Exil." In Mittelmann and Wallas, *Österreich-Konzeptionen*, 171–93.

———. "Seelenaufschlitzer und Gottsucher: Die Krisen jüdischer Identität im österreichischen Expressionismus." *Das jüdische Echo* 48 (October 1999): 34–53.

Walser Smith, Helmut. "Anti-Semitic Violence as Reenactment: An Essay in Cultural History." *Rethinking History* 11, no. 3 (2007), 335–51.

———. *The Butcher's Tale: Murder and Anti-Semitism in a German Town*. New York: W.W. Norton, 2002.

Wassermann, Janek. "Black Vienna, Red Vienna: The Struggle for Intellectual and Political Hegemony in Interwar Vienna, 1918–1938." Ph.D. diss. Washington University, 2010.

Weinzierl, Erika, and Otto D. Kulka, eds. *Vertreibung und Neubeginn: Israelische Bürger österreichischer Herkunft*. Vienna: Böhlau, 1992.

Weitz, Eric. *Weimar Germany: Promise and Tragedy*. Princeton: Princeton University Press, 2007.

Werses, Shmuel. "An-ski's 'Tsvishn tsvey veltn (Der Dibbuk)'/'Bein shney olamot'/'Hadybbuk'/'Between Two Worlds (The Dibbuk):' A Textual History." In *Studies in Yiddish Literature and Folklore*, 99–185. Jerusalem: Hebrew University, 1986.

Wertheimer, Jack. *Unwelcome Strangers: East European Jews in Imperial Germany*. New York: Oxford University Press, 1987.

Wimmer, Adi, ed. *Strangers at Home and Abroad: Recollections of Austrian Jews Who Escaped Hitler*. Translated by Ewald Osers. Jefferson, NC: McFarland & Company, Inc., 2000.

Wistrich, Robert S., ed. *Austrians and Jews in the Twentieth Century: From Franz Joseph to Waldheim*. New York: St. Martin's Press, 1992.

———. "Social Democracy, Antisemitism, and the Jews." In Oxaal, et. al., *Jews, Antisemitism, and Culture in Vienna*, 111–20.

———. Review of *The Anti-Journalist: Karl Kraus and Jewish Self-Fashioning in Fin-de-Siècle Europe*, by Paul Reitter. *American Historical Review* 114, no. 5 (2009): 1565–66.

———. *Socialism and the Jews: The Dilemmas of Assimilation in Germany and Austria-Hungary*. East Brunswick, NJ: Associated University Press, 1982.

Yates, W.E. *Theatre in Vienna: A Critical History, 1776–1995*. Cambridge: Cambridge University Press, 1996.

Zakim, Eric. "Between Fragment and Authority in David Fogel's (Re)Presentation of Subjectivity," *Prooftexts* 13, no. 1 (1993): 103–24.

INDEX

Made in United States
North Haven, CT
25 January 2023